In Byzantium monks did not form a separate caste, apart from society. They held loyalties not only to their own houses or monastic leaders, but also formed part of a nexus of social, economic and spiritual relationships which bound together the 'powerful' in the middle Byzantine state. Monasticism displayed a highly individualistic streak, unlike the western religious 'orders'.

Using hagiography, chronicles and, in particular, the newly-available archives of the Athonite monasteries, this book reassesses the role of monks in Byzantine society and examines the reasons for the flowering of the monastic life in the period from the end of iconoclasm to the beginning of the twelfth century. It is the first study of its kind in English, and is aimed at anyone interested in either the western or the Byzantine early medieval religious life.

Monks and laymen
in Byzantium, 843–1118

Monks and laymen in Byzantium, 843–1118

Rosemary Morris

Lecturer in History, University of Manchester

CAMBRIDGE
UNIVERSITY PRESS

Published by the Press Syndicate of the University of Cambridge
The Pitt Building, Trumpington Street, Cambridge CB2 1RP
40 West 20th Street, New York, NY 10011–4211, USA
10 Stamford Road, Oakleigh, Melbourne 3166, Australia

© Cambridge University Press 1995

First published 1995

Printed in Great Britain at the University Press, Cambridge

A catalogue record for this book is available from the British Library

Library of Congress cataloguing in publication data
Morris, Rosemary.
Monks and laymen in Byzantium, 843–1118 / Rosemary Morris.
p.   cm.
Includes bibliographical references and index.
ISBN 0 521 26558 4
1. Monasticism and religious orders. Orthodox Eastern – Byzantine
Empire – History. 2. Byzantine Empire – Church history. 1. Title.
BX385.B9M67 1995
271'.8–dc20   94–36325   CIP

ISBN 0 521 26558 4 hardback

To my parents

Contents

Maps

———◆———

x

Tables

———◆———

Acknowledgements

◆

The completion of this book in its final form is due to the kindness and support of a number of friends and colleagues. James Howard-Johnston supervised the thesis from which the book evolved; Anthony Bryer has, from the first, acted as a wise and supportive 'spiritual father' to the project. Many friends have provided bibliographical help. In particular, Catia Galatariotou supplied offprints at a moment's notice; Jonathan Shepard disinterred Russian periodicals; Peter Gatrell illuminated Slavonic transcription systems and Paul Magdalino kindly allowed the use of much important unpublished material on Alexios Komnenos. Margaret Mullett not only shared with me her vast knowledge of the eleventh century, but has, over the years, sustained me with her enthusiasm and friendship. I have greatly profited from the comments of members of the Byzantine Seminars of the Universities of Birmingham and Oxford and the Queen's University, Belfast on sections of this work and members of the 'Bucknell Group' will, I hope, recognise many of the issues upon which their contributions have helped to shape my views. I have felt it important that the book should appeal to the general medievalist and, to this end, two distinguished 'Latins', Wendy Davies and Chris Wickham, have read the entire text in draft. Leslie Brubaker has also brought to it the keen 'eye' of the art historian. The comments of all three have greatly improved the work. Financial assistance from the British Academy and the Leverhulme Trust enabled me to work in Paris in 1987 at the Centre de Recherche d'histoire et civilisation de Byzance of the Collège de France. I must thank its Director, Gilbert Dagron, for his kind hospitality; Jacques Lefort, who, with great generosity, supplied me with transcriptions of the (then unpublished) eleventh-century Acts of Iviron and Michel Kaplan who provided – then as now – many insights into the landed fortunes of Byzantine monasteries. The task of finding often arcane works has been greatly eased by the assistance of the librarians of the Bodleian Library, the Cambridge University Library, the John Rylands University Library, Manchester, the Bibliothèque Nationale and the Bibliothèque Byzantine, Paris. This book has been long in the writing and the fact that it has been finished at all is due in no small measure to the encouragement of my colleagues in the Department of History at the University of Manchester. Jeffrey Denton never allowed me to doubt for very long that the work would be completed; Richard Davies was a staunch travelling companion through the desert of many a Long Vacation. The final draft was corrected in the unlikely surroundings of the British Antarctic Survey, Cambridge and I must thank my sister, Liz Morris, for providing this much-needed oasis of calm. My husband, Alan Forrest, has patiently borne with this book over the years. He has both shared in my enthusiasm for things Byzantine and taught me much about social relationships in the past, albeit those of *un autre pays*! My profoundest debt of gratitude, however, is to those to whom this book is dedicated, at once my most perceptive critics and my greatest support.

Note on transliteration and citation

———◆———

As Byzantinists well know, there is no standard system for the transliteration of Greek, but I have, in general, transliterated Greek names and terms as closely as possible, except in the case where there are familiar English versions. The sixth century has been taken as the division between the Latinised and the pure Greek. I have made no distinction between long and short vowels. Those who know Greek will be familiar with the words concerned; those who do not will not welcome a clutter of confusing accents.

Works cited in abbreviated form are listed in full in the abbreviations at the beginning of the work. All others are in the bibliography at the end.

Abbreviations

◆

AASS	*Acta Sanctorum* (Antwerp, 1643–)
AB	*Analecta Bollandiana* (Brussels, 1882–)
Alexiad	Anna Comnène, *Alexiade*, ed. and translated B. Leib (3 vols, Collection byzantine, Paris, 1937–45), IV; index by P. Gautier (Collection byzantine, Paris, 1976)
Attaliates	*Michaelis Attaliotae Historia*, ed. I. Bekker (CSHB, Bonn, 1853)
B	*Byzantion* (Brussels and Paris, 1924–)
BCH	*Bulletin de Correspondance Héllenique* (Paris, 1877–)
BEMP	*Byzantina Engrapha tes Mones Patmou.* I: *Autokratorika*, ed. E. Vranoussi; II: *Demosion leitourgon*, ed. M. Nystazopoulou-Pelekidou (Athens, 1980)
BF	*Byzantinische Forschungen* (Amsterdam, 1966–)
BMGS	*Byzantine and Modern Greek Studies* (Oxford, 1975–83; Birmingham, 1984–)
BNJ	*Byzantinisch-Neugriechische Jahrbücher* (Berlin and Athens, 1920–)
BS	*Byzantinoslavica* (Prague, 1929–)
BZ	*Byzantinische Zeitschrift* (Leipzig and Munich, 1896–)
CA	*Cahiers Archéologiques* (Paris, 1945–)
Carbone	G. Robinson, 'History and Cartulary of the Greek monastery of S. Elias and S. Anastasius of Carbone', *Orientalia Christiana*, 11/5, 271–348 (History), 15/2, 121–275 (Cartulary) (Rome, 1928)

CFHB	Corpus Fontium Historiae Byzantinae (Series Washingtonensis, Washington, 1967– ; Series Berolinensis, Berlin and New York, 1967– ; Series Vindobonensis, Vienna, 1975– ; Series Italica, Rome, 1975– ; Series Bruxellensis, Brussels, 1975–)
Chilandar (*Supplementa*)	*Supplementa ad acta graeca Chilandarii*, ed. V. Mošin and A. Sovre (Ljubljana, 1948)
Chronicle of George the Monk	*Georgii monachi Vitae imperatorum recentiorum*, ed. I. Bekker, in Theophanes cont., 763–924
Chronicle of the Logothete	*Leonis Grammatici Chronographia*, ed. I. Bekker (CSHB, 1842)
Chronicle of Pseudo-Symeon *magistros*	*Symeonis Magistri ac Logothetae Annales a Leone Armenio ad Nicephorum Phocam*, ed. I. Bekker, in Theophanes cont., 603–706
CIC	*Corpus Iuris Civilis*. I: *Institutiones*, ed. P. Krüger, *Digesta*, ed. T. Mommsen; II: *Codex Iustinianus*, ed. P. Krüger; III: *Novellae*, ed. R. Schöll and W. Kroll (Berlin, 1892–5; reprinted 1945–63)
CSHB	Corpus Scriptorum Historiae Byzantinae (Bonn, 1828–97)
DAI	*Constantinus Porphyrogenitus, De Administrando imperio*. I: *Text*, ed. G. Moravcsik, translated R. J. H. Jenkins, revised edn. (CFHB, I, Ser. Washington., Dumbarton Oaks Texts, I, Washington, DC, 1967); II: *Commentary*, ed. R. J. H. Jenkins (London, 1962)
Diataxis of Attaliates	P. Gautier, 'La diataxis de Michel Attaliate', *REB*, 39 (1981), 4–143
Diatheke of Christodoulos	*Testamentum et codicillus Sancti Christoduli*, MM, VI, 81–5
Diatyposis of Athanasios	*He diatyposis tou hosiou kai makariou patros hemon Athanasiou*, in Meyer, *Haupturkunden*, 123–30
Diegesis merike	*Diegesis merike ton epistolon Alexiou Basileios kai Nicholaou Patriarchou genomene kata diaphorous kairous*, in Meyer, *Haupturkunden*, 163–84
Dionysiou	*Actes de Dionysiou*, ed. N. Oikonomidès (*Archives de l'Athos*, IV, Paris, 1968)
Docheiariou	*Actes de Docheiariou*, ed. N. Oikonomidès (*Archives de l'Athos*, XIII, Paris, 1984)
Dölger, *Regesten*	F. Dölger, *Regesten der Kaiserurkunden des oströmischen Reiches von 565–1453* (3 vols.,

	Munich/Berlin, 1924–32, reprinted Hildesheim, 3 vols. in 1, 1976)
DOP	*Dumbarton Oaks Papers* (Cambridge, Mass. and Washington, 1941–)
EB	*Etudes Byzantines*, 1–3 (Bucharest, 1943–5)
EEBS	*Epeteris Hetaireias Byzantinon Spoudon* (Athens, 1924–)
Esphigménou	*Actes d'Esphigménou*, ed. J. Lefort (*Archives de l'Athos*, VI, Paris, 1973)
Evergétis	P. Gautier, 'Le typikon de la Théotokos Evergétis', *REB*, 40 (1982), 5–101
Genesios	*Iosephi Genesii regum libri quattuor*, ed. A. Lesmüller-Werner and I. Thurn (CFHB, XIV, Ser. Berolin., Berlin/New York, 1978)
GRBS	*Greek, Roman and Byzantine Studies* (San Antonio, University of Mississippi, Cambridge, Mass. and Durham, 1958–)
Grumel, *Régestes*	*Les régestes des actes du patriarcat de Constantinople.* I: *Les actes des patriarches* (3 vols., Chalcedon/Bucharest/Paris, 1974)
Hiéra-Xérochoraphion	N. G. Wilson and J. Darrouzès, 'Restes du cartulaire de Hiéra-Xérochoraphion', *REB*, 26 (1968), 5–47
Hypotyposis of Christodoulos	*Regula edita a Sancto Christodulo pro monasterio sancti Ioannis Theologi in insula Patmo ab eo condito.* MM, VI, 59–80
IRAIK	*Izvestiia Russkogo Arkheologicheskogo Instituta v Konstantinopole* (Odessa and Sofia, 1896–1912)
Ivirôn, I, II	*Actes d'Ivirôn*, I, II, ed. J. Lefort, N. Oikonomidès, D. Papachryssanthou with H. Métrévéli and V. Kravari (*Archives de l'Athos*, XIV; XVI, Paris, 1985; 1990)
JÖB	*Jahrbuch der österreichischen Byzantinistik*, 18– (Vienna, Graz and Cologne, 1969–)
JÖBG	*Jahrbuch der österreichischen Byzantinischen Gesellschaft* (Graz and Cologne, 1951–68), 1–17
John Klimakos, *Ladder of Divine Ascent*	John Climacus, *Scala Paradisi*, *PG*, 88, cols. 632–1208; English translation C. Luibheid and N. Russell (London, 1982)
John of Antioch, Against the charistike	P. Gautier, 'Réquisitoire du patriarche Jean d'Antioche contre le charisticariat', *REB*, 33 (1975), 77–132
JRS	*Journal of Roman Studies* (London, 1911–)

Kécharitôménè   P. Gautier, 'Le typikon de la Théotokos Kécharitôménè', *REB*, 43 (1985), 5–165

Kedrenos   George Cedrenus, *Compendium historiarum*, ed. I. Bekker (2 vols., CSHB, Bonn, 1838–9)

Kellerana   *Saint-Nicodème de Kellerana (1023/1024–1232)*, ed. A. Guillou (*Corpus des actes grecs d'Italie du sud et de Sicile. Recherches d'histoire et de géographie*, II, Vatican City, 1968)

Kodikellos of Christodoulos   *Testamentum et codicillus Sancti Christoduli*, MM, VI, 85–90

Laurent, *Sceaux*   V. Laurent, *Le corpus des sceaux de l'empire byzantin*. V: *L'église* (3 vols., Paris, 1963–72)

Lavra, I   *Actes de Lavra*, I, ed. P. Lemerle, A. Guillou, D. Papachryssanthou and N. Svoronos (*Archives de l'Athos*, V, Paris, 1970)

Leo the Deacon   *Leonis diaconi Caloënsis Historiae libri decem*, ed. C. B. Hase (CSHB, Bonn, 1828)

Life of the Patriarch Euthymios   *Vita Euthymii Patriarchae CP*, ed. and translated P. Karlin-Hayter (Bibliothèque de Byzantion, III, Brussels, 1970)

Life of St Athanasios (A) and (B)   *Vitae duae antiquae sancti Athanasii athonitae*, ed. J. Noret (Corpus Christianorum, Ser. Graec., IX, Louvain, 1982)

Life of St Basil the Younger   *Vita S. Basilii junioris*, *AASS*, Mar. III, pp. *24–*39

Life of St Christodoulos   John of Rhodes, *Bios kai politeia tou hosiou patros hemon Christodoulou*, in K. Boïnes, *Akolouthia hierea tou hosiou kai theophorou patros hemon Christodoulou* (3rd edn., Athens, 1884)

Life of St Cyril Phileotes   E. Sargologos, *La vie de saint Cyrille le Philéote, moine byzantin (†1110)* (Subsidia Hagiographica, XXXIX, Brussels, 1964)

Life of St Elias Spelaiotes   *Vita S. Eliae Spelaeotae in Calabria*, *AASS*, Sept. III, 848–87

Life of St Elias the Younger   *Vita di Sant' Elia il Giovane*, ed. and translated G. Rossi Taibbi (*Vite de Santi Siciliani*, III, Istituto Siciliano di Studi Bizantini e Neoellenici, *Testi e monumenti*, *Testi*, 7, Palermo, 1962)

Life of St John Xenos   N. B. Tomadakis, 'Ho Hagios Ioannes ho Xenos kai he diatheke autou', *Kretika Chronika*, 2 (1948), 47–72

Life of St Lazaros   *Vita S. Lazari Galesiotae*, *AASS*, Nov. III, 508–88

Life of St Leo-Luke of Corleone	*Vita S. Leonis-Lucae, AASS*, Mar. I, 98–102
Life of St Luke of Demena	*Vita S. Lucae abbatis, AASS*, Oct. XIII, 337–41
Life of St Luke the Stylite	*Vita S. Lucae Stylitae*, ed. H. Delehaye, *Les saints stylites* (Subsidia Hagiographica, XIV, Brussels/Paris, 1923), 195–237
Life of St Luke the Younger	*Vita S. Lucae junioris, PG*, 111, cols. 441–80 supplemented by E. Martini, 'Supplementum ad acta Sancti Lucae junioris', *AB*, 13 (1894), 81–121
Life of St Michael Maleïnos	L. Petit, 'Vie et office de S. Michel Maleïnos', *ROC*, 7 (1902), 549–68
Life of St Nikephoros	'Vita S. Nicephori episcopi Milesii', ed. H. Delehaye, *AB*, 14 (1895), 133–61
Life of St Nil	*Vita et conversatio sancti et deiferi patris nostri Nili, PG*, 120, cols. 15–166
Life of St Paul the Younger	'Vita S. Pauli Iunioris in Monte Latro cum interpretatione latina Iacobi Sirmondi S.J.', ed. H. Delehaye, *AB*, 11 (1892), 19–74, 136–81
Life of St Peter of Argos	*Vita et conversatio s. patris nostri Petri episcopi Argivorum, NPB*, IX/3 (1888), 1–17
Life of St Philaretos	M.-H. Fourmy and M. Leroy, 'La vie de S. Philarète', *B*, 1 (1934), 85–170
Life of St Sabas	J. Cozza-Luzi, 'Orestes patriarcha Hierosolymitana de historia et laudibus Sabae et Macarii Siculorum', *Studi et documenti di storia e diritto*, 12 (1891), 37–56, 135–68, 312–23
Life of St Symeon the New Theologian	*Un grand mystique byzantin. Vie de Syméon le Nouveau Théologien (942–1022) par Nicétas Stéthatos*, ed. and translated J. Hausherr and G. Horn (*Orientalia Christiana*, XII/45, 1928)
Life of SS John and Euthymios	B. Martin-Hisard, 'La *Vie de Jean et Euthyme* et le statut du Monastère des Ibères sur l'Athos', *REB*, 49 (1991), 67–142 (84–134, translation of Life)
Life of SS Niketas, John and Joseph	*Bios kai politeia ton hosion kai theophoron pateron hemon, Niketa, Ioannou kai Ioaseph*, in G. Photeinos, *Ta Neamonesia* (Chios, 1864)
Meyer, *Haupturkunden*	P. Meyer, *Die Haupturkunden für die Geschichte der Athos-Klöster* (Leipzig, 1894)
MM	F. Miklosich and J. Müller (eds.), *Acta et diplomata graeca medii aevi* (6 vols., Vienna, 1860–90)

NE	*Neos Hellenomnemon* (Athens, 1904–27)
Nicholas Mystikos, *Letters*	*Nicholai I Constantinopolitani Patriarchae, Epistolai*, ed. and translated R. J. H. Jenkins and L. G. Westerinck (CFHB, 6, Ser. Washington., Dumbarton Oaks Texts, XI, Washington, DC, 1973)
NPB	*Novum Patrum Bibliotheca*, ed. A. Mai, vols. I–VII (Rome, 1852–4); ed. I. Cozza-Luzi, vols. VIII–X (Rome, 1871–1905)
OCA	Orientalia Christiana Analecta (Rome, 1935–)
OCP	*Orientalia Christiana Periodica* (Rome, 1935–)
ODB	*Oxford Dictionary of Byzantium*, ed. A. Kazhdan *et al.* (New York and Oxford, 1991)
Pakourianos	P. Gautier, 'Le typikon du sébaste Grégoire Pakourianos', *REB*, 42 (1964), 5–145
Pantéléèmôn	*Actes de Saint-Pantéléèmôn*, ed. P. Lemerle, G. Dagron and S. Ćircović (*Archives de l'Athos*, XII, Paris, 1982)
Peira	*Practica ex actis Eustathii Romani*, Zepos, IV, 11–260
PG	*Patrologiae Cursus Completus, series Graeco-latina*, ed. J. P. Migne (Paris, 1857–66; 1880–1903)
Philothée	*Actes de Philothée*, ed. W. Regel, E. Kurtz and B. Korablev, *VV*, 20 (1913), *Prilozhenie*, 1
PP	*Past and Present* (London, 1952–)
Prôtaton	*Actes du Prôtaton*, ed. D. Papachryssanthou (*Archives de l'Athos*, VII, Paris, 1975)
REA	*Revue des Etudes Arméniennes*, n.s. (Paris, 1964–)
REB	*Revue des Etudes Byzantines*, 4– (Paris, 1946–)
REG	*Revue des Etudes Grecques* (Paris, 1888–)
ROC	*Revue de l'Orient Chrétien*, ser. 1, 1–10 (Paris, 1896–1905), ser. 2 (Paris, 1906–1915/17), ser. 3, 1–10 (Paris, 1918/19–1935/6)
RP	K. Rhalles and M. Potles, *Syntagma ton theion kai hieron kanonon* (6 vols., Athens, 1852–9)
Skylitzes	*Ioannis Scylitzae Synopsis historiarum*, ed. I. Thurn (CFHB, V, Ser. Berolin., Berlin/New York, 1973)
Stroumitza	L. Petit, 'Le monastère de Notre Dame de Pitié en Macédoine', *IRAIK*, 6 (1900), 1–153, Part II, pp. 69–93 (*typikon*) and pp. 106–9 (commentary)
Testament of Boïlas	S. Vryonis, 'The will of a provincial magnate, Eustathios Boïlas (1059)', *DOP*, 9 (1957), 263–77,

	reprinted in *Byzantium, its internal history and relations with the Muslim world* (London, 1971), article v; ed. P. Lemerle, *Cinq études sur l'XIe siècle byzantin* (Le monde byzantin, Paris, 1977), 20–9
Theophanes	*Theophanis Chronographia*, ed. C. de Boor (2 vols., Leipzig, 1883–5, reprinted Hildesheim, 1963)
Theophanes cont.	Theophanes continuatus, Ioannes Caminiata, Symeon Magister, Georgius Monachus continuatus, ed. I. Bekker (CSHB, Bonn, 1825)
TIB	*Tabula Imperii Byzantini* (Vienna, 1976–)
TM	*Travaux et Mémoires* (Paris, 1965–)
Trinchera	F. Trinchera, *Syllabus Graecarum membranarum* (Naples, 1865)
Typikon of Athanasios	*Typikon etoi kanonikon tou hosiou kai theophorou patros hemon Athanasiou tou en Atho*, in Meyer, *Haupturkunden*, 102–30
Vatopedi	M. Goudas, 'Byzantiaka engrapha tes en Atho hieras mones tou Batopediou', *EEBS*, 3 (1926), 113–34; 4 (1927), 211–48
VV	*Vizantiiskii Vremmenik*, 1–25 (St Petersburg/ Leningrad, 1894–1927), n.s. (Moscow, 1947–)
Xénophon	*Actes de Xénophon*, ed. D. Papachryssanthou (*Archives de l'Athos*, xv, Paris, 1986)
Xéropotamou	*Actes de Xéropotamou*, ed. J. Bompaire (*Archives de l'Athos*, iii, Paris, 1964)
ZRVI	*Zbornik Radova Vizantološkog Instituta* (Belgrade, 1952–)
Zepos	J. and P. Zepos, *Jus graeco-romanum* (8 vols., Athens, 1931–6, reprinted Aalen, 1962)
Zonaras	*Ioannis Zonarae Epitomae Historiarum libri XIII usque ad XVIII*, ed. M. Pinder and T. Büttner-Wobst (3 vols., CSHB, Bonn, 1897)

Introduction

———◆———

The figure of the monk was a familiar one in the Byzantine world. But what he represented and his place in society changed in response to the tensions and challenges, the fears and aspirations, the doubts and certainties of Byzantines through the centuries. The lack of any comprehensive modern study of Byzantine monasticism should therefore come as no surprise; such a task is well nigh impossible given the variety of monastic forms within the medieval Greek church. But this study aims to examine one of the most important aspects of Byzantine monasticism, the way in which it interacted with the lay world, and to focus on the ways in which these worlds impinged upon one another.

Monasticism in the abstract was something that Byzantines of all social classes admired and respected. It is no accident that most of the saints of the church in the period after Christianity had become the official religion of the Roman empire were monks. For monks had taken the place of martyrs as those willing to undertake a death in the world, to renounce human ties and associations and to replace them by a new life in the spirit, a life 'in the world but not of it', which in its most devout practitioners could lead to the 'life of the angels', where the flesh was of so little importance as to be almost subsumed into the spirit. But monks did not constitute a separate caste within Byzantine society. They might follow different ways of life, or adhere to different spiritual priorities, but monks had all once been laymen and many laymen, after long years in the secular world, became monks. 'Abandoning the world' thus often meant not the abandonment of human relationships such as family feeling or friendship, or the discarding of claims to leadership in society, but the recasting of them in a different, spiritually orientated context.

Although liturgical observances, theological education, spiritual training and private prayer and meditation were central to the life of Byzantine monks, these were essentially internal concerns. Each

I

monastic founder organised such matters in his own way and each monastery carefully preserved its own customs, for Byzantine monasticism was highly individualistic. Although adherence to the monastic precepts of St Basil of Caesarea was widespread and although the liturgical and organisational influence of such houses as the Stoudios Monastery in Constantinople was of importance, there were no monastic 'orders' on the Western model, and thus a variety of customs was to be found within monastic life. It is not the purpose of this book to examine in any great depth the internal workings of Byzantine monasteries, since it is unlikely that many potential novices were aware of the finer details of the liturgical, ceremonial and daily routine of the house they proposed to enter, although they afterwards certainly spent a great deal of time in learning and practising them. What attracted recruits to specific monastic houses was sometimes their geographical position – most nuns were found in urban convents near their homes, for example – but often the reputation of the founder of the house and the general style of monasticism practised in it. For founders themselves decreed what kind of life should be lived within their establishments. They laid down whether the community should be entirely or essentially coenobitic, whether it should comprise a group of solitaries or whether it should encompass a variety of monastic 'styles'. They oversaw the first building programmes and admitted the first recruits. They received the first donations of cash and land and set the tone for the future development of the house.

The first part of this book is therefore devoted to the question of what kinds of monasticism were most popular in the Middle Byzantine period, both with those who themselves entered the religious life and with those who remained in the lay world, yet through patronage expressed their interest in, and concern for, its prosperity. The importance of what has been termed 'hybrid' monasticism, the combination of elements drawn from the coenobitic and lavriote traditions, is very striking and the reasons for its attraction in the two centuries after the triumph of orthodoxy in 843 are important to identify, not the least in order to lay to rest the view that Byzantine monasticism developed chronologically from the lavriote to the coenobitic styles. Monastic life in this period was much more flexible than this model would allow.

But while monastic 'style' was important in attracting lay recruits and patronage, there is little doubt that the personalities of the monastic founders of the tenth and eleventh centuries did much to enhance the reputation of the religious life. There is, however, a contrast to be drawn between the charismatic holy men of the tenth century, responsible both for the re-establishment of the monastic life in parts of the empire ravaged by invasion and dislocation in the eighth and ninth centuries and for the foundation of important monastic communities such as those on Mount Athos, and the lay founders who come to prominence in the eleventh century. Their contrasting backgrounds, careers and attitudes to the monastic life are important to emphasise because of the element of choice always present among potential novices and patrons. What might attract men and women to participation in and promotion of the monastic life varied from time to time and from place to place. But the reputation of monastic leaders always played an important part in influencing lay decisions.

The relationship between monks and the laity, so important in assuring the patronage which would provide for the continuing existence, if not prosperity, of monasteries was, of course, expressed in a number of different ways. The nexus of relationships involved in spiritual father-hood was but one of the ways in which monks and laymen came together; but with its political as well as spiritual overtones it was one of the most important. But others, also discussed in the early chapters of this book, included those of friendship, family connection and communal associ-ation on both a local and empire-wide level. For the implications of the imperially articulated protection of monasticism throughout the Byzantine state need to be compared and contrasted with more locally based associations, so that the importance of monks at all levels of Byzantine society can be clearly illustrated and understood.

While the first part of this book is essentially a story of commitment – commitment by monastic founders to furthering the ideals and virtues of the monastic life and by their disciples and patrons to their founder's original vision – Part II tells a tale of compromise. Under the pressure of the increasing popularity of monasticism, the spiritual orientation of the early founders, especially their emphasis on solitude (*eremia*), was compromised by the pressure of numbers and by the need to acquire property to feed extra mouths. This territorial expansion brought with it a change in monastic orientation which led both to increased contact and conflict with the neighbouring laity and to the involvement of more distant political authority. Monastic expansion and monastic ambitions played their part in the much discussed agrarian crisis of the tenth century; the activities of the monastic *dynatoi* have long needed to be analysed against the background of the general debate about the 'poor' and the 'powerful' which has been of such interest to modern commen-tators. The weapons used to defend monastic interests, the law, lay patronage, financial management and the sheer weight of spiritual tradition can all be seen in action, both then and in the eleventh century.

The implications of monastic survival and expansion for the health of the Byzantine polity are discussed in the latter part of the book. There is no doubt that, by the eleventh century, monastic interests were often acting to the disadvantage of the Byzantine state administration. Imperial officials were circumvented in their tasks of imposing taxation and justice by the vested interests of monasteries and their supporters. Exemptions and privileges seemed to be eating away at the resources of the state. Yet even in the reign of Alexios Komnenos (1081–1118), when an apparently much tougher line was being taken (with imperial approval) towards religious houses, we are still left with the apparent paradox of the imperial power allowing, by privileges, the very practices which appeared to be reducing the central power of the state. To attempt to explain this paradox, Alexios' own attitude to the monastic life (and that of his increasingly important family) has been discussed and his reign used as a landmark from which to survey the development of monastic–lay relationships over the previous two centuries.

As with all works on Byzantium, the shape of the present study has been dictated by the available source material. Rather than present a survey of sources in isolation from the questions which they may be used to illustrate, I have felt it more useful to pause from time to time to discuss the significance of various types of source material as and when they are relevant to the questions posed. I have cast my net widely, as all Byzantinists are bound to do, but have particularly focused my attention on archival material and on hagiography, since these are the two major groups of sources which give us information about the Byzantine countryside. Of course, the use of hagiographical texts presents enormous problems, but I remain convinced that they can with profit be used by the social and economic historian so long as a critical (and flexible) attitude is taken to the material they contain. The problems of *topoi* can, I think, be resolved by asking simple questions about the likelihood of the reliability of the information contained in the individual hagiography; about its style, its message and its provenance. I have taken the view that information should not be automatically disbelieved, simply because it appears in a hagiography; nor should it be unquestionably accepted, since the genre of a source always dictates the presentation of its contents.

This is no less true of the archival material, chiefly from the acts of the monasteries of Athos, and the evidence of the foundation charters (*typika*) which have been mainly deployed in the second part of the book. Without the steady publication of the *Archives de l'Athos*, this book could not have been written and I hope that one of its small achievements may be to bring the more recent volumes of this outstanding series to the attention of an English-language readership. The precision and detail of the French editors have enabled later commentators to be fully aware of the wide variety of types of document contained in the Athonite archives. Again, I have attempted to give each document I have used an 'identity' of its own, rather than merely 'quarrying' it for detail. The same is true of the *typika*;

while they all clearly conform to a recognisable pattern of composition, each one has its own character and individuality and this needs to be borne in mind when reading them.

The period covered by the book is that from the triumph of orthodoxy, the re-establishment of icon veneration within the Byzantine church and final defeat of iconoclasm in 843, to the end of the reign of Alexios Komnenos. It is a period which shows a dramatic rise in monastic foundation and an enthusiasm for the various forms of the monastic life which was in no small measure the result of the heroic role that monks were believed to have played in the fight against the iconoclasts. It is a period during which source material of all kinds becomes much more plentiful: the surviving Athonite archives begin at the end of the ninth century; hagiography is plentiful (and, more importantly, unstereotyped) throughout the tenth century, although of less value in the eleventh; imperial legislation is preserved in significant quantities and personal foundation documents, such as *typika*, begin to appear. Of course, there is much that has been lost. We know very little about the workings of the patriarchate, still less about the secular church in town or countryside and its relationship with monastic houses. Many monastic archives were destroyed either by Seljuk invasion in the eleventh century, or by later depredations of Franks and Ottomans. The documents kept in the central administrative bureaux in Constantinople have, almost without exception, been lost. It is only the mercifully bureaucratic methods of Byzantine officials, with their tidy-minded issuing of duplicates and triplicates, which have enabled us to reconstruct imperial activity via copies preserved in the archives of the recipients of imperial communications.

But given all these disadvantages, the tenth and eleventh centuries are a period when monasticism and its development may be studied in a variety of sources, and it is this very variety that can provide us with an important range of insights. And these insights are not just communicated by the written word. For the monastic monuments of the period also have their story to tell, albeit one that is often puzzling and incomplete. I have tried to present their visual evidence – architecture, decoration and inscriptions – as well as that from other artistic media whenever it has seemed relevant to my major themes. The book has been unashamedly 'source led'; it does not pretend to an overall theory or interpretation, but rather to a methodology which takes as a premise the importance of source analysis and criticism. Where there are no sources the reader will find little discussion.

Most studies of Byzantine history and society omit the study of Byzantine southern Italy from their considerations. Usually this is justified by the comment that southern Italy was in some way 'different', that it had traditions of its own which set the region apart from the Byzantine lands further to the east. But all the Byzantine provinces had their own particular characteristics. Some areas – such as the eastern themes (administrative districts) – invariably included as 'properly' Byzantine in any survey, contained linguistic, religious and social variations every bit as complicated as those of Italy. I have felt it important to include as much material about Byzantine monasticism in Apulia, Lucania and Calabria as possible (and there are some great and regrettable *lacunae* in our knowledge), not only because these regions *were* without question part of the empire until the late eleventh century, but because southern Italian sources help to demonstrate many of the similarities of monastic style, development and contact visible throughout the Byzantine world.

What linked the monks of southern Italy with their brethren further to the east was, above all, their use of a common language. They were part of the Greek-speaking and writing world and this is the world upon which I have concentrated. Though the monastic life of the Slavs is of great importance in this period and was a reflection of the 'Byzantinisation' of the Balkans and Russia, it deserves a study of its own by one competent to appreciate the Slavonic sources. So this book is not so much about monks and laymen in the 'Byzantine Commonwealth' as monks and laymen in the Byzantine heartlands. For they provided the setting for the establishment of the spiritual values, the personal commitment and the administrative support upon which orthodox monasticism was built. Although monasticism was one of Byzantium's most significant cultural and political 'exports' to the Slav world, it was created in the Greek-speaking lands and its development needs, above all, to be studied there.

PART ONE
Founders and benefactors

CHAPTER ONE

The resurgence of the monastic life

◆

We have had, we have indeed had our winter – and what a winter!
. . . But see that spring has burst into bloom, promising divine
favours and finds us all assembled to offer a prayer of thanksgiving
in return for a happy harvest![1]

T HE ENTHRONEMENT OF THE NEW patriarch Methodios of
Constantinople on 11 March 843 marked the beginning of a new era
in the Byzantine church. For the triumph of the iconodules, those who
supported the veneration of religious images was now, finally, achieved
and this practice was re-established as a crucial element in orthodox
worship. The Feast of Orthodoxy, which came to be celebrated on that
day (the first Sunday in Lent) with processions and celebrations, brought
together the forces which were deemed to have conquered iconoclasm:
the imperial family, which, in the person of the Empress Theodora acting
for her young son, Michael III, had finally cast aside error; the orthodox
clergy who had stayed faithful through the long years of persecution and,
last, but certainly not least, the monks from Constantinople and beyond,
who had provided the most stubborn and steadfast opposition to the
iconoclasts in the previous two centuries.[2]

This, at least, was the picture familiar to pious Byzantines by the
end of the ninth century. By this time, the iconoclast clergy had been
purged; iconoclast writings and conciliar decrees had been systematically
destroyed and a programme of figural redecoration of the most important
churches of the empire had begun. The *Synodikon of Orthodoxy*, a

---

[1] J. Gouillard, '*Le Synodikon de l'Orthodoxie*, édition et commentaire', *TM*, 2 (1967),
1–316, see 45. Translations are by the author unless otherwise stated.
[2] For an introduction to the history of the iconoclastic period, see A. A. M. Bryer and
J. Herrin (eds.), *Iconoclasm* (Birmingham, 1977). A useful summary of events can be found
in J. M. Hussey, *The orthodox church in the Byzantine empire* (Oxford, 1986), pp. 30–68.

document most probably drawn up by the Patriarch Methodios himself, was read aloud in the churches of the empire each year by senior clerics and served as a lasting reminder of the official version of events. The iconoclasts had 'outraged the Lord and dishonoured the holy veneration given to Him in the holy images' but had finally been defeated by the Lord's response to the pleas of the outraged saints and apostles. Iconodule doctrines were placed on a par with other fundamental tenets of the faith, such as the doctrine of the Incarnation and the 'heralds of the faith', the 'champions and doctors of Orthodoxy' were praised and commemorated by name.

Naturally, these names included the four Patriarchs of Constantinople – Germanos I (715–30); Tarasios (784–806); Nikephoros I (806–15) and Methodios I (843–7) – who had remained faithful to iconodule beliefs. But other names, those of the monks Theodore of Stoudios (759–826); Joannikios of Mount Olympos (b. ?752–4, d. 846); Hilarion and Dalmatos, *hegoumenoi* (abbots) of Constantinopolitan houses (both d. 845); 'Isaac' (d. 817) and Symeon (d. 844) were also to be commemorated as doughty fighters for the faith. Even though these names were carefully chosen to represent the leaders of the most important monastic groups in the empire, and thus to emphasise the unified support of the monks for the restoration of icon veneration, this was not merely propaganda. For it was among the monks that the iconoclasts had found some of their most tenacious opponents and at the triumph of orthodoxy these men were transformed into the heroes of hagiographic legend and their way of life gained new strength and popularity.[3]

By the beginning of the tenth century, the 'official' view of both historians and hagiographers (in many cases hardly to be distinguished from each other) was that the monks had not only bravely borne the insults, privations and even martyrdom inflicted upon them by the iconoclast emperors, but had played a major part in the events which led to the re-establishment of the icons in 843. One source fed upon another, as is well illustrated by the two versions of the events of 842–3 in the *Synodikon Vetus*, a compendium of accounts of councils held up to the ninth century. The first version, written at the end of the ninth century, simply related that a council had been held at the house of a high court official and that the courtiers and churchmen present there had approved the appointment of the new Patriarch Methodios by the Empress Theodora acting in the name of her three-year-old son, Michael III. The

---

[3] Gouillard, '*Synodikon*', 130–3 for the institution of the Feast of Orthodoxy, whose ceremonial was well established during the last years of the ninth century, and pp. 144–6 for the monastic commemorations. The monk 'Isaac' may have been a reference to the much more famous Theodore the Confessor under his secular name.

second version, found in the historian Genesios in the tenth century, told of a delegation of monks from the Stoudite house in Constantinople who visited a high official, Manuel, when he was sick and promised him recovery if he restored the icons. He then persuaded Theodora, who called upon Methodios, who himself 'still bore the marks of persecution upon his body'. A great assembly of monks from the spiritual centres of the empire – the holy mountains of Ida, Olympos, Athos and Kyminas – then took part in the processions of the first Feast of Orthodoxy in 843. Crucial elements in the 'official' version were thus established: the important rôle of monks in general (and the Stoudites in particular) in persuading the secular authorities to see the error of their ways; the references to the physical sufferings of the iconodules and the hint of the miraculous concerning the healing of the courtier, Manuel, indicating the support of Divine Power for the restoration of the icons.[4]

While it would be going too far to maintain that Byzantines of the late ninth and tenth centuries completely rewrote the history of the iconoclast centuries and the part played by monks in it, it is certainly the case that modern scholarship has been able to identify a number of areas in which the reliability of the existing sources can be questioned. In the realm of monastic hagiography, for example, it has been demonstrated that, of twelve saints' lives dealing with the first period of iconoclasm from 730–87, only one was written at the time. Three were composed before 843 and *eight* at a much later date. Only the Life of St Stephen the Younger (d. 764), a highly problematic text which was written in 806, gives some contemporary information. In the second half of the ninth century the history of the first iconoclastic period was yet to be written.

The same problem is present, to a somewhat lesser extent, when we consider the lives of the saints of the second period of iconoclasm (813–43). There are some twenty odd texts, of which some, certainly, are contemporary – such as the Letter of Theodore Graptos, which describes his brother's summons before the Emperor Theophilos and subsequent branding on his forehead for his refusal to give up his iconodule beliefs – and the lives of Theophanes the Confessor (d. 818), Michael the Synkellos (d. 846) and St Joannikios (d. 846), all of which were written by hagiographers of the next generation. But the earliest version of the life of a man considered by later generations of Byzantines to have been the focus of opposition to the iconoclasts – St Theodore the Stoudite – turns out not to have been written until after 868, some forty years after his

---

[4] C. Mango, 'The liquidation of iconoclasm and the Patriarch Photios', in Bryer and Herrin, *Iconoclasm*, pp. 133–40, reprinted in Mango's *Byzantium and its image: history and culture of the Byzantine empire and its heritage* (London, 1984), article XIII. See Genesios, p. 58 for the holy mountains.

death.[5] Many saints' lives actually *written* during the second iconoclasm did not concern themselves at all with the question of the icons. Works such as the Life of St Philaretos (d. 792), which was written about 822, portrayed the Job-like sufferings of a private citizen (not a monk until the end of his life) who lost his wealth and estates, but who still managed to maintain his faith through a period of great adversity. The iconoclasts themselves, indeed, were not opposed to the writing of hagiography which, after all, had as a main purpose the presentation of holy men whose virtuous lives could be imitated.[6]

The systematic effort to commemorate the iconodule saints did not begin until the end of the ninth century, when, as it has been aptly put, 'only the victors were left to celebrate their own heroes'.[7] The creation of a potent tradition of heroic suffering, especially among the monks, was, however, to have influential and durable consequences. By the time Symeon Metaphrastes made his collection of saints' lives in the late tenth century, much hagiography about the iconoclast period already existed and the perceptions of educated Byzantines – both laymen and ecclesiastics – about the rôle played by monks were already well formed.

The most powerful of these tenets was that the iconoclast emperors had been deeply opposed to the monastic life as well as to the veneration of icons. Until recently most historians have been agreed that the most serious period of persecution took place during the reign of Constantine V (741–75) who, it was argued, despised the ascetic way of life and who viewed the monks as an insidious force which criticised imperial policy (especially on the matter of icons) under the guise of religious instruction.[8] *The Chronicle of Theophanes*, compiled in the years 810–14, provided graphic descriptions of his anti-monastic activity. Under the years 765–7, it reported how monks from the great houses of Constantinople, such as that of Dalmatos, had been expelled from their monasteries; how holy objects, books and the landed property of the monasteries with their animals had been confiscated by the emperor. But there was worse: monks and nuns had been herded into the Hippodrome at Constantinople and ordered to marry, under the threat of blinding

---

[5] See I. Ševčenko, 'Hagiography of the iconoclast period', in Bryer and Herrin, *Iconoclasm*, pp. 113–31, reprinted in Ševčenko's *Ideology, letters and culture in the Byzantine world* (London, 1982), article v, for a forthright discussion of this problem.

[6] Ševčenko, 'Hagiography', p. 119 suggests that there are identifiably iconoclast saints' lives. See also M.-F. Rouan, 'Une lecture "iconoclaste" de la vie d'Etienne le Jeune', *TM*, 8 (1981), 415–36. For Philaretos, see Life of St Philaretos.

[7] Ševčenko, 'Hagiography', p. 129.

[8] S. Gero, 'Byzantine iconoclasm and the failure of a medieval reformation', in J. Gutman (ed.), *The image and the word: confrontations in Judaism, Christianity and Islam* (Missoula, Mont., 1977), pp. 49–62, for a concise statement of this view.

and exile to Cyprus. Those who tried to rescue holy books from the flames were themselves punished by beating, blinding or death. The persecutions spread as far afield as Mount Olympos in Asia Minor, where the *strategos* (military governor) of the Thrakesion theme, Michael Lachanodrakon, was accused of having taken a particularly active rôle in these attacks.[9]

It is very difficult to know what to make of these accounts, which have a strong flavour of atrocity stories compiled long after the event. In addition, interesting, if contradictory, evidence is contained in the Life of St Anthusa of Mantineon which, while depicting the attempts of Constantine V to persuade the saint to accept iconoclast teachings and his subsequent persecution of her double monastery when she did not, also contains an account of St Anthusa's help to the emperor's wife Eudocia, brought to the house during a crisis in her pregnancy when the emperor was on campaign. The empress subsequently richly endowed the monastery. This may not have been an isolated example and should warn us against assuming that Constantine was resolutely 'anti-monastic' as well as 'pro-iconoclast'. After the emperor's death, however, the attacks on monasticism, such as they were, seem, for the most part, to have ceased. In fact, some monastic houses actually espoused iconoclasm. But even for those that did not, the difficulties seem not to have been over-whelming. In 787, when a council re-established icon veneration, monks were present to support the iconodule cause and, during the second period of iconoclasm, Niketas the Patrician, an iconodule, had only to travel some twenty miles from Constantinople to find shelter with like-minded monks.[10]

What is important to establish, however, is not what modern scholar-ship can demonstrate to have happened, but what many educated Byzantines had been taught *had* happened. And by the beginning of the tenth century, they certainly believed that one of the greatest of the iconodule heroes had been the *hegoumenos* Theodore the Stoudite, whose voluminous correspondence, hymns and collections of homilies – the greater and the lesser *Catecheses* – provide a mine of information about his

---

[9] Theophanes, I, pp. 443–6; see also *The Chronicle of Theophanes: an English translation of* anni mundi *6095–6305 (AD 602–813) with introduction and notes*, ed. and translated H. Turtledove (Philadelphia, 1982), pp. 125–31.

[10] C. Mango, 'St Anthusa of Mantineon and the family of Constantine V', *AB*, 100 (1982), 401–9, reprinted in his *Byzantium and its image*, article IX. For a re-assessment of the monastic experience during iconoclasm, see M. Kaplan, *Les hommes et la terre à Byzance du VIe au XIe siècle. Propriété et exploitation du sol* (Byzantina Sorbonensia, X, Paris, 1992), pp. 297–300. See also C. Frazee, 'St Theodore of Studios and ninth-century monasticism in Constantinople', *Studia Monastica*, 23 (1981), 27–58, 30, and C. Mango, 'Historical introduction', in Bryer and Herrin, *Iconoclasm*, pp. 5–6.

teaching on a range of spiritual matters, including the veneration of icons, as well as the correct ordering of the monastic life.[11] Theodore, his brother Joseph (later metropolitan of Thessalonike) and their uncle, Plato, *hegoumenos* of the Monastery of Sakkoudion in Bithynia, consistently refused to accept iconoclast teachings. Even when the ideological climate became somewhat more favourable at the end of the first period of iconoclasm in 787, they also refused to accept that any leniency should be shown towards iconoclast clergy who had not maltreated the iconodules. They declined to take part in any discussion in which iconoclast views *might* be expressed. They were exiled from Constantinople and imprisoned on numerous occasions, although virtually always for what might be termed 'political offences', such as fomenting opposition to the divorce of the Emperor Constantine VI and his remarriage in 795 and refusing to join in the customary good wishes expressed by the clergy to the Emperor Nikephoros I as he was about to leave on campaign in 808. Even that saintly ascetic, Joannikios of Mount Olympos, himself an ardent iconodule, was driven to criticise Theodore's 'lack of humility' when, in 820, he yet again refused to attend a council (which was, in fact, to declare the iconoclast Second Council of Nicaea in error) because of the likely presence there of those he considered unregenerate heretics.[12]

But by the end of the ninth century, such attitudes were not viewed in official circles as stubborn intransigence and a refusal to assist in the delicate and difficult task of rebuilding the shattered hierarchy of the church, but as admirable steadfastness and courage in adversity. This was not only because the iconodule cause had triumphed, but also because Theodore had already been recognised as a great monastic leader and the Stoudite style of monasticism was already gaining in popularity.[13] Theodore's initial sphere of activity was in western Asia Minor, in the region around Mount Olympos where he succeeded his uncle Plato as *hegoumenos* of the Monastery of Sakkoudion in 794. In 798, Theodore became *hegoumenos* of the Monastery of St John the Baptist in the district

[11] *Theodori Studitae opera omnia*, *PG*, 99, but see P. Speck, *Theodoros Studites. Jamben auf verschiedene Gegenstände* (Supplementa Byzantina, I, Berlin, 1968), for his verse and most recently, *Theodori Studitae epistolae*, ed. G. Fatouros (CFHB, xxxi, ser. Berolin. Berlin/New York, 1992), which I have not been able to consult.

[12] See Hussey, *Orthodox church*, pp. 46–57; 61. Frazee, 'St Theodore of Stoudios', pp. 36–7 and C. van der Vorst, 'Le translation de S. Théodore Studite et de S. Joseph de Thessalonique', *AB*, 31 (1913), 27–62, 39–40.

[13] It is surprising that there is no full-length modern study of Theodore the Stoudite, though his career is summarised in *ODB*, iii, pp. 2044–5. For Stoudite monasticism, see J. Leroy, 'La reforme studite', in *Il monachesimo orientale* (OCA, 153, Rome, 1958), pp. 181–214 and 'La vie quotidienne du moine studite', *Irénikon*, 27 (1954), 21–50.

tou Stoudiou in Constantinople, not, as his biographer indicated, because Arab raids had forced the monks to flee from Sakkoudion (in fact a number remained and the Monastery of Sakkoudion continued to receive novices for the Stoudite houses), but because important figures in the capital, possibly including the Empress Irene, were keen to encourage such a notable iconodule to undertake the reorganisation of an existing monastery there.[14]

Although it is customary to speak of the Stoudite 'reform', this may be something of a misnomer as we have little information about how monasteries were organised and upon what spiritual principles they were run in the period before Theodore. Certainly (like the eleventh-century reformers in the West), the saint himself always emphasised that he was *restoring* the old monastic ways which time had eroded:

> I seek the divine and human aid which will enable me to gain my own salvation . . . and will be capable of restoring that life which obtains salvation, to lay down the path, to put our affairs in order and to return to the old way of life.[15]

Thus Theodore preached a return to the past and that a literal adherence to the teachings of the Fathers – particularly St Basil, St Dorotheos of Gaza, Barsanouphios and John, John Klimakos and Mark the Monk – was the best guarantee of the purity of the monastic life. In his emphasis on tradition he was following a well-established ecclesiastical practice of avoiding any claims to an originality which could all too easily be considered heretical novelty.

Theodore's teaching on monasticism concentrated on three elements: the creation of a monastic rule to restore the teachings of the Fathers, a return to the coenobitic spirit and an emphasis on poverty. The 'Rule of the Fathers', in his view, was concerned not to acquire knowledge of God by contemplation, but to realise the old ideals of primitive monasticism, where the monastery was a 'Christian village' of an essentially practical type. Work rather than meditation was the order of the day, for work was seen as a measurement of spiritual fervour and 'love of work' (*philergia*) and 'frequent work' (*polyergia*) were seen as virtues to which every monk should aspire. 'He who is fervent in bodily tasks', wrote Theodore, 'is also fervent in spiritual ones.' Work was to be considered as both the liturgy

---

[14] Leroy, 'Reforme studite', pp. 202–4 demonstrates the inaccuracy of the information contained in the second Life by Michael the Monk: *Vita et conversatio sancti patris nostri et confessoris S. Theodori abbatis monasterii Studii, PG*, 99, cols. 233–328, cols. 257–60, which sought to dramatise the episode perhaps to demonstrate that Theodore, like all saints, enjoyed God's especial protection.

[15] *Great Catechesis*, II, as quoted by Leroy, 'Reforme studite', p. 186.

and the offering of the monk and could include activity such as the copying of manuscripts, for which the Stoudite house in Constantinople became celebrated and which was not considered to be in any way qualitatively different from other forms of manual labour. The monastic day included at least four and a half hours' work of some kind in winter and at least eight hours' in summer. Work had a distinct social purpose, too: that of helping the poor and the unfortunate. Hospices for the sick and for travellers were always to be found in monasteries which followed Stoudite customs.[16]

The coenobitic or communal monasticism which Theodore favoured was not a recent development, for it was modelled on the communities set up by St Pachomios in fourth-century Egypt. The definition of the *koinobion* familiar to Theodore was that provided by St Basil in his *Monastic Constitutions*:

> I term the common life that in which personal property is discarded, the struggle of wills is eradicated and all tumult, strife and conflicts are trampled underfoot. All is held in common: souls, thoughts, bodies.[17]

The physical surroundings in which this spiritual unity might be achieved were described in the sixth-century Justinianic legislation on monasticism: 'In all monasteries which are called *koinobia*, we order that, according to the monastic canons, all should live in one habitation and sleep in one dormitory.'[18] The emphasis in the *koinobia* was on the collective battle of the community against the forces of evil and the community was conceived of as a 'mystic body', with the *hegoumenos* at the head, but with other monks providing the 'eyes', 'hands' and 'feet'.

Theodore's main contribution to monasticism was his designation of the 'limbs' of the community, by establishing in detail the various ranks of the monastic hierarchy within each house and assigning to each its specific duty. The *hegoumenos*, as well as being in general charge of the affairs of the monastery, was particularly concerned with the spiritual guidance of the monks and each day, as spiritual father to the community, heard the private revelation of each member's thoughts, concerns and confessions. Beneath him was a deputy, originally known as the *deuteron*, but by the tenth century most often referred to as the *oikonomos*, whose task was to oversee the property and temporal organisation of the monastery. He was assisted by other officials, the most important of

---

16 Leroy, 'Reforme studite', pp. 188–90, see 191–7; 'Vie quotidienne', p. 46.
17 Basil of Caesarea, *Constitutiones monasticae*, XVIII, 1, *PG*, 31, cols. 1321–1428, col. 1381.
18 Justinian, *Novella*, CXXIII, 36 in *CIC*, III.

whom was probably the *kellarites*, in charge of the provision of food and the supervision of the kitchens and bakehouse. The discipline of the house was under the charge of another series of officials: the *epistemonarches*, the *taxiarches* and the *epiteretes* all concerned with the maintenance of discipline at services, the correct order of processions and more mundane (but doubtless common) occurrences such as the rousing of somnolent monks for early services, the eradication of worldly gossip and cliques and, in particular, the strict prohibition of personal possessions, even something so apparently insignificant as a needle. The rule of absolute poverty was to be demonstrated by the collection and redistribution each week of the monks' clothes and, on the wider scale, by adherence to the idea that the house should only aim to be self-sufficient in produce and at all costs avoid waste.[19]

There has been much debate about whether a written rule existed for the houses of the Stoudite 'federation' in Constantinople and Asia Minor during Theodore's lifetime. The existence of a penitential, providing punishments for those who transgressed monastic customs, suggests that some sort of set code of behaviour had been laid down, but it is only with the so-called *Hypotyposis* (composed after Theodore's death, but doubtless strongly influenced by his teachings), that his views on monasticism began to be widely spread.[20] Although Byzantine monasticism never possessed 'rules' that were common to families of houses (such as those of the Benedictines or Cistercians in the West), the Stoudite way of life and liturgical customs became the basis for the regulations (*typika*) of many houses, although they were often associated with other traditions from Palestine and clauses drawn more directly from the writings of the Fathers, particularly St Basil, on the monastic life. It is clear from manuscript evidence that the *Hypotyposis* had reached southern Italy by the end of the ninth century and it later became the basis for the *typika* of many of the Greek houses there.[21] In the eleventh century, the revised edition made by the Patriarch Alexios Stoudites (1025–43) was translated into Slavonic and introduced into the Cave Monastery near Kiev in Russia by its famous *hegoumenos*,

---

[19] Leroy, 'Reforme studite', pp. 199–201 for the officers of the monastery; p. 191 for the adherence to common possessions and poverty. See chapter 7 for a further discussion of monastic poverty.

[20] Leroy, 'Reforme studite', pp. 208–10.

[21] See A. Guillou, 'Grecs d'Italie du sud et de Sicile au moyen âge: les moines', *Mélanges d'archéologie et d'histoire de l'Ecole Française de Rome*, 75 (1963), 79–110, see 105, reprinted in A. Guillou, *Studies in Byzantine Italy* (London, 1970), article XII, and A. Pertusi, 'Rapporti tra il monachesimo italo-greco ed il monachesimo bizantino nell' alto medio evo', in *La chiesa greca in Italia dall' VIII al XVI secolo. Atti del convegno storico interecclesiale, Bari, 1969*, published as *Italia Sacra*, 20 (1972–3), 473–520, 501.

Theodosios (c. 1062–74). In later centuries, Stoudite influence was to be found in houses throughout the Balkans and in northern and central Russia.[22]

Within the empire itself, Stoudite customs soon came to play an important part in monastic life. Their spread was aided by the cult which sprang up around Theodore and his brother Joseph, after their bodies were brought back to Constantinople for reburial in their own monastery in 844.[23] From the large number of manuscripts of Theodore's homilies (the *Catecheses*) which survive from the medieval period (over seventy in the case of the *Lesser Catecheses*), it is clear that they were a popular source of monastic reading, often in the form of excerpts to be read on particular days of the year. Copies of the *Greater Catecheses* also spread widely and again selections were made from them for reading aloud, such as that compiled in the eleventh century by Paul of Evergetis for his refounded Monastery of the Theotokos Evergetis in Constantinople. Passages from the *Hypotyposis* also made their appearance in monastic *typika* in Constantinople, as well as on Mount Athos, although whether Theodore's emphasis on the coenobitic life took hold here in its original form is a matter of some debate.[24] In any case, it would be mistaken to view the Stoudite 'rule' as an unchanging set of regulations. It, too, was subject to the same kinds of evolution in the tenth century as were the customs of other houses which were certainly influenced by the other main tradition of Byzantine monasticism, that of the foundations of St Anthony in Palestine – the *lavrai* – where monks lived in individual cells (*kellia*) during the week and only gathered together for the weekly liturgy, to collect food and materials for handiwork and on great festivals. Here the emphasis was on individual *hesychia* (solitude) in which each monk developed his own relationship with God and fought with his own spiritual strength against the onslaughts of the demons.[25]

But the improved fortunes of the Stoudite monks after the restoration of the icons and the high esteem in which they were held, although one of the most obvious cases of a characteristic association by Byzantine public opinion of past exploits with present virtue, were not phenomena confined to a single monastic group. Throughout the empire, monasti-

---

[22] For the Stoudite rule in Russia, see A. P. Vlasto, *The entry of the Slavs into Christendom* (Cambridge, 1970), p. 304; D. Obolensky, *The Byzantine commonwealth* (London, 1971), pp. 298–300 and *The Paterik of the Kievan Caves Monastery*, translated M. Heppell (Harvard Library of Early Ukrainian Literature, English translations, 1, Cambridge, Mass., 1989).

[23] Van der Vorst, 'Translation de S. Théodore Studite', pp. 27, 35.

[24] Leroy, 'Reforme studite', p. 213, note 256.

[25] For further discussion of the extent of Stoudite influence on Mount Athos and the development of monastic 'styles' in the tenth century, see chapter 2.

cism revived and flourished after the mid-ninth century and the variety
of life-styles practised testifies to the enthusiasm with which Byzantines
(male and female alike) sought to find a suitable outlet for their individual
spiritual aspirations. Imperial approval and patronage of the monastic life
was of the first importance, however, and the post-iconoclastic 'boom'
in religious foundation owed much of its impetus to the activities of
individual rulers.[26] Basil I's biographer, the Emperor Constantine
Porphyrogennetos (913–59), was at particular pains to emphasise his rôle
as a benefactor of ecclesiastical institutions, especially in Constantinople,
and the tradition of mentioning the founding activities of his successors
was maintained by the chroniclers who dealt with the tenth and eleventh
centuries. This was part and parcel of the portrayal of the orthodox ruler,
although, like many imperial qualities, it was criticised if taken to excess.[27]
The twelfth-century historian, Zonaras, explained the exhaustion of the
imperial treasury at the accession of the Emperor Isaac I Komnenos
(1057–9) by stating that, since the death of Basil I, the emperors had
dissipated their resources in paying for 'their own pleasure and the
construction of religious houses'.[28]

Many of these monasteries were extremely grand foundations and the
imperial lead was followed on a slightly more modest scale by aristocrats
and high ecclesiastical officials. The part played by Constantinopolitan
patrons in the resurgence of monastic foundation in the period from 843
onwards is relatively simple to plot in the pages of the court-orientated
chronicles, and the painstaking work of modern scholars in identifying
the location of these houses and, in some important cases, excavating
and restoring them, has also made an important contribution to our
knowledge. Two famous examples may suffice. The monastic complex
of the Myrelaion (Bodrum Camii) was built by Romanos I Lekapenos
(920–44), probably on the site of his own house in Constantinople, and
completed about 922. It was an extensive set of buildings which included
a church in which Romanos decreed that he should be buried. Slightly
later on, the *patrikios* (court official) Constantine Lips built and endowed
a monastery and a hostel for travellers on a site near the River Lykos in
the city.[29]

But the monastic geography of the provinces is much more difficult to

---

[26] See, for instance, R. S. Cormack, *Writing in gold: Byzantine society and its icons* (London, 1985), chapter 4.

[27] Theophanes cont., V, pp. 211–353 for the reign of Basil I and pp. 321–41 for his building and restoration programme.

[28] Zonaras, III, p. 667.

[29] See C. Striker, *The Myrelaion (Bodrum Camii) in Istanbul* (Princeton, 1981) and T. Macridy, A. H. Megaw, C. Mango and E. J. W. Hawkins, 'The Monastery of Lips (Fenari Isa Camii) at Istanbul', *DOP*, 18 (1964), 249–315.

elucidate. The existence of many monastic and eremitic communities may be demonstrated from saints' lives and charters of donation, but for some regions such documentary evidence is either sparse or entirely lacking. In southern Italy, for example, where extensive survey work has been continuing since the pioneering work of Emile Bertaux early this century, inscriptions and allusions in hagiographies inform us of the existence of houses such as those of the Monastery of St John Prodromos at Vietri on the Gulf of Salerno, ceded by its founder Jaquintus (a Lombard?) to two Greek monks, the *hegoumenos* Sabas and the hieromonk (monk in priestly orders) Kosmas in 986; the Chapel of Sant' Angelo near San Chirico in the Monte Raparo region of Lucania which was probably part of a monastery founded by St Vitalis in the tenth century; and the Monastery of San Giovanni Vecchio near Stilo, in Calabria, which expanded greatly in the eleventh century as a consequence of the activity of a local saint, John Theristes (d. 1090–5).[30]

There are other areas, however, where the significance of caves and what may be other ecclesiastical complexes may only be surmised. The existence of numerous grottoes (some painted) around Rossano in Calabria has led to the suggestion that the region was a 'holy mountain', inhabited by monks. Other monastic centres have been located in the caves around the Rivers Sauro, Salandrella, Basento and Bradono in Lucania as well as in the southernmost tip of the Terra d'Otranto (the 'heel' of Italy). That considerable debate continues about the precise significance of many of these grottoes (some commentators preferring to see them as churches and chapels rather than the sites of eremitic monasticism) is an indication of how difficult it is to interpret these monuments from visual evidence alone.[31]

Such is also the case with the monastic centres of Cappadocia, where the late tenth-century chronicler, Leo the Deacon, mentioned 'troglo-dyte' dwellers in the area although he did not include monks among them, but where the survival of richly decorated monuments cut into the soft volcanic rock of the area testifies to the existence of flourishing monastic

---

[30] E. Bertaux, *L'art de l'Italie méridionale de la fin de l'empire romain à la conquête de Charles d'Anjou* (3 vols., Paris, 1903). Reprinted in A. Prandi (ed.), *L'art dans l'Italie méridionale, Aggiornamento dell'opera di Emile Bertaux* (6 vols., Rome, 1978), IV–VI. See also A. Wharton, *Art of empire: painting and architecture of the Byzantine periphery: a comparative study of four provinces* (University Park, Pa., 1988), chapter 5. For the Monastery of St John Prodromos at Vietri, see Prandi, *Aggiornamento*, IV, p. 295; for the Chapel of St Angelo on Mount Raparo, *Aggiornamento*, IV, pp. 312–14; Wharton, *Art of empire*, p. 139; for San Giovanni Vecchio, *Aggiornamento*, IV, pp. 124–5 and for the suggestion that the Cattolica at Stilo was also a monastic church, p. 305 and Wharton, *Art of empire*, p. 140.
[31] Prandi, *Aggiornamento*, IV, pp. 308–10, 331–7; Wharton, *Art of empire*, pp. 130–9.

communities.[32] The omission of references to Cappadocia as a monastic
centre in Byzantine, Arab and Turkish texts is baffling, since inscriptions
in many of the churches and monasteries show a lively interest in their
decoration on the part of a local aristocracy which played an important
rôle in the politics of the empire at this time. Although controversy has
long raged over the precise dating of many of the frescoes, the consensus
of opinion among art historians indicates that the earliest foundations may
date from the seventh century and that some may have survived the most
dangerous period of Persian and Arab raiding in the region in the seventh,
eighth and ninth centuries. But the most prosperous period for the rock
monasteries was undoubtedly the tenth and eleventh centuries. It has
been estimated that, of the churches and monasteries built between the
seventh and fourteenth centuries, 45 per cent can be dated to the ninth
and tenth centuries and 25 to 30 per cent to the period between 1000 and
the Battle of Mantzikert in 1071.[33]

In many other areas of Asia Minor, however, the detailed regional
surveys which would help to identify and date monastic structures and
which could be used in conjunction with literary evidence still remain to
be done, although recent work on the region of Trebizond and the
Pontos shows something of what can be achieved. The convoluted history
of the cult of St Eugenios of Trebizond is a case in point. A monastery
dedicated to this saint (martyred under Diocletian) was established in the
city by the ninth century and was rebuilt by the Emperor Basil II in
1021–2. We know from the account of later miracles associated with the
saint written by the patriarch of Constantinople, John Xiphilinos
(1064–75), who was a native of Trebizond that the monastery possessed
considerable property near Paipertes (modern Bayburt). But it is now also
clear that St Eugenios of Trebizond was a 'composite' saint, merging
in hagiographical tradition with St Eugenios of Arauraka (also in the

[32] Leo the Deacon, III.1, p. 35. See G. de Jerphanion, *Une nouvelle province de l'art byzantin. Les églises rupestres de Cappadoce* (3 vols., Paris, 1925–42); N. Thierry, 'Monuments de Cappadoce de l'antiquité romaine au moyen âge byzantin', in N. Thierry, *Le Aree omogenee della civiltà rupestre nell'ambito dell'impero bizantino. La Cappadocia* (Galatina, 1981), pp. 39–73; Wharton, *Art of empire*, chapter 2 and, for the best recent study and full bibliography, L. Rodley, *Cave monasteries of Byzantine Cappadocia* (Cambridge, 1985).
[33] For the patrons, see Rodley, *Cave monasteries*, pp. 250–2 and N. Thierry and M. Thierry, *Nouvelles églises rupestres de Cappadoce. Région de Hasan Dagi* (Paris, 1963), p. 3. Patronage is further discussed in chapter 5. For the survival of monuments through the period of arab raids, R. S. Cormack, 'Byzantine Cappadocia: the archaic group of wall-paintings', *Journal of the British Archaeological Association*, 3rd ser., 30 (1967), 19–36, reprinted in R. S. Cormack, *The Byzantine eye* (London, 1979), article VI, see pp. 29–36. For building statistics, N. Thierry, 'L'art monumental byzantin en Asie Mineure du XIe siècle au XIVe', *DOP*, 29 (1975), 73–111, reprinted in N. Thierry, *Peintures d'Asie Mineure et de Transcaucasie aux Xe et XIe siècles* (London, 1977), article VII, p. 96.

Pontos). The monks of the monastery dedicated to him in Trebizond took good care to foster the saint as a miracle-working guardian of the city and its region, even to the extent, in the late ninth century, of moving his festival from the inconvenient site of 21 January (the traditional date of his martyrdom) to that of 24 June (his birthday), when as well as celebrating St John the Baptist's feast, they could also 'eclipse' the reputation of another local saint, Orestes of Rhizaion. Caravans could also, of course, much more easily reach Trebizond with goods for the saint's *panegyris* (fair), thus adding to the revenues of the monastery. When other regions have been subjected to this sort of detailed analysis, it may be possible to extend our knowledge of the monastic geography of the interior of Asia Minor. For the moment it remains depressingly sparse.[34]

The history of the monastic communities of the western regions of Asia Minor, is, happily, more accessible, although problems about the precise location of individual houses still remain. The 'holy mountains' of Ida, Latros, Kyminas, Mykale, Auxentios and Olympos are all attested in literary sources by the beginning of the tenth century and testify to an interesting 'migration' of the focus of monastic life in the region from the Bithynian coastline (where the Stoudites had been active and where their houses and other *koinobia* still remained), to the mountainous hinterland.[35] The origins of these monastic centres probably lay in the movement of the monastic populations of the eastern provinces away from Persian and Muslim attack. The hagiographers of the tenth and eleventh centuries believed that the first inhabitants had been monks fleeing from Palestine, and there may be some truth in this tradition,

---

[34] See A. A. M. Bryer and D. C. Winfield, *The Byzantine monuments and topography of the Pontos* (2 vols., Dumbarton Oaks Studies, xx, Washington, DC, 1985), I, pp. 166–9 (see pp. 222–4 for the cult and houses dedicated to St Eugenios); and B. Martin-Hisard, 'Trébizonde et la culte de Saint Eugène (6e–11e s.)', *Revue des Etudes Arméniennes*, n.s. 14 (1980), 307–43, for a more detailed study of the textual evidence.
[35] R. Janin, *La géographie ecclésiastique de l'empire byzantin. Section one: Le siège de Constantinople et le patriarcat oecuménique* (2 vols). ii: *Les églises et les monastères du grands centres byzantins* (Paris, 1975). Genesios, as we have seen (p. 11, and note 4), reported the presence of monks from Olympos, Athos, Ida and Kyminas at the processions celebrating the restoration of images in 843, but he may have been 'reading back' from what was customary on the Feast of Orthodoxy in the tenth century. Theophanes cont. cites the holy mountains of Olympos, Kyminas, Chryse Petra and Barachios as monastic centres in 933 (pp. 418–19) and Olympos, Kyminas, Athos, Barachios and Latros in 945 (p. 430). The so-called Continuation of the Chronicle of George the Monk cites Olympos, Kyminas, Latros, Chryse Petra and Barachios (p. 910). For Mount Auxentios, see J. Pargoire, 'Mont Saint-Auxence. Etude historique et topographique', *ROC*, ser. 1, 8 (1903), 15–31, 240–79, 426–58, 550–76. For the monasteries of the Bithynian coastline, see Janin, *Grands centres*, and C. Mango and I. Ševčenko, 'Some churches and monasteries on the southern shore of the Sea of Marmara', *DOP*, 27 (1973), 235–77.

although the suggestion of an association with the Holy Land may also, of course, have been added to enhance their spiritual prestige. Another possible explanation for the appearance of groups of monks in these mountains is that they were refugees from iconoclast persecution in the great monasteries of the capital and Michael Lachanodrakon's activities in the Thrakesion theme. By the end of the tenth century, large numbers were leading the contemplative life there, and the significant influence of the founders of these houses began to stretch across the islands of the Aegean to the mainland of the Balkans.[36]

An important factor in the resurgence of monasticism in the Aegean islands, as in other regions of the empire, was the re-establishment of Byzantine military and administrative control in areas lost to Muslim or Slav attacks in the 'dark ages' from the sixth to the ninth centuries. Two examples may suffice to illustrate this trend. The island of Crete, lost in 827, was finally reconquered by Byzantium in 961 and the military success was immediately followed by a campaign to reconvert the indigenous population and to re-establish the monastic life.[37] Similarly, the reconquest of Cyprus in 965, after its three-hundred year period of Muslim influence, created conditions of security vital to the promotion of monasticism and was followed in the eleventh century by the foundation of a number of important houses, such as the Monastery of St Chrysostom at Koutsovendis founded in 1090 by the *hegoumenos* George and later patronised by the general Eumathios Philokales, and the complex containing the Church of the Panagia Phorbiotissa at Asinou, founded in the last years of the century.[38] The establishment of security on the Aegean islands in the late tenth century, as well as providing conditions in which indigenous monasticism could flourish, was also to prove of particular importance in the eleventh century when the raids

---

[36] The hagiographers of the saints on Mount Latros in the tenth century maintained that monks from Rhaïthu on the Red Sea had founded their communities, see Life of St Paul the Younger, chapter 8, p. 33; Life of St Nikephoros, chapter 14, p. 145. St Paul of Latros lived for a time in a cave which had once been inhabited by a hermit, Athanasios, who had fled from Constantinople during the 'persecutions' of Michael II (820–9). See Life of St Paul the Younger, chapter 13, pp. 42–3.

[37] See *Life of St Nikon*, ed. and trans. D. F. Sullivan (Brookline, Mass., 1987), chapters 20–1, pp. 82–9; Life of St John Xenos, and chapter 2.

[38] For a general survey of Cyprus in the eleventh century, see C. Galatariotou, *The making of a saint: the life, times and sanctification of Neophytos the Recluse* (Cambridge, 1991), chapter 3. For the monuments, see Wharton, *Art of empire*, chapter 3; A. and A. J. Stylianou, *The painted churches of Cyprus: treasures of Byzantine art* (London, 1988), pp. 456 (Koutsovendis) and pp. 114–40 (Asinou); C. Mango and E. J. W. Hawkins, 'Report on field work in Istanbul and Cyprus, 1962–3', *DOP*, 18 (1964), 319–40 and C. Mango, E. J. W. Hawkins and S. Boyd, 'The Monastery of St Chrysostomos at Koutsovendis (Cyprus). Part I: description', *DOP*, 44 (1990), 63–94.

of the Turks reached the western coasts of Asia Minor and forced the monastic communities there to flee elsewhere for safety.[39]

The creation of more secure conditions in the Balkans was also the result of an association of military action, imaginative diplomacy and missionary activity in which the monastic life had its part to play. Although this study is primarily concerned with the fortunes of monastic houses within the borders of the empire which were part of a Greek-speaking cultural tradition, it is important to bear in mind how important an 'export' Greek monasticism was. For Byzantine monks travelling among the Slavs of the Balkans and the peoples of Russia and the steppes brought with them not only the teaching of the Gospels and the liturgy, traditions and moral teachings of the eastern church, but the cultural and political attitudes of Constantinople. Monks from centres such as Mount Olympos in Bithynia were used as ambassadors and messengers in distant parts; they enjoyed the confidence of emperors and could be relied upon to preach the autocracy and supremacy of the Byzantine ruler as God's viceregent on earth. The value placed by the imperial government on the activities of monks in distant lands is not only a testament to their skills in evangelism and diplomacy, but also a mark of the high esteem in which monasticism, as a way of life, was held.[40]

Nowhere is this more evident than in the careers of the 'Apostles of the Slavs', the two brothers SS Constantine-Cyril and Methodios, who were key figures in the Byzantine cultural advance into the Balkans in the mid-ninth century and who both embraced the monastic life. Methodios took his vows on Mount Olympos and Cyril followed his example at the very end of his life. In their first area of activity, Moravia, evangelisation had already begun from the great Latin monasteries in Bavaria, but archaeological evidence indicates that orthodox monasticism developed as a consequence of their missionary work. A church at Sady in Bohemia, for instance, probably built about 830, was extended to include the more Byzantine elements of a large narthex and a round apse in the years after 863. It has been suggested that this extra space was needed to house a school for monastic catechumens and that this house should be identified with Velegrad – the residential centre of the Cyrillo-Methodian missions in the region.[41]

[39] On the reconquest of the islands, see E. Malamut, *Les îles de l'empire byzantin, VIIIe–XIIe siècles* (2 vols. Byzantina Sorbonensia, VIII, Paris, 1988), I, pp. 72–91 and chapter 2.

[40] See, in general, F. Dvornik, *Byzantine missions among the Slavs* (Brunswick, NJ, 1970).

[41] Vlasto, *Entry of the Slavs*, p. 299. For the church at Sady, p. 71. For a summary of the activities of Constantine-Cyril and Methodios, see Obolensky, *Byzantine commonwealth*, pp. 137–46.

The tradition of monastic foundations in the lands bordering the empire was continued by the disciples of Cyril and Methodios, SS Clement and Naum. It was in Bulgaria that perhaps their most outstanding success was achieved. After the expulsion of the Byzantine missionaries from Moravia in 885, a group of them (including Clement and Naum) had travelled down the Danube to Belgrade, where they entered the lands controlled by the Bulgars. Having been welcomed there, they travelled to the Bulgar capital at Pliska, where they became close advisers of the Tsar, Boris, who had been baptised in 864 or 865 and had taken as his Christian name that of the reigning emperor, Michael III. The battle for the 'hearts and minds' of Bulgarian Christians which had hitherto raged between the missionary representatives of Rome and Constantinople had to a large extent been resolved by the time of their arrival, since in 870 a council held in Constantinople formally placed the Bulgars under the control of the Byzantine patriarch, and the Patriarch Ignatios appointed an archbishop (whose rank and degree of autonomy set him above many of similar rank within the empire) and numerous subordinate clergy. Clement and Naum were thus able to assist Boris-Michael with his task of creating and educating a Slav-speaking clergy who could help in the spread of Christianity. At Boris-Michael's request, Clement moved south to Macedonia, while Naum remained in Bulgaria until 893, where he was active in promoting the increasing amount of literary production in Old Slavonic which was taking place in the monasteries of Pliska and in the tsar's foundation of St Panteleimon at Preslav.

An important mark of the early success of orthodox monasticism in Bulgaria was the fact that Boris-Michael himself retired into the Monastery of St Panteleimon in 889, and although he was forced to emerge to quell a pagan rebellion led by his eldest son, Vladimir, he did finally end his days as a monk in 907. By the second decade of the tenth century, indigenous Bulgarian monasticism was well established in all its forms. As well as the royal *koinobia*, solitary ascetics could also be found. The most famous of them, St John of Rila (born c. 876), first organised a monastic group in the hills above Sofia and then moved on to practise an extremely ascetic life in the mountains of southern Bulgaria. He founded the Rila Monastery in c. 930 and spent the last years of his life as a solitary hermit in a cave nearby. He became a figure of local Bulgarian devotion; an office to commemorate him was composed at Rila soon after his death in 946 and his relics were eventually moved to Sofia in about 980.[42]

Clement (b. about 840), a pupil of St Methodios during his time as a monk on Mount Olympos, moved south and first established himself at

[42] Vlasto, *Entry of the Slavs*, pp. 165–8; Obolensky, *Byzantine commonwealth*, pp. 93–7.

Devol to the south-west of Lake Ohrid, afterwards becoming a bishop in the region of the Upper Vardar river in about 893. On his death in July 916, he was buried in his own monastic foundation of St Panteleimon in Ohrid. His assistant, Naum, took over the work of preaching and teaching when Clement became a bishop and also founded monasteries at Devol and on the shores of Lake Prespa. Ten years before his death in 910 he retired into the monastic life and his relics were later transferred to a monastery dedicated to him at the southern end of Lake Ohrid.[43] So in the Ohrid region, too, the traditions of the monastic life were closely linked with the process of preaching the Gospel and conversion. As in northern Bulgaria, the presence of the relics of these monastic saints in the regions they had helped to convert emphasised the honour in which the spiritual life was held. Indeed, there was never any thought of separating out the various 'elements' of the Christian life; with the acceptance of orthodox Christianity came the recognition that the monastic life presented the most pure form of the Christian life that could be practised. The establishment of Byzantine monastic houses was to prove of great significance when (as in Moravia) the missions themselves suffered political set-backs, for they provided bases from which orthodox preaching could begin again when the time was ripe and establishments where the indigenous populations could begin to experience as well as learn about orthodox spiritual and cultural values.

Associated with the establishment of Christianity on the empire's northern borders was an attempt to reassert imperial control within the empire in the southern Balkans. By the end of the tenth century, the threat of Slav, Magyar and Bulgar raiding had passed from the Greek themes, but that conditions at the beginning of the century had been precarious may be attested not only from chronicle sources, but from the lives of the saints of the area.[44] 'Barbarians' (it is not clear who was meant) attacked the residence of the bishop of Argos in the Peloponnese in the early years of the tenth century; a bishop of Kerkyra (Corfu) was abducted by the 'Scyths' – possibly Croatian pirates.[45] The religious foundations of Attica suffered Bulgar attacks in 917–18 and 978–96 and Magyar raiding in 943. Danger came not only from outside the boundaries of the empire, but also from within: Slavonic tribes, long settled in the Peloponnese, revolted in the reign of Romanos I Lekapenos (920–45).[46]

[43] Vlasto, *Entry of the Slavs*, p. 170; Obolensky, *Byzantine commonwealth*, p. 96.

[44] G. da Costa-Louillet, 'Saints de Grèce aux VIIIe, IXe et Xe siècles', *B*, 31 (1961), 309–69, summarises the lives.

[45] Life of St Peter of Argos, p. 8; da Costa-Louillet, 'Saints de Grèce', pp. 321, 328.

[46] Life of St Luke the Younger; Martini, p. 94, *PG*, col. 449; da Costa-Louillet, 'Saints de Grèce', pp. 337, 339. For the Slav revolts, *Life of St Nikon*, chapter 62, pp. 206–13; da Costa-Louillet, 'Saints de Grèce', p. 363; *DAI*, II, pp. 186, 232–4; R. J. H. Jenkins, 'The

It is hardly surprising, then, that we hear little of the *settled* monastic life in Greece in the tenth century, although the importance of wandering monks was considerable. The Monastery of Hosios Loukas in Phokis contains the only known church to have been founded in mainland Greece in the tenth century. But with the defeat of Bulgaria in 1018 and its incorporation into the Byzantine empire, the way stood open for further foundations in more secure conditions. From the early eleventh century date the expansion and decoration of Hosios Loukas, the Monastery of the Saviour at Lakedaimon (c. 1027) and a number of houses in or near Athens: the two monasteries of the Asomatos, and those of the Soteira Lykodemou (1044), St Theodore (1049), Theotokos Kapnikarea (1075–1100) and St Meletios (c. 1105). Numerous churches were also built and decorated in this period.[47] The case of Athens is particular interesting since the city, once highly vulnerable to Slavonic and Arab raids, now moved into a period of prosperity marked by a rise in ecclesiastical patronage. The peaceful conditions in the southern Balkans in the eleventh century are epitomised by the buildings at Hosios Loukas and the expensive reconstruction of the Monastery at Daphni near Athens (before 1048), an enterprise which would not have been undertaken in earlier, more troubled times.[48]

Further to the north, in the lands of Thrace and Macedonia stretching northwards and westwards from Constantinople, relative security from Bulgar and Magyar raiding was not established until the end of the tenth century and, with one significant exception, monastic foundations did not

date of the Slav revolt in the Peloponnese under Romanos I', *Late classical and medieval studies in honor of A. M. Friend, Jr.* (Princeton, 1955), pp. 204–11, reprinted in R. J. H. Jenkins, *Studies in Byzantine history of the ninth and tenth centuries* (London, 1970), article xx.

[47] J. Darrouzès, 'Le mouvement des fondations monastiques au XIe siècle', *TM*, 6 (1976), 156–76, 165–6. For Hosios Loukas, see N. Oikonomidès, 'The first century of the monastery of Hosios Loukas', *DOP*, 46 (1992), 245–55 and for the debate about the dating of the buildings, D. I. Pallas, 'Zur Topographie und Chronologie von Hosios Lukas: eine kritische Übersicht', *BZ*, 78 (1985), 94–107 and, controversially, C. L. Connor, *Art and miracles in medieval Byzantium: the crypt at Hosios Loukas and its frescoes* (Princeton, NJ, 1991), chapter 3, pp. 102–21. For the Monastery of the Saviour, see D. Zakynthinos, 'Kastron Lakedaimonos', *Hellenika*, 15 (1957), 95–111. For church construction and decoration, see K. Skawran, *The development of middle Byzantine painting in Greece* (Pretoria, 1982) and D. Mouriki, 'Stylistic trends in monumental painting of Greece during the eleventh and twelfth centuries', *DOP*, 34–6 (1980–1), 77–124.

[48] See the comments of A. Frantz in *The Church of the Holy Apostles* (The Athenian Agora, xx, American School at Athens, 1971), on the archaeological evidence for the increasing prosperity of Athens at this period. A. Bon, *Le Péloponnèse byzantin jusqu'en 1204* (Bibliothèque byzantine, Etudes, I, Paris, 1951), chapter 4, pp. 119–53 examines the growth of other Greek towns at the time. For Daphni: G. Millet, *Le monastère de Daphni. Histoire, architecture, mosaïques* (Paris, 1899), more recent discussion in *ODB*, I, pp. 587–8.

flourish in the countryside until the eleventh. The exception is, of course, the 'holy mountain' of Athos, where hermits were well established by the mid-ninth century.[49] But Athos' early development as a centre of contemplative life may chiefly be attributed to its rugged and inaccessible landscape, which made it a safe haven from attack. Further to the north there were few new foundations until the threat of Bulgar attack had been curbed at the beginning of the eleventh century. Houses such as that founded by Michael Attaliates at Rhaidestos, the modern Tekirdağ (1079), the Monasteries of the Theotokos Eleousa at Stroumitza (present-day Veljusa) dating from 1080, of Kataskepe at Philea in Thrace (near modern Cape Kara Burnu, c. 1050) and of Petritzos (Bačkovo in modern Bulgaria, 1083) were all founded at a period when the Bulgarian lands were firmly under Byzantine control.[50] The consolidation of the considerable landed wealth of these houses (and of those on Athos) in the eleventh century testifies to the peaceful conditions prevalent in the region until the general upheavals in the last twenty years of the eleventh century, associated with the attacks by the Normans of southern Italy on the western Balkans and by the nomadic Petchenegs on the lands south of the River Danube.[51]

In the empire's most westerly territories, the themes of southern Italy, the same link between military fortune and monastic foundation can be established. The late ninth century was the period of Byzantine counter-attack against the Muslim forces which had taken control of Sicily earlier in the century and which were established in many areas of the mainland, especially in Calabria. In the 880s, forces were sent out from Constantinople to reconquer Calabria, Apulia and parts of the Lombard principality of Benevento. By the late tenth and early eleventh centuries, the imperial government had re-established military, administrative and ecclesiastical control over large areas of the mainland and reorganised their administrative and religious structures, although the challenges to their authority from both Lombard princes and the expansionist German empire were a perpetual threat, often not fully appreciated by distant rulers in Constantinople. But the reconquest of Sicily always eluded the Byzantines and the persistent presence of the Muslim emirates there

[49] The monastic church of St Andrew at Peristerai was established at the end of the ninth century, presumably in a lull in the warfare between Byzantium and Bulgaria, see Wharton, *Art of empire*, pp. 101–4, but other foundations seem to have been in larger and more protected towns such as Thessalonike and Kastoria, see Wharton, pp. 93–101. See *Prôtaton*, part I, pp. 6–17, for religious life on Athos before the foundation of the monastic communities, and further discussion in chapter 2.
[50] See chapter 2.
[51] General survey in M. Angold, *The Byzantine empire, 1025–1204: a political history* (London, 1984), chapter 6.

meant that the danger of attack from that quarter was never entirely lifted from the mainland.[52]

While the survival of Greek monasticism in the towns of southern Italy can be attested throughout the period, although the evidence is often fragmentary, the significance of this ever-present insecurity for the development of monastic life in rural southern Italy has been the subject of some debate among modern historians. In many hagiographies there are references to monks moving away from the predominantly Greek regions of Sicily and the southernmost parts of Italy further to the north into Campagna and Lazio, and it is tempting to associate this with flight from Arab attack. Certainly there were Greek monasteries in the Lombard principality of Capua which were founded by refugees from Sicily. But some Sicilian and Calabrian houses certainly did survive Muslim raiding, and even conquest, and it may be that, in some cases, the monastic migrations of southern Italy had more to do with a quest for monastic solitude (and even, in some cases, a wish to visit the apostolic shrines in Rome), than with any *immediate* physical danger, although the devastation of the land and food shortages resulting from attack often caused monks as well as laity to move away. Whatever the reasons, the houses founded in the countryside in the late ninth and tenth centuries – such as those in the regions of Salinoi, Merkourion, Latinianon and Carbone in Calabria, Tricarico in Lucania and the Val Demena in Sicily – were mainly to be found in remote spots; a fact which had important implications for the type of monasticism practised in them and their rôle in the community.[53] The Greek monks of southern Italy, whether in town or countryside, never enjoyed anything like the security of their eastern brethren and were to see many of their houses taken over by the militant Latin monasticism which came hard on the heels of the Norman conquests in southern Italy in the eleventh century.[54]

---

[52] For the political background, A. Guillou, 'L'Italie byzantine du IXe au XIe siècle. Etat des questions', in Prandi, *Aggiornamento*, IV, pp. 3–47, see 3–5 and V. von Falkenhausen, 'I bizantini in Italia', in G. Cavallo, V. von Falkenhausen, R. F. Campanati, M. Gigante, V. Pace and F. D. Rosati, *I bizantini in Italia* (Milan, 1982), pp. 1–136. Demographic and cultural implications are discussed in A. Guillou, 'Italie méridionale byzantine ou byzantins en Italie méridionale?', *B*, 44 (1974), 152–70, reprinted in A. Guillou, *Culture et société en Italie byzantin (VIe–XIe siècles)* (London, 1978), article xv.

[53] The question of the causes of monastic migration is debated in Guillou, 'Grecs d'Italie du sud', p. 82 and Pertusi, 'Rapporti', p. 474. The southern Italian and Sicilian houses are further discussed in chapter 2.

[54] See L. White, Jr., *Latin monasticism in Norman Sicily* (Cambridge, Mass., 1938) and L. R. Ménager, 'La byzantinisation réligieuse de l'Italie méridionale (IX–XIIe siècles) et la politique monastique des Normands d'Italie', *Revue d'Histoire Ecclesiastique*, 53 (1958), 747–74; 54 (1959), 5–40, reprinted in the same author's *Hommes et institutions de l'Italie normande* (London, 1981), article i.

There is thus an important association to be made between the general fortunes of the Byzantine state and the popularity and spread of orthodox monasticism. On the one hand, the church played an important part in spreading or re-establishing a 'Byzantine way of life', a centrally promoted set of cultural and social values, in which monasticism, the highest form of the Christian life, had a central part to play, especially in those regions which had suffered from the invasions of the 'dark ages' and from the incursions of 'unbelievers'. On the other, the resolution of the iconoclast controversy, although accompanied by considerable upheavals within the hierarchy of the secular church, only served to strengthen the cause of monasticism within the empire, a monasticism which its adherents could now portray as the force which had done more than any other (even the imperial power) to defend the true teachings of orthodoxy. The official imperial and ecclesiastical view of monasticism at the turn of the ninth and tenth centuries was that it was an entirely beneficial and admirable institution. From this base of popularity (engineered perhaps, but none the less genuine), monastic life in the empire expanded and developed in a variety of forms over a wide geographical area.

CHAPTER TWO

Groups, communities and solitaries

◆

THE TWO CENTURIES following the triumph of orthodoxy saw a remarkable revival in the fortunes of Byzantine monasticism. Not only did the numbers of those following the contemplative life increase, but the sheer variety of monastic practices testifies to its success in providing a range of experience that could appeal to all sectors of society. For monasticism was never the sole prerogative of the aristocratic or the educated; the small oratory built by a group of two or three pious peasants who wished to devote themselves to the religious life was deemed to be just as valid and as honourable a monastery as the rich, well-populated house founded by members of the upper ranks of society or the imperial family.[1] The availability of these various types of monastic life-style made it necessary for potential monks and nuns to make an active and individual choice about which they proposed to follow.

Such a choice could already be made in western Asia Minor by the end of the ninth century, a matter of considerable importance in the development of monasticism throughout the empire in the following centuries since many of the most celebrated monastic leaders of the period either lived there or passed through the region in a formative period of their ministry. The contrasting forms of monasticism may be placed here, as elsewhere, in a geographical context. The fertile, flat lands bordering the Sea of Marmara and the Aegean Sea supported large communal houses, such as those founded by St Theodore of Stoudios and his uncle; by contrast, the inhospitable ranges to the east could provide a natural

---

[1] P. Charanis, 'The monk as an element in Byzantine society', *DOP*, 25 (1971), 63–84, reprinted in his *Social, economic and political life in the Byzantine empire* (London, 1973), article II, attempted to calculate the number of monks in the empire, an enterprise doomed to failure because of a lack of enough statistical information; but there is certainly evidence for numerical expansion in specific houses. For imperial concern to protect small rural houses from episcopal interference, see the novel of Basil II (996), Zepos, I, pp. 249–52.

setting for those who sought *eremia* (solitude), a prerequisite for followers
of the kind of life first led by St Anthony in the fourth century.[2]

The concept of the mountain as a holy place had been implanted in
Hellenistic consciousness long before the coming of Christianity. But St
Anthony's progression higher into the mountainous wilderness of Egypt
as he entered advanced planes of spiritual experience was the specific
exemplar both for later Byzantine hermits and for many influential
monastic founders. For the theological significance of 'nearness to God'
in both the physical and metaphysical sense, which height (whether
mountains, rocks or stone columns) could provide, was associated with
a far more primitive admiration for those who could survive in the
harshness of the mountain landscape. In an age before the Alpine became
fashionable, living in such conditions by choice was a mark of unusual
spiritual dedication to solitude. Survival in the unpredictable dangers of
climate and nature was itself a mark of sanctity.[3]

Life alone in the mountains or in other desolate spots was the setting
for the most extreme form of asceticism which Byzantine monasticism
could offer, but there were many, such as the Stoudites, who doubted
whether solitary wrestling with the temptations of the flesh and the
demons was the best method of aspiring to the *angelikos bios*, the 'life of
the angels', the ultimate goal of all monasticism, a life in which the
demands of the body and the human will were completely subordinated
to those of the spirit.[4] For them, the most completely spiritual life could
only be lived in the *koinobion*, a community where the imposition of
obedience, the denial of personal property and the subordination of the
individual will to that of the group could lead to a positive 'dehumanis-
ation', which avoided the risk of taking any pride in extreme forms of
individual asceticism. In addition, the *hegoumenos* of the *koinobion*, as both
shepherd and 'spiritual father' of his flock would, it was thought, ensure
the ascetic development of all the monks and their adherence to orthodox
practices. His years of experience and wisdom would, indeed, make him
a more reliable spiritual guide than the self-taught and perhaps self-
deluded solitary. Theodore of Stoudios' suspicion of anchorite monasticism was clearly derived from the writings of St Basil, who felt that the
solitary life could lead to self-absorption and that only in communal

2 St Athanasius of Alexandria's *Life of St Anthony*, a crucial text in the history of Byzantine monasticism, may be consulted in the English translation of R. T. Meyer (Ancient
Christian Writers, x, Westminster, Md., 1950).
3 See the short discussion in A. Kazhdan and G. Constable, *People and power in
Byzantium: an introduction to modern Byzantine studies* (Washington, DC, 1982),
pp. 41–2.
4 G. W. H. Lampe, *A patristic Greek lexicon* (Oxford, 1961), s.v. *angelos* gives important
early references. The concept of *angelikos bios* deserves its own study.

houses could Christ's commandment of 'Love thy neighbour' fully be practised.[5]

On the other hand, Theodore himself would have been the first to recognise that there were some monks who progressed more quickly up the spiritual ladder than others. How could such men be helped to reach a higher spiritual plane which would, of necessity, set them apart from their fellows in the monastery? It is in these circumstances that even the firmest proponents of the communal life could envisage an element of the solitary within it. The Justinianic legislation, which banned the foundation of non-coenobitic houses, did allow that a few monks would be capable of 'leading a perfect life in contemplation', and that they should be permitted to do so within the confines of their monasteries.[6] The Council *in Trullo* (692) declared that the solitary life could be practised after at least four years of communal life, but again only within a religious community.[7] This admission, however, opened up the way towards the official acceptance of lavriote houses formed from members living alone for most of the time in individual cells (*kellia*), but meeting together weekly to worship and collect food and materials for handiwork and on feast days and thus reflecting to a certain degree the unity required by St Basil.

The most important characteristic of Byzantine monasticism by the end of the ninth century was, in fact, its very *lack* of clearly defined forms. An institution long considered by modern scholars to have developed over time from the lavriote to the coenobitic style, had always, in fact, demonstrated an ability to adjust and adapt itself to changing circumstances.[8] The different traditions amalgamated in a variety of ways: hermits could live in a loose, but recognisable relationship with communities; the more experienced members and even the *hegoumenoi* of houses which were clearly *koinobia* often lived a solitary life some little distance away from them. It is these very cross-fertilisations which have led to the impossibility of providing any precise semantic definitions for

---

[5] See chapter 1, p. 16, for St Basil's definition of a *koinobion*. His suspicions of lavriote monasticism are discussed in L. Amand, *L'ascèse monastique de Saint Basile. Essai historique* (Maredsous, 1948), pp. 118–28. For a general discussion of the spiritual advantages of the various forms of the monastic life, see T. Špidlík, *The spirituality of the Christian east*, trans. A. P. Gythiel (*Cistercian Studies*, LXXIX, Kalamazoo, Mich., 1986), chapter 8.

[6] Justinian, *Novella*, v. 8, in *CIC*, III.

[7] RP, II, pp. 401–6.

[8] The idea of a 'chronological' development of Byzantine monasticism was successfully laid to rest in D. Papachryssanthou, 'La vie monastique dans les campagnes byzantines du VIIIe au XIe siècles', *REB*, 43 (1973), 158–82. For more recent comments on the flexibility of Byzantine monasticism, see A. P. Kazhdan, 'Hermitic, cenobitic and secular ideals in Byzantine hagiography of the ninth century', *Greek Orthodox Theological Review*, 30 (1985), 473–87, 476.

the various words used in contemporary sources to describe monastic houses in this period. Efforts to point fine distinctions between the terms *koinobion, mone, monasterion, phrontisterion* and, indeed, *lavra* are doomed to failure simply because many houses contained elements of both the eremitic and the communal life. But this is not to say that monastic founders and the lay public did not have quite well-defined ideas of which tradition they found most admirable and which they wished to predominate in the houses they founded and patronised.[9]

Even though they had no notion of what the original *lavrai* of fourth-century Palestine actually looked like, and could only have formed an opinion of the way of life led in them from patristic and hagiographical writings, many of the most influential monastic founders of Asia Minor, Athos and Patmos believed that they were founding houses in the age-old lavriote tradition. By this they meant that an important emphasis was given to the possibility of individual spiritual experience which did not replace that offered by the *koinobion*, but existed in addition to it. As in many areas of Byzantine life, the concept of hierarchy was also present in monasticism: men could progress from the communal life to that of the solitary within the community and finally to that of the hermit, though women were never encouraged to aspire to a religious life beyond the group as, it was believed, their weaker wills could not be expected to stand up to its demands.[10] The influence of lavriote monasticism spread in the tenth and eleventh centuries and there is clear evidence that many monastic founders wanted to include these opportunities for individual *askesis* in the regulations that they drew up for their houses, regulations which themselves always reflected to a certain extent their own spiritual predilections.

A strong tradition prevailed in tenth-century western Asia Minor that the communities there had been founded by monks fleeing from the Muslim attacks on the Holy Land.[11] Certainly, the Lavra of St Sabas in Palestine remained a place of pilgrimage for monastic founders such as St Lazaros of Mount Galesion, who visited it in c. 1009, and, in the late eleventh century, St Christodoulos, previously a monk on Mount Olympos and a *hegoumenos* on Mount Latros, required his monks on the island of Patmos to follow the liturgical customs of St Sabas. Although it is not possible to establish a firm personal link between the Lavra of St Sabas and the 'holy mountains' of Bithynia in the seventh century, when any migration must have taken place, the continuation of a 'spiritual

[9] Papachryssanthou, 'Vie monastique', p. 168, note 3. For a discussion of patronage, see chapter 5.
[10] Kazhdan, 'Hermitic, cenobitic and secular ideals', p. 479.
[11] See chapter 1, pp. 22–3.

attachment' to the customs of St Sabas in the eleventh century could well indicate the existence of a stronger association at an earlier period.[12]

But if direct links with Palestine are difficult to establish, those between the monastic centres of western Asia Minor and other houses are not, and it is in tracing the links in this spiritual chain that the influence of the lavriote way of life may most clearly be shown. Of the 'holy mountains' mentioned by Genesios in his account of the processions to mark the Feast of Orthodoxy in 843 – Olympos, Kyminas and Ida – and those added to the list of the chronicles of Theophanes continuatus and the Continuation of George the Monk – Barachios/Mykale, Chryse Petra, Athos and Latros – the longest recognised was undoubtedly Mount Olympos (modern Ulu Dağ) a mountainous region of Bithynia roughly coterminous with the metropolitanate of Prousa (modern Bursa, see map 1).[13] Unfortunately, little archaeological excavation has been done in this region, so it is impossible to know what the architectural plans of the many houses which the sources refer to as *lavrai* actually were, but it is clear that they were much higher in the mountains than the great *koinobia* of Sakkoudion or Horaia Pege and therefore much more likely to have been smaller establishments with more scattered living quarters.[14] For the houses nearer the coast are usually referred to as *monasterion* or *mone*, an indication (although not always an infallible one) that they were coenobitic. There are a number of them whose existence can be noted in the tenth century, such as Elegmoi, which also served as places of confinement for political prisoners; Medikion, a flourishing house in the ninth century, but whose fortunes had declined by the eleventh; Smilakia, founded by the future patriarch, Nicholas Chrysoberges, some time before 979, and a group of eleventh-century houses: a house founded by the *protovestiarios* Symeon about 1034; the Monastery of the Theotokos of Kalamion (c. 1054), and the Monasteries of Trapeza and Horaia Pege, the last-named of which was founded by Nicholas, who had been a monk of Stoudios between 1035 and 1045.[15]

---

[12] Life of St Lazaros, pp. 514, 516; *Hypotyposis* of Christodoulos; MM, VI, pp. 59–80, see p. 71.

[13] Janin, *Grands centres*, pp. 127–91, goes some way towards replacing the misleading study of B. Menthon, *Une terre de légende. L'Olympe de Bithynie* (Paris, 1935), but we await the relevant volume of *TIB*. Olympos was mentioned as a religious centre in the fifth-century Life of St Hypatios, but its fame was most widespread in the eighth and ninth centuries, see Janin, *Grands centres*, pp. 127–8.

[14] See Janin, *Grands centres*, p. 129 for Sakkoudion; p. 191 for Horaia Pege. P. Gautier, 'Eloge funèbre de Nicolas de la Belle Source par Michel Psellos, moine à Olympe', *Byzantina*, 6 (1954), 9–69, establishes the location of Horaia Pege and what is known of its founder.

[15] For security reasons, if nothing else, Elegmoi was almost certainly an enclosed *koinobion*. Among its reluctant inhabitants were the *sakellarios* Anastasios, relegated there after

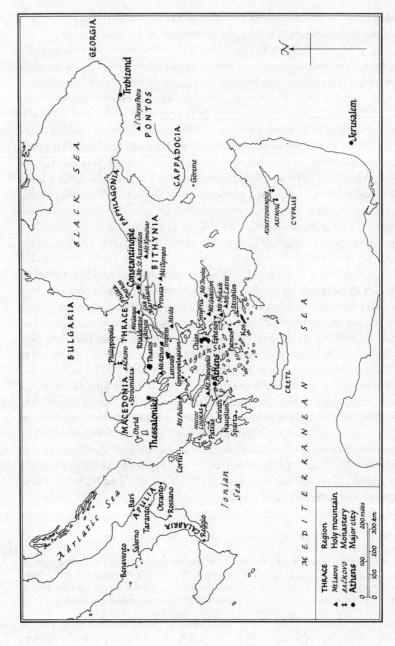

Map 1 *Monastic geography of Byzantium, ninth to eleventh centuries*

It was to the lavriote houses of Olympos that many of the most important figures of tenth-century monasticism gravitated. By the end of the ninth century, monks from as far away as Georgia had been attracted to the area. A Georgian hermit, Hilarion, built a church with the help of neighbouring coenobitic monks, who were probably Greek. Hilarion was soon joined by three of his compatriots and by the tenth century the house, possibly to be identified with the 'Lavra of Krania', was probably largely Georgian, as were two other houses, the Monasteries of SS Kosmas and Damian and of Spelaion ('the Caves'), whose name suggests that it consisted of a series of cave cells.[16] Though little is known of the subsequent history of these houses, they were of particular importance since Olympos sheltered, at various times, three influential Georgian monastic leaders: SS John and Euthymios, the father and son who founded the Georgian monastery of Iviron on Mount Athos, and John Tornik, the co-founder of Iviron and the monastery's most generous early benefactor.[17] Earlier in the tenth century, St Luke the Younger, later a stylite, spent some time at the Greek Lavra of St Zacharias and the Lavra of St Elias received as a postulant the monk Basil, the elder brother of the celebrated St Paul of Latros and the man who introduced him to the religious life.[18] So although the Olympos *lavrai* make only fleeting appearances in contemporary sources, and, in many cases, their sites have not yet been identified, their influence on the development of monasticism was considerable, since their practices and customs were exported to other parts of the empire.

The mountain of Latros (modern Beş Parmak Dağ, see map 1) provides the next link in the chain of lavriote development. Like Olympos, it provided an area of seclusion and harsh terrain which conformed to lavriote ideals, while remaining easily accessible from the more populated areas of the Maeander Valley below. Little is known of the monks of the region before the tenth century, though there were certainly hermits on

plotting against the Emperor Romanos Lekapenos in 921 (Theophanes cont., VI, p. 400); Romanos Saronites, who plotted unsuccessfully against Romanos II, c. 960 (see Kedrenos, II, p. 343) and the Emperor Michael V who entered the house after being dethroned and blinded in 1042 (Kedrenos, II, p. 540). Janin, *Grands centres*, for references to all these houses: pp. 144–6 for Elegmoi; p. 165 for Medikion (Mango and Ševčenko, 'Some churches and monasteries', pp. 240–2; 274–6 for architectural details); p. 181 for Smilakia; p. 183 for the house of the *protovestiarios* Symeon; p. 154 for that of Kalamion or Kalamon; p. 184 for Trapeza.
[16] Janin, *Grands centres*, pp. 156–7.
[17] Life of SS John and Euthymios, pp. 87, 88.
[18] Life of St Luke the Stylite, p. 203; Life of St Paul the Younger, chapter 2, p. 22; chapter 4, pp. 24–5; see Janin, *Grands centres*, pp. 151, 157.

the mountain in the ninth.[19] The Life of St Paul the Younger (written c. 969–75) mentions three tenth-century houses: those at Kellibaron and Karyes and a monastery dedicated to Christ the Saviour. It is very probable, however, that there were considerably more monasteries in the area by this time, since the chronicle of Theophanes continuatus reports that the Emperor Romanos Lekapenos (920–44) gave monastery donations to them as a group.[20]

The Monastery at Karyes (possibly dedicated to the Holy Cross) was a coenobitic house, in which Paul of Latros was placed by his brother Basil in about 900. It was, the Life of St Paul relates, 'large and highly populated' and the young man was first put to work in the kitchens. Paul's ascetic tendencies were discouraged here (but only on account of his youth) which suggests that the main body of the monks, and certainly the novices, led a communal life, while only a few older monks were allowed to withdraw from the *koinobion*. The two other houses mentioned in the Life were clearly influenced by lavriote practices. Both had solitaries living at some distance from the houses, but attached to them. At Kellibaron, Paul consulted the monk Matthew, who had built a small church dedicated to St John the Theologian near the monastery; close to the Monastery of the Saviour he encountered the monk Athanasios, who indicated to him the rock which was to become the centre of his own foundation.[21]

The Monastery of the Stylos provides an important example of a house which combined the lavriote and coenobitic traditions. Paul, who initially lived as a hermit in the pinnacle of rock, which he referred to as his *stylos* (literally 'column') in imitation of the earlier stylite saints such as the two Symeons and Daniel, was soon joined by disciples, some of whom lived communally, others in *kellia*. The writer of the Life of St Paul clearly indicates the co-existence of both types of monastic life: 'He [Paul] divided it wisely and well between those seeking to live alone and by themselves and those embracing the common existence of the spiritual flock.'[22] It was not even necessary for the solitaries to live very far from the community, for the rocky cave in which Paul himself lived seems to

---

[19] Janin, *Grands centres*, pp. 217–40 for the houses on Mount Latros and Appendix, pp. 441–53 for a list of the surviving acts of the Latros monasteries. The German expedition to the region in the late nineteenth century produced much archaeological information on the monastic sites: T. Wiegand, *Milet. Ergebnisse der Ausgrabungen und Untersuchungen seit dem Jahre 1899*, III/1; *Der Latmos* (Berlin, 1913).

[20] Theophanes cont., VI. 44, p. 430.

[21] Life of St Paul the Younger, chapter 6, p. 26; chapter 7, pp. 29–31. Wiegand, *Der Latmos*, pp. 25–9 identified the Monastery of Kellibaron with the ruins at Jediler. For the monks Matthew and Athanasios, Life of St Paul the Younger, chapter 10, pp. 36–40; chapter 13, pp. 42–3.

[22] Life of St Paul the Younger, chapter 17, p. 52.

have been easily incorporated into the monastic enclosure after his death. Evidently, solitude could be more a spiritual than a physical reality and the lavriote *eremia*, initially sought in mountainous and desert places could, in fact, be maintained in close proximity to a flourishing communal life. At the Stylos Monastery there was one rule uniting both groups: that they should all accept Paul's spiritual guidance.

This way of life was still practised in the eleventh century, when it was clearly described in the *Hypotyposis* (Regulations) of St Christodoulos of Patmos, who began his monastic career on Mount Olympos, but who was later *hegoumenos* of the Stylos Monastery and who took its customs to his own foundation. He related that the monks lived both the communal and the eremitic life, but that the coenobitic rules of poverty and common ownership curbed any excessive tendencies to *idiorrhythmia* (self-direction). All the members of the community gathered together on Sundays, and Christodoulos nostalgically remembered a very happy state of affairs: 'Each led the other to a higher form of life.'[23] Although by the end of the eleventh century, the growth in the number of monasteries on Mount Latros meant that the mountain had, in a sense, lost its role as a spiritual 'desert', it is clear that throughout the previous two centuries Latros, like Olympos, provided an area where coenobitic and kelliote monastic traditions merged together and where, as in the case of the Stylos Monastery, a deliberate effort was made to preserve this way of life.[24]

Two other 'holy mountains' mentioned in the tenth-century sources – Mykale or Barachios (modern Samsun Dağ above the ancient city of Priene) and Kyminas (probably on the borders of Bithynia and Paphlagonia, precisely where is not clear) – also supported houses which followed this 'hybrid' style of monasticism. The tenth-century Life of St Nikephoros (Nikephoros was a one-time bishop of Miletos and then a monastic founder in the area) tells how Nikephoros retired first of all to Latros 'so that uninterruptedly and in solitude, he might converse with God', finding his way to the Stylos Monastery in the days of Paul's successor, the *hegoumenos* Symeon. He finally moved on to Mount Mykale, where he founded (or took charge of) two houses: Erebinthos and Hiera-Xerochoraphion. If, as is likely, he took with him the customs he

---

[23] *Hypotyposis* of Christodoulos, pp. 60–1.
[24] Christodoulos' stated reason for leaving Mount Latros was that he wished 'to go in search of an entirely eremitic and hesychastic life [and] communion alone with God, untroubled by the cares of life': *Hypomnema* of Patriarch Nicholas III Grammatikos, June 1087, MM, VI, pp. 32–3; see Grumel, *Régestes*, no. 944. For the emergence of other houses on Latros (the Monastery of the Theotokos of Lamponion, associated with Kellibaron by 1049; the Monastery of St George at Schynon and two monasteries *tou Asomatou*), see Janin, *Grands centres*, pp. 222–3.

had found on Mount Latros, then both these houses would have allowed for the solitary as well as the communal life but, since by the mid-eleventh century Hiera-Xerochoraphion possessed considerable estates and the number of its inhabitants had risen to three hundred, the vast majority of the monks clearly lived a coenobitic life.[25]

Mount Kyminas, of which nothing is known until the early tenth century, was the destination of another well-connected young man seeking eremitic solitude, St Michael Maleïnos. He received the monastic *schema* (habit) from the *hegoumenos* of a small lavriote monastery, John Elatites, and gave the share of property inherited from his father to this house. Michael's way of life clearly conformed to lavriote custom: on Sundays he joined in worship with his brethren, but the remainder of the week he spent in seclusion on a rock.[26] At some time before 917, Michael founded his own monastery, whose church was dedicated to the Theotokos, but which was always known as the *lavra* or *mone* of Maleïnos. According to his biographer, the saint transmitted to the brethren the 'laws of asceticism' and 'most harsh customs', which certainly seems to suggest a lavriote-influenced régime. Conclusive evidence is (like that for Latros) supplied 'retrospectively'; the regulations laid down by St Athanasios for his foundation of the Great Lavra on Mount Athos, and the use of the term *lavra* to describe his house, testify to the nature of the house where he himself spent his novitiate and of which Michael Maleïnos, his 'spiritual father', was the founder.[27]

The last important monastic centre of western Asia Minor was that of Mount Galesion (Alaman Dağ, north of Ephesos, see map 1) where hermits were active in the tenth century, though there is no precise record of any monasteries in the region before the mid-eleventh century, when St Lazaros began his work there. The houses he founded – the monasteries of St Marina (1005–12) near Mount Galesion and the Saviour

---

[25] The identification of Barachios with Mykale is made in Life of St Paul the Younger, chapter 8, p. 33. Numerous 'ecclesiastical' ruins were noted in the late nineteenth century but remain unexcavated; T. Wiegand and H. Schrader, *Priene. Ergebnisse der Ausgrabungen und Untersuchungen in den Jahren 1895–98* (Berlin, 1904), p. 487 and map 2, where large numbers of 'monasteries' are marked. Life of St Nikephoros, chapter 14, p. 145; chapter 17, pp. 148–9; chapter 18, pp. 149–50. What survives of the archives of the Monastery of Hiera-Xerochoraphion (possibly modern Monastir, above the Maeander Valley) was pieced together by Wilson and Darrouzès, 'Hiéra-Xérochoraphion', *REB*, 26 (1968), 5–47. For the difficulty of locating Mount Kyminas, see Janin, *Grands centres*, pp. 115–18.

[26] Life of St Michael Maleïnos, chapter 6, pp. 552–3; chapter 10, p. 556. For the endowment, see Kaplan, *Les hommes et la terre*, pp. 301–2.

[27] Life of St Michael Maleïnos, chapter 15, p. 560 for the Church of the Theotokos, which was founded before the Byzantine defeat by the Bulgars at the Battle of Acheloos in 917, which Michael, already established, predicted. For the customs of the Great Lavra on Mount Athos, see pp. 45–6, below.

Map 2 Monastic geography of southern Italy

(1012–12), the Theotokos and the Anastasis actually on the mountain – were probably subject to the same lavriote-influenced administration as that on Olympos, Latros and Kyminas since Lazaros seems to have been concerned to limit the number of monks in each house to prevent them from becoming large *koinobia*. He himself lived on a column near the houses while the day to day running of affairs was carried out by an *oikonomos*. His rôle as *hegoumenos* was, in the lavriote tradition, more advisory than administrative. Associated with the houses on Mount Galesion and providing them with revenues, was the Monastery of the Theotokos at Bessai, probably near Ephesos, which was founded between 1046 and 1050 with the assistance of money given to Lazaros by Maria Skleraina, the mistress of the Emperor Constantine IX Monomachos.[28]

The links which can be drawn between the 'holy mountains' testify to two important characteristics of lavriote monasticism: first, that the landscape played a vital rôle in determining what kind of monastic life was practised, since the quest for *eremia* was of paramount importance and mountainous regions were eminently suitable for the solitary life and, secondly, that the movements of monks and postulants between the mountains were not haphazard. The reputation of the holy men spread quickly beyond their immediate area and the arrival of disciples to seek the spiritual guidance of specific individuals meant that their self-professed 'solitude' was, as in the case of Stylos, often more spiritual than physical.[29] These disciples, in turn, carried the tradition to other parts of the empire and thus the association between the various centres of lavriote-influenced monasticism may be placed in a definite chronological context. Olympos served as the consolidating point for the new monastic style. Coenobite monks, some refugees from iconoclastic persecution, were placed in surroundings in which they might gain experience of the religious practices of the solitaries. From Olympos the idea of a mixed community of communal and eremitic monks passed to Latros, Mykale and Kyminas, a process made possible by the remarkable mobility of

---

[28] For the houses on or near Mount Galesion, Janin, *Grands centres*, pp. 241–9. Holy men active before St Lazaros' arrival: Life of St Lazaros, chapter 41, p. 522 (a stylite); chapter 59, p. 528 (a very rare female stylite); chapters 37–9, pp. 521–2; chapter 62, p. 529 (the hermit Paphnutios, whose relics had been taken to Constantinople by Lazaros' day); chapter 59, p. 529 (an unnamed solitary, who built churches dedicated to the Holy Trinity and the Prodromos). Lazaros' foundations are all mentioned in his hagiography: St Marina, chapters 31–6, p. 519; Monastery of the Soter, chapters 42–3, pp. 522–3; chapter 100, p. 539; Monastery of the Anastasis, chapter 162, p. 557; chapter 246, p. 585 and Monastery of the Theotokos, chapter 64, p. 529; Monastery at Bessai, chapters 238–9, p. 582. Constantine IX donated land to it in memory of Maria Skleraina. For the location, see E. Malamut, 'A propos de Bessai d'Ephèse', *REB*, 43 (1985), 243–51. Lazaros' monastic régime is mentioned in Life of St Lazaros, chapter 246, pp. 585–6.
[29] See chapter 3.

monks at the time. The last link in the chain in western Asia Minor, to Galesion, can surely be established by monastic tradition, if not in precise personal terms.

There is no doubt that the most famous of the 'holy mountains' was Mount Athos, the most easterly of the three promontories of the Chalkidike peninsula to the east of Thessalonike (see map 1). Its most famous monastic founder, St Athanasios, was the favoured disciple of Michael Maleïnos on Mount Kyminas and, in his foundation known as the Great Lavra, incorporated many of the practices familiar in the mountains of Asia Minor. Mount Athos was already a celebrated spiritual centre before Athanasios' arrival in about 958, for even though Genesios' reference to the monks of Athos taking part in the celebrations for the restoration of the icons in 843 may be anachronistic, St Euthymios the Younger left the Monastery of Pissadinon on Mount Olympos for Athos in about 859, because he had 'heard of its tranquillity'.[30] Unlike the case of Olympos, iconoclast persecution was probably not an important factor in bringing monks to Athos. It is more likely that peaceful conditions in the Chalkidike at the end of the eighth century (a state of affairs which, unhappily, was not to last for long) attracted monks to Athos, which, like the other holy mountains, was a region of possible *eremia*, physically close to, but spiritually beyond, more settled regions, in this case Thessalonike and its hinterland.[31]

Athos in the ninth century was a place of hermits and small religious groups rather than large houses. St Euthymios the Younger lived a life of seclusion there before moving on to Thessalonike; St Peter the Athonite is described in a ninth-century canon as living there in *hesychia*, hidden amongst the mountains and caves, as did another two of the earliest known ascetics, John Kolobos, by 865 'already advanced in spirituality' and the monk Symeon, who were both disciples of St Euthymios. Some monks seem to have come to the mountain specifically to undertake a period of seclusion before returning to their own houses, but many lived there permanently.[32] By the time Athanasios arrived in the mid-tenth century, a certain amount of land clearance had already begun in the interior of the peninsula, where many of the hermits had moved to escape

---

[30] *Prôtaton*, p. 72 for the date of Athanasios' arrival on Mount Athos. *Vie et office de Saint Euthyme le Jeune*, ed. L. Petit, *ROC*, 8 (1903), 168–205, summarised by D. Papachryssanthou in *Prôtaton*, pp. 22–31. See also her article 'La vie de Saint Euthyme le Jeune et la métropole de Thessalonique', *REB*, 32 (1974), 225–45.

[31] *Prôtaton*, pp. 6–19.

[32] For Peter the Athonite, see two articles by D. Papachryssanthou: 'L'office ancien de Saint Pierre l'Athonite', *AB*, 88 (1970), 27–41 and 'La vie ancienne de Saint Pierre l'Athonite. Date, composition et valeur historique', *AB*, 92 (1974), 19–61. *Prôtaton*, pp. 29–31 for Euthymios' disciples.

the raids of Muslim pirates on the coastline and Bulgars and Magyars inland.[33]

The earliest extant documents concerning Athos indicate that at the end of the ninth century solitaries and monastic groups lived side by side, while to the north, in the Chalkidike, more permanent houses were being established. A *sigillion* of the Emperor Basil I (June 883) drew a distinction between the Athonites 'living *outside* the monasteries' and 'those who have pitched their frugal tents there' (probably a reference to the early foundations). A chrysobull of Romanos Lekapenos also contrasted the houses beyond Athos and the hermits living on the peninsula.[34] This evidence, then, reveals a pattern very similar to that of Bithynia: a mountainous region inhabited by hermits and small communities, with, nearby, more permanent establishments founded on more fertile land. The history of Athos before the arrival of Athanasios was characterised by increased contact and growing tension between those in monasteries and the hermits. To defend themselves, the hesychasts began to evolve a loose organisation of their own and by 908 a certain Andrew, referred to as *protos hesychastes* (literally 'chief hermit'), complained to Constantinople about the encroachments of the flocks of the monasteries beyond Athos on to the mountain itself.[35]

The concern of the hermits for the protection of their solitude was brought to a head by the establishment of coenobitic monasteries on the mountain itself; a stage corresponding to eighth- and ninth-century developments on Olympos. The foundation of the rather confusingly named Monastery *tou Athonos* was probably the cause of the protests of 908 and two other early houses, those of Xeropotamou (already founded by 956) and Bouleuteria (whose *hegoumenos*, Poimen, was reported in 1010 to have held office 'for more than fifty years'), were both situated on land which had previously been the preserve of solitaries.[36] They provide the best known examples of an important development taking place on Athos in the first half of the tenth century: the establishment of a number of communal houses. This tendency is clearly demonstrated by the

[33] Life of Athanasios (A), chapters 38–43, pp. 18–22. The 'Cretan pirates' may have been the band led by the Muslim convert Leo of Tripolis, which sacked Thessalonike in 904 and was finally dealt with in 921–2. See Theophanes cont., VI. 14, p. 405 and Nicholas Mystikos, *Letters*, no. 23, pp. 164–6 (Grumel, *Régestes*, no. 705). For land clearance, see *Prôtaton*, p. 70.
[34] *Prôtaton*, no. 1 (883) and p. 33; *Prôtaton*, no. 3 (934).
[35] *Prôtaton*, no. 2 (908).
[36] *Prôtaton*, no. 4 (942) and see pp. 61–4 for the distinction between early references to the mountain of Athos and the monastery of the same name. The complex early history of Xeropotamou was first elucidated by S. Binon, *Les origines legendaires et l'histoire de Xéropotamou et de Saint-Paul* (Louvain, 1942). See now *Xéropotamou*, pp. 4–8 and *Prôtaton*, pp. 65–9. For Bouleuteria, see *Prôtaton*, pp. 68–9.

number of signatures to the *Typikon* of John Tzimiskes (a document regulating life on Athos commonly known as the *Tragos* or 'goat' because it was written on a large piece of goat-skin), issued between 970 and 972. Forty-seven *hegoumenoi*, heads of recognisable monastic communities, signed this document, so it is clear that large numbers of Athonite monks were by now grouped in *koinobia*.[37]

Why should this change in emphasis have taken place? Certainly, the establishment and early success of the Great Lavra and the personal influence of Athanasios (which his biographers were keen to emphasise) can provide part of the answer; but it is more likely that the peaceful conditions in Thrace and the hinterland of Athos after the dying down of Bulgar and Magyar attacks in the mid-tenth century, allowed greater numbers to come to the mountain, numbers which could not be absorbed by eremitic ways. The *Tragos* itself put an end to the period of individual asceticism on Athos, for it declared that 'those coming to Athos to take up the monastic life should be received inside monasteries and are not to stay outside the holy enclosures'. The *hegoumenoi* alone were to decide on suitable candidates for the solitary life in each monastery. Without recruits, the numbers of hermits dwindled and it is probable that the last group of hesychasts, those at Chaldou in the south of the peninsula, had formed themselves into a *koinobion* by 991.[38]

The rise of the communal life of Athos at the expense of individual spiritual experience is all the more ironic since the expressed purpose in coming to the mountain of Athanasios, the man chiefly responsible, was to seek peace and solitude. His biographers maintained that he only reluctantly abandoned his life as a hermit on the southern tip of the peninsula. But the foundation of an essentially communal house, though a considerable change in spiritual and emotional emphasis, could well have been contemplated by one who had already experienced – on Mount Kyminas – a way of life which combined the elements of *koinobion* with opportunities for individual *hesychia*. The use of the word *lavra* to describe his foundation is a strong indication of what he had in mind.

There has, however, been considerable discussion about Athanasios' alleged 'conversion' to coenobitic monasticism, for the striking similarities between the *Diatyposis* (liturgical rules) which he drew up for the Great Lavra, the *Hypotyposis* of Theodore of Stoudios and even the Rule of St Benedict, have led to a widespread view among modern scholars that Athanasios was converted to coenobitic ways in general and Stoudite customs in particular. This argument seems to gain strength

[37] *Typikon* of John Tzimiskes, *Prôtaton*, no. 7, pp. 95–102 for analysis and discussion. It was issued either January 970–April 971 or August 971–summer 972.
[38] *Prôtaton*, no. 7, ll. 45–53; ll. 72–4.

from a telling phrase in another document, based on one left by Athanasios, the *Hypotyposis*: 'After much trial and strife, it has been borne in on us that the best style of life is the *koinobion* . . . for the *koinobion* has one heart, one will and one desire.'[39]

It is certainly true that the Stoudite influence on the liturgical and disciplinary regulations of the Great Lavra is indisputable; but if we examine the early buildings of the monastery (described in some detail in Athanasios' *typikon* for the house), it is clear that he was constructing a place in which a mixed style of monasticism would be practised. The first building was a *hesychasterion* (hermitage) which was intended for Nikephoros Phokas, an important aristocrat and later emperor, still, at that time, expected to join the house. An oratory and churches then followed, then *kellia*, a refectory, a hospice and its bath-house for the sick, irrigation and water-mills and *hesychasteria* and other buildings for the Lavra's dependent houses (*metochia*).[40] Thus provision was made both for communal life and charitable work *and* for the practice of the solitary life. So the coenobitic life was not seen as an alternative, but as an indispensable stage in the search for true asceticism. Athanasios himself probably planned to withdraw outside the Lavra in his old age, but was accidentally killed in a fall from a building under construction before he could do so. Although his *Typikon* only made provision for five hesychasts at any one time out of a then total of 120 monks, it did make provision for the 'hybrid' form of monasticism which he had brought from Mount Kyminas.[41]

The history of the endowments and political influence of the houses on Athos based on the Lavra's pattern is evidence enough for the approval of many monastic founders and their patrons for this style of monasticism.[42] This is particularly true in the case of the Georgian house, Iviron, founded by two disciples and friends of Athanasios, the father and son John and Euthymios, and their relative John Tornik. John the Iberian had spent his early years as a monk in the Lavra of the Four Churches, in the

---

[39] *Typikon* of Athanasios, p. 115. The argument for a 'conversion' to coenobitic ideals has been most cogently put by J. Leroy: 'La conversion de S. Athanase l'Athonite à l'idéal cénobitique et l'influence studite', *Le millénaire du Mont-Athos 963–1963. Etudes et mélanges* (2 vols., Chevetogne, 1963–4), I, pp. 101–20 and 'S. Athanase et la Règle de S. Benoît', *Revue d'Ascétique et de Mystique*, 29 (1953), 108–22.
[40] *Typikon* of Athanasios, pp. 103–5, see Life of St Athanasios (A), chapter 23, p. 38; chapter 25, pp. 34–6. Athanasios here enumerates all the building work which had taken place up to the time of writing; it is impossible to establish any precise time scale.
[41] Athanasios died between 997 and 1006, and possibly even before 1000; see Life of St Athanasios (A), p. cx. The numbers of monks and hesychasts contained in the *Typikon* (p. 114) refer to the period between 969 and 979, the date of the document. See *Lavra*, I, p. 17, where the date of 973–5 is suggested.
[42] See chapter 5.

46

Georgian region of Tao-Klardjeth, some 200 km east of Trebizond. Fear
that his solitude would be compromised led him to flee westwards to
Mount Olympos and from there, having been re-united with his son who
had been held as a hostage in Constantinople, the two travelled to Athos
between 963 and 969. They joined Athanasios, whose reputation had
begun to spread and whose Pontic origins were probably known to them,
and lived for a time in the Great Lavra before leaving (with Athanasios'
permission) to live in a group of eight *kellia* some little distance away
(the existence of which certainly supports the argument for 'hybrid'
monasticism in the Great Lavra). It was through the benefactions and
influence of John Tornik that the Georgian monks received the
Monastery of Clement on Mount Athos, which was to form the basis of
what later came to be described as the Lavra *or* Monastery of the Iberians.
And although the rules drawn up by Euthymios (the second *hegoumenos*)
were not written down at the time, it is clear from his biography that the
house followed a similar pattern to that of the Lavra: a community to
house the majority of the monks, with a number of hermitages in which
more experienced monks lived the hesychastic life.[43]

The process of the transformation of areas sought out for their *eremia*
into flourishing monastic communities can also be seen in the development of the most important island monasteries of the Aegean. For just as
Athanasios' foundation on Athos shows distinct similarities to that of the
Lavra of Maleïnos on Mount Kyminas, so, too, did the early experiences
of St Christodoulos on Mounts Olympos and Latros influence the
constitutions of his Monastery of St John the Theologian on Patmos.
The real reason for Christodoulos' departure from Latros is unclear, but,
at all events, he does seem to have been seeking an environment similar
to that to which the monastic founders of western Asia Minor had
gravitated: a place of solitude, a 'desert' in both the literal and metaphysical sense.[44] After a short period as *hegoumenos* of a monastery at
Strobilos (modern Aspat or Çifut Kalesi) on the western coast of Asia
Minor, founded by one Arsenios Skenoures, Christodoulos moved on
with a band of monks to the island of Kos. Invited by Skenoures to found

[43] Life of SS John and Euthymios, pp. 75–83 on the problems caused by the lack of a
written *typikon*; p. 99, notes 69 and 71 for hermits outside Iviron. The early, highly
complex history of the Monastery of Iviron is discussed in detail in *Ivirôn*, I and II: I,
pp. 3–102. See I, pp. 13–21 for the arrival on Athos of John the Iberian, Euthymios and
John Tornik and their friendship with Athanasios; p. 25 for the Monastery of Clement and
the foundation of Iviron; pp. 39–40 for the name and character of the house. A shorter
summary in J. Lefort and D. Papachryssanthou, 'Les premiers Géorgiens à l'Athos dans
les documents byzantins', *Bedi Kartlisa*, 41 (1983), 27–33.
[44] E. Vranoussi, *Ta hagiologika keimena tou hosiou Christodoulou hidrytou tes en Patmo
mones. Philalogike paradosis kai historikai martyriai* (Athens, 1966), surveys the saint's
career. For Christodoulos' departure from Latros, see chapter 3.

a house on one of his family estates, it is significant that he chose to settle near Kastrianon on Mount Pelion, the highest and most rugged point on the island 'for it was surrounded by ravines, with valleys all around, a citadel, as it were . . . I wished to stand aside from the affairs of the multitude and enjoy the hesychastic life until my death'.[45]

Christodoulos was searching for an environment similar to that of Latros, and it seemed for a while as if he had been successful. The group built a church dedicated to the Theotokos and some cells and other buildings for the monastery. An imperial *pittakion* (privilege) granted him the possession of two places (*topia*) on the island: Kastellion (the name by which Kastrianon was officially known) and Pile, indication enough that he originally intended to remain on Kos. What is more, Christodoulos' was not the first of such settlements on the island. His patron, Arsenios Skenoures had already founded two *kellia* on the wilderness of Mount Dikaion and had lived the hesychastic life there. His support for Christodoulos indicates that they were kindred spirits.[46]

The houses on Kos thus provide examples of embryonic monastic communities on the Bithynian pattern. But its peaks never developed into celebrated 'holy mountains', probably because of the departure of Christodoulos for Patmos. His reason was, once again, the intrusion of the affairs of the world into his monastic solitude. Friendships began to be formed between his monks and their lay neighbours, a state of affairs which, in his account of these events in the *Hypotyposis*, prompted him to make an interesting monastic 'policy statement': 'You will never achieve solitude [*eremos*] unless you find a place from which the laity has been completely removed; a place of *hesychia* for yourself and your brethren which can contribute to the work of the spirit.' Here was a distinct change in the quest for *eremia*. Christodoulos was not prepared to withdraw himself from the world; the world had now to be excluded.[47]

The island of Patmos was initially chosen as a monastic site by Christodoulos because of its tranquillity and the fact that it was unfrequented by shipping. The customs of the Monastery of St John the Theologian which he founded clearly place it among the houses

---

[45] *Hypotyposis* of Christodoulos, pp. 12–63. His explanation for leaving Strobilos was that it was liable to Turkish attack. Certainly, it had fallen before 1103, when it was described as 'devastated' by the English pilgrim, Saewulf, but the precise year is unknown. See C. Foss, 'Strobilos and related sites', *Anatolian Studies*, 38 (1988), 147–74, see 149. The location of the Monastery on Kos is given in a chrysobull of Alexios Komnenos (March 1085), *BEMP*, I, no. 4, pp. 33–4.
[46] *Pittakion* of Nikephoros Botaniates (March, 1080), now lost, is mentioned in the chrysobull of Alexios Komnenos of 1085 (p. 33), see note 45, above. See also *Kodikellos* of Christodoulos, p. 88.
[47] *Hypotyposis* of Christodoulos, pp. 63–4.

practising the mixed monastic life. Its constitutions were very similar to those of the Great Lavra on Mount Athos, although, curiously, no mention of Patmos appears in the published Athos archives of the period or vice versa. The house was basically coenobitic and Christodoulos followed St Basil in his approval of the common life: 'Those who have truly striven after the life of the angels are the ascetics who have lived the common life through great difficulties, showing in their communal existence a pure *mimesis* (imitation) of the angelic state.' But he also provided regulations for those following the hesychastic life. Twelve monks were to be permitted to live on rocks, or in caves or *kellia* not only because the island was particularly suited to this way of life, but also, significantly, because Christodoulos did not wish to imply that this aim was unobtainable.[48]

The monastic settlements of Athos and Patmos may be firmly linked with the traditions of Asia Minor. But there were other houses for which circumstantial evidence also suggests a link with the earlier 'holy mountains'. In a chrysobull of the Emperor Constantine IX Monomachos (1042–55) for the foundation he patronised on the island of Chios (the so-called Nea Mone, which may, in fact, have originally been a double monastery of monks and nuns and whose *typikon* is now lost), the emperor expressed a concern to preserve the seclusion of those 'who live a life near to God and, according to their ability, follow the way and existence of the angels . . . so that they may have solitude and joy in all things'. There may, too, have been more personal links between the monks of Chios and those of Olympos. For Constantine Monomachos also granted the Chiotes a *xenodocheion* (hostel) in Constantinople to be used when the monks visited the capital on business, which was also frequented by those from Olympos. He may in this case have sought to place together monks of similar disciplines; he was certainly also a patron of the lavriote-influenced community of St Lazaros on Mount Galesion.[49]

[48] *Ibid.*, pp. 64, 69, 76–7.
[49] For a general history, C. Bouras, *Nea Mone on Chios. History and architecture* (Athens, 1982). For the archives, E. Vranoussi, 'Les archives de la Néa Moni de Chios. Essai de reconstitution d'un dossier perdu', *BNJ*, 22 (1977–84), 267–84; *Chrysoboullos logos* of Constantine IX Monomachos (June 1045), Zepos, I, Appendix, document VII, 629–31 (Dölger, *Regesten*, no. 868). For the *xenodocheion*, see Constantine Monomachos' *Chrysoboullon sigillion* of 1046, Zepos, I, Appendix, document VIII, 631–2 (Dölger, *Regesten*, no. 878) and his *Chrysoboullon sigillion* of 1048, Zepos, I, Appendix, document IX, p. 632 (Dölger, *Regesten*, no. 887). The *xenodocheion* was a building belonging to the monastic and administrative complex of St George of the Mangana in the district *ta Angouriou*; see Janin, *Eglises et monastères*: R. Janin, *La géographie ecclésiastique de l'empire byzantin. Section one: Le siège de Constantinople et le patriarchat oecumenique* (2 vols). III: *Les églises et les monastères* (2nd edn., Paris, 1969), pp. 9, 70–6. N. Oikonomidès, 'L'évolution de l'organisation administrative de l'empire byzantin au XIe siècle', *TM*, 6 (1976), 125–52, reprinted in his *Byzantium from the ninth century to the Fourth Crusade* (Aldershot, 1992), article X, p. 140

Mention should finally be made of two obscure holy mountains outside Asia Minor. The first, Mount Ganos in Thrace (near modern Gaziköy), is first mentioned in the tenth century, though by the mid-eleventh there was a Protos on the mountain, a clear indication of the existence of a monastic federation on the lines of Latros or Athos. The second of these mountains, the so-called 'Mountain of the *kellia* of Zagora' (modern day Mount Pelion in Thessaly) is of particular interest because the Emperor Alexios Komnenos (1081–1118) originally wished Christodoulos to go there, rather than to Patmos. He was offered the *prostasia* (possibly the office of *Protos*) of the community in order to reform the way of life of the monks, who were reported to have turned away from the proper life. This would suggest either that they had originally practised a way of life familiar to him from Asia Minor or that the Bithynian 'way' was now deemed to be a style worth imitating.[50]

There is little difficulty, then, in establishing the spread of the monastic traditions of western Asia Minor in the eastern Mediterranean. The task is somewhat more difficult in the case of Italy, as clear relationships between the monastic leaders there and more distant houses in the east cannot be established with any degree of precision. But there are a number of factors which indicate that in the more mountainous parts of southern Italy, the same kind of emphasis on *eremia* and *hesychia* could be found. The evidence of the tenth-century saints' lives of the region reveals a number of examples of those who first followed a peripatetic existence in the mountains and then founded small lavriote-influenced monasteries. St Elias of Enna, after many years wandering in the East, founded small monastic houses in the Salinoi region of Calabria before leaving again for Greece. St Elias Spelaiotes (as his name indicates) spent many years in a cave at Melicuccà, north-east of Reggio, which later, in a pattern very similar to that of Paul of Latros' foundation, became a monastic centre. St Vitalis of Sicily, after living the communal life for fifteen years, then spent much of the remainder of his life as a hermit: in ruined baths at St Severina, on a hill top in Sicily and in a grotto near Armento in Calabria.[51]

---

and Kaplan, *Les hommes et la terre*, pp. 315–16, deal with the administrative functions of the Mangana. See Life of St Lazaros, chapter 230, p. 597 (Dölger, *Regesten*, no. 855) for Monomachos' patronage of houses on Mount Galesion.

[50] Mount Ganos is mentioned in the Chronicle of Pseudo-Symeon *magistros*, p. 615. The seal of its Protos is given by Laurent, *Sceaux*, ii, nos. 1228–31. See also M. Gedeon, 'Mnemeia latreias christianikes en Ganochorois', *Ekklesiastike Aletheia*, 32 (1912), 304, 311–13, 325–7, 352–5, 389–92, Vranoussi, *Ta hagiologika keimena*, pp. 128–9 for the Monastery of the Kellia of Zagora. See also *Hypotyposis* of Christodoulos, p. 64.

[51] These saints are discussed further in chapter 3. The parallels between monastic developments in ninth- and tenth-century southern Italy and Asia Minor are pointed out by Pertusi, 'Rapporti', pp. 474–5 and Guillou, 'Grecs d'Italie', p. 97.

In addition, there is abundant evidence of frequent monastic contacts between the eastern and western themes of the empire. Many, from the eighth century onwards, came to Rome on pilgrimage, most probably landing at the southern Italian ports on the way. As well as the Stoudite and other books and customs which they brought, they may well have transmitted news and information about the houses of Bithynia and elsewhere.[52] There were certainly close contacts between Athos and Italy, for apart from the Benedictine Amalfitan Monastery on the mountain, Athonite documents provide the signatures of *hegoumenoi* of the Monastery 'of the Calabrians' (1080–1108) and that 'of the Sicilians' (986–1108), both Greek houses. The biographer of John the Iberian and his son, Euthymios, wrote in approving terms of the monks on Athos who followed the Benedictine rite and there seems to have been a mutual admiration, in both Greek and Latin circles in southern Italy, for the form of monastic life found on the Holy Mountain.[53] In the main, the customs and traditions of 'hybrid' monasticism were carried by those who had been trained in them in youth and whose personal commitment to them was transferred to the foundation of new houses. Although the 'ideological content' of this way of life may well have appealed to many Byzantines, it was the personalities of the holy men who practised it which drew recruits to it in such numbers.[54]

The consequences of the development of hybrid monasticism in many parts of the empire were considerable. First, the necessity to find a physical environment in which individual *hesychia* might be achieved led to deliberate settlement in hitherto desolate or abandoned areas and provided them with some stimulus for economic development. Secondly, as a consequence of the growing popularity of this type of religious life, many joined the houses in which it was practised. They were thus often transformed, by sheer force of numbers, into institutions which played a dominant economic and social rôle in the areas in which they were situated. Complex and often difficult relationships with the surrounding lay and religious communities arose partly from the need to ensure an adequate food supply for their survival. This was achieved by land acquisition, by trade or from the charitable impulses of the laity. A conflict also arose from the attempts, visible in many areas where the founding principle had been the quest for *hesychia*, to preserve solitude

[52] Pertusi, 'Rapporti', pp. 562–3 discusses pilgrimages to Rome.
[53] Life of SS John and Euthymios, pp. 109–10. Pertusi, 'Rapporti', pp. 497–8 for the 'orthodox' Italian houses on Mount Athos. For the Amalfitan house, P. Lemerle, 'Les archives du monastère des Amalfitains au Mont Athos', *EEBS*, 23 (1953), 548–66 and A. Pertusi, 'Nuovi documenti sui Benedettini Amalfitani dell' Athos', *Aevum*, 27 (1953), 1–30.
[54] See chapter 3.

51

when unavoidable economic expansion brought too close a contact with neighbouring groups. The paradoxes of living a life 'in the world but not of it' were particularly evident in the case of the houses combining the coenobitic and the lavriote styles.[55]

Although the evolution of a style of monasticism which combined the eremitic and coenobitic traditions was a development of considerable spiritual importance, houses completely devoted to the communal life maintained their appeal. Though literary references are irritatingly short in the tenth and first half of the eleventh centuries – we have no detailed urban *typika*, for example, except for that of Stoudios – visual evidence suggests a growth in urban foundations during the two centuries after 843. Particularly in the towns and cities, the coenobitic way would have remained the style of monasticism most familiar to Byzantines. Furthermore, the increase in numbers of those entering the 'hybrid' houses (particularly on Mount Athos) cannot be taken to imply a corresponding diminution in the numbers entering coenobitic houses. It may simply be that in the tenth and eleventh centuries there were more monastic vocations. Certainly, as far as women were concerned, the coenobitic life remained the only style available for the overwhelming majority. It is somewhat revealing in this context that it was a holy *woman* who told the Italian St Leo-Luke of Corleone that true virtue was not to be found by wandering and that he should enter a *koinobion* and imitate the lives of previous saints. But it is a melancholy fact that we know next to nothing about female monasticism in the period up to c. 1100; from the beginning of the twelfth century, the figure of the Byzantine nun appears much more frequently in the sources.[56]

---

[55] See chapters 6 and 7.
[56] Life of St Leo-Luke of Corleone, chapter 5, p. 99. There are, of course, hagiographies of female saints, many of whom took the veil, but they provide little in the way of trustworthy detail about monastic life for women at this time. See, for example, *Life of St Irene of Chrysobalanton*, ed. and trans, J. O. Rosenqvist (Acta Universitatis Upsaliensis, Studia Byzantina Upsaliensis, i, Uppsala, 1986); *Life of St Athanasia of Aegina*, ed. and English summary L. Carras, in *Maistor: Classical, Byzantine and Renaissance studies for Robert Browning*, ed. A. Moffat (Byzantina Australiensia, v, Canberra, 1984), pp. 199–224, 212–24 (text); Life of St Theodora of Thessalonika, E. Kurtz, 'Des Klerikers Gregorios Bericht über Leben, Wunderthaten und Translation der hl. Theodora von Thessalonich', *Zapiskie imp. Akad. Nauk., ist.-fil. otdel.*, 8th ser., 6/1 (1902), 1–49, pp. 37–49 (text) and see E. Patlagean, 'Theodora de Thessalonique. Une sainte moniale et un culte citadin (IXe–XXe siècle)', in S. B. Gajano and L. Sebastiani (eds.), *Culto dei santi, istituzioni e classi sociali in età preindustriale* (Rome, 1984), pp. 37–67. Further discussion: D. deF. Abrahamse, 'Women's monasticism in the middle Byzantine period: problems and prospects', *BF*, 9 (1985), 35–58; A. E. Laiou, 'Observations on the life and ideology of Byzantine women', *BF*, 9 (1985), 59–102; A.-M. Talbot, 'A comparison of the monastic experience of Byzantine men and women', *Greek Orthodox Theological Review*, 30 (1985), 1–20 and C. Galatariotou, 'Byzantine women's monastic communities: the evidence of the *typika*', *JÖB*, 38 (1988), 263–90.

There was always a great deal in the communal life to attract prospective religious of either sex, as is revealed in the surviving *typika* of five of these coenobitic houses, all dating from the end of the eleventh century or the beginning of the twelfth. Not surprisingly, they come from regions in or near Constantinople and the Northern Balkans which did not suffer such destruction in the Turkish invasions as the houses of Asia Minor. But there is no reason to doubt that they were echoed by foundation documents, now lost, from houses throughout the empire. The *typika* of the monasteries of the Theotokos Evergetis near Constantinople (c. 1054); the Theotokos of Petritza in Bačkovo (1083); the Theotokos Eleousa at Stroumitza (1085–1106); the Nunnery of the Theotokos Kecharitomene in Constantinople (c. 1118) and the charitable institution with associated monastery founded by Michael Attaliates at Rhaidestos and Constantinople (1077) all provided detailed regulations for the running of coenobitic houses. But their founders also expressed their opinions on the merits of the coenobitic life and in this respect they form part of the tradition that stretched back via the Stoudite rule to the precepts of St Basil.[57]

Like Theodore of Stoudios, all these monastic founders emphasised adherence to the 'laws of the Fathers', by which they, too, understood the monastic constitutions of St Basil. The spiritual benefit of the monastic life could not fully be achieved if the coenobitic style were not strictly followed. The individual's desires and aspirations had to be subordinated to the common will and it is in the emphasis on obedience (*hypotage*), found so often in these *typika*, that a fundamental difference between their concept of the religious life and that of the lavriotes may be perceived. The lavriotes could envisage a state in which the individual could reach communion with God; the strict coenobites believed that the subordination of the individual will was the path to the truly ascetic life. Attaliates' *Diataxis* (regulations) expressed the aim of this kind of self-abnegation:

> I deem greater than all things *hesychia* [inner spirituality], obedience [*hypotage*], humility [*tapeinosis*] and mutual love amongst the brethren. I wish the monks to make peace, one with the other, each evening. Let the *hegoumenos* or *oikonomos* appointed by my heir look to it diligently that no monk should go to bed annoyed or angry with anyone, in accordance with the saying, 'Let not the sun go down upon thy wrath.'[58]

---

[57] *Typika*: Evergétis; Pakourianos; Stroumitza; Kécharitôménè; *Diataxis* of Attaliates. It is worth noting how many coenobitic houses at this time were dedicated to the Virgin, a matter which deserves further study.

[58] *Diataxis* of Attaliates, p. 61. See also Evergétis, chapter 15, p. 57.

The individual will was to be subordinated by the imposition of uniformity in dress, in diet, in labour and in limitations on movement. In each of these areas, a contrast may be made with the customs of the hesychasts.

The monastic habit, each part of which symbolised an aspect of the spiritual duties of the monk, was common to the great coenobitic houses. The *Typikon* of Stroumitza describes the significance of the tonsure, of the dark robes indicating penance, the *analabos* (scapular) with its cross to remind the wearer of the Crucifixion, and the *koukoulion* (cowl), covering the head in humility.[59] This is a marked contrast with the figure of St Lazaros of Mount Galesion in his hair shirt or St Luke the Stylite, dressed in skins and weighed down by chains, and vividly marks the difference in their monastic approach.[60] For the lavriotes, part of the charisma of many of their leaders lay in the fact that they donned the dress of the first hermit, John the Baptist, and added to it the mortifying chains of the early Syrian monks. For the coenobitic monks, such action would have implied an unacceptable concern with *individual* spirituality and *typika* generally stated that there should be no differences in dress among the brethren.[61] Similarly, the excesses of frugality practised by some ascetics were not possible in the atmosphere of the *koinobion*, where diet was strictly controlled and fasting monitored. Out of the five *typika*, only the *Diataxis* of Attaliates permitted any variation in diet between the *hegoumenos* and the rest of the monks; in all the others, the value of the common table was emphasised.[62]

But the most profound contrast between the *koinobia* and the *lavrai* or lavriote-influenced houses was in the tasks to which their members devoted themselves. While the founders of *lavrai*, such as Paul of Latros or Lazaros of Mount Galesion, followed a life of solitary prayer and the adjudication, from some distance, of the affairs of their houses and the surrounding countryside, the *hegoumenoi* of these eleventh-century *koinobia* were actively concerned in the affairs of their houses. Particular tasks and offices might be given to some, as established by Theodore of Stoudios, but the basic equality of the community was preserved by the fact that all of its members could aspire (in theory at least) to hold even

---

[59] Stroumitza, chapter 9, pp. 77–9 and commentary.
[60] Life of St Luke the Stylite, chapter 5, p. 200; Life of St Lazaros, chapter 35, p. 520.
[61] Stroumitza, chapter 9, pp. 77–8; Evergétis, chapter 26, p. 59; Kécharitôménè, chapter 56, p. 107.
[62] Stroumitza, chapter 4, p. 72; chapter 12, pp. 85–6; Evergétis, chapter 9, pp. 33–9; chapter 26, p. 59; Pakourianos, chapter 4, pp. 45–51; Kécharitôménè, chapter 44, pp. 91–3; chapter 56, p. 107; *Diataxis* of Attaliates, p. 69.

the highest office.[63] Moreover, the highest pinnacle of spiritual achievement was not seen to lie in a solitary life outside the monastery. On the contrary, the detail with which the liturgical duties of the monks were laid down in the coenobitic *typika* underlined the emphasis which their founders and patrons placed on united, orderly and, most important of all, multiple intercession with the Deity.[64] But though the performance of the liturgy and prayers was of supreme importance in monastic communities of whatever type, a much stronger emphasis was placed in the *koinobia* on the spiritual virtues of labour. In the tradition of the Stoudites, the *Typikon* of the Theotokos Evergetis Monastery, for example, exhorted the monks to carry out their work with the thought 'I have not come to command, but be commanded.' The *Typikon* of Bačkovo put it somewhat more succinctly, when it declared that the monks should work with their hands, but have psalms on their lips.[65] Similarly, although the *lavrai* did open their doors to strangers and the needy, charitable work was undertaken to a much greater extent in the *koinobia*.[66]

The unity of the *koinobion* was most firmly emphasised by the prohibition on monks leaving the house. The *Typikon* of the Theotokos Evergetis Monastery forbade the *hegoumenos* venturing into Constantinople (some three kilometres away), unless he had been specifically summoned by the emperor or the patriarch, or when an enemy attack might have forced everyone to leave the house. This prohibition was emphasised by other founders of communal houses and was in keeping with the accepted teachings of the Councils of the Church.[67] It was in great contrast,

[63] For the appointment of *hegoumenoi* or abbesses, see Stroumitza, chapter 11, pp. 81–121; chapters 15–16, pp. 87–9; Kécharitôménè, chapter 11, pp. 47–51; Pakourianos, chapter 5, pp. 51–3; Evergétis, chapter 13, pp. 47–9. The *hegoumenos* Timothy, interestingly, considered the possibility of the appointment of two *hegoumenoi*, one living in seclusion, one with the monks, but in the end decided on one. The *hegoumenos* was, in theory, allowed to choose whether or not to be a solitary, but, in giving details of his administrative duties, Timothy seems to have assumed he would not be. *Diataxis* of Attaliates, p. 57, and further discussion in chapter 3.
[64] Stroumitza, chapters 6–7, pp. 73–6 and commentary; Evergétis, chapters 4–6, pp. 19–29. There was also a liturgical *typikon*; see A. Dmitrievskii, *Opisanie liturgicheskikh rukopisei kharaniashchikhsia v bibliotekakh pravoslavnago vostoka* (2 vols., Kiev, 1895; 1901, reprinted Hildesheim, 1965), I, *Typika*, pp. 256–614; Pakourianos, chapter 11, p. 71; chapters 21–2, pp. 97–103; Kécharitôménè, chapters 32–9, pp. 79–89. The liturgical *typikon* for Michael Attaliates' foundations is now lost; see *Diataxis* of Attaliates, p. 67.
[65] Evergétis, chapter 33, pp. 73–5; Pakourianos, chapter 14, p. 77.
[66] See, generally, D. Constantelos, *Byzantine philanthropy and social welfare* (New Brunswick, NJ, 1968). Michael Attaliates' foundations were ostensibly founded for charitable purposes, and Gregory Pakourianos made provisions for refuges on the estates at Bačkovo; see Pakourianos, chapter 29, pp. 111–15.
[67] Evergétis, chapter 13, p. 49. The general principles are discussed in E. Herman, 'La "stabilitas loci" nel monachismo bizantino', *OCP*, 21 (1955), 115–42, see 115–20.

however, to the practices of the lavriote founders. Paul of Latros, Lazaros of Mount Galesion and Christodoulos of Patmos all spent their early years wandering from house to house. Athanasios of Athos, indeed, took care to order his monks not to despise those who came to Athos from other houses. It is in this matter, above all, that the lavriote insistence on individual *askesis* might have come into conflict with the traditional coenobitic emphasis on communal spirituality, had it not been for the fact that the new 'hybrid' monasticism deliberately limited the number of those living the eremitic life.[68]

The dislike of emphasising the individual spiritual achievement, shown in so many ways in the *typika* of communal houses, is perhaps most strikingly expressed by the attitude taken to their founders and leaders by both monks and laity. None of them gave their own names to their houses and although they were to be venerated as founders with due gratitude and their donations were to remain inviolate, only in rare cases were they later to be considered as saints.[69] The only case from this period of a recognised saint favouring the practice of the communal life alone would appear to be that of St Cyril of Philea, whose Monastery of the Saviour at Derkos in Thrace was founded about 1050. He was reported to have given instructions that any future *hegoumenos* who tried to transform the existing coenobitic monastery into a kelliote house should be removed. Cyril himself had lived the ascetic life in his early years as a monk, but had been persuaded to abandon its harsh rigours by his own spiritual father, the monk Hilarion, because 'some virtuous men are inclined to over-estimate those ascetics, from which follows vainglory'.[70]

The *hegoumenoi* of the *koinobia* were rarely founders but they were, in all cases, the spiritual directors of the monks, so the opportunity provided in the lavriote system for monks to choose and group themselves around their own spiritual father was again a contrast with the communal houses and helps to explain the apparent dearth of charismatic spiritual directors within that system, with the important exception of the tenth-century *hegoumenos*, Symeon the New Theologian.[71] The purely coenobitic communities thus formed far more static units than did those houses

68 Herman, '"Stabilitas loci"', 122–6; *Typikon* of Athanasios, p. 109.
69 Kécharitôménè, chapter 34, pp. 83–5; Pakourianos, chapter 21, pp. 97–103; Evergétis, chapter 35, p. 77; *Diataxis* of Attaliates, pp. 47, 49, 65. For the terminology applied to founders, see chapter 3, p. 88.
70 *Life of St Cyril Phileotes*, chapter 16, p. 89 (312); chapter 39, p. 173 (399) and introduction, p. 39 for the date of the foundation of the monastery. Page numbers in brackets refer to the French translation, which follows the Greek text.
71 See chapter 4, pp. 92–102 for spiritual fatherhood. For the *hegoumenos* as sole spiritual guide, Evergétis, chapter 15, p. 57; Kécharitôménè, chapter 12, p. 53, where the abbess is referred to as 'spiritual mother'. The nuns were, however, also to have a single male *pneumatikos pater*, who had to be a eunuch; chapter 16, p. 69.

which allowed some elements of the solitary life. Their organisation obviously affected the numbers that might be accommodated in them, since every expansion in numbers had to be based on a parallel increase in both food supplies and revenue to pay for the extensions to communal monastic buildings.

At all levels, then, the founders and leaders of the communal houses made it clear that they wished the coenobitic life to be followed without alteration. In many cases, they represented the adherents to traditional modes of piety, a conservative group to be contrasted with the founders and patrons of the *lavrai* in both the social and spiritual sense. They believed more in a strict adherence to the teachings of the Fathers of the Church of the past, than in the prowess of the spiritual athletes of their own times:

> For they [the Fathers of the Church] were well aware and, indeed, firmly laid down that the communal life should be undertaken and that those fleeing from the storms of the world and seeking the peaceful haven of the monastic life, should renounce their own desires and should devote themselves to submission. They are in need of a helmsman and a guide for the eyes of their souls are blind and they are not able to help themselves . . . [72]

Few saints appeared from the *koinobia*, but the traditional ideals of monasticism were perhaps better fulfilled there.

The final group of monks to play an important part in the spiritual life of tenth- and eleventh-century Byzantium was comprised of individuals whose careers did not *primarily* involve the founding or organisation of religious houses, but who spent their lives in three other spiritual activities: preaching, healing and prophecy. They were usually peripatetic and played a major part in bringing spiritual guidance, communal leadership and often the Gospel itself to those in areas in which the Christian life had been disrupted by invasion. In particular, Greece, Crete and southern Italy provided the background for the activities of a series of major figures. In Greece, the threat came from the Bulgar and Magyar raids of the early and last years of the tenth century, which severely disrupted rural life, as did the incursions of the Muslims in southern Italy. In Crete, the challenge to the church was to re-establish Christianity after the Byzantine reconquest of the island from the Muslims in 961.[73]

One of the most striking aspects of this type of monastic ministry is the immense distances that were covered. St Luke the Younger (896–953) spent his childhood near Delphi, then travelled throughout the Peloponnese before returning to his native Phokis to die at Stiris. St John

---

[72] Kécharitôménè, chapter 2, p. 31.   [73] See chapter 1, pp. 23–4.

Xenos, a contemporary of the Patriarch Alexios Stoudites (1025–43), travelled through western Crete setting up small oratories (*eukteria*), often with only one monk in them, as 'relay-stations' in the re-Christianisation of the island. He probably confined his activity to this area because the groundwork of preaching had already been laid in the central and eastern regions by St Nikon *Metanoeite* ('Repent Ye!'), who had issued his famous call to the island's population to repent of their lapses into 'idolatry' (by which he meant conversion to Islam) shortly after 961. Nikon then went on to Greece, where he concentrated his evangelism in the Peloponnese.[74] The same kind of continual migration was found among the wandering saints of tenth-century southern Italy. Here, too, the dangers of attack were all too real and the saints provided a very important focus of spiritual guidance and leadership for communities ravaged by incessant raiding.[75]

The incessant travelling was in direct contravention of the legislation of church councils and was certainly alien to the traditions of the coenobitic houses. And even though many of the later lavriote-influenced founders spent their early years wandering from monastery to monastery or on pilgrimage (Lazaros of Galesion and Christodoulos to Jerusalem; Cyril Phileotes to Rome), there is no one among these later examples to compare with the tenth-century holy men, who spent the whole of their lives on the move. It was a need which died out as political conditions became more peaceful and as other sources of leadership and communal guidance began to present themselves, and does not ever seem to have been a source of direct criticism of the saints concerned.[76]

The wandering holy men of the tenth and early eleventh centuries represented the final flowering of a long tradition. Their major functions of preaching, arbitration and leadership, coupled with the spiritual qualities common to all of them – such as the ability to predict the future and to heal the sick – followed a pattern well familiar to Byzantines. They acted according to long-held spiritual customs, moving from community

---

[74] Life of St Luke the Younger, *passim*. Da Costa-Louillet, 'Saints de Grèce', pp. 333, 335, 338–9 identifies the place names in the Life. See Life of John Xenos, p. 194, for dating. The place names in it were first identified as Cretan by L. Petit, 'St Jean Xénos ou l'Ermite d'après son autobiographie', *AB*, 42 (1924), 5–20. The preaching of Nikon Metanoeite and the reconquest of Crete is discussed by E. Voulgarakis, 'Nikon Metanoeite und die Rechristianisierung der Kreter von Islam', *Zeitschrift für Missionswissenschaft und Religionswissenschaft*, 417 (1963), 192–269.

[75] For Italian wandering saints, see note 51, above. Useful summaries of lives in G. Da Costa-Louillet, 'Saints de Sicile et d'Italie méridionale aux VIIIe, IXe et Xe siècles', *B*, 29–30 (1959–60), 89–173.

[76] Life of St Lazaros, chapters 14–29, pp. 513–18; *Hypotyposis* of Christodoulos, p. 60; Life of St Cyril Phileotes, chapter 20, pp. 100–4 (325–9).

to community, 'standing outside the ties of family and economic unity' just as their predecessors had done as long ago as the fourth and fifth centuries; they added an element of security in a world which was just as dangerous for many in the tenth century as it had been then. In some cases, the holy men apparently refused to reveal their origins, a device used by their hagiographers to emphasise their quality of separateness, their distance from worldly ties based on blood and thus their ability to arbitrate justly in both spiritual and social terms. St Basil the Younger, for instance, who died in the mid-tenth century, consistently refused to reveal either his place of birth or his parentage, even when tortured by a high official in Constantinople and St John *Xenos* ('Stranger') was so known because of his wandering life. Nicholas Kataskepenos, the biographer of St Cyril Phileotes, gave some indication of the importance of the *xenos* figures when describing his hero's illness during a pilgrimage to Rome: 'He stayed stretched out like a *xenos*, separated from everything in order to guard his thoughts and constantly united with God.'[77] In other words he was one whose spiritual strength derived from his conspicuous refusal to invoke the ties associated with family and *patris*.

In their lifetimes, these rather mysterious figures gained popularity precisely because they 'stood outside the ties of family', but this independent position was ended by the very existence of the foundations which they caused to be established. In John Xenos' case, several small hermitages which he set up, originally containing only one monk each, were gathered together at the end of his life into one entity, complete with patriarchal documents of confirmation. Basil the Younger founded no house during his own lifetime, but on his death, his body was buried in a monastery in Constantinople, after his followers had scotched a plan by an erstwhile patron, Constantine Barbaros, to remove the remains of the saint to a church on his own estate outside the city. Neither Luke the Younger, nor Peter of Argos had foundations associated with them until after their deaths and little is known of the monastery founded by St Nikon during his lifetime. Chrysobulls of establishment and exemption from state dues were only obtained after the saint's death, by its *hegoumenos*, Gregory Paphlago. Peter of Argos' corpse was fought over

[77] P. R. L. Brown, 'The rise and function of the holy man in late antiquity', *JRS*, 61 (1971), reprinted in *Society and the holy in late antiquity* (London, 1982), pp. 103–52, p. 91. *Life of St Basil the Younger*, to be completed from A. N. Veselovskii, 'Zhitie sv. Vasiliya Novogo', in *Sbornik Otdeleniya Russkogo Yazyka i Slovesnosti Imp. Akad. Nauk*, 46 (1890); 53 (1892), *Prilozheniya*. The version published by S. G. Vilinski, *Zhitie sv. Vasiliya Novogo v russkoi literature* (2 vols., Odessa, 1911–13), has eluded me. See in *AASS* version, chapters 3–7, p. *20; Life of St Cyril Phileotes, chapter 20, p. 102 (327); and see J. Leclercq, 'Monachisme et pérégrination du XIe au XIIe siècle', *Studia Monastica*, 3 (1961), 33–52, for Western parallels.

by the citizens of Argos and Nauplia, before it was finally buried at Argos.[78]

Although three of these wandering monk-saints, Peter of Argos, Nikon Metanoeite and Luke the Younger, appear in the *Synaxarion of Constantinople* (an extensive list of saints according to the days on which they should be celebrated), an indication of their wider appeal, their initial spheres of influence were local. Nikon's biographer clearly indicates that, though he had travelled widely, he was primarily a holy man for the people of Sparta: 'for he protected them from all evil on land and sea'. Peter of Argos was, and is, the particular patron saint of that city.[79] The contrast with the early, widespread fame of monastic founders such as Athanasios of Athos is marked. Though these wandering saints had some disciples, their main efforts were devoted towards the concerns of the surrounding laity. Rather than attracting a large number of followers into the localities where they were active, they were themselves later 'exported' to other regions after their deaths, a process which was only made possible by their initial *lack* of a permanent, territorial establishment. The popularity of these saints reflected their achievement of the old-established goals of the holy men of the past. Only one other group, the stylites (those who traditionally lived on stone columns), practised the life 'apart' to a greater extent.

It would be tempting to correlate the decline in the stylite population of the empire with the rise in the number of monastic foundations headed by charismatic figures, but there is no obvious relationship between these two factors. References to stylites, however, do become much sparser in the hagiographical literature of the tenth and eleventh centuries and only one full-length biography of a stylite – that of St Luke of Chalcedon – exists for this period, though there are fleeting glimpses of them in other sources. St Luke the Younger was the servant of a stylite at Zemena near

---

[78] Life of John Xenos, p. 64 for the chrysobulls and see Kaplan, *Les hommes et la terre*, p. 301, for a further discussion of the accumulation of properties. Life of St Basil the Younger, chapters 54–5, pp. *37–8. The monastery was situated in the western part of the city, in the region known as *ta Meltiadou*; see R. Janin, *Constantinople byzantin* (Paris, 1950), p. 361 and *Eglises et monastères*, pp. 496–7. Life of St Luke the Younger, chapter 69, p. 475. *Life of St Nikon*, chapters 36–7, pp. 124–30; chapter 58, p. 184. Life of Peter of Argos, chapter 22, pp. 14–15.

[79] See H. Delehaye, *Synaxarium Ecclesiae Constantinopolitanae e Codice Sirmondiano* (Brussels, 1902), 26 November, p. 260 (Nikon); 7 February, p. 449; 8 February, p. 453 (Luke the Younger); 2 May, p. 649; 3 May, p. 652 (Peter of Argos), *Life of St Nikon*, chapter 76, pp. 264–6 and see S. Papaoikonomos, *Ho poliouchos tou Argous hagios Petros episkopos Argous ho thaumatourgos* (Athens, 1908), especially plates showing processions associated with the saint in the early years of this century. For the mosaic portrayal of Nikon in the Katholikon at Hosios Loukas, see *Life of St Nikon*, introduction, p. 18 and Pallas, 'Topographie und Chronologie von Hosios Loukas', p. 98.

Patras in the Peloponnese for about ten years (c. 916–26); St Lazaros of Mount Galesion, in the mid-eleventh century, came across one stylite on the mountain and heard of another female one. His companion on his return journey from Jerusalem (c. 1009), the monk Paul, remained behind at Laodicea in Syria to become a stylite. So the traditional stylite life was still being practised and with the same rationale as in earlier times. As Luke Stylites' biographer put it: 'These men abandoned, as being too base a habitation, the earth upon which we all crowd, and placed themselves on pillars.'[80]

But the stylite life was now often significantly adapted to suit the purposes of the new 'hybrid' monasticism. In some cases, even the physical environment was altered. St Paul of Latros spent twelve years on what he termed his *stylos*. It was, in fact, a cave at the top of a steep rock. St Cyril Phileotes constructed a cell in a pine forest near Derkos (c. 1051–6) on the spot where he had seen the *vision* of a *stylos*. The traditional withdrawn existence of the stylite was sometimes replaced by a more active involvement in the day-to-day affairs of a neighbouring monastery, rather than a mere reliance upon it for food. Paul of Latros directed a monastery from his *stylos*, which was actually within the monastic enclosure. So, to a certain extent, did St Lazaros who lived on at least two *styloi* and in a cave which may have been at the top of a rock. The latter's biographer, his disciple Gregory, also refers to one Laurence – 'a stylite in my own time' – who probably took over one of the columns vacated by Lazaros.[81]

In the same way that the concept of *eremia* played a vital part in the thinking of monastic founders in the tenth and eleventh centuries, so, too, did the most extreme form of ascetic exercise epitomised by the life of the stylites. But even in its modified form, this life was no longer available to all those who might wish to follow it and could withstand its rigours. The *stylos* became another symbol of spiritual leadership; the life of the stylite was a coveted accolade to be awarded (like the right to live as a hesychast) to the most outstanding among the monastic brethren. In this way, a life which was originally intended to bring its practitioners nearer to heaven and away from terrestrial concerns, became itself an adjunct to a religious life led firmly in the world.

The variety of religious experience available to pious Byzantines of the

---

[80] Life of St Luke the Stylite, especially chapters 2–3, pp. 196–9, for the author's discussion of earlier famous stylites. Life of St Luke the Younger, p. 99 (Martini); Life of St Lazaros, chapter 22, p. 517; chapter 41, p. 522; chapter 59, p. 528. H. Delehaye, 'Les femmes stylites', *AB*, 27 (1908), 391–2 cites only three other examples of female stylites.
[81] Life of St Paul the Younger, chapter 13, pp. 43–4; chapter 20, p. 57 and map in Wiegand, *Der Latmos*; Life of St Cyril Phileotes, chapter 22, p. 107 (332); Life of St Lazaros, chapter 31, p. 519; chapter 138, p. 549.

tenth and eleventh centuries was thus considerable. Much of it was firmly rooted in tradition, but there are distinct indications from the tenth century onwards that many of the old ways were being adapted and changed. Certainly, some of the more extreme and individualistic forms of asceticism were being absorbed into a communal framework and adapted by it. At the same time as the stylites began to fade into respectability, the *saloi*, the 'fools for the sake of God' who feigned insanity, also seem to have declined in influence.[82] While the life of St Andreas Salos may have been composed in the mid-tenth century (though there remains considerable controversy on this point), its author wanted to place its events firmly in the past. This may have been, of course, to give a patina of tradition to the activities of his hero, but it may also have reflected the fact that such men were rarely to be seen in the Constantinople of his own day.[83] A few references to *saloi* appear in the sources: Lazaros of Mount Galesion's biographer, the monk Gregory, mentions the monk of the Monastery of the Anastasis, Luke, 'who lived pretending to be a fool, so that he might be found wise in Christ' and planned to write about him.[84] Symeon the Stoudite, the spiritual father of St Symeon the New Theologian has been characterised as 'a part-time holy fool', particularly for his 'dispassion' in the face of human nudity, but neither Symeon the New Theologian, nor his biographer Niketas Stethatos actually used the word *salos* to describe him. Cyril Phileotes pretended to be dumb on one occasion when questioned by an imperial official and ended up in prison for his pains.[85]

By the twelfth century, positive hostility to what might be termed 'extremist' spirituality became very evident.[86] The late eleventh-century general Kekaumenos was deeply suspicious of *saloi*, but warned against hitting or insulting them, perhaps an indication that this was by now a

---

[82] Cf. I. Cor. 3: 18; 'If any one among you thinks he is wise in this age, let him become a fool that he may become wise.' General discussion in D. Saward, *Perfect fools: folly for Christ's sake in catholic and orthodox spirituality* (Oxford, 1980).

[83] L. Ryden, 'The date of the *Life of Andreas Salos*', *DOP*, 32 (1978), 127–55 and 'The *Life* of St Basil the Younger and the *Life* of St Andreas Salos', in *Okeanos. Essays presented to Ihor Ševčenko on his sixtieth birthday by his colleagues and students* (Harvard Ukrainian Studies, vii, Cambridge, Mass., 1983), pp. 568–86, but see C. Mango, 'The Life of St Andrew the Fool reconsidered', *Rivista di Studi Byzantini e Slavi*, 2 (*Miscellanea A. Pertusi*, II, Bologna, 1982), 297–313, repr. in Mango's *Byzantium and its image*, article VIII.

[84] References collected in J. Grosdidier de Matons, 'Les thèmes d'édification dans la vie d'André Salos', *TM*, 4 (1970), 277–328, 280, 300–2.

[85] H. J. M. Turner, *Symeon the New Theologian and spiritual fatherhood* (Byzantina Neerlandica, XI, Leiden/New York/Copenhagen/Cologne, 1990), pp. 62–4. Life of St Cyril Phileotes, chapter 15, p. 86 (309).

[86] P. Magdalino, 'The Byzantine holy man in the twelfth century', in S. Hackel (ed.), *The Byzantine saint* (Studies subordinate to Sobornost, v, London, 1981), pp. 51–66, for some telling and unsavoury evidence.

common reaction! In the twelfth century, the canonist Theodore Balsamon mentioned a *salos*, Staurakios Oxeobaphos, whom he regretted not having met, but Eustathios, Metropolitan of Thessalonike, in contrast, emphasised the essential 'selfishness' of the eremitic life and even questioned the standards of monasticism itself.[87] Many of the customs of the hermits and stylites were still followed in the monastic world – the periods spent in seclusion, the rough clothing and the vigorous spiritual exercises – but in a new context. In fact, in many of the new foundations, the prevailing mood was flexibility and compromise. The strict lavriote tradition was compromised in order to receive the larger numbers of postulants; the coenobitic tradition was modified to allow for the existence of a few 'advanced' monks outside the walls. This compromise held great appeal for the Byzantine laity. For it enabled them to continue to place their trust in charismatic individuals and to continue a flourishing tradition of religious activity which, in many cases, took place outside the diocesan framework. But in addition, the communal aspects of the 'mixed' houses created that sense of security and companionship in spiritual endeavour which had always been the great strength of the *koinobion*. The outstanding contribution of the lavriote-influenced houses to Byzantine monasticism was this very flexibility. It allowed the individual full opportunity to begin his spiritual development within a community without ever denying him the eventual prospect of a progression into the solitary life.

---

[87] Grosdidier de Matons, 'Thèmes d'édification', pp. 280, 300; A. Kazhdan (with S. Franklin), 'Eustathius of Thessalonica: the life and opinions of a twelfth-century Byzantine rhetor', in *Studies on Byzantine literature of the eleventh and twelfth centuries* (Cambridge/Paris, 1984), article IV, pp. 115–95, pp. 150–4.

CHAPTER THREE
Monastic founders

◆

THE VARIETY OF MONASTIC styles available to Byzantines of the tenth and eleventh centuries brought with it a serious problem of choice. Although the question of which house to enter, or which to patronise, was often solved by geographical proximity or family loyalty, a very strong influence on recruitment was the personality and outlook of the monastic founders themselves. Knowledge of the precise régime followed in any particular house was perhaps limited, whereas the charisma of individual holy men was both more widespread and more accessible. Dry, technical discussions of the virtues of the *koinobia* in relation to those of the *lavrai* could not in themselves attract men and women to follow the monastic life; they sought human examples of monastic virtue and ascetic achievement upon which to model themselves, and those of their own times were often more attractive than those of the past. It is, therefore, of considerable importance to attempt to discover what kind of men (for women were rarely involved) provided this attraction and had such an important influence on the continued growth of monasticism in this period.

There are, of course, many pitfalls in such a study. The main source of information about the lives and careers of most of these monastic founders is hagiography written after their deaths and, more importantly, after the houses associated with them had been founded. Indeed, the role of these biographies was both to commemorate the spiritual qualities of their heroes and to circulate information about their achievements which would help to attract more recruits to their monasteries and confirm the vocations of those already there. Just as icons preserved the visual memory of the saints of the past, so hagiography was a form of literary icon, which presented a verbal picture of its subject. And as the icon provided a summary of the attributes of the saint – white hair to indicate age, particular dress to indicate ecclesiastical position or the monastic profession and even the instruments of martyrdom to remind the observer of the climax of the saint's life – so the hagiography attempted to portray in words the salient points of the career of its subject while relating them to accepted norms of spiritual behaviour. For this reason, there is often considerable difficulty in many saints' lives in disentangling any kind of historical reality from the idealised spiritual portrait, and the essentially didactic nature of the genre must be continually borne in mind. Whatever else hagiographers of the tenth and eleventh centuries were attempting to achieve, 'balanced' biography in the modern sense was not one of them.[1]

Some things, however, are certain. There could be no possible advantage to be gained by including material in hagiography which every reader or listener would know to be factually inaccurate, just as there was little point in describing episodes or attitudes which would overstrain the credulity of the audience. Hagiography was a vehicle to express views and attitudes which were commonly held: about faith, about spiritual experience and, most importantly of all, about the qualities of religious leadership. If the vast majority of the saints' lives written in this period deal with monks rather than the holders of high offices in the secular church, this is a strong indication of where sanctity was, in the eyes of contemporaries, most likely to be found, although hagiography was also, of course, one of the tools used by monks to promote their own houses and their founders.[2]

The monastic founders of the period are best considered in two groups: those who were the subject of hagiography and those who were not, for the lack of a subsequent hagiography (always taking into account the possibility of the loss of the text) is an important factor in assessing the posthumous reputation of a founder and the potential success of his house. It was not the only one, for matters such as endowment and

---

[1] Pioneering work in establishing the genres of Byzantine hagiography was done by H. Delehaye, *Les légendes hagiographiques* (Subsidia Hagiographica, XVII, 3rd edn., Brussels, 1927) and L. Bréhier, 'L'hagiographie byzantine des VIIIe et IXe siècles', *Journal des Savants*, 14 (1916), 458–67. But the use of hagiography as a source for the history of social and spiritual attitudes is now also widespread. For the Byzantine context, see F. Halkin, 'L'hagiographie byzantine au service de l'histoire', *Proceedings of XIII International Congress of Byzantine Studies, Oxford, 1966* (Oxford, 1968), pp. 345–9 and, in particular, the work of E. Patlagean, 'Ancienne hagiographie byzantine et histoire sociale', *Annales, ESC*, 23 (1968), 104–24, reprinted in *Structure sociale, famille, Chrétienté à Byzance* (London, 1981), article V, and 'Sainteté et pouvoir', in Hackel, *Byzantine saint*, pp. 88–105. For the relationship between hagiographical and pictorial representation, see A. Kazhdan and H. Maguire, 'Byzantine hagiographical texts as sources on art', *DOP*, 45 (1991), 1–22.
[2] For a useful checklist of hagiographies dealing with ninth- and tenth-century saints (though those dealing with Southern Italy and primarily with the struggle against iconoclasm or the conversion of the Slavs are omitted), see Patlagean, 'Sainteté et pouvoir', pp. 88–92.

patronage also played their part, and no amount of saintly aura could compensate for bad economic (or political) management on the part of the founders' successors. But those for whom no hint of a hagiography survives were generally different kinds of people: men and women who had lived mainly in the world before turning to the monastic life in their own foundations, not those who had devoted themselves to it from an early age and for whom foundation of a house was only part of a wider and deeper spiritual experience which a full-scale hagiography could chronicle.

The historian of the tenth and eleventh centuries is particularly fortunate in the number and quality of the hagiographies available, for the period saw the last real flowering of this genre of Byzantine literature. After Symeon Metaphrastes made his collection of rather stilted lives at the end of the tenth century, the decline into a mannered and imitative style was accelerated, although the Life of St Lazaros of Mount Galesion (written in the second half of the eleventh century) and the Life of St Cyril Phileotes (written after 1143 but dealing with events which mainly took place in the eleventh century) are two notable, though contrasting, exceptions to this trend. The existence of officially sponsored collections, such as those of Metaphrastes and the *Synaxarion of Constantinople*, may also have led to a view in certain quarters that, as has been cogently remarked, 'the communion of saints was a closed society, whose numbers were now more or less complete'.[3]

As with the monastic records of the period, the geographical spread of hagiography from the tenth to the early twelfth centuries is not wide. Leaving aside the Slavonic hagiographical tradition of Bulgaria, the largest groups deal with saints whose main area of activity was southern Greece (St Peter of Argos; St Luke the Younger and St Nikon Metanoeite); the western coast of Asia Minor (St Paul of Latros; St Nikephoros; St Michael Maleïnos and St Lazaros of Mount Galesion); from Athos (St Athanasios; SS John and Euthymios and St George the Hagiorite, an eleventh-century *hegoumenos* of Iviron) the Aegean Islands (St Christodoulos of Patmos and possibly the prototype for the existing biography of SS Niketas, John and Joseph, the Chiote saints associated with the Nea Mone) and southern Italy (St Elias the Younger; St Elias Spelaiotes; St Vitalis of Sicily; St Sabas the Younger and his relatives SS Christopher and Makarios; St Luke of Demena and St Nil of Calabria

---

[3] The stultifying effect of the Metaphrastic collections is described by H.-G. Beck, *Kirche und theologische Literatur im byzantinischen Reich* (Handbuch der Altertumswissenschaft, XII/2.1, Munich, 1959), pp. 570–5. It has been persuasively argued that, by the twelfth century, hagiography was 'authorised according to style' and that 'amateurish efforts' or those not considered to have done justice to the subject *stylistically* were 'disposed of'. See Magdalino, 'Byzantine holy man in the twelfth century', pp. 61–2 and note 61.

being the most important). The lives of a few saints living in or near Constantinople have also survived (St Luke the Stylite; St Basil the Younger and St Symeon the New Theologian).[4]

That one of the areas least well represented in Greek hagiography of this period is that of the northern themes of the empire outside Athos, may perhaps be explained by the dangerous conditions of the tenth and the end of the eleventh centuries, which were not conducive to the peaceful pursuit of the monastic life in unfortified places. In addition, the linguistic orientation of their populations may have been more Slavonic than Greek and it is in this tradition, perhaps, that we should look for popular saints. But Thrace and Macedonia in the eleventh century were also places were coenobitic monasticism seems to have been most prominent and there is surely a link to be made between the type of monasticism practised here and the type of monastic literature produced. Where the emphasis was placed on holy men, individual asceticism and, to a lesser extent, the lavriote or hybrid monastic styles, there hagiography, as part and parcel of the process of spreading the reputation of the holy men, also flourished. Coenobitism, on the other hand, did not seek to focus on individual monks, a prerequisite for successful hagiography. There are, of course, exceptions to this general rule. The Life of St Cyril Phileotes is a most elegantly written hagiography, but one which also presents a wealth of detail about contemporary happenings and especially the court of Alexios Komnenos. It is set in Thrace, an area not at all associated with lavriote houses, but, significantly, does deal with one of the last figures in this period who fulfilled the criteria for the 'holy man' and thus assisted in the traditional way in the preservation of his memory and reputation.

The uneven geographical distribution of the surviving hagiographical literature (particularly trying in such areas as Cappadocia, where ample physical and artistic remains of a flourishing monastic culture survive) does not, however, present as much of a challenge to the historian as the varying nature of that literature. Some hagiographical accounts were clearly intended to be read aloud to an audience of monks, laity or both, often to celebrate the anniversary of the death of the saint. In the case of the Life of St Elias the Younger, the writer addresses his audience directly, characterises them as coming from both town and country and remarks that they will be able to verify what he is about to say from their own knowledge for 'you have seen him and known him; you will not doubt what I say'.[5] The author of the Life of St Luke the Stylite urged his

---

[4] Bibliographical details of these hagiographies are (or have been) given with the first reference to each source.
[5] Life of St Elias the Younger, chapter 2, p. 4.

audience to pay attention to his account of the rescue of three Western merchants accused of stealing a statue known as 'The Bath-Attendant' from the Hippodrome in Constantinople and condemned to three years in gaol, by the intervention of St Luke: 'Listen to this story, which is the best in my recital.'[6]

Some hagiographers clearly intended to entertain as well as to edify a general audience. The Life of St Basil the Younger, by his disciple Basil, is full of recognisably 'folk-tale' and loosely Biblical elements: accounts of how Basil, persecuted by the high official Samonas, was thrown to the lions in the Hippodrome (who refused to eat him) and then into the Bosphoros, where he was rescued by dolphins.[7] The Life of St Luke the Younger is considerably enlivened by a series of animal stories. A deer is admonished by the saint for eating carefully nurtured vegetables and then saved by the holy man's intervention from a hunting party; two large fish leap out of the sea and present themselves as food; and a viper, hanging on Luke's toe, is politely asked to desist. 'Let us each take our own paths [remarks the saint] since we are all creatures of the one Creator and must not perform that which is forbidden by Him.'[8]

Other hagiographies, written in a more literary and rhetorical style, were clearly aimed at a more educated audience, which could appreciate a text sprinkled with quotations from ecclesiastical and rhetorical literature and members of which might have been able to read the text for themselves. The author of the Life of St Nikephoros, written in the late tenth century, quoted tags from writers such as Homer, Philostratus and Apollonius of Rhodes, although he was ignorant of some of the most important information about his subject, such as the identity of the house on Mount Latros where Nikephoros became a monk. He regretted that he could not provide more details of his hero's ascetic exploits.[9] In this case, it seems clear that the writing of a hagiography was necessary to preserve the reputation of the saint and his foundation, but that the chosen author had to disguise his ignorance of his subject matter under a cloak of erudition.

In other cases, however, the learning displayed by the hagiographers was deployed to enhance the achievements of their subjects by judiciously chosen references from the Bible, from patristic writings and from other saints' lives. The Life of St Cyril Phileotes by Nicholas Kataskepenos,

[6] Life of St Luke the Stylite, chapters 25–6, pp. 221–2, especially p. 221.
[7] Life of St Basil the Younger, chapters 6–7, p. *21.
[8] Life of St Luke the Younger, chapter 21, pp. 92–3 (Martini); chapter 24, col. 448 (*PG*); chapter 43, col. 457 (*PG*).
[9] Life of St Nikephoros, chapter 3, p. 135 (quotations from *Iliad*, I, 155; *Iliad*, VII, 238); chapter 15, p. 147 (Philostratus, *Life of Apollonius of Tyana*, I, 34, 37); chapter 22, p. 154 (Apollonius of Rhodes, *Argonautica*, I, 154).

an elegant and informative piece of work clearly aimed at a monastic audience, interspersed episodes from the saint's life with linked homilies which included a wide range of quotations (with which his listeners were doubtless familiar) from the works of St Basil the Great, John Chrysostom, Gregory Nazianzos, John Klimakos, Mark the Monk, Maximos the Confessor and a number of other monastic favourites.[10] The purpose was to place Cyril in the context of these great men of the past and to show how his life and teachings were but a continuation of theirs. But here the author was in command both of his biographical material and of the literary references which he used to enhance it. In other cases, such as the first Life of St Athanasios of Athos, written by the monk Athanasios of Panagiou (who may have been a lawyer in his secular life), the ecclesiastical references were chiefly from Biblical passages associated with the liturgy and thus made familiar by constant repetition, though he was also familiar with monastic 'classics' such as Athanasius' Life of St Anthony and Cyril of Scythopolis' Life of St Sabas and could not resist a few secular references too.[11]

It would, however, be mistaken to suggest any correlation between the stylistic elegance of any particular hagiography and the accuracy of the information contained in it. In many of the works written in simple, accessible language, there are distinct signs of considerable research having been undertaken into the career of the subjects. Though 'eye-witness' reports are, of course, part and parcel of hagiographic technique and we must be properly wary of them, this does not mean that they should be automatically discarded. For often the hagiographer was a disciple of the saint and would have been entrusted with the task precisely because of his first-hand knowledge or his ability to gather contemporary reports. As the monk of Latros who composed the Life of St Paul the Younger put it:

> We have made use of those who were eye-witnesses, not just one or two, but no fewer than twenty, who lived with Paul and were greatly loved not only for their truth, but for their virtue.[12]

But his interests were not merely confined to oral testimony and he seemed to be aware of its potential pitfalls, for when dealing with the

---

[10] Life of St Cyril Phileotes, introduction, pp. 32–87, for a discussion of the quotations. A.-J. Festugière, 'Notes sur la vie de Saint Cyrille le Philéote', *REG*, 80 (1967), 430–44; 81 (1968), 88–109, commented on the language and sources of the Life, characterising it somewhat intemperately as a 'hotch-potch'. For a more favourable assessment, see P. Karlin-Hayter, 'L'édition de la vie de S. Cyrille Philéote par E. Sargologos', *B*, 34 (1964), 607–11 and note her dating of the saint's death to 1120, not 1110 (see p. 610).

[11] Life of St Athanasios (A) and (B), introduction, p. cxxxiii.

[12] Life of St Paul the Younger, chapter 6, p. 27.

supposed eastern origins of the monastic communities on Latros, he remarked:

> This is not just a silly story or legend which is carelessly related by all and sundry and can thus be called into question, but a carefully researched account, pieced together from the archives [*hypomnemata* literally 'documents'] of Mount Latros.[13]

In other cases, too, there is clear evidence of existing documentary sources being used as source material for the hagiography. The Life of St Athanasios (B), written on Athos between c. 1050 and c. 1150, used material from documents composed by Athanasios himself: from the *Typikon* when dealing with monastic regulations and from the *Hypotyposis* on church services and ecclesiastical discipline.[14] These texts would have been available to the author on Athos itself, as would the colophons (end notices) from Georgian manuscripts and the *synaxaria* in the Monastery of Iviron used by George the Hagiorite as material for his Life of SS John and Euthymios.[15]

But perhaps the most convincing proof that hagiographies were not, as a rule, comprised of fanciful and, indeed, fictional, anecdotes fleshed out with a modicum of learning, can be provided by examining the circumstantial detail contained in them. A particularly good example is the late eleventh-century Life of St Lazaros written by Gregory, one of his disciples on Mount Galesion. Not only is this Life full of lively details of monastic life, situations in which the author himself appears and episodes from the saint's past life which Lazaros himself had related to him, but Gregory seems never at a loss for material. He knows exactly how many years Lazaros spent at various locations throughout Asia Minor and the Levant. He shows an intimate knowledge of the village names and geographical features in the region of Ephesos, of the routes taken by Lazaros and his companions to Jerusalem and back and of the local laity who visited the saint (and their doings in Constantinople and beyond). But he also consecrates a long section of his work to a series of pen-portraits of monks who were in the houses on Mount Galesion when Lazaros was their *hegoumenos* and afterwards. If the hagiography was originally intended for 'home' consumption on Mount Galesion, then it would certainly have provided an engaging and encouraging 'group portrait' of the holy founder, surrounded by a successful and purposeful community. And since one of the surviving manuscripts of this Life

---

13 Life of St Paul the Younger, chapter 8, p. 34.
14 Life of St Athanasios (B), chapter 29, pp. 157–9.
15 See Life of SS John and Euthymios, chapter 4, p. 85 and discussion by Martin-Hisard, 'La *Vie de Jean et Euthyme*', p. 82. See also *Ivirôn*, I, introduction, pp. 4–8.

comes from Athos, it can be suggested that Gregory's account of monastic life (with all its ups and downs) under the wise leadership of St Lazaros also struck a chord there.[16]

If the wealth of detail in some hagiographies (often corroborated from other sources) goes a long way towards strengthening their credibility, there are some – in some cases the very same works – where apparently startling omissions have to be explained. In the earliest of the two Lives of Athanasios, for instance, a generally well-informed account, there is no mention of the Georgian monks who we know from Athanasios' own writings were his close associates and friends on Mount Athos. Indeed, John the Iberian and his son, Euthymios were left as *epitropoi* (guardians) of the Lavra after Athanasios' death by the saint himself – a considerable mark of his trust and esteem. Why, then were they apparently deliberately ignored by his biographer? The only reasonable explanation seems to be that the *hegoumenos* Anthony of the Monastery of Panagiou in Constantinople, where the work was written, had been Athanasios' successor in the Lavra, but had left the post after conflict in the house. The *epitropoi*, John and Euthymios, must have played a major rôle in his departure and were thus, through pique perhaps, ignored in a work written by one of Anthony's own monks. In this case, it was deemed better to say nothing, than to risk open criticism of men whom Athanasios himself clearly admired. A similarly surprising set of omissions is to be found in the Life of St Michael Maleïnos. Here there is no mention of the time spent on Mount Kyminas by St Athanasios, nor of the fact that he was the favoured spiritual son of Michael himself and still less of his subsequent foundation on Mount Athos. In addition, the Emperor Nikephoros Phokas, Michael's nephew, is only alluded to once in the Life and his frequent visits to Mount Kyminas (mentioned in the *Typikon* of Athanasios) are ignored. There is no suggestion of any animosity in this case. It is simply that the writer wished to concentrate on Michael's monastic achievements and his own community, and perhaps also felt that writing about a controversial emperor would have presented a number of difficulties.[17]

[16] For an example of information given to Gregory by Lazaros, see chapter 16, p. 514: 'He stayed, as he often told me, six years there.' For Lazaros' relationships with the laity and Gregory's information about them, see chapter 4. See chapter 74, col. 532 for an account of a miraculous seal with an effigy of the Theotokos involving Gregory himself and chapters 159–80, pp. 555–61; chapters 193–202, pp. 566–71 for two groups of monastic pen-portraits.
[17] J. Noret, 'La vie la plus ancienne d'Athanase l'Athonite confrontée à d'autres vies des saints', *AB*, 103 (1985), 243–51, discusses these omissions. For Nikephoros Phokas' reputation, see R. Morris, 'The two faces of Nikephoros Phokas', *BMGS*, 12 (1988), 83–115.

The problems presented by these two texts (which only became clear since other material concerning their subjects was also, fortunately, in existence) are a cogent reminder of the fact that the concern of the hagiographers was not *primarily* either with factual accuracy or with the presentation of a wide-ranging and impartial record, though they often seem to have achieved both. Such information as they had (and there is no real evidence to suggest that it was deliberately falsified) was deployed as part of a deeper message conveyed in the hagiography. In most cases, this was clearly stated at the beginning of the work. The deeds of the champions of the faith should be recorded, wrote the author of the Life of St Elias the Younger because 'they incite us to virtue by their deeds'. The first version of the Life of St Nikon, using a favourite Byzantine nautical metaphor, put it somewhat more poetically: 'Those who navigate without landmarks look to the stars, but those who travel in the ship of life look to the deeds of earlier holy men.'[18] The erudite hagiographer of the Life of St Nikephoros took the argument a stage further: the lives of the saints should encourage lesser mortals to engage in their own battle against evil, summoned by the trumpet call of sanctity.[19] Even if Lazaros of Mount Galesion's hagiographer could report, in answer to his own question about the lack of miracle-working monks in their own day, his master's view that 'we are not of the calibre of the early fathers; we are as lead to their gold', there were others who disagreed. Paul of Latros' biographer, writing about 975, commented that although many contemporary writers argued that no virtue was to be found in their own day, and looked to the past for it, he disagreed: 'For even in our own day there exist large numbers devoted to a virtuous life and Paul of Latros was one of them.'[20]

The major task of hagiography was, then, to show how the lives of the saints could act as a model for ordinary men and even though there might be modest disclaimers that the heights reached by the saints of the past could ever be regained, the very existence of these saints' lives testifies to an implicit belief that it was possible to emulate these men and that, in theory at least, sanctity was available to all. But it certainly could not easily be achieved in the lay world, and the fact that the vast majority of the saints of this period were monastic founders is indication enough of the environment in which these writers considered the most virtuous life could be led. It is not surprising, therefore, that a great deal of information

---

[18] Life of St Elias the Younger, chapter 1, p. 2; *Life of St Nikon*, chapter 1, p. 26; for dating, see introduction, pp. 7–18.
[19] Life of St Nikephoros, chapter 1, pp. 133–4.
[20] Life of St Lazaros, chapter 186, p. 565; Life of St Paul the Younger, chapter 1, pp. 19–20.

is provided about their teachings on the practice of the monastic life and, in particular, on the challenges and difficulties of asceticism. Elias the Younger apparently spent three years on Mount Sinai observing the various qualities of the monks he found there: the 'humanity' of one, the 'calm' of another, and the 'intensity of prayer' of a third.[21] George the Hagiorite included in his Life of St Euthymios a series of short chapters in which Euthymios' concern for the maintenance of monastic discipline was illustrated and his stipulations on such varied matters as mutual discussions, peace-making between monks, care for the less able brethren and even details of clothing and diet were presented in some detail.[22] Nicholas Kataskepenos interspersed his account of the life of Cyril Phileotes with short homilies based on the saint's spiritual advice to him. Vigils were of great value, because they refined the perception of the monk and rendered him more suitable for intelligent contemplation. Prayer should be aided by bearing in mind short, homiletic phrases such as 'Talk to God as a friend or son', or 'Pray as if you were the adopted brother of Christ' and thus it could be compared with the kind of familiar behaviour expected of relatives and kin. Alms-taking was to be strictly controlled. According to Cyril, ascetics never accepted alms and 'ordinary' monks should never request donations, but, if they were spontaneously offered, could accept them. If a monk was in a weakened state, however, he might ask with humility and consistently blame himself for accepting.[23]

It was not only ideals of monastic behaviour which were described. For in most hagiographies the saint was portrayed as the wise counsellor as well as the spiritual shepherd of his flock. The Life of St Lazaros, for instance, contains a series of accounts of various forms of demonic possession and hallucination suffered by the monks on Mount Galesion. The monk John, praying at night, was terrified by the sound of a wild pig and its young; another, Philippikos was troubled by phantoms and phantasms which caused great winds to rush through the monastic church; Sabas, a third, saw what he thought were a band of robbers, but which turned out to have been an attack of demons. In all these instances, understandable in the context of a monastery built in a wild, mountainous area, the saint was on hand with explanation and reassurance and his hagiographer was there to note the details of how Lazaros himself coped with the kinds of experience which would have been common to many of

[21] Life of St Elias the Younger, chapter 20, p. 30.
[22] Life of SS John and Euthymios, chapters 34–53, pp. 112–18. As Martin-Hisard has shown, this was an attempt to provide – retrospectively – a written *typikon* for Iviron, see chapter 2, p. 47 and note 43.
[23] Life of St Cyril Phileotes, chapter 3, p. 53 (275) (vigils); chapter 9, pp. 72–4 (294–6) (prayer); chapter 17, p. 31 (315) (alms).

those living a life of austere diet and sleep deprivation. Here, practical examples could serve to strengthen monastic morale.[24]

In some cases, the particular concerns of a founder for his house were reflected by his hagiographer. The conflicts between the hesychasts on Mount Athos and the founders of the new, hybrid monasteries are clearly at the origin of the praise for the coenobitic life attributed to Athanasios of the Lavra by both his biographers. Both the Lives emphasised the 'conversion' of the hesychasts to the kind of monasticism followed by Athanasios, by having them voluntarily abandoning their old lives in favour of being directed by the saint.[25] Similarly, the difficult period of hostility between Greeks and Georgians on Mount Athos in the early eleventh century, is clearly evident in the exhortation of George the Hagiorite, at the end of his account of the lives of John and Euthymios, to the monks of Iviron to defend their Georgian tradition:

> If it should happen that any one of our people, *hegoumenos*, *oikonomos* or anyone else, by whatever means or artifice – through avarice, love of the Greeks or simply to gain favour – should betray this holy territory and should traitorously alienate one of its lands on the Mountain or outside, or should become a traitor to the Iberians and should have them dispersed ... let him be cursed, anathematised and expelled from Christian worship ... Eternal glory to those who work for the increase of the Iberians and the prosperity of the house.[26]

By placing these remarks in the context of this hagiography, he associated the honoured founders of the house with his own sentiments.

There was guidance, too, for the laity. If circumstances prevented them entering the monastic life, then they could draw their own conclusions from accounts of the period some saints had spent in the world as to the sort of behaviour deemed most conducive to salvation. It might not need to be quite so extreme as the way of life followed by Cyril Phileotes before he became a monk, when he lived a celibate life within his own family for some years, but temperance, the 'continence of sense and spirit', as his biographer put it, was certainly to be aimed at.[27] Luke the Stylite served for some years in the army at the beginning of the tenth century, but still managed to perform his prayers and ascetic exercises even in these

---

[24] Life of St Lazaros, chapter 42, p. 522; chapter 44, p. 523; chapter 48, pp. 523–4. In fact, chapters 42–54 is a section of the work entirely devoted to the activities of demons and how best to deal with them. See C. Mango, 'Diabolus byzantinus', *DOP*, 46 (1992), 215–23, who points out (p. 219) that demons were thought to be particularly active in the countryside, where their chief enemies were the monks.

[25] Life of Athanasios (A), chapter 159, pp. 75–9; (B), chapter 43, p. 176.

[26] Life of SS John and Euthymios, chapter 88, p. 133.

[27] Life of St Cyril Phileotes, chapter 3, pp. 48–51 (270–3).

difficult circumstances, as did both he and Paul of Latros when they were reduced by ill-luck to herding pigs. Even the most humble, therefore, were not debarred by their station from receiving manifestations of God's grace.[28] Charitable giving was also certainly something that the laity could always bear in mind; the monk Gregory used his account of the cure performed by St Basil the Younger on the *patrikia* Anastasia, a high-born lady in Constantinople, to introduce a short homily by the saint on the virtue of charity and post mortem donations for, as Basil remarked, 'nothing helps a soul departing from this life as much as the extent of its charity'.[29]

There is no doubt, then, that these monastic saints were looked upon as 'living icons', the best possible examples of the spiritual life. But although the didactic themes and idealised character studies are easily identified by the textual analyst, much information about the lives of these men does remain, and remains in enough factual detail to satisfy all but the most severe critics. Often, indeed, it is necessary to ask whether material which seems to be in accordance with common *topoi* of hagiographical style, might not, in fact, reflect the true state of affairs. A case in point is the family background of these monks. In the vast majority of cases, they are said to have been the children of parents who were like those of Elias the Younger 'of noble family', or 'well-born and rich', like those of St Athanasios of Athos, or even holders of military estates, as were the parents of Luke the Stylite. They were sometimes identified even more clearly as members of the middle to upper ranks of Byzantine society: Paul of Latros' father, Antiochos, was a *komes* in the navy and Michael Maleïnos' hagiographer was well aware of his subject's exalted connections, and his descent from *patrikioi* on both sides of the family.[30] In addition, the hagiographer usually knew his subject's place of origin, the names of his parents and often those of his brothers and sisters as well. It is only in cases such as that of St Basil the Younger, who made a point of refusing to disclose his origins, that no information at all is given about the family background of the saint, although in some cases it is thin. Nicholas Kataskepenos, for instance, does not seem to know the names of the parents of St Cyril Phileotes, though he knew that the saint had been born at Philea in Thrace.

Though there is no reason to doubt the information about places of

---

28 Life of St Luke the Stylite, chapter 5, p. 200; chapter 20, pp. 203–4; Life of St Paul the Younger, chapter 3, p. 23.
29 Life of St Basil the Younger, chapter 25, p. *25. Donations and patronage are discussed at greater length in chapter 5.
30 Life of St Elias the Younger, chapter 36, p. 6; Life of St Athanasios (A), chapter 5, p. 5; (B), chapter 2, p. 128; Life of St Luke the Stylite, chapter 5, p. 200; Life of St Paul the Younger, chapter 2, p. 20; Life of St Michael Maleïnos, chapter 3, pp. 550–1.

birth and family names, it has often been suggested that the 'well born and of comfortable means' description was used so often as to make it suspect. But there is no real reason why this sort of description should not have fitted the facts. *Topoi*, after all, are the means of expressing the accepted, but, more importantly, the *expected*. It is hardly likely that many male members of poor peasant families could have been spared from the land that demanded maximum manpower to ensure the survival of the family, nor that they themselves would have abandoned their families to certain starvation by becoming monks. The very rich would have known that their continuing prosperity might well depend on placing as many of their sons as possible in lucrative and powerful positions in the bureaucracy and armed forces – though here there were exceptions, Michael Maleïnos and the Georgian founders John and Euthymios being obvious cases in point. It is precisely from the ranks of the reasonably well off that these monastic leaders could come, for in every case they had an easy *entrée* into the provincial society in which they later found themselves (and were therefore clearly not country bumpkins) and often, too, had the resources to donate money to the houses that originally took them in and, indeed, to finance the earliest buildings of their own foundations.[31] Michael Maleïnos used the share of money and property inherited from his father, Eudokimos, to finance the expansion of his house on Mount Kyminas and Symeon the New Theologian, although renouncing in writing any claims to his paternal inheritance, was still able to offer, in 976 or 977, the *apotage* (entrance donation) of 2 *litrai* (equivalent of 144 gold *nomismata*) apparently required by the Monastery of Stoudios.[32]

A further indication of the comfortable family background of many of these monastic leaders is the information given by their biographers about their education. In the tenth century, St Peter of Argos was learned enough to have been offered the post of bishop of Corinth (which he refused) before accepting that of bishop of Argos in later life. He may well also have been the author of a series of florid orations on St Anne, St Athanasios of Methone and SS Cosmas and Damian. St Nikephoros was bishop of Miletos before retreating into the monastic life. Such high positions were only possible because parents had taken good care to obtain for their sons the kind of education which would gain entry into the ranks of Byzantine professional society – both clerical and lay.[33] It could begin

---

[31] Relations with the local laity are further discussed in chapters 4 and 5.
[32] Life of St Michael Maleïnos, chapter 11, pp. 557–8; Life of Symeon the New Theologian, chapter 9, p. 16; chapter 11, p. 18. Symeon entered the Monastery of Stoudios at the age of about twenty-seven, though the Life puts it at twenty; see Turner, *St Symeon the New Theologian*, p. 27.
[33] Life of St Peter of Argos, chapter 9, p. 6. For his rhetorical works, see A. Vasiliev, 'The "Life" of St Peter of Argos and its historical tradition', *Traditio*, 5 (1947), 163–90, 168, 172.

locally; Paul of Latros and his elder brother Basil were both taught *ta grammata* (letters) at the Monastery of St Stephen near their home in Bithynia; St Athanasios of Athos received his early education at home in Trebizond, and St Elias Spelaiotes studied the Scriptures in his home town of Reggio Calabria in southern Italy. In the eleventh century, St Lazaros was taught firstly by his parents and then by a priest, Leontios, on the instructions of his uncle, the monk Elias. After three years' further training with a *notarios*, he joined his uncle in the Monastery *ton Alathon*. By this time he would have studied the Scriptures in detail and some theology. His notarial training would have familiarised him not only with the techniques of drawing up documents, but also, probably, with basic legal terminology and financial calculation. St Christodoulos, according to his biographer John of Rhodes, was sent to a *grammatistes*, but does not seem to have had any 'higher' education before entering the monastic life. Cyril Phileotes, appointed to the rank of reader in his local church by the archbishop of Derkos, had clearly risen above the ranks of the barely literate.[34]

Like other Byzantines of good family, the parents of many of these monastic saints knew that it was only by sending their sons to continue their education in the capital that their future success in life might be obtained. St Nikephoros, already an able mathematician at the age of eight, was sent to Constantinople to continue his studies and was lodged in the household of the *magistros* Mouseles, whose steward he afterwards became. Symeon the New Theologian was sent to the capital from Paphlagonia by his grandparents to be perfected in 'profane culture and rhetoric'. He was taken in by an uncle who was a *koitonites* (a chamberlain in charge of the bodyservants of the emperors Basil II and Constantine VIII) and subsequently himself entered the imperial service, gaining the rank of *spatharokoubikoularios* (official of the bedchamber). The quality of the education he received and his own intellectual ability is more than evident in the large body of writings which he left. But perhaps the most shining example of academic success was that enjoyed by St Athanasios

---

Life of St Nikephoros, chapter 11, p. 143. See P. Lemerle, *Byzantine humanism: the first phase: notes and remarks on education and culture in Byzantium from its origins to the 10th century*, translated H. Lindsay and A. Moffat (Byzantina Australiensia, III, Canberra, 1986), chapter 9, pp. 281–308, for a discussion of the education system of the tenth century.
[34] Life of St Paul the Younger, chapter 2, p. 21; Life of St Athanasios (A), chapter 9, p. 7; (B), chapter 3, p. 129, see Lemerle, *Byzantine humanism*, p. 299. Life of St Elias Spelaiotes, chapter 3, p. 849; Life of St Lazaros, chapters 2–3, cols. 509–10. The Monastery of Kalathai may have been near Magnesia, see Janin, *Grands centres*, p. 242, note 5; Life of St Christodoulos, John of Rhodes, *Bios kai politeia tou hosiou patros hemon Christodoulou*, in K. Boïnes, *Akolouthia hierea tou hosiou kai theophorou patros hemon Christodoulou* (3rd edn., Athens, 1884), pp. 109–33; Life of St Cyril Phileotes, chapter 2, p. 44 (266).

of Athos, who having reached Constantinople in the household of the *strategos* Zephinezer, whose son had been married to a childhood friend of the saint, proceeded to show such brilliance that he was first made assistant to his own teacher (another Athanasios) and then became the master of his own educational establishment during the reign of the Emperor Constantine VII Porphyrogennetos. His success was such that the emperor requested him to move his school to another part of Constantinople, to avoid causing offence to the teachers already established in the district.[35]

The importance of education for the subsequent careers of many of these holy men cannot be over-stressed. It was of obvious benefit to such men as Symeon the New Theologian or, indeed, Euthymios of Iviron, whose translation work from Greek into Georgian provides eloquent testimony of his linguistic and theological skills. But it also had a more wide-ranging consequence. For it placed these monks within a particular social stratum – albeit a wide one in the Byzantine context – that of the literate and reasonably well educated, and was one aspect of contact with the world that could never be discarded. The hagiographers might attempt to gloss over their heroes' familiarity with a high level of secular as well as theological study, but it was this which enabled them to communicate easily with disciples even of high social standing, to receive their confidences and give them advice. It is hardly likely that members of the Byzantine aristocracy, so important from the point of view of patronage, would have entrusted their spiritual guidance to illiterates. The ability of a holy man to create a rapport with his followers – both the simple and the sophisticated – was a major part of his spiritual strength and education had an important part to play in this.[36]

Whether or not they had received a high level of education and whatever their precise family circumstances might be, there came a moment when the future saints entered the monastic life. For some, this came at an early age as the result of family decisions. St Lazaros' parents were

---

[35] Life of St Nikephoros, chapter 4, pp. 136–7; Lemerle, *Byzantine humanism*, pp. 282–3 and note 6. For the family of Moseles/Mouseles, see J.-C. Cheynet, *Pouvoir et contestations à Byzance (963–1210)* (Byzantina Sorbonensia, IX, Paris, 1990), pp. 223, 256, 271. Life of Symeon the New Theologian, chapter 2, p. 2. For the *koitonites* and the *koubikoularioi*, see N. Oikonomidès, *Les listes de préséance byzantines des IXe et Xe siècles* (Le monde byzantin, Paris, 1972), pp. 301, 305. These posts had to be held by eunuchs. Life of St Athanasios (A), chapter 11, pp. 7–8; (B), chapter 5, pp. 130–1 (household of Zephinezer); (A), chapter 14, p. 9; (B), chapter 7, pp. 132–5 (Athanasios' success as a *didaskalos*), see Lemerle, *Byzantine humanism*, pp. 299–302. Athanasios' talent for engineering was later amply demonstrated in the irrigation systems he devised for the Lavra and his invention of a mechanical dough-beating machine worked by oxen; see Life of St Athanasios (B), chapter 25, pp. 151–2.

[36] For the saint as spiritual father, see chapter 4.

perhaps already planning a 'traditional' monastic career for him, as they sent him to various houses to be instructed in the Scriptures and 'religious matters'. The two sons of the southern Italian St Sabas, Christopher and Makarios, both entered the monastic life, as did both the parents, two of the three brothers and the sister of St Peter of Argos. John the Iberian insisted that his son, Euthymios, whom he himself had abandoned when he had become a monk in Georgia and who had subsequently been taken as a hostage to Constantinople (where he could well have expected a successful career in imperial service), should be allowed to join him at a Georgian house on Mount Olympos and was given imperial permission to take him away from the capital against the wishes of his maternal grand-father.[37] For others, however, the flight from the world implied, in a very real sense, flight from their families.

Here again is a theme beloved of the hagiographers and therefore one which needs to be subjected to some scrutiny. Time and again, they fill their pages with rhetorical accounts of parental opposition, anger, tears and pursuit. When, after St Nikon Metanoeite had spent twelve years in the Monastery of Chryse Petra on the border of Pontos and Paphlagonia, his father finally tracked him down, he was forced to flee from the house and only escaped his father's clutches because the River Parthenion (Barlan-su), which lay between them, was in flood and cut off the pursuit. St Michael Maleïnos' mother apparently fainted from the shock on hearing the news that her son had become a monk on Mount Kyminas, while his father, infuriated by the sympathetic comments of his neigh-bours, went to Kyminas and stationed an armed guard around his son's monastery while he attempted to persuade him to return. Stories of grief abound. St Luke the Younger's mother was said to have appeared to him in a dream and tearfully begged him to return to his family – which his *hegoumenos* in Athens urged him to do. But after staying only four months at his home in Thessaly, he left again. Symeon the New Theologian refused to support his father in his old age and one of his monks, Arsenios, refused to see his own mother, even though she waited for three days at the gates of Stoudios.[38]

It is not difficult to see why the hagiographers employed all the rhetorical skills at their disposal to describe these moments of family parting. They wanted to convey the message that the monastic family

[37] Life of St Lazaros, chapters 3–6, pp. 509–10; Life of St Sabas, pp. 37–56, 135–68, 312–23; chapter 6, p. 50; Life of St Peter of Argos, chapter 5, p. 3. For Euthymios' early life, see *Ivirôn*, I, introduction, pp. 4–5. See generally, A.-M. Talbot, 'The Byzantine family and the monastery', *DOP*, 44 (1990), 119–29.
[38] *Life of St Nikon*, chapters 11–17, pp. 56–74; Life of St Michael Maleïnos, chapters 8–9, pp. 554–6; Life of St Luke the Younger, chapters 14–16, pp. 87–9 (Martini); Life of St Symeon the New Theologian, chapter 8, p. 16; chapter 46, p. 68.

was a more worthy institution than the secular one; that the spiritual father should take the place of the natural one and that natural love in all its forms (including that of parents for their children) was, unlike spiritual love, ultimately the inspiration of the Devil.[39] But the attitude of the families is certainly understandable. In many cases, expensive education and the exertion of considerable social influence (especially to get their offspring a foot on the ladder of Constantinopolitan society) were apparently wilfully discarded. In others, the loss of a son to a widowed mother (like that of St Nikephoros) must have seemed a heavy burden to bear. Nevertheless, there is no doubt that conventional Byzantine piety admired those who apparently achieved such lasting abandonment not only of the snares of the world, but also of its sentimental attachments. The question to be asked, however, is whether they really did so.

It is a truism, but one worth restating, that all Byzantine monks had once been laymen, usually until their late teens, since we do not hear of child oblates at this period. We should not, therefore, expect them ever to have completely cast off all the social attitudes with which they were familiar, even though their hagiographers might have been at pains to persuade us otherwise. But in some important cases, it is quite clear that relationships which had existed 'in the world' were continued out of it. This was particularly the case in the great coenobitic foundations, especially those in towns. Often members of the same families took their vows at the same house and the *Typikon* of Kecharitomene, for example, allowed the nuns visits from female relatives once or twice a year. But even amongst the lavriotes, some family contacts can be traced. St Nikephoros' mother seems to have spent her time collecting funds for his foundation of Hiera-Xerochoraphion and was present at his death, which strongly suggests that they kept in touch. The Convent of Eupraxia, near Mount Galesion, took in the female relatives of neighbouring monks; we do not know whether the two groups were in any kind of direct association. The frequent visits of the Phokas brothers, Nikephoros and Leo, to their uncle Michael Maleïnos on Mount Kyminas indicate that they knew quite well where to find him and that they considered his spiritual advice to be particularly important. This essentially family concern was later extended to Michael's spiritual son, Athanasios, to whom Nikephoros was particularly close. When Athanasios fled from Kyminas to Athos to seek a place where his fame might not follow him, it was Leo Phokas who used his considerable influence to track him down

---

[39] See A. P. Kazhdan, 'Hagiographical notes (5–8)', *B*, 54 (1984), 176–92, reprinted in *Authors and texts in Byzantium* (Aldershot, 1993), article IV, pp. 190–1.

and it was Nikephoros who then energetically supported his foundation there in its early years.[40]

Even saints who appeared to have abandoned their families for ever are sometimes reported to have been in contact with one or two members: St Lazaros returned to his home after twenty years of travelling and was, apparently, immediately recognised by his mother; St Luke the Younger is reported to have been joined for a time by his sister, and later provided with bread by her. Only those monks who made a particular point of being without roots – St John Xenos, St Basil the Younger and St Nikon Metanoeite provide the best examples – seem ever to have completely divorced themselves from their families, and here again we have only their hagiographers' word for it.[41]

The most striking example of continuing family solidarity, however, is provided by the early founders of the Georgian Monastery of Iviron on Mount Athos. Again, the flight from the world was not comprehensive, and although the hagiographers say nothing of the intelligence system that kept the members of this monastic and secular élite in contact with one another, there is enough evidence to indicate its existence. John the Iberian, a member of a noble Georgian family, became a monk in the 960s at the Lavra of the Four Churches in Tao-Klardjeth. After his fame began to spread, he moved on to a Georgian house on Mount Olympos (and the fact that he knew of it is another indication of the web of Georgian contacts which seemed to extend throughout the empire) where he learned of his son Euthymios' presence as a hostage in Constantinople – again evidence of the circulation of news. At some time between 963 and 969, father and son went to Athos to join Athanasios and there they were shortly joined by the man responsible for the foundation and first endowment of Iviron, the ex-general, Tornik, who also took the monastic name of John. It is very likely that John Tornik was a cousin of the wife of John the Iberian and he could also have been his brother-in-law, since the third *hegoumenos* of Iviron, George I, who was certainly John the Iberian's nephew, is described in a Georgian text as being nephew to Tornik as well. Certainly, the direction of Iviron in its first fifty years (c. 979–1029) was in the hands of men who were closely related to the founder. Thus a pattern of family monasticism, already in existence in Georgia, was transferred to Athos and the closest secular

[40] Talbot, 'Byzantine family and the monastery', pp. 119–20. Life of St Nikephoros, chapter 21, p. 153; chapter 29, pp. 150–60; Life of St Athanasios (A), chapters 28–30, p. 15; (B), chapter 11, pp. 136–8 (visits); (A), chapter 55, p. 27; (B), chapter 20, pp. 145–6 (Leo Phokas' search).
[41] Life of St Lazaros, chapter 30, pp. 518–19; Life of St Luke the Younger, chapter 30, col. 448 (*PG*); chapter 54, p. 104 (Martini).

relationships were thus perpetuated in a monastic context, rather than abandoned.[42]

It may well be that the monastic 'clannishness' of the Georgians was an extreme case (it was certainly something the eleventh-century Georgian founder, Gregory Pakourianos, warned against in the *Typikon* of Bačkovo), but as little is known of Byzantine monastic prosopography, it would be unwise to conclude that the Greeks behaved in a markedly different way. Indeed, the direction of their monastic patronage was often towards houses with which family connections already existed, and many *typika* assumed that the founding family would continue to play an important part in the running of the house by stipulating that *hegoumenoi* should, as far as possible, be chosen from among its members. It is thus important to bear in mind that professed 'flight from the world' often amounted to no such thing. Family relationships were replicated in monastic houses and associations continued with those in the lay world and were of great assistance in assuring the continued prosperity of monastic houses.[43]

Monastic founders were certainly not unacquainted with the wider world, for after an early period of monastic apprenticeship, it is frequently reported that they undertook a period of travel. This was sometimes characterised as flight from their growing fame (as in the case of Athanasios or John the Iberian), but often seems to have been a response to the old-established Christian traditions of pilgrimage and preaching. The Italian St Elias the Younger, active at the end of the ninth century, travelled to Palestine, Egypt and Persia, before returning via North Africa, Sicily, the Peloponnese and Epiros to a monastery near Reggio in Calabria. In the tenth century, St Nikon, after preaching widely in Crete, travelled the length and breadth of the Peloponnese, as did St Luke of Stiris. St Lazaros undertook an extensive journey in the early eleventh century which took him across Asia Minor to Jerusalem and Syria, where he had hoped to remain in the Monastery of St Sabas, but was driven away (with the rest of the monastic community) by the Arab attacks under al-Aziz which culminated in the pillaging of the Church of the Anastasis in Jerusalem and the desecration of the relics of the Cross in 1009. St Christodoulos may have visited Rome and certainly travelled to

---

[42] The complex family history of SS John and Euthymios is discussed in *Ivirôn*, I, introduction, pp. 17–21 and see II, p. 15 for a suggestion that the *hegoumenos* Gregory (c. 1035–1041) was also related to them.

[43] Pakourianos, chapter 18, p. 93; chapter 25, pp. 105–7. For the appointment of family *hegoumenoi*, see, for example, Life of SS John and Euthymios, chapter 20, p. 99, where, at the end of his life, John designated first his son, Euthymios and then his nephew, George, as his successors in the hegoumenate. See Talbot, 'Byzantine family and the monasteries', pp. 121–3, for further examples of family groups within the same monastery.

Jerusalem. St Cyril Phileotes visited the shrine of St Michael at Chonai in Asia Minor, as well as the tombs of the Apostles in Rome. In all these cases, the canonical prohibitions on monks leaving the houses in which they had first taken the habit seem not only to have been completely ignored by the hagiographers, but their heroes' journeys also seem to have been considered (like those of the early Irish monks) as praiseworthy manifestations of a wish to travel the world doing God's work.[44]

Even when such men had settled in their own foundations, their contacts with the outside world were by no means cut off. St Michael Maleïnos and St Christodoulos both made visits to Constantinople and St Paul of Latros received letters from there; but these examples pale into insignificance in comparison with the evidence of monastic journeys to the capital provided by the detailed archives of Athos. Though Athanasios might have stipulated in his *Typikon* that the *hegoumenos* of the Lavra should travel little, his own behaviour hardly conformed with this instruction. In 961, on the request of Nikephoros Phokas, the commanding general, he had joined the armies invading Crete almost as his personal chaplain, and in 963, after hearing that his protégé had become emperor, he disguised his intention to flee from Athos by telling his monks that he intended to travel to Constantinople on business concerning the Lavra. When he finally returned to Athos at the pleading of his monks, his route certainly took him via the capital and to a meeting with the emperor which resulted in an important chrysobull of privileges for the monastery. As conflict with other houses on Athos grew in the 970s, Athanasios made a visit to the new emperor, John Tzimiskes, which resulted in an enquiry being held on the mountain by Euthymios, the *hegoumenos* of Stoudios and the issuing of the *Tragos*. John the Iberian was also reported to have been 'frequently' to Constantinople and to have met all the emperors from Nikephoros Phokas to Constantine VIII and Basil. He personally received from their hands privileges and monetary gifts for the Iberians.[45]

---

[44] For a summary of St Elias the Younger's travels, see Guillou, 'Grecs d'Italie', pp. 101–9; *Life of St Nikon, passim*; Life of St Luke the Younger, *passim*; Life of St Lazaros, chapters 20–9, pp. 516–18; Life of St Cyril Phileotes, chapter 18, pp. 94–8 (317–22); chapter 20, pp. 101–4 (325–9).

[45] Life of Athanasios (A), chapters 19–20, pp. 11–12; (B), chapter 8, pp. 133–4 for Michael Maleïnos in Constantinople; Life of St Paul the Younger, chapter 34, pp. 146–7 (monks on business in Constantinople); chapter 37, pp. 150–2 (letters); for Christodoulos in Constantinople, see R. Morris, 'Divine diplomacy in the late eleventh century', *BMGS*, 16 (1992), 147–56; *Typikon* of Athanasios, pp. 112–14; Life of Athanasios (A), chapter 68, p. 32; (B), chapter 22, pp. 147–8 (Crete); (A), chapters 90–9, pp. 42–8; (B), chapters 30–3, pp. 159–65 (flight). For the privileges to the Lavra, see Morris, 'Two faces', p. 104; for events leading up to the issuing of the *Tragos*, *Prôtaton*, no. 7 (972) and *Lavra*, I, introduction, pp. 22–3. Life of SS John and Euthymios, chapter 18, p. 97.

It is particularly noticeable that the *hegoumenoi* on Athos worked hard to maintain good relations not only with the rulers in Constantinople, but also with their more important officials. Athanasios appointed as *epitropoi* (lay protectors) of the Lavra after his death not only the two Georgians, John and Euthymios, but also Nikephoros Ouranos, the imperial *epi tou kanikleiou*, an official in charge of the final authentication of all imperial documents. Probably in imitation of this move, John the Iberian, as death approached, declared that he wished the Emperors Basil II and Constantine VIII to be the *epitropoi* of Iviron; certainly they looked with particular benevolence on the house. Less august figures were, however more usual. In 1052, the Lavriotes again requested from the Emperor Constantine Monomachos the designation as *epitropos* of the *epi tou kanikleiou* John as 'a protection against the fisc and against the indiscipline of other monks', as precise a statement as one could wish of the use of such appointments. The existence of lay *epitropoi* for Attaliates' houses and (probably) the Monastery of the Panagiou at Constantinople indicates that this was a popular method of gaining lay protection for the monasteries concerned. It is certainly evidence of close contact between the founder and important secular figures.[46]

Links with powerful lay interests were thus envisaged from the earliest days of some foundations. Certainly, as time went on and the fame of their founders spread, it became virtually impossible to keep the secular world at bay and although the hagiographers often formally lamented this loss of solitude, they also used the number and importance of lay visitors as a means of illustrating the spiritual influence of their subjects. Fame, however, brought patronage and patronage brought donations of money and land and this, above all, meant that any theoretical separation of monastic communities from the secular world could not, in practice, be maintained. Those monasteries which were lasting and successful were those in which the founders and their successors realised that the lay world of tax-collectors, army commanders, provincial governors and influential courtiers (not to mention the imperial power itself) had not only to be accepted, but also to be managed.[47]

On some occasions, however, affairs of the world impinged in a quite startling fashion on the lives of monastic leaders. St Athanasios' journey to Crete as spiritual adviser to Nikephoros Phokas during his conquest of the island is a case in point, though it could be argued that he was

---

[46] The *epitropoi* of the Lavra are discussed in *Lavra*, I, p. 21 and *Lavra*, I, no. 31 (1052). See Life of SS John and Euthymios, chapter 20, pp. 99–100. For the Monastery of Panagiou, see the passage borrowed from its *Typikon* in Pakourianos, chapter 16, p. 85. *Diataxis* of Attaliates, pp. 97, 127.

[47] See chapter 5.

fulfilling the traditional duty of monks to aid the imperial armies with their counsel and prayers. But the extraordinary summons of his Georgian contemporary, John Tornik, to the aid of the young emperors Basil II and Constantine VIII in 978 demonstrates that, when matters of imperial concern were at stake, even monastic vows could not be held absolute. Tornik, who had joined John and Euthymios on Mount Athos in the early 970s after a very successful career as a member of the Georgian military élite which had gained him the Byzantine title of *patrikios*, came from a family in the immediate circle of the rulers of Georgia. His father, Tchordvaneli (referred to in Byzantine sources as the *patrikios* 'Zourbaneles') had been a member of the suite of the *kouropalates* Ashot who visited the Emperor Constantine Porphyrogennetos in Constantinople in c. 950. Three of his nephews are known to have had military careers and one of them, Tornik Varasvatze could well have been the man known to the Byzantines as 'Barazbatze the Iberian', the *katepan* (military governor) of the important eastern city of Edessa in 1037–8.[48]

It was undoubtedly Tornik's close family and professional connections with the rulers of Georgia that prompted the *parakoimomenos* Basil, in charge of the government of Constantinople at a period in the mid-tenth century when the reigning emperors (Basil II and Constantine VIII) were still both minors and when two serious revolts had broken out in Asia Minor, to send an imperial messenger to Athos summoning Tornik to Constantinople, whence it was intended he should take an appeal for help to the Georgian ruler, the *kouropalates* David of Iberia. Tornik, as the Life of SS John and Euthymios relates, was reluctant to go, but was, significantly, persuaded by Athanasios and John the Iberian that it would be in the best interests of the Athonite monks for him to obey the imperial command. Thus far, Tornik was only acting as a messenger – a task often entrusted to monks who could pass through hostile territory more easily than the imperial officials. But his role changed dramatically when he reached Georgia, for the *kouropalates* David appointed him commander of the Georgian troops and promised him all the booty should the campaign be successful. On 24 March 979 Tornik and his troops inflicted a crushing defeat on those of the usurper Bardas Skleros. He was rewarded by the Byzantine government with the title of *synkellos* and returned in triumph to Athos.[49]

But it was not only the gratitude of the emperors that Tornik brought

[48] John Tornik's family and career are summarised in *Ivirôn*, I, introduction, pp. 15–16, 21–4.
[49] Life of SS John and Euthymios, chapters 9–11, pp. 89–91. For the *parakoimomenos* Basil, see W. Brokaar, 'Basil Lekapenus', *Studia Bizantina et Neoellenica Neerlandica*, 3 (1972), 199–234.

back with him: the Life of SS John and Euthymios reports that even after his soldiers had been rewarded, Tornik returned with 'precious objects' as well as twelve *kentenaria* (1,200 lb) of gold, the equivalent of some 86,400 *nomismata*. It was this fortune which enabled the Georgians to set about the establishment of their own house on Athos. They made use of the existing site of the Monastery of Clement, dedicated to John the Baptist, some 11 km north of Lavra, which was part of monastic lands both on and outside Athos granted to Tornik by the grateful emperors in the years 979–80. Among them was the Monastery of Kolobos, long sought after by the Athonites and now granted to the favoured Georgians. Tornik's temporary emergence from the monastic life thus brought considerable short-term gains to the Georgian monks (although it stored up a legacy of jealousy among the Greeks which was soon to boil over into criticism and attack) and he was always honoured as the true *ktetor* (founder) of the house.[50]

Other monastic leaders who had previously held high positions in the world also found themselves involved in delicate diplomatic missions where their status could ensure discretion and neutrality. Symeon the Sanctified, *hegoumenos* and refounder of the Monastery of Xenophon on Mount Athos in the late eleventh century had been *droungarios* of the Watch (a high legal official) until he came to Athos in 1078, probably as a consequence of the coup which had brought Nikephoros Botaniates to power. But Symeon could still be of use to the new régime in Constantinople, for shortly afterwards he was involved in negotiations between the new *megas domestikos* (and later emperor) Alexios Komnenos and one Basilakios, a supporter of another usurper, Nikephoros Bryennios, who had taken refuge in Thessalonike. His activity later stood him in good stead, as it was Alexios Komnenos himself who intervened in 1089 to compel the Athonite authorities to take back Symeon and his monks after they had been expelled from the mountain. Indeed, Symeon seems to have been a widely known figure, being cited by Theophylact, archbishop of Ohrid, as 'a most agreeable monk, charming and well-informed'.[51]

But, as in all areas of Byzantine society, it paid monastic leaders to be circumspect about their choice of friends. The 'time of troubles' which afflicted the Monastery of Iviron in the mid-eleventh century, though a consequence of growing hostility between Greek and Georgian monks

[50] Life of SS John and Euthymios, chapter 14, p. 93. Iviron's early land acquisitions are identified in *Ivirôn*, I, introduction, pp. 24–30. Tornik and John the Iberian probably ran the house together in its early days, John as *hegoumenos* and Tornik as *ktetor* (founder). *Ivirôn*, nos. 3, 4 and 5 (all of 982) are acts involving both of them on equal terms.
[51] *Xénophon*, pp. 12–14 for the early career of Symeon. See further discussion and references in chapter 10, pp. 279–80.

within the monastery, was sparked off by the unfortunate involvement of the *hegoumenos* George I in an unsuccessful revolt in 1029 against the reigning emperor, Romanos III Argyros. A number of easterners and Georgians were involved in the affair and it seems that, on this occasion, the close relationship between the Georgian laity and 'their' monastery had disastrous consequences. George the Hagiorite, *hegoumenos* some twenty years later, commented sadly, 'What then happened, God knows'. George I was paraded through Constantinople and then exiled to the Monastery of Monobata; the Monastery of Iviron was initially subject to serious confiscations.[52]

In most cases, of course, relationships between monastic founders and the laity were on a much less elevated plane. But the most important point is that they did exist and that Byzantine society did not find it unusual that they should. Monastic vows might set men apart from their families and previous lives, but they did not cut them off. What did effect a separation was the consideration of certain monks as saints, while others, doubtless just as devoted to their calling, were simply considered as particularly good men. It is to them we must now turn. Apart from the members of the imperial families whose foundations were often cited in the chronicles, or the great monastic patrons whose *typika* have survived, it is particularly difficult to identify these 'unsaintly' monastic founders, since they were never the subject of hagiography or visual commemoration; but some traces of them do remain, in the Athonite archives, for example, the founders of some of the less prestigious houses make momentary appearances. The founder of the Monastery of Docheiariou, first mentioned in 1013, could well have been John, the *docheiarios*, or cellarer of the Monastery of Xeropotamou. The first founder, Xenophon, of the monastery that subsequently bore his name, had a brother, Theodore, who was cured of an illness by St Athanasios, a small detail which immediately helps to establish the chronology of their own foundation. And the Monastery of the Theotokos of Xylourgou, which later became part of the Russian Monastery of St Panteleimon, may have been founded by the *hegoumenos* Gerasimos (possibly one of the Russian carpenters or *xylourgoi* who came to Athos in the great building phase at the end of the tenth century) and who is known from a Lavriote document dated to 1016.[53]

Elsewhere, where archival evidence, particularly that of signatures to documents, is lacking, other information is sparse. Where it does exist, it sometimes takes surprising forms. An inscription, possibly dating to the

---

[52] *Ivirôn*, I, introduction, pp. 22–3. Life of SS John and Euthymios, chapter 81, p. 127.
[53] *Docheiariou*, pp. 5–6; *Xénophon*, introduction, pp. 3–5; *Pantéléêmôn*, introduction, pp. 3–4 and *Lavra*, I, no. 19 (1016).

end of the tenth century, found in western Asia Minor on Mount Tmolos (Boz Dağ), recorded the foundation of the Monastery of the Mother of God and an associated *gerokomeion* (old people's home) by one Nikephoros Erotikos. Another, noted on a bridge at Lakedaimon in the Peloponnese in the eighteenth century and now lost, commemorated not only the building of the bridge by the monk Nikodemos, but also the establishment, in 1027, of a monastery on the left bank which would act as a protection for it. Nikodemos, in what was (like the inscription on Mount Tmolos) to all intents and purposes a *typikon* written on stone, placed it under the protection of the emperor and the officials – the *strategos* and *krites* – in charge of the theme, requesting these two to oversee the subsequent choice of *hegoumenoi*. Nothing else is known of Nikodemos, whose ability to finance the building of both a bridge and a monastery must surely indicate him to have been from a wealthy and influential family.[54]

At the other end of the social scale, none of the rural founders of the humble monasteries of fewer than ten monks referred to in Basil II's novel of 996 has left any individual documentary trace, and the founders of many of the smaller cave monasteries in Cappadocia and southern Italy remain equally obscure.[55] It was the monastic founders marked out by sanctity whose reputations survived their deaths and entered into the literary and artistic traditions of Byzantium. Those like Tornik and Symeon the Sanctified, whose lives had been a little too 'active' for them to be fitted into the hagiographer's mould, were honoured, but never deemed to have been saints. Nor did the founders of coenobitic houses live lives which contemporary opinion felt were above the level of the admirable. They were worthy patrons of an old and honourable tradition; but it was the lavriotes, or those who practised the mixed forms of monasticism, who gained popular appeal by being in the forefront of spiritual endeavour. No hagiographical biographies of Gregory Pakourianos, Michael Attaliates or Irene Doukaina have survived. Their names were remembered and venerated, but they were referred to as *makarios* (blessed), *aoidimos* (famed), and *hosios* (holy), whereas the true subjects of hagiography were described as *hosios pater* (holy father) and, most significantly, *hagios* (saintly).

In some cases, too, the reputation of an individual founder was further enhanced by the inclusion of his name in the *Synaxaria*, the calendars of

---

[54] See T. Drew-Bear and J. Koder, 'Ein byzantinischer Kloster am Berg Tmolos', *JÖB*, 38 (1988), 197–215 and D. Feissel and A. Philippides-Braat, 'Inventaires en vue d'un recueil des inscriptions historiques de Byzance; III, Inscriptions du Peloponnèse (à l'exception de Mistra)', *TM*, 9 (1985), 267–395, no. 43, pp. 301–3.

[55] Novel of Basil II (996), Zepos, I, no. 29, pp. 249–52.

saints celebrated more widely than in the immediate vicinity of their houses. St Luke the Stylite, St Luke the Younger and St Paul the Younger were all included in versions of the *Synaxary of the Great Church*, an indication that their fame had reached Constantinople, and it may well be that the stylite portrayed in the sumptuous manuscript of the *Menologion of Basil II* at the date of 11 December is Luke himself.[56] Others were very soon portrayed in icons. The noble John Malakenos, comforted by St Nikon Metanoeite when he felt that imperial displeasure would soon be his ruin, had an icon made of the saint after his death and both Nikon and St Luke the Younger were portrayed in the mosaics of the house dedicated to Luke. The father of Athanasios of Panagiou paid for a copy to be made of the icon of St Athanasios of Athos already in his possession at the request of Kosmas, the *ekklesiarches* of the Lavra, who often stayed with him when on business in Constantinople. The painter, Pantoleon, at work on an imperial commission, was said to have been miraculously forewarned to undertake the task.[57] The criticism faced in the eleventh century by Symeon the New Theologian, who honoured his own spiritual father, Symeon the Stoudite by having icons made of him and his likeness painted on the wall of Stoudios, is a strong indication that such visual representation was only acceptable when there was no doubt that its subject really was a saint. But the most obvious sign of sanctity was the power to intervene with the Deity, that *parresia* (access) that those who prayed to the monastic saints after their deaths or venerated their images clearly believed they possessed. It was a power which set them apart from their fellow monks, although it was the monastic life which had provided the conditions in which it could be achieved, and it was a power continually demonstrated in their relationships within the society in which they lived.

[56] Patlagean, 'Sainteté et pouvoir', p. 103, provides a useful table of entries in the *Synaxaria* for ninth- and tenth-century saints. For the possible portrait of St Luke the Stylite, see *Il menologio di Basilio II (Cod. Vaticanus greco 1613)* (2 vols., Codices e Vaticanis Selecti, Turin, 1907), I, no. 238, pp. 64–5; II, pl. 238.

[57] *Life of St Nikon*, chapters 43–4, pp. 148–56; Life of Athanasios (A), chapter 254, pp. 122–3; (B), chapter 78, pp. 211–12. English translation of part of the episode in C. Mango, *The art of the Byzantine empire 312–1453: sources and documents* (Englewood Cliffs, NJ, 1972, reprinted Toronto, 1986), pp. 213–14 and see I. Ševčenko, 'On Pantoleon the painter', *JÖB*, 21 (1972), 241–9, reprinted in *Ideology, letters and culture*, XII; Life of Symeon the New Theologian, chapters 72–94, pp. 98–130.

CHAPTER FOUR

Monasticism and society

◆

ALTHOUGH THE MONASTIC state brought with it a different way of life and conferred distinct responsibilities on those who followed it, it would be wrong to consider monks as constituting a separate caste in Byzantine society. Their contacts with the secular world were often close and frequent and, though monastic tradition might decree the opposite, complete seclusion – a life 'in the world but not of it' – was, in fact, rarely practised. All the monks recorded in hagiography maintained contacts with the lay world around them and, indeed, their biographers expected that they should and were eager to chronicle such associations. For it was through their relationships with others, both religious and secular, that the power of the monastic saints could be demonstrated and, on a less elevated plane, that the rôle of monastic houses as centres of importance to the local community could be maintained. Two kinds of power were involved: the power that *parresia*, access to God and almost a familiarity with Him, could bring to monks, who thus provided a channel between the ordinary believer and the Deity, and, secondly, the practical influence always wielded by those individuals or institutions which could provide local and immediate leadership. But although it is initially necessary to discuss the relationships of monks and laity on these two levels, they should not be too sharply distinguished, since it was the honour in which the religious life was held by Byzantines that could, in theory, raise up *any* monk to a position of authority. Byzantine lay society, though remarkably fluid in many ways, offered no comparable honours.

Central to the relationship between monks and laity was the rôle of the monk as spiritual guide. This position of honour, however, was not enjoyed by nuns, always perceived as inferior because of the disadvantages of their sex, which transcended the honour of their calling. It was a rôle which might properly have been considered the province of the parish priest, given that the administration of the sacrament of confession was usually involved. But although lamentably little is known of the Byzantine secular clergy, especially in the provinces, their humble origins, peasant life-style and, above all, married state did not differentiate them to any great extent from their lay flocks. A basic level of education was necessary for the performance of the liturgy and instruction in the faith (though Alexios Komnenos found it necessary to recruit a special group of *didaskaloi* – 'teachers' – because he felt the level of instruction inadequate among the Constantinopolitan clergy at the beginning of the twelfth century) and the local priest is sometimes heard of providing elementary teaching for children; but literacy and a competent understanding of the Bible, the liturgy and religious literature were not confined to him.[1] Many lay Byzantines of the 'middling sort' were perfectly able to read and understand such matters for themselves and affairs often confined to priests in the West, such as the drawing up of charters or legal documents were, in Byzantium, quite often the province of the laity.[2]

So though doubtless able to give comfort and advice in the normal course of their duties, priests do not seem to have been those to whom the laity turned for deeper spiritual guidance. Indeed, outside the towns and larger settlements, it is not at all clear that many priests could be found, or whether they were easily accessible to the population at large, since many churches at this period seem to have been the private foundations of landowners, or attached to monasteries, rather than *katholikai ekklesiai*, or 'public' churches. The lure of Constantinople for ambitious clerics who wished to gain a post in the patriarchal or imperial administrations, or become the chaplain of a rich household, had already been noted by the time of the Second Council of Nicaea (787) which forbade priests to leave their own dioceses, especially in order to go to the capital and 'live with

---

[1] This chapter builds on material first published in R. Morris, 'The political saint in the tenth and eleventh centuries', in J. Petersohn (ed.), *Politik und Heiligenverehrung in Hochmittelalter* published as *Vorträge und Forschungen*, 42 (1994), 384–402 and 'Spiritual fathers and temporal patrons: logic and contradiction in Byzantine monasticism in the tenth century', in *Le monachisme à Byzance et en occident du VIIIe au Xe siècle. Aspects internes et relations avec la société*, ed. A. Dierkens, D. Misonne and J.-M. Sansterre, published as *Revue Bénédictine*, 103 (1993), 273–88. On literacy in general, see M. E. Mullett, 'Writing in early medieval Byzantium', in R. McKitterick (ed.), *The uses of literacy in early medieval Europe* (Cambridge, 1990), pp. 156–85. See Hussey, *Orthodox church*, pp. 329–35 for a short survey of the secular clergy. The eleventh-century landowner, Eustathios Boïlas, expected the clergy in the churches he founded to be able to instruct the boys on his estates, see Testament of Boïlas, p. 271 (Vryonis); p. 27 (Lemerle). For the Novel of Alexios Komnenos on *didaskaloi*, see P. Gautier, 'L'édit d'Alexis Ier sur la réforme du clergé', *REB*, 31 (1973), 165–201.

[2] For hagiographical accounts of education in the countryside, see chapter 3, pp. 76–7.

princes and celebrate the divine liturgy in their chapels'.[3] Those who stayed in small provincial settlements were probably those whose intellectual or spiritual talents could take them no further. They were often peasant small-holders with liturgical functions and thus not those to whom landowners or officials wished to turn for intimate spiritual guidance.

The full history of 'spiritual' relationships in Byzantium has yet to be written, but recent research has demonstrated how important non-blood ties could be. Friendship among the educated classes, for instance, was a highly structured affair, where both parties were well aware of the duties and responsibilities they held to one another; the relationship of god-parents not only to their godchildren, but to these children's families and kinship groups, were deemed to be so close that they involved the same prohibitions on marriage as affected those related by blood. The relation-ship of spiritual father to spiritual son or daughter was thus part of a whole nexus of relationships which employed the vocabulary of the family (as, indeed, did the monastic community itself) and in a sense replicated it, but always on a higher plane. The mere accident of blood relationship, a matter of the most basic worldly significance, was replaced by a deliberate choice based on spiritual criteria. The number of 'children' guided by a monastic spiritual father was a mark of his own merit, a recognition of powers beyond the ordinary and thus implied a willing acceptance of his authority. What power Roman Law decreed for the *pater familias* as of right, was bestowed on the spiritual father by the choice of his children. But it was, like the links that bound godparents and the families of their godchildren, a twoway relationship: the 'son' complimented his spiritual father by requesting his guidance; the 'father' bestowed favour and access to his spirituality by accepting the task of guiding the 'son'.[4]

---

[3] Hussey, *Orthodox church*, pp. 331–2. In the countryside the notary might sometimes be a priest, but in cities, especially Constantinople, specialised corporations took on general legal drafting work, see R. Morris, 'Dispute settlement in the Byzantine provinces in the tenth century', in W. Davies and P. Fouracre (eds.), *The settlement of disputes in early medieval Europe* (Cambridge, 1986), pp. 125–47, especially pp. 140–1. See *Iviron*, II, p. 168, for notarial bureaux attached to churches in the capital. For the priest as peasant landowner, see Kaplan, *Les hommes et la terre*, pp. 228–31.

[4] See M. E. Mullett, 'Byzantium: a friendly society?', *PP*, 118 (1988), 3–24 and, for baptismal relationships, E. Patlagean, 'Christianisme et parentés rituelles: le domaine de Byzance', *Annales ESC*, 32 (1978), 625–36, reprinted in *Structure sociale, famille, Chrétienté*, XII; and R. Macrides, 'The Byzantine god-father', *BMGS*, 11 (1987), 139–62. It is significant that monks were canonically forbidden to act as godparents (though on occasion they did) since they were deemed to have renounced 'simply every blood-relationship'; see *ibid.*, p. 144 and note 24; p. 154.

Like the monastic life itself, spiritual fatherhood did not exist in isolation from secular society and was, indeed, closely intertwined with it. Both monks and laymen were deemed to need spiritual guides. Theodore the Stoudite had argued that there was an equality among Christians when it came to the demands of the inward, spiritual life, summing up this view in his use of the phrase 'All things are equal.' Common to all, too, was the aim of this inner life: 'the transformation of soul and body and their translation into the sphere of the Spirit, that is, the spiritualisation of soul and body'.[5] What was different, however, was the fact that monks had placed themselves in physical circumstances in which they could give themselves up to God once and for all, and this had been done by virtue of their vows of poverty, obedience and chastity. As Hausherr remarked, 'if there were differences between spiritual direction for monks and that given to Christians in the world, they lie not in the doctrine or in the goal professed, but in the means to be used to reach it'.[6]

True, only a priest could administer the sacrament of confession. But what was involved in spiritual guidance was not simply this. Apart from the self-accusation of sins made with a view to receiving absolution, Byzantines were also familiar with the idea of the 'manifestation of thoughts' (*exagoreusis*) made in order to receive guidance. It was, as has rightly been emphasised, a therapeutic rather than a forensic relationship. *Exagoreusis* could be made to any persons (male or female), but only if their spirituality was beyond question.[7] As Symeon the New Theologian put it: 'Do not seek to be mediators on behalf of others until you have come to know the king of all through the conscious experience of your soul.'[8] In his view, those (including priests) who had not attained such experience therefore had no power to grant absolution or to bind and loose, but monks with suitable spiritual standing could (and indeed should) exercise such a ministry, even if they were not priests. Symeon's was an extreme view, since it implied a denial of the validity of sacraments administered by unworthy priests, but hagiographic evidence does seem to suggest that those who were in a position to choose, often wished

---

[5] Špidlík, *Spirituality*, p. 33; I. Hausherr, *Spiritual direction in the early Christian east*, translated A. P. Gythiel (Cistercian Studies, 116, Kalamazoo, Mich., 1990), p. 308.

[6] Hausherr, *Spiritual direction*, p. 309.

[7] Turner, *Symeon the New Theologian*, pp. 57, 135–6.

[8] Symeon the New Theologian, Letter i, text in K. Holl, *Enthusiasmus und Bussgewalt beim griechischen Monchtum. Eine Studie zu Symeon dem Neuen Theologen* (Leipzig, 1898), pp. 110–27, as cited in Bishop Kallistos (Ware) of Diokleia, 'The spiritual father in Saint John Climacus and Saint Symeon the New Theologian', *Studia Patristica*, 8/2 (1990), reprinted as foreword to Hausherr, *Spiritual direction*. Citations will be made from Bishop Kallistos' translation.

to be guided in their spiritual lives by monks, not all of whom were ordained.[9]

So in contrast to the official ministry of the priesthood, the provision of spiritual guidance was essentially a charismatic one and could be best carried out by those living a life which allowed them to be granted the gifts of the spirit: monasticism. For they had rejected all purely human knowledge and had embarked on a life of self-denial and the surrender of self-will, of mortification of the body and the senses.[10] The life of the monk was considered as the equivalent of martyrdom in the world and, if lived to the full in chastity and humility, it could lead to the achievement of the *angelikos bios*, the 'life of the angels'. The most respected practitioners of the monastic life had obtained dispassion (*apatheia*): the ability to remain unaffected by all that they saw, to stand above the most dangerous human emotions and to help others to do the same. Their spiritual expertise was on a higher plane than that of the clergy.[11]

Although the most widely spread form of spiritual fatherhood was that exercised by the *hegoumenos* of a monastery over the monks within it (although in nunneries a priest might assume this function in place of the female – and thus less spiritually 'adequate' – *hegoumene*), the most influential was that which existed between major figures amongst the laity and a small, celebrated group of spiritual advisers.[12] They were among the closest confidants of men in positions of power and influence in Byzantium and the advice they gave was often instrumental in shaping affairs of state. So while the spiritual importance of these relationships should always be borne in mind and, indeed, has often been commented upon, their political significance should not be overlooked. It is therefore

[9] Turner, *Symeon the New Theologian*, pp. 57–8; Špidlík, *Spirituality*, p. 284; Hausherr, *Spiritual direction*, p. 192. There is no evidence that Nikon Metanoeite, Basil the Younger or John Xenos were priests. Symeon the New Theologian's own spiritual father, Symeon Eulabes, a monk of Stoudios, is described as one who 'had no ordination from men', see Turner, *Symeon the New Theologian*, p. 57.

[10] Špidlík, *Spirituality*, pp. 73–5 (on charismatic activity); pp. 180–2 (self-denial and mortification).

[11] Cf. Matt. xx: 80: 'For in the resurrection they neither marry, nor are given in marriage, but are as the angels of God in Heaven.' For monasticism and virginity on a par with martyrdom, see Špidlík, *Spirituality*, pp. 75–7; 220–1. Dispassion (*apatheia*) is well defined by Špidlík, *Spirituality*, p. 100, as 'the mind's freedom from and independence of the fleshly *pathos* (passion), the victory over sexuality and thence virginity with all its prerogatives'. For its importance as a 'skill' of the spiritual father, see Turner, *Symeon the New Theologian*, pp. 170–7.

[12] For the references to the *hegoumenos* as spiritual father to his monks, see C. Galatariotou, 'Byzantine *ktetorika typika*: a comparative study', *REB*, 45 (1987), 77–138, pp. 108–9 and for nuns, see chapter 2, pp. 52 and note 56.

important to establish the nature of the spiritual relationship and what could be gained by either party.[13]

The most celebrated spiritual father of the period was undoubtedly Symeon the New Theologian, *hegoumenos* of the great Constantinopolitan Monastery of St Mamas (which he restored) from 980 to 1005. It is from his copious collection of homilies and other spiritual writings that evidence for the workings of the institution can be collected as the duties and demands of spiritual fatherhood were matters frequently discussed in them. In addition, the Life of Symeon the New Theologian, by his disciple Niketas Stethatos, provides other information about Symeon's views on spiritual fatherhood.[14] But, interesting though his views are, it is important to bear in mind that he was a somewhat controversial figure and a man of uncompromising, not to say abrasive, character. He was a 'hard-liner' on the subject of spiritual fatherhood and others were more accommodating with their charges, as Symeon himself frequently pointed out.[15]

Although much of his writing on the subject dealt with the relationship between monks and their spiritual fathers – usually the *hegoumenoi* of their monasteries – Symeon was also quite clear about the need for lay people to have spiritual guides too, and his views on the spiritual relationship are, to a degree, equally applicable to them. The motives for establishing it were common to both states: first, a general need for spiritual help with the problems of the inner life and what were often referred to as *logismoi* ('black thoughts');[16] secondly, even among those who did not try to improve their spiritual status by leaving the world,

[13] See Hausherr, *Spiritual direction* and Turner, *Symeon the New Theologian*.
[14] See Life of St Symeon the New Theologian, introduction, pp. i–xciii and Symeon's works: *Catechèses*, ed. B. Krivochéine, translated J. Paramelle (3 vols., Sources Chrétiennes, 104, 113, Paris, 1963–5), English translation by C. J. deCatanzaro, *The Discourses* (New York, 1980); *Chapitres théologiques, gnostiques et pratiques*, ed. and translated J. Darrouzès and L. Neyrand (Sources Chrétiennes, 51, 2nd edn., Paris, 1980), English translation P. McGuckin, *The Practical and Theological Chapters and the Three Theological Discourses* (Cistercian Studies, 41, Kalamazoo, Mich., 1982); *Traités théologiques et éthiques*, ed. and trans. J. Darrouzès (2 vols., Sources Chrétiennes, 122, 129, Paris, 1966–7), translated McGuckin, see above. Only one of the Letters has been published: see Holl, *Enthusiasmus und Bussgewalt*, pp. 110–27. For unpublished Letters I and III, see excerpts in B. Krivochéine, *In the light of Christ. St Symeon the New Theologian 949–1022: life, spirituality, doctrine*, translated A. P. Gythiel (Crestwood, NJ, 1986) and Turner, *Symeon the New Theologian*.
[15] See Life of Symeon the New Theologian, chapters 36–9 and 75–7, pp. 48–52, 102–6 for Symeon's problems with his own monks and the ecclesiastical hierarchy. For 'lax' spiritual fathers, see Turner, *Symeon the New Theologian*, pp. 238–41.
[16] Turner, *Symeon the New Theologian*, p. 70. On *logismoi* (literally 'thoughts', but usually translated in a pejorative sense), see Spidlík, *Spirituality*, especially p. 248, where the 'eight principal thoughts' – akin to the Seven Deadly Sins – are discussed.

there remained an urge to find the assurance of salvation. For the question 'How may I be saved?' lay at the root of the relationship of both monks and laymen and their spiritual guides.[17] It was important to find someone who could aid an individual's chance of achieving this goal. This was clearly expressed in the sixth-century *Ladder of Divine Ascent* of John Klimakos, a book with a wide circulation in both monastic and lay circles in Byzantium and one which we know Symeon had found in his own father's library: 'A ship with a good navigator comes safely to port, God willing. A soul with a good shepherd climbs easily heavenward, even if it has earlier done much wrong.'[18]

If monks could lose their way on the spiritual road without proper direction, it was even more likely that laymen would do so. But it was not just the hope of salvation and the fear of hell-fire that was at issue. For what could be achieved by proper spiritual counselling was nothing less than the 'radical healing of every disease of the soul together with fullness of life for the soul in Christ'.[19] Logically, then, every layman needed a spiritual father. In practice, however, as Symeon pointed out in his articulate and intellectual way, without some degree of self-knowledge, no one could realise the importance of having one and anyone who thought he was in no need of such guidance only demonstrated his own ignorance. In his Epistle 3, written to a layman, Symeon made clear that self-examination should precede the search for a suitable spiritual father:[20]

> Having considered all this in yourself . . . and having learned the distinct and sure use of things, make haste as long as you have strength to become a Christian, not only in word but through your very actions. Secure a father, acquire a teacher, find an ambassador, a guarantor before God.[21]

---

[17] Turner, *Symeon the New Theologian*, p. 70 rightly points out that this was a question not entirely confined to those entering the monastic life. See Galatariotou, 'Byzantine *ktetorika typika*', pp. 91–5 for the concern of lay patrons for their salvation.

[18] John Klimakos, *Ladder of Divine Ascent*, col. 1089 (*PG*), p. 259 (Luibheid and Russell). For Symeon's familiarity with John Klimakos, see Ware, 'Spiritual father', pp. xi–xii and notes 19 and 20. For the *Ladder of Divine Ascent* in Byzantine lay libraries, see e.g. Life of Symeon the New Theologian, p. 12; Testament of Boïlas, p. 270 (Vryonis); p. 25 (Lemerle); *Ivirôn*, ii, no. 47 (1098), will of the nun Maria/Kale Pakouriane. It was a work very commonly found in monastic libraries, see Luibheid and Russell, introduction, pp. 66–8.

[19] I. Hausherr, 'Vocation chrétienne et vocation monastique selon les Pères', in *Etudes de spiritualité orientale* (OCA, 183), pp. 403–85, p. 405, translated Turner, *Symeon the New Theologian*, p. 72.

[20] Lengthy extracts in Krivochéine, *In the light of Christ*, chapter 6; cf. Turner, *Symeon the New Theologian*, pp. 235–41.

[21] Krivochéine, *In the light of Christ*, p. 97.

Thus the layman himself had to initiate the process of spiritual improvement after a process of complex self-analysis and this surely meant that spiritual fathers were mostly to be found advising the educated, higher ranks of the laity, those who had leisure to contemplate the state of their souls and to undertake counselling sessions. Symeon also laid great importance on the fact that the spiritual son (or daughter) must completely open his or her heart in order to make the relationship possible. For it was unfair, he maintained, to place the burden of spiritual direction on the 'father' unless this could be guaranteed. But how could such a person be selected?

The process of choosing a spiritual father was one in which a layman had much more freedom than did a monk or nun, bound by monastic tradition to hold the head of the house in this position.[22] But Symeon believed that not all monks could be considered suitable spiritual guides, for, 'in truth those who have the skill properly to direct and heal rational souls are rare, especially at the present time.'[23] An inexperienced 'physician of souls' should at all costs be avoided 'lest he either plunge you into the depths of despair through excessive severity and inopportune surgery and cauterisation [of the soul], or else, through overmuch tenderness leave you in your sickness but thinking that you are healthy'.[24] The terms frequently used by Symeon to describe such a person indicate the skills he felt should be deployed by the reliable spiritual father. He was a 'physician' (*iatros*); a 'skilled worker' (*technites*); one who was *empeiros*, who had 'accumulated' spiritual knowledge.[25] The use of medical imagery had, of course, a penitential connotation, since penance was the method of 'healing the wounds of sin which harmed both the individual Christian and the community'.[26] 'Let us run to the spiritual physician', wrote Symeon in one of his letters, 'and, by means of confession vomit out the poison of sin, spitting out the venom.'[27] But the father should also be possessed of certain important traits of character: *diakrisis* (discernment) enabling him to listen to, truly understand and, if necessary, correct, the thoughts of his spiritual child; 'charity' (*agape*) towards his clients by

---

[22] Turner, *Symeon the New Theologian*, pp. 54–5. For nuns, see *Life of St Irene of Chrysobalanton*, chapter 9, pp. 40–1 and Hausherr, *Spiritual direction*, pp. 268–306.
[23] Symeon, Catechesis xx, 7, *Catechèses*, II, p. 346, translated deCatanzaro, *The Discourses*, p. 236.
[24] Letter I, ed. Holl, p. 117, translated Turner, *Symeon the New Theologian*, p. 81.
[25] Turner, *Symeon the New Theologian*, chapter 6.
[26] R. J. Barringer, *Ecclesiastical penance in the church of Constantinople: a study of the hagiographical evidence to 983 AD* (doctoral thesis, University of Oxford, 1979), p. 32.
[27] Letter I, ed. Holl, pp. 115–16, translated Turner, *Symeon the New Theologian*, p. 101.

which the love of God could be expressed and, most important of all, 'dispassion' (*apatheia*).[28]

It was to be expected that every experienced monk should have been able to show such spiritual qualities, but Symeon warned of unsuitable and unworthy persons who wished to recruit spiritual children for self-interested reasons. Hagiographers always mentioned the attraction of crowds of followers by true saints in approving tones; it is thus not surprising to hear of those with spiritual ambitions trying to emulate them from less pure motives.[29] But how, then, could the layman recognise a proficient and truly spiritual father? John Klimakos had advised that the seeker must attempt to find someone to match his own character:

> We should analyse the nature of our passions and of our obedience so as to choose our director accordingly. If lust is your problem, do not pick for your trainer a worker of miracles who has a welcome and a meal for everyone. Choose instead an ascetic, who will reject any of the consolation of food . . . We should not be on the look out for those gifted with fore-knowledge and foresight, but for those who are truly humble and whose character and dwelling place match our weakness.[30]

This is an interesting indication that, for John Klimakos, the more startling signs of sanctity, such as miracles and second sight, need not necessarily indicate a gifted spiritual guide. But this was not a view supported by the hagiographers and their audiences, for whom, as we shall see, such manifestations were clear evidence of a higher spirituality.[31] But Symeon also emphasised the importance of prayer in finding a spiritual father. He explained the mystic process by which he felt the choice would be made:

> Go and find the man whom God, either mysteriously through Himself, or externally through His servant, shall show you. He [the spiritual father] is Christ Himself. So must you regard him and speak to him; so must you honour him; so must you learn from him that which will be of benefit to you.[32]

[28] See note 25, above, and Špidlík, *Spirituality*, pp. 244–5 (discernment); 165–6 (charity in correcting sinners); 270–95 (curbing of the passions).
[29] Letter iii, *passim*, see Turner, *Symeon the New Theologian*, pp. 238–9. For crowds around saints, see, for instance, *Life of St Nikon*, chapters 20, 24, 26. There are many other examples.
[30] John Klimakos, *Ladder of Divine Ascent*, chapter 4, col. 725 (*PG*), p. 119 (Luibheid and Russell).
[31] See pp. 102–16, below.
[32] Symeon, Catechesis xx, 2, *Catechèses*, ii, p. 335; translated deCatanzaro, *The Discourses*, p. 232.

In practical terms, however, this must surely have implied someone with whom the layman felt some affinity, or, in some cases, a charismatic figure who had already become a sought after confessor. It might, in fact, be someone to whom the layman was already closely related (as in the case of the Phokas brothers and St Michael Maleïnos), or someone with whom he felt he could undertake such an intimate relationship – a man of learning (either intellectual or intuitive) and of the experience and proven ability to respond to considerable emotional demands.

The relationship between the two parties was to be, from the first, one of complete openness and trust and of unquestioning acceptance of the advice of the spiritual father. For, according to Symeon, the layman had himself to attempt to cure his soul and receive Christ into his heart and he could only begin to do this by undertaking a strict spiritual regimen directed by his 'father'. Thus practical matters, such as abstinence and fasting, were dealt with. On a metaphysical level, Symeon also gave advice about how to pray, how to prepare oneself for participation in the liturgy, how to receive Communion and how to show compunction and sorrow for sin.[33] Unless he was sure that he was spiritually ready, Symeon also declared, the layman should leave after the first part of the Eucharist and stand in the narthex of the church.[34] But was this really what happened? Would a lay person really have taken upon himself the risk of communicating in an unsatisfactory state? Far more likely was a procedure by which the spiritual father himself indicated when he thought his client was ready to receive communion.

Total commitment on the part of the spiritual son was required at all times. In his unpublished Epistle 3, Symeon warned against assuming that conventional religious observance would be enough:

> But since they were baptised as infants, they think themselves innocent
> ... and because from childhood they have learnt the Holy Scriptures, they
> suppose that this is piety enough for them and are of the opinion that for
> salvation, it is sufficient simply to tell and confess their sins and receive
> pardon from their spiritual father.[35]

What Symeon, and other spiritual fathers were working towards was nothing less than the total spiritual transformation of the disciple, whether monastic or lay: 'the man is entirely changed; he knows God and is first known by Him . . . it makes him a friend of God and a son of

---

[33] Letter II, summarised and translated in Turner, *Symeon the New Theologian*, pp. 133, 164, 166.
[34] Turner, *Symeon the New Theologian*, p. 165.
[35] Letter III, translated Turner, *Symeon the New Theologian*, p. 236.

the Most High and, as far as this is attainable to men, a god'.[36] The consequence of this docility and obedience, particularly important in the monastic context, would be the achievement of complete self-renunciation: 'For accomplishing an act not of their own will, but of their spiritual father's will, led just as much to self-renunciation as to death in the world.'[37]

Symeon the New Theologian's writings thus provide an invaluable source for the theory of spiritual fatherhood. But we can also see it in action in two episodes related in the Life of St Cyril Phileotes. The first is an episode of spiritual counselling, which probably owed a great deal of its detail to the imagination of Cyril's biographer, Nicholas Kataskepenos, but was, nevertheless, what the writer, himself a distinguished monk, knew happened on such occasions. An unnamed woman (who was clearly Anna Dalassene, mother of the future Emperor Alexios Komnenos), asked the saint to provide her with a spiritual *aide mémoire* which would be suited to her abilities. Cyril responded with a series of short *apophthegmata*, quotations from Basil the Great on the virtues of charity and, among others, from John Klimakos and the desert father, Barsanouphios. At this point the woman confessed that 'I wish to reveal my thoughts to your holiness, but I am afraid of not staying faithful to your words and thus offending God.' Cyril assured her that the unveiling of one's innermost thoughts (*exagoreusis*) to spiritual fathers was the first indication of wishing to reform one's way of life and proceeded to give her a series of moral precepts which she should attempt to follow.[38]

In this episode, the foundations of a spiritual relationship were being laid, but the association could develop into something rather more complex. Spiritual fathers could become constant companions of their spiritual children, not merely their occasional counsellors. On a visit to Cyril Phileotes, Alexios Komnenos, by this time emperor, described the devotion of an earlier spiritual father, the monk Ignatios, who was appointed by Anna Dalassene to accompany the young Alexios on one of his first campaigns, against the Norman rebel Roussel of Bailleul in 1074, and who comforted him when he was suffering from cold and illness. Ignatios was clearly a member of the household and close both physically and emotionally to the young soldier. Alexios' daughter and biographer, Anna Komnene, mentioned another monk, Joannikios, as her father's *pater pneumatikos* during his campaign against the rebel Basilakios in 1078, though the historian Nikephoros Bryennios named the Athonite

---

[36] Symeon, Catechesis XX, 6, *Catechèses*, II, p. 346, translated deCatanzaro, *The Discourses*, p. 236.
[37] Symeon, *Traités théologiques et ethiques* IV, vol. II, p. 18.
[38] Life of St Cyril Phileotes, chapter 17, pp. 91–4 (314–17).

hegoumenos Symeon the Sanctified in this capacity. He was certainly employed as a trusted and discreet negotiator and thus could well have also been a close spiritual adviser to Alexios. It is unlikely, given the intimacy of the relationship, that it was usual to have more than one spiritual father at a time, but the death of one would, of necessity, have entailed the search for another.[39]

The choice of a spiritual father, although, as we have seen, often arising from existing family links, could also depend on other factors. Groups already bound together by friendship strengthened these ties by associating themselves with the same spiritual father. Thus Basil the Younger, active in the tenth century, became the spiritual adviser to a group of aristocratic ladies in Constantinople and was introduced by one of them to the Empress Helena, wife of Constantine VII Porphyrogennetos. Symeon the New Theologian was spiritual father to a circle which met at the house of Christopher Phagoura, the donor of the Oratory of St Marina in which Symeon took refuge for a time. The canonical prohibitions against leaving monasteries were clearly not observed by these monks and, in Basil's case, it was seemingly quite acceptable for a spiritual father to spend a great deal of time in the company of a group of women whose status would normally have demanded a great deal of seclusion.[40]

The existence of a common spiritual father was thus an important aspect of the creation of social and political alliances among the aristocracy as well as an indication of prevailing fashions in spirituality. But it must not be seen as an exclusively aristocratic institution. An act of donation from the archives of the Lavra on Mount Athos, that of Constantine and Maria Lagoudes (February 1014), was made 'because of the strongest attachment' the couple had felt throughout their lives to their spiritual father Theodoret, the *hegoumenos* of the monastery. There is no evidence to suggest that they were either particularly wealthy or aristocratic. Similar humble donations were made by single monks or hermits to the monasteries of their spiritual fathers on Athos. In such cases, the gift was often in return for shelter being provided for the grantor in his old age. The monastic community fulfilled the protective

[39] Life of St Cyril Phileotes, chapter 47, pp. 233–4 (459–60). For the campaign against Roussel of Bailleul, see *Alexiad*, I. i–iii, pp. 9–17 and against Basiliakios, *Alexiad*, I. viii, 2, p. 32; I. ix, 3, p. 35 and Bryennios, *Nicephori Bryennii Historiarum libri quattuor*, ed. and translated into French, P. Gautier (CFHB, IX, Ser. Bruxellen., Brussels, 1975), L. iv, 27, p. 155. For Symeon the Sanctified, see chapter 3, p. 86 and chapter 10, pp. 279–80.
[40] Life of St Basil the Younger, chapters 21–2, pp. *29–*30; Life of St Symeon the New Theologian, chapter 100, p. 135; chapter 109, p. 142. Spiritual relationship conferred the social freedom enjoyed by blood relations and could, in the secular world, even be used as a cover for sexual relationships. See Macrides, 'God-father', p. 154.

rôle which would usually have been undertaken by the family in lay society.[41]

The provision of expert advice and guidance made certain spiritual fathers famous but there were difficulties about the acceptance as saints of those who were merely revered advisers – Symeon the New Theologian's insistence on venerating an icon of his own spiritual father, Symeon Eulabes, who does not seem to have had any following beyond the monastery, produced a clash with the episcopacy – but it is clear that the spiritual children of outstanding 'fathers' did consider that they had supernatural powers. Nikephoros Phokas, according to the historian Skylitzes, was accustomed to sleep wrapped in a bearskin which had once been worn by his uncle, Michael Maleïnos. Another of Michael's spiritual children, St Athanasios of Athos, took with him Michael's *koukoulion* (cowl) when he left Kyminas and 'wore it as a protection in life and when dying had it placed in his tomb'. Such talismans could bridge any physical separation between the spiritual father and his child and were a form of relic which could be created even before the death of the original owner.[42]

The protection thought to be provided by such items of clothing, as by relics, was a sign of a spiritual power which placed the monks concerned in a rank above the human but below the divine. Their holiness gave them an increased access to God and made of them His chosen channels of communication with the world below. This *parresia* could, it was believed, be translated into eminently practical terms. A commonly accepted mark of sanctity was, in fact, an ability to predict the future. It was a gift primarily associated with those who led the eremitic life; their long periods of solitary contemplation could allow them to reach a higher degree of nearness to God than could a coenobitic *hegoumenos*, always to some extent distracted by the organisational problems of his monastery.

There is very often an association to be drawn between the recipients of prophecy (always, of course, correct, otherwise it would have remained unrecorded) and their subsequent patronage of a monastic house. But it was a phenomenon which seems to have occurred at all social levels, although, naturally enough, the hagiographers usually only reported instances concerning important figures of the day. In the Life of St Luke the Younger, however, there are episodes in which the saint used his powers of prophecy for the benefit of the community, rather than for the

---

[41] *Lavra*, I, no. 18 (1014). The link between spiritual fatherhood and donation is examined in chapter 5.
[42] Life of Symeon the New Theologian, chapter 72, p. 98; chapter 78, p. 106 and chapter 3, p. 89; Skylitzes, chapter 22, p. 280; Life of Athanasios (A), chapter 240, p. 115; (B), chapter 12, p. 139; chapter 65, p. 200.

guidance of any powerful individual. He apparently predicted the Bulgar attack of 917 which culminated in the Byzantine defeat at the Battle of the Acheloos and a later 'barbarian' invasion into the Peloponnese, probably the Magyar raids of 934. The people treated him as a prophet and none of the inhabitants around the area of Mount Joannitza (where the saint was based at the time) would leave their homes until he gave the signal of impending attack. St Peter of Argos had a vision of John the Baptist warning him of trouble in the Peloponnese (a probable reference to Slav rebellions) and St Nikon Metanoeite predicted to the anxious *strategos* of the Peloponnese that a 'barbarian' attack would be turned back: a reference to the raid led by the Bulgarian leader, Samuel, in 996, which was defeated by Nikephoros Ouranos in the following year.[43]

What can be made of these predictions? They were, of course, reported by hagiographers after the event, but this is no real reason to dismiss them out of hand as mere fabrications. The accounts are doubtless embroidered and certainly fulfilled an important rôle in the construction of the hagiographical portrait, although it is important to bear in mind that both the visionaries and their listeners believed in direct divine revelation; but they may well also have been based on the saints' access to important and wide-ranging intelligence systems. In the instances discussed here, contact with spiritual children among the ranks of the military would have given access to information of both attack and planned response and if any form of 'early warning system' such as that which is known to have existed in Asia Minor was also present in the Balkans, then the provision of up-to-date information about the position of the enemy would have been quite possible. But the form in which the information was later 'presented' – dreams and visions – was, of course, particular to a specific form of spiritual life.[44]

---

[43] Little has been written on the subject of the Byzantine interest in prophecy, oracles, horoscopes and other prognostications. But see P. J. Alexander, ed. D. deF. Abrahamse, *The Byzantine apocalyptic tradition* (Berkeley/Los Angeles/London, 1985) for books of prophecy in the mid-tenth century. C. Mango, 'The legend of Leo the Wise', *ZRVI*, 65 (1960), 59–93, reprinted in *Byzantium and its image*, article XVI, discusses early Macedonian attitudes to divination. On horoscopes, see D. Pingree, 'The horoscope of Constantine VII', *DOP*, 27 (1973), 219–31. A horoscope for the coronation of that most apparently devout of Emperors, Alexios Komnenos, is contained in D. Pingree, 'Gregory Choniades and Palaeologan astronomy', *DOP*, 18 (1964), 135–60. Life of St Luke the Younger, chapter 25, p. 94 (Martini); 52, col. 462 (*PG*); 63, col. 468 (*PG*); Life of St Peter of Argos, chapter 19, p. 13. For a suggested dating of this episode (probably between 924 and 927), see Vasiliev, '"Life" of St Peter of Argos', pp. 184–5; *Life of St Nikon*, chapter 40, pp. 140–2, pp. 288–9.

[44] P. Pattenden, 'The Byzantine early-warning system', *B*, 53 (1983), 258–99, discusses the beacon system which stretched from the eastern frontier to Constantinople. Byzantine military officers would also have known of older, Roman signalling systems involving mirrors or semaphore and were expected to gather intelligence of all kinds, see, for

Access to 'privileged information' probably also lies at the root of the success with which spiritual fathers often predicted the fortunes of those Byzantines whose rank placed them in positions of authority, those in court circles and those who held, or eventually gained, the imperial rank. Numerous examples, often borne out by the chroniclers of the period, can be culled from the tenth and eleventh centuries; only a few can be cited here. St Basil the Younger warned two young *protospatharioi* (court officials) not to take part in the doomed revolt of Constantine Doukas in 917; was he already aware from other court sources that the imperial government knew of the plans and had already taken suitable counter-measures? St Luke the Younger may have been able to predict that the *strategos* of Hellas, Pothos Argyros, an appointee of the Emperor Romanos Lekapenos, would come to no harm under the restored régime of Constantine Porphyrogennetos and that Krinites, the next *strategos*, would later be given control of the Peloponnese, because, as a bishop, he had enough contacts in church circles in the capital to keep him informed of the way the political wind was blowing. Both these *strategoi* were clearly among his spiritual children.[45]

In the eleventh century, St Lazaros of Mount Galesion stood at the centre of a network of local officials in the Thrakesion theme. His circle included Nikephoros Proteuon, the *krites* (literally 'judge' but by this time administrator) of the theme and John Mitas the *dioiketes* of Ephesos in charge of the financial management of the property of the *sekreton* (governmental bureau) of the Myrelaion in the same theme, who came to

---

example, *Three Byzantine military treatises*, ed. and translated G. Dennis (CFHB, xxv, Ser. Washington, Dumbarton Oaks Texts, ix, Washington, DC, 1985); Anonymous Byzantine treatise *On Strategy*, chapter 3, p. 26 (beacons); *On Skirmishing*, chapter 2, p. 152; 7, p. 162 (spies); *On Campaign Organization and Tactics*, chapter 18, p. 290 (spies).

[45] Life of St Basil the Younger, chapters 10–14, pp. *26–8. For the revolt of Constantine Doukas, see Chronicle of Pseudo-Symeon *magistros*, in Theophanes cont., pp. 718–21; Life of the Patriarch Euthymios, chapter 21, pp. 131–3 and S. Runciman, *The Emperor Romanus Lecapenus and his reign* (Cambridge, 1929, reprinted 1963), pp. 49–50. The account of the Life of Basil the Younger is remarkable for its virulent hostility towards the patriarch Nicholas Mystikos (then in charge of the government), a trait also reflected in the Life of the Patriarch Euthymios, see Commentary, pp. 227–8. Could Constantine Doukas have been a spiritual son of Basil's? For Pothos Argyros and the *strategos* Krinites, see Life of St Luke the Younger, chapters 58–9; col. 464–8 (*PG*) and Chronicle of Pseudo-Symeon *magistros*, p. 732. For Pothos Argyros' family, see J.-F. Vannier, *Familles byzantines. Les Argyroi (IXe–XII siècles)* (Byzantina Sorbonensia, i, Paris, 1975), no. 5, pp. 27–8. Pothos had real cause for concern, as his brother Leo Argyros' son was married to Romanos Lekapenos' daughter, Agatha. Krinites, according to Da Costa-Louillet, 'Saints de Grèce', p. 340, note 1, should *not* be identified with Krinites Arotras (see Bon, *Péloponnèse byzantin*, p. 189, no. 17) who was *strategos* of Hellas, then Peloponnese, then Hellas again and was sent by Constantine Porphyrogennetos to put down revolts by the Slavic tribes in the Peloponnese in 952, see *DAI*, chapter 50, pp. 232–4; *Commentary*, p. 186 and Runciman, *Romanus Lecapenus*, pp. 73–4.

request a cure for his uncle, Eustathios. But he also had contacts in Constantinople. He warned the eparch, Nikephoros Kampanarios, of an imminent revolt against the Emperor Michael V; he prophesied the downfall of Constantine Barys (who had wished to make a present of gold-decorated court tunics – *scaramangia* – to the saint, but was refused) who later led an abortive revolt against Constantine IX Monomachos, although he foretold the political survival of his associate, Nikephoros 'son of Euthymios'. He also received visits from the *strategos* Romanos Skleros and from Kosmas Konidiares, two figures well known from contemporary chronicles and from the legal compilation of the *Peira*. On an even higher level, he was consulted by Maria Skleraina, the sister of Romanos Skleros and the influential mistress of the Emperor Constantine Monomachos and by a certain Makrembolites – clearly a relative of the Empress Eudocia Makrembolitissa, the consort of both Constantine X Doukas (1059–67) and his successor, Romanos IV Diogenes (1067–81).[46] Other examples can be found in the hagiography of the early twelfth century, notably, perhaps, the contacts between St Cyril Phileotes and the Komnenos family. Cyril was the spiritual father of Anna Dalassene, the mother of the future emperor (whose accession to the purple he prophesied); of the emperor himself and of his brother-in-law George Palaiologos. He was also consulted by the celebrated general Eumathios Philokales and by Constantine Choirosphaktes, the scion of an eminent Byzantine family.[47]

[46] Life of St Lazaros, chapter 120, p. 543 (Nikephoros Proteuon); chapter 103, p. 539 (John Mitas); chapter 102, p. 539 (Nikephoros Kampanarios – the 'Kampares' of the text should be emended). Nikephoros Proteuon later became *katepan* (governor) of Bulgaria, attempted to seize the throne as Constantine IX lay dying in 1055, but was thwarted and imprisoned in the Monastery of Kouzenos, interestingly enough quite near Mount Galesion, the home of St Lazaros; see Cheynet, *Pouvoir et contestations*, pp. 65, 194. Nikephoros Kampanarios is mentioned in Skylitzes, p. 420 and is probably the *krites* (judge) Kampanarios of the *Peira*; see Cheynet, *Pouvoir et contestations*, p. 55, no. 56. For the plot of Constantine Barys, see Life of St Lazaros, chapter 105, p. 540 and Cheynet, *Pouvoir et contestations*, pp. 64–5, no. 74, who also identifies other members of the family. For the Skleros family, Life of St Lazaros, chapter 87, p. 538 (Romanos Skleros); chapter 245, p. 554 (Maria Skleraina) and see W. Seibt, *Die Skleroi. Eine prosopographisch-sigillographische Studie* (Byzantina Vindobonensia, IX, Vienna, 1976) and N. Oikonomidès, 'St George of the Mangana, Maria Skleraina and the "Malyj Sion" of Novgorod', *DOP*, 34–5 (1980–1), 231–45, reprinted in *Byzantium from the ninth century*, XVI. For Kosmas Konidiares, a monk who later returned to the world to take part in the rebellion of Isaac Komnenos in 1057, see Life of St Lazaros, chapter 97, p. 538 and Cheynet, *Pouvoir et contestations*, p. 689 and for Makrembolites, Life of St Lazaros, chapter 101, p. 539 (for a possible identification with John Makrembolites who rebelled with the future patriarch Michael Keroularios in 1040, see Cheynet, *Pouvoir et contestations*, pp. 51–2).

[47] Life of St Cyril Phileotes, chapter 17, pp. 90–4 (314–17) (Anna Dalassene); chapter 52, pp. 231 (469) (Alexios Komnenos); chapter 48, p. 237 (463–4); (George Palaiologos); chapter 34, pp. 143–6 (370–2) (Constantine Choirosphaktes); chapter 35, pp. 146–54

Founders and benefactors

It is clear, then, that monastic leaders were often visited by members of the laity for consultation on all sorts of matters, although their visits were ostensibly for spiritual reasons. St Lazaros of Mount Galesion, indeed, apparently turned away a *topoteretes* (military officer) who wanted to talk to him 'about wars and other worldly happenings', because he had not taken the saint's advice on spiritual matters. From members of the Byzantine administrative 'middle management' as far up as the imperial families themselves, the clients represented a cross-section of the Byzantine ruling class. They consulted their spiritual fathers either in person or by letter, and it is very likely that they were well aware of others who also sought guidance from the same source. It is not clear whether spiritual sons and daughters of the same 'father' considered themselves related, as did those linked by other forms of spiritual relationship such as baptism, but the example of the spiritual children of Cyril Phileotes, all of whom were close to, if not members of, the Komnenan 'clan', strongly suggests that spiritual and political alliances were often not very far apart. If this were so, it would help to explain the accuracy of the specifically secular guidance dispensed by the saints. The relationship of 'father' to 'son' or 'daughter' and the protection afforded by one to the other could transcend any scruples about the divulging of information and modern perceptions of the 'sanctity of the confessional' should not unquestioningly be transferred into the Byzantine context.[48]

Of particular interest, since they concerned the political fortunes of the empire, were the predictions made to certain individuals of their imminent accession to the imperial power. Michael Maleïnos reportedly described a dream he had had to a group of courtiers from Constantinople, in which he had seen five small boxes on the altar of Hagia Sophia. He interpreted this as meaning that the usurper Romanos Lekapenos and his four sons would soon be toppled from power and Constantine Porphyrogennetos would be again left as sole ruler. Constantine Monomachos' accession in 1042 was predicted while he was in exile on the island of Mytilene by, it would appear, monks from both Galesion and Chios and Cyril Phileotes predicted the accession of

(372–80) (Eumathios Philokales). For all these personalities, see B. Skoulatos, *Les personnages byzantins de l'Alexiade. Analyse prosopographique et synthèse* (Université de Louvain. Recueil de Travaux d'Histoire et de Philologie, 6th ser., fasc. 20, Louvain, 1980).

[48] Life of St Lazaros, chapter 118, p. 544. George Palaiologos was the brother-in-law of Irene Doukaina, wife of Alexios I Komnenos, see Cheynet, *Pouvoir et contestations*, p. 275 (family tree of the Doukai); Eumathios Philokales was one of Alexios' most important military commanders and Constantine Choirosphaktes one of his *oikeioi* (close advisers). See Cheynet, *Pouvoir et contestations*, pp. 230, 257, 297 and note 47 above.

Alexios Komnenos.[49] The act of making this kind of prediction was not
essentially different from that of advising less august figures on their
future political actions, and again may have depended to a large extent on
an efficient intelligence system; but the consequences were much more
significant. All the establishments of the holy men concerned later
received donations and privileges from the successful candidates.[50]

The personal relationships established between leading monks and
members of the Byzantine élite were one aspect of the very close association which had long been established between the welfare of monastic
institutions and that of the state itself. This two-way process was clearly
described by Michael Attaliates, when, like many monastic founders, he
decreed in his *Diataxis* the offering of prayers for the Emperors:

> For it is fitting for him [the Emperor] to look to the wishes of the founders
> and to protect the holy establishments [*sebasmia*] and maintain the
> holy chrysobulls granted to them . . . so that the holy men may commend
> their lives to God and offer prayers for their safety and for the raising of
> the military standards, the campaigning and victory of the army, the
> governance of the commonwealth and its spiritual welfare and those things
> pleasing to God.[51]

It is also possible that prayers for the emperors were also specifically
requested by the founders of small monastic houses, though it is
impossible to know for certain since no *typika* for these humble establishments survive. But concern for the emperor, and through him the
state, was one of the most fundamental links between personal and state
piety, between spiritual observance and political duty. In fact, since the
political premise of the Byzantine state was that it represented a *mimesis*
(shadowing) of the Heavenly Kingdom, it is unwise to attempt to separate
out these 'religious' and 'political' aspects in too precise a way. Certainly
the responsibility of the emperor to ensure the spiritual welfare of the
Byzantine people had been established since the days of Justinian and was
accepted just as much in the tenth and eleventh centuries as it had been
in the sixth. The *Typikon* of Constantine Monomachos for Mount Athos
(September 1045) provides a list of imperial responsibilities very similar

[49] Life of St Michael Maleïnos, chapter 23, pp. 565–6; Life of St Lazaros, chapter 230,
p. 579; Life of SS Niketas, John and Joseph, in *Bios kai politeia ton hosion kai theophoron
pateron hemon, Niketa, Ioannou kai Ioaseph*, in G. Photeinos, *Ta Neamonesia* (Chios, 1864),
p. 24. It is suspicious that this prophecy is attributed to two monastic groups and the story
may have been 'borrowed' by Photeinos from the eleventh-century tradition in the Life of
St Lazaros. Note the profound (and justified) suspicion of this text expressed by Vranoussi,
'Archives de Néa Moni', pp. 269–72. Life of St Cyril Phileotes, chapter 17, p. 91 (314).
[50] See chapter 5.
[51] *Diataxis* of Attaliates, p. 81.

to that enumerated by Attaliates: to control political affairs; to concern himself with the welfare of the army; to wage foreign wars; to conquer cities; to protect the holy canons of the church and to ensure the welfare of 'those who have fled the world, especially to the holy mountains'.[52]

The monastic life was also a means by which the most numerous (and most efficacious) prayers could be offered on behalf of the state. The *typika* of Attaliates and Pakourianos, among others, make it clear that this was one of the important functions of the great coenobitic houses.[53] There is also evidence to suggest that it was a prime concern of the *lavrai* of the holy mountains, too. The necessity for this type of intercession was clearly strongest in time of war, and on a number of occasions in the tenth century, when the Byzantine state was facing a serious military challenge, imperial appeals were made for the spiritual assistance of the monks. In a speech to be delivered to the armies of the eastern themes as they left to campaign against Tarsos in 952–3, Constantine Porphyrogennetos assured his troops that:

> having called upon the most worthy and holy fathers who sit upon the mountains and in caves and holes in the ground, for their prayers, and having exhorted them for their supplications, we have ordained that they should unceasingly and unsleepingly offer prayers on your behalf. We have also commanded that the same shall be done in the churches and monasteries of the God-guarded City.[54]

Letters requesting such intercession have also survived from the same period. One, drafted by the *magistros* and logothete of the Drome, Symeon, was directed to the communities of Olympos, Latros, Kyminas and Athos and also (for reasons which are not clear) to the metropolitan of Kyzikos. A second mentions the particular spiritual gifts of a certain monk of Olympos, Dermokaïtes, while making a general plea for prayers for the army about to leave for Calabria.[55] Such actions reveal an important official motive for the patronage of monasteries – the belief that

---

[52] See L. Bréhier, *Le monde byzantin* (3 vols., Paris, 1949, reprinted 1970), II: *Les institutions de l'empire byzantin*, chapters 1–2, pp. 1–89, especially pp. 63–5. Justinian, *Novella*, CXXXIII, in *CIC*, pp. 666–76; *Prôtaton*, no. 8 (1045).

[53] *Diataxis* of Attaliates, pp. 65, 81; Pakourianos, chapter 18, p. 91.

[54] H. Ahrweiler, 'Un discours inédit de Constantin VII Prophyrogénète', *TM*, 2 (1967), 343–404; see 395, 402.

[55] J. Darrouzès, *Epistoliers byzantins du Xe siècle* (Archives de l'Orient Chrétien, VI, Paris, 1966), I, no. 83, pp. 146–7; no. 88, p. 149. Dermokaïtes is mentioned in Theophanes cont., VI, p. 440 as interceding for the soul of the Emperor Romanos Lekapenos, so that the pages of a mysterious book containing his sins were made blank. For other members of the family, see D. M. Nicol, 'The Byzantine family of Dermokaïtes, c. 940–1453', *BS*, 35 (1974), 1–11 and A. P. Kazhdan, 'The Byzantine family of Dermokaïtes. Additions to the article by D. M. Nicol in *BS* (1974), 1–11', *BS*, 36 (1975), 192.

the monks could provide reinforcements on a non-combative, but not inactive, level. Though such requests were most frequently made in time of war, the importance of monastic prayers for the emperor and the empire was a constant theme of monastic documents. An early document from the Lavra on Mount Athos (972) makes use of the familiar imagery of ships in a storm, but in this case the monastery is seen as the haven from which the monks send up prayers for the beleaguered ship of state. And far from regarding these duties as detracting from their individual spiritual development, the monks accepted such generalised intercession as an important part of their spiritual labours. In a letter sent to the Emperor Alexios Komnenos, which only now survives in part in another collection, the so-called *Diegesis merike*, the monks of the Lavra themselves emphasised their concern for his welfare: 'For in your peace we live our eremitic life, praying for the rule of your Imperial Majesty, that God will grant it many years.'[56] Individual founders and benefactors were commemorated in monastic liturgies as those whose personal efforts had brought the house into being and ensured its survival; the emperor was commemorated as the symbol of that stability and protection which allowed all religious life in the empire to flourish.

It would, however, be both unjust and inaccurate to conceive of the monasteries and their leaders as simply concerning themselves with the spiritual welfare and guidance of the aristocracy, even though this brought considerable returns in the form of donations, privileges and protection. For monastic leaders, especially in the tenth century when the peripatetic life was still practised and when the small, locally based houses predominated, were also communal leaders. They, too, possessed the power of prophecy, but it was often devoted to much more mundane affairs than foretelling the political fortunes of powerful individuals and their hagiographers were touchingly concerned to relate happenings of local interest, an indication, perhaps, that they intended their work for local consumption. In areas where safety could not be guaranteed by the military forces of the state – southern Italy and Greece are two cases in point – the holy men provided guidance and reassurance for anxious and displaced communities. In some cases, they acted as intercessors between rural communities and the representatives of the state. St Nil, in southern Italy, protected the inhabitants of Rossano from the over-enthusiastic attentions of imperial officials (probably tax-collectors) and St Elias Spelaiotes, when travelling through Greece, was not averse to sharing his unflattering opinion of the local *strategos*, John Mouzalon, with the notables of Patras with whom he was dining. Elsewhere, Paul of Latros intervened in the case of John, a villager from the Thrakesion

---

[56] *Lavra*, I, no. 7 (972); *Diegesis merike*, see p. 166.

theme, who had taken part in some kind of minor revolt and was in the process of being taken away in chains for punishment by a *dikazon* (judge), and who, after praying to the saint, felt his fetters miraculously drop away (or perhaps had them removed when the saint's displeasure became known).[57]

But holy men also concerned themselves with other, more personal troubles. Luke the Younger directed two brothers to the site of their father's buried treasure in order to end a family feud; he also identified the thief of a large amount of gold stolen from an imperial official en route for Africa and thus saved the weight of imperial justice falling on the community as a whole. St Nikon freed Sparta of plague apparently by the simple expedient of expelling the Jews, a somewhat hazardous move as Jews enjoyed official tolerance and protection, but one which may well have reflected widespread Christian popular opinion. Peter of Argos acted as negotiator with Cretan pirates at Nauplia (c. 930) in order to ransom Christian captives.[58] Other examples can be cited from Italy: St Sabas tactfully refused a gift of honey offered him by a man who, the saint knew, had stolen it from his neighbours' hives and thus avoided contributing to a potentially serious feud; in the mid-980s St Luke of Demena organised a foray of townspeople from the *kastron* of Armento which successfully saw off a Saracen raiding force; St Elias the Younger ended a five-month drought by first lecturing the villagers on the virtues of the brotherly love that had hitherto been lacking and then praying for rain, to immediate effect.[59]

It was, in fact, to monks that Byzantines of all ranks turned in times of crisis, when self-help or existing communal and kinship structures were of no avail and when the officials of the state seemed powerless to intervene or were, themselves, the cause of the problem. Periods of attack and insecurity were one important time when the practical expedient of allowing terrified villagers inside the fortified walls of monasteries could be bolstered by the morale-boosting effects of preaching and the expression of the certainty of ultimate Christian triumph, even though

---

[57] Life of St Nil, cols. 96–7. I have not been able to obtain the more recent *Bios kai politeia tou hosiou patros hemon Neilou tou Neou, testo originale greco e studio introduttivo*, ed. G. Giovanelli (Grottaferrata, 1972), or his Italian trans., *Vita di S. Nilo, fondatore e patrono di Grottaferrata* (Grottaferrata, 1966). Life of St Elias Spelaiotes, p. 857; Life of St Paul the Younger, chapter 50, pp. 179–80.

[58] Life of St Luke the Younger, chapter 27, p. 95 (Martini); chapter 44, pp. 99–100 (Martini); *Life of St Nikon*, chapter 33, pp. 110–32 and see J. Starr, *The Jews in the Byzantine empire* (Texte und Forschungen zur byzantinisch-neugriechischen Philologie, xxx, Athens, 1939), who dates this episode to c. 985, pp. 167–8. Life of St Peter of Argos, chapter 14, p. 10.

[59] Life of St Sabas, chapter 28, pp. 153–4; Life of St Luke of Demena, II, chapters 10–11, p. 340; Life of St Elias the Younger, chapter 58, pp. 90–2.

this had to be tempered with warnings that it was first necessary to undergo extreme suffering. In the Balkan and southern Italian contexts, such warnings were only too merited as urban and rural communities struggled to cope with the effects of Bulgar, Magyar and Muslim raids, particularly serious in the early tenth century before the Byzantine military response had gained any real momentum.[60] Though periods of both offensive and defensive warfare saw the holy men come into their own as spiritual bulwarks of the civilian population as well as encouragers of the military, there were two other circumstances in which, if the consistent concern of the hagiographers is anything to go by, their assistance was particularly requested: climatic disaster and illness, both physical and mental.

The climate of the south of Italy and of the Eastern Mediterranean is often one of extremes. The number of disputes about water rights found in archival material is proof enough of the problems caused by the characteristic hot and dry summers of many of the coastal and plateau regions. In contrast, winters are often plagued by snows, high winds and heavy rains. The Byzantines, like their ancient predecessors, had accustomed themselves to these vagaries and made attempts to combat them in terms of agriculture and habitat. But what they could not be expected to cope with were periodic climatic excesses: freak weather conditions beyond their normal experience or more serious phenomena such as earthquakes and the appearance of comets and other heavenly bodies. It is this sort of experience which was often recorded in the chroniclers (since they were interested in all kinds of unusual natural phenomena, although not, of course in recording day-to-day observations) and a variety of alarming events can be noted in their accounts.[61]

The chronicle written about 1057 by John Skylitzes may serve as an example. He noted extremes of heat and cold: in 928, for example, a great cold (possibly the famous 'long winter' referred to in imperial legal material) began on Christmas Day and lasted, 'ice bound' and with sub-zero temperatures, for forty days, that is until mid-February. In 1010, the rivers, marshes and even the seas froze and in southern Italy heavy snow 'burned' the olive trees and killed birds and fish. In 1048–9, the Danube froze, allowing Petcheneg tribesmen to cross and raid the northern

---

[60] Life of St Elias the Younger, chapters 45–6, pp. 68–70 are a sermon on the virtues of suffering. Trinchera, no. 15 (January 1015) is a grant of a *kastellion* (fortified place) to Luke, *hegoumenos* of the Monastery of St Ananias in Calabria on condition that the local population would be allowed to take refuge there in time of attack; see V. von Falkenhausen, *La dominazione bizantina nell'Italia meridionale dal IX al' XI secolo* (Bari, 1978), pp. 146–7.

[61] For climatic conditions in the lands of the Byzantine empire (except Italy), see Kaplan, *Les hommes et la terre*, chapter 1, especially pp. 10–21. For southern Italy, see Guillou, 'Italie byzantine', p. 30.

provinces of the empire. In contrast, Skylitzes recorded a long and fierce drought in 1036 and a 'great heat' that killed people and animals in the summer of, probably, 1054. He also commented, as did others, on the effects of these phenomena, especially in terms of mortality. He linked the drought of 1036 with famine in Thrace, Macedonia, Strymon, Thessalonike and Thessaly the following year. He noted that the strong winds which had destroyed many fruit trees in May 968, led to shortages the following year.[62]

Serious climatic variations could thus disrupt both rural and urban economies for some time afterwards. In the aftermath of the 'great winter' of 928, for instance, the destitute poured into Constantinople to receive the imperial food doles distributed by the monks of the capital and to take refuge from the cold in the arcades of the main streets which were boarded over to provide some shelter. The hardship caused by the famine which followed the cold was the stated reason for large numbers of peasant landholders selling their lands to richer owners in return for food. The Life of St Luke the Stylite, in a passage which could well refer to the same period, describes the saint opening up his family's storage pits (*lakkoi*) and distributing 4,000 *modioi* of corn to the needy as well as fodder for their animals. In the mid-tenth century, St Luke of Demena ordered the monastic stores of his house in southern Italy to be opened to the hungry who flocked there from the region of Marsicorum (modern Marsico) near the River Agri.[63]

But more immediately damaging, in both a material and psychological sense, were sudden disasters such as earthquakes, to which the lands of the Byzantine empire were particularly prone and which seem to have been particularly frequent in this period. Twelve earthquakes affecting Constantinople and its immediate region in the years 860–1118 have been recorded and there were others where the main damage seems to have been in the provinces, such as an earthquake which destroyed five villages in the Bukellarion theme in Asia Minor in 1035 and one in January of 1040 which destroyed Smyrna and other towns. In the Balkans, a serious tremor hit Lovec in Bulgaria in 1059 and a long period of seismic activity which affected Constantinople in 1010 had already caused earthquakes in southern Italy in 1004–5 and was to affect Armenia in 1011–12. A series of earthquakes recorded by Arab and Crusader chroniclers in Cilicia and Syria in 1114–15 were also felt in Piacenza in Italy and across the Po

---

[62] Skylitzes, p. 225 ('long winter'), p. 347 ('freezing rivers and marshes'), p. 400 (drought), p. 402 (famine of 1037–8), p. 477 (fierce heat).
[63] For the effects of the 928 famine, see R. Morris, 'The powerful and the poor in tenth-century Byzantium: law and reality', *PP*, 73 (1976), 3–27 and Kaplan, *Les hommes et la terre*, pp. 421–2, 461–2; Life of St Luke the Stylite, chapter 7, pp. 201–2; chapter 10, p. 205. Life of St Luke of Demena, I.7, p. 338.

valley. And these abnormalities rarely seemed to have occurred singly. Thus the earthquake of 1010 was followed by a period of intense cold and those of 1041 and 1106 by violent winds and heavy rains. In all cases, too, the water tables of the regions concerned were seriously affected, thus altering their fertility, sometimes permanently.[64]

The very suddenness of earthquakes, combined with their devastating destruction and the trauma suffered by the survivors, served to convince Byzantines of all classes (like their Western counterparts) that they were clear manifestations of Divine displeasure. So, too were the astronomical portents – eclipses, shooting stars and pillars of fire so assiduously noted by the chroniclers. In these circumstances, as with climatic disasters, it is hardly surprising that Byzantines turned to those whom they felt could interpret these signs and their meanings, identify their immediate causes and, most importantly, instruct them how to atone for the moral lapses which they knew lay at their root. To request assistance from monks was to recognise that among them lay the more profound understanding that could explain God's will. Thus after a particularly serious drought in the region around Miletos, in the mid-tenth century, the inhabitants of forty villages assembled for a mass pilgrimage to Mount Latros, to request the assistance of St Paul the Younger, who, according to his hagiographer, showed his immediate power to assist them by causing, in Biblical fashion, an amphora to be continuously and miraculously refilled with water to refresh those exhausted by the journey. St Sabas, in contrast, diverted the floods in Latium in Italy which threatened vineyards and a church by praying before them like Moses parting the Dead Sea.[65]

It was not only the weather which could disrupt the precarious balances of rural life. In the tenth century, in particular, the Balkan and Italian themes suffered constant raiding, and although the guidance provided by the saints could often avert serious loss of life, their power could not always be exercised in time and their powers of leadership could often only be deployed in comforting and supporting communities shattered by attack. The Life of St Peter of Argos describes the grim aftermath of an

[64] Skylitzes, pp. 107, 271, 331, 347, 386, 399, 405, 414 (earthquakes in 860, 967, 987, 1010, 1032–3, 1036, 1038–9, 1041); Kedrenos, pp. 657–8 (earthquake in 1063); Zonaras, XVIII, 22, p. 740 (earthquake in 1090); *Alexiad*, XII.4, pp. 66–7 (earthquake or strong storm in 1106) and XV.8, pp. 222–3 (earthquake in 1118). For the 1059 earthquake in Bulgaria, see Zonaras, XVIII.6. The wider climatic phenomena associated with earthquakes are discussed by A. Ducellier, 'Les séismes en Méditerranée orientale du XIe au XIIIe siècle. Problèmes de méthode et résultats provisoires', *Actes du XVe Congrès Internationale d'Etudes Byzantines* (4 vols., Athens, 1980), IV: *Communications*, pp. 103–13. For the Byzantine literature on earthquakes, see G. Dagron, 'Quand la terre tremble', *TM*, 8 (1985), 87–103, reprinted in *La Romanité chrétienne en Orient. Heritages et mutations* (London, 1984), article III.
[65] Life of St Paul the Younger, chapter 18, p. 53; Life of St Sabas, chapter 13, pp. 55–6.

Arab raid into the Peloponnese, probably after 924: 'Houses, streets, lanes and fields were filled with dead bodies and there were no living men to bury them.' The crops and stores were pillaged and people ate grass and plants. Rhetorical *topoi*, perhaps, but credible none the less. During this time, Bishop Peter distributed doles of flour, his stocks apparently miraculously increased to cater for the demand. In the late tenth century, St Sabas instructed the *oikonomos* of his monastery to provide for the needs of refugees from Saracen attacks on Calabria, even though complaints were made that there was not enough food remaining to cater for the needs of the monks themselves. A large jar (probably a storage *pithos*) was subsequently found full of grain.[66]

Although the miraculous element in these stories and the likelihood that the hagiographers elaborated their descriptions of the death and destruction caused by attacks for dramatic effect mean that they have to be treated with some caution, there are common themes which run through all of them. In times of crisis, monasteries clearly provided sources of instant help, especially in terms of food and shelter, and this was not only because of the charitable works urged on them by their own tradition. They were often large enough institutions with enough land to provide a surplus of produce, which did not have to be earmarked for dues to superiors or for seed and thus was available when smaller landholders were in need. Their *hegoumenoi* were generally honoured and trusted leaders of local society who could be relied upon, it was hoped, to deal fairly with each according to his need and to be free from the petty corruption and greed of lay officials and landowners. People fled to monasteries in time of trouble because the lay world had failed them: the military had been defeated or shown to be powerless to protect them; their landlords could not or would not provide help, and their own communal solidarities had broken down under the pressure of sudden or unmanageable disaster.

In a similar way, the involvement of holy men in cures was also an indication of the failure of existing lay mechanisms. Though lamentably little is known of Byzantine folk medicine, and not much about the professional doctors who were, in any case, only to be found in larger towns, there were clearly many cases in which available skills were thought to be inadequate. Miraculous cures – necessary and undeniable marks of sanctity – were, by definition, cures which were for some reason unexpected or surprising, although their very existence in hagiographies indicates not only a wish to conform to Biblical prototypes, but at least a distant familiarity with doctors and medicines. In many cases, without

---

[66] Life of St Peter of Argos, chapter 13, pp. 8–9; Vasiliev, '"Life" of St Peter of Argos', pp. 172, 176–7; Life of St Sabas, chapter 14, pp. 135–7.

the intervention of the saint, it was clearly believed that the victims would have died. The diseases concerned were often those particularly associated with the eastern Mediterranean. Studies of early Byzantine hagiography have revealed concentrations of certain types of diseases in certain geographical areas. Alexandrine saints' lives revealed numerous cures for eye complaints (clearly associated with Nilotic bilharzia), cancers and leprosy; in Constantinople, cancers, growths and leprosy were brought to the saints and in Antioch, the deaf, the dumb and those suffering from paralysis were successfully treated.[67]

The hagiography of the tenth and eleventh centuries reveals a similar range of diseases. The *kandidatos* Floros was cured of leprosy by St Luke the Stylite; St Luke the Younger cured sufferers from hydropsy, lameness and St Anthony's fire (severe skin disease and ulcerations); St Sabas dealt with stomach disorders, cancer of the face, haemorrhages and chest infections and St Elias the Younger with snake bite. And throughout the pages dealing with miracle cures lurks the ever present threat of demonic possession, dealt with at one time or another by all those later considered to be saints. In many cases, the symptoms described were clearly those of epilepsy or other types of fits, as in the case of the monk cured by the sign of the cross administered by St Sabas as he fell foaming at the mouth, or the woman, also helped by the saint, who foamed at the mouth and uttered strange cries. But others are not so easily explained. 'Possession by devils' is often characterised by modern historians as a way of describing mental illness; the prevalence among Byzantines of all levels of society of prophylactic charms and amulets to ward off this dire possibility is evidence enough of their own fear of evil spiritual forces attacking them even when they enjoyed rude health, attacks which could only be combated by the strength of the aura transmitted by the holy men. Demons could appear at the most inopportune moments: the Devil, in the guise of a beautiful woman, was said to have appeared at the sick bed of St Lazaros of Galesion and offered, in a bizarre reversal of roles, to cure him, 'for [as she said] I am the healer of Emperors and patriarchs and all the court and I have come to heal you, so let me touch your body'. War against the demons had to be perpetually waged; the holy monks were in the vanguard of the Christian forces.[68]

[67] For the earlier periods, see J. Seiber, *The urban saint in early Byzantine social history* (British Archaeological Reports Supplementary series, xxxvii, Oxford, 1977); E. Patlagean, *Pauvreté économique et pauvreté sociale à Byzance, 4e–7e siècles* (Paris, 1977), pp. 105–20; H. Magoulias, 'The lives of Byzantine saints as sources of data for the history of magic in the 6th and 7th century AD: sorcery, relics and icons', *B*, 38 (1967), 228–67.
[68] Life of St Luke the Stylite, chapter 29, pp. 225–6; Life of St Luke the Younger, chapter 77, p. 110 (Martini); chapter 85, p. 117 (Martini); chapter 86, p. 118 (Martini); Life of St Sabas, chapter 17, p. 140 (chest problems and paralysis); chapter 32, pp. 157–8;

Details of the process of cure are often lacking, but where they do exist it is quite clear that the methods were closely associated with the person of the saint. In many cases he was actually present in person to perform the cure, often by smearing oil from church lamps on the afflicted part or by making the sign of the Cross, or, in the case of demons by some form of exorcism. The curing of snake bite or broken bones or even haemorrhages could well have depended on medical skills passed down in monasteries combined with the immeasurable and beneficial psychological effects of the reassurance provided by the concern and prayers of the saint and his community. But the true mark of sanctity was, of course, the ability of some holy monks to continue to perform cures even after death. The sick were cured, it was believed, merely by a sight of St Sabas' corpse and after St Elias the Younger died in Thessalonike, his relics were carefully brought back to southern Italy, where they performed miracles on their slow progress to his monastery in the Salinoi. A fragrant oil, which apparently oozed from the corpse of St Nikon in Sparta was successfully used by the *strategos* Basil Apokaukos to cure his servant Gregory and among those cured by a vigil in front of the tomb of the saint was the *stratiotes* Michael Argyromites, hitherto given to uncontrollable fits of violence. Even in the Life of St Athanasios (A), a work which reflects its author's own caution on the subject of miracles, the necessary details of Athanasios' post mortem miracles are provided to establish irrevocable proof of his sanctity. Blood was collected from the fatal wounds he suffered in a fall from the roof of the new building in the Lavra whose construction he was supervising, and this precious liquid was the source of many cures.[69]

The creation of shrines, a potent mark of popular esteem for the saint, was not, however, uniformly welcomed. The monk Symeon begged Paul of Latros *not* to perform miracles after his death, so that the monks of his monasteries should be left in peace (perhaps a device employed by the hagiographer to explain the fact that there are few of the saint's post mortem miracles recorded in the Life of St Paul the Younger), but the oratory built after his death soon became a centre for pilgrimage, and oil from the lamps burning over his tomb cured both leprosy and cattle

chapter 37, p. 162 (tumours); chapter 34, p. 159 (throat tumours); chapter 44, p. 314 (female illnesses); Life of St Elias the Younger, chapter 52, p. 80; Life of St Lazaros, chapter 208, p. 572.
[69] St Sabas used oil from the lamps above the tomb of St Pankratios, near Rome, to cure a man possessed by demons; Life of St Sabas, chapter 19, p. 143 and that from a shrine to St Philip built by his brother Merkourios, an epileptic woman, chapter 40, pp. 165–6. Post mortem cures (from many examples): Life of St Sabas, chapter 50, p. 231; Life of St Elias the Younger, chapters 73–4, pp. 116–18; *Life of St Nikon*, chapter 50, pp. 166–8; chapter 65, pp. 222–4; Life of St Athanasios (A), chapter 238, pp. 114–15.

disease. It was also on the site of the early burial places that later, more lavish churches and monastic houses were built; houses such as Hosios Loukas at Stiris, dedicated to St Luke the Younger, or the monastery that grew up in Sparta at St Nikon's place of death, which attracted patronage and donation not only from local worshippers, but from much further afield. It is not surprising to read of the ferocious competition between the inhabitants of Nauplia and Argos for the corpse of St Peter of Argos, or of the exhumation and burial of the head of St Cyril Phileotes in the sanctuary of a neighbouring religious house, for the possession of wonder-working relics was one of the most potent attractions of any monastery and an almost infallible aid to its survival.[70]

The emergence of new centres of worship based on the cults of the monastic saints was only one of the means by which the spiritual and human geography of the empire was altered by the expansion of monasticism. The new shrines attracted pilgrims and worshippers who helped to swell the populations of the settlements in which they were situated, but the mere existence of a monastic house could also have significant effects on local demographic patterns. The quest for monastic solitude, coupled with the long tradition of monastic labour (particularly emphasised by the Stoudites) meant that hitherto inaccessible and uncultivated areas were often first brought into productive use by monks. At first, these enterprises were small scale, and often the work of solitary hermits. St Luke the Younger cleared a small garden in his refuge in the Peloponnese and the theft of his 'grinding mill' (a pair of grinding stones) by a group of marauding sailors would also indicate that he grew a little grain. In the eleventh century, St Lazaros of Mount Galesion was given a small patch of land by the metropolitan of Ephesos soon after he arrived on the mountain, on which he planted one *modios* (measure) of beans. In a forest near Derkos in Thrace in the late eleventh century, St Cyril Phileotes cleared a small plot and grew vegetables on it.[71]

In the mountains of Southern Italy, the process was the same. The tenth century seems to have been the main period for monastic clearances; a mark not only of the popularity of monasticism, but of the demographic increases which partially contributed to it. At the Monastery of St Nikodemos of Kellerana (Gallinaro, near Mammola), founded in the

---

[70] General discussion, see P. R. L. Brown, *The cult of the saints* (London, 1981). Life of St Paul the Younger, chapter 46, p. 167; Life of St Luke the Younger, cols. 473–6 (*PG*); 476–7 (*PG*) for the earliest church and buildings on and near the site of St Luke's burial and see Connors, *Art and miracles*, pp. 77–80. The dating is much discussed, see chapter 1, p. 27. *Life of St Nikon*, chapter 58, pp. 188–90. For St Peter of Argos, see chapter 2, p. 76. Life of St Cyril Phileotes, chapter 55, p. 262 (491). For later patronage, see chapter 5.
[71] Life of St Luke the Younger, chapter 51, p. 103 (Martini); Life of St Lazaros, chapter 34, p. 520; Life of St Cyril Phileotes, chapter 23, pp. 109–10 (334).

tenth century, the monks took it in turns to use a communal hoe (*skalidion*) to clear the area around their cells, and lived on a diet of beans and chick-peas which they cultivated, augmented by chestnuts from the surrounding woods and occasionally by salt fish from the coast, some four hours' walk away. St Elias Spelaiotes supervised tree felling near his monastic community in Calabria and SS Sabas and Makarios cleared in the Merkourion region and in the valley of the River Sinni in the *tourma* of Latinianon.[72]

The process by which the original monastic clearances developed into new communities centred on the religious houses can be clearly traced in the case of the Monastery of the Theotokos of Refuge near Tricarico in the theme of Lucania. In 998, the *hegoumenos*, Kosmas, received a *sigillion* from the katepan, Gregory Tarchaneiotes, which confirmed the monastery's possession of a village (*chorion*) which the monks had founded on their own territory to receive the poor and fugitives from other areas. Twenty-five years later it was reconfirmed by the katepan Basil Boïoannes, a sure indication that the settlement was still in existence. The monks had succeeded in attracting a supply of that most useful of all agrarian commodities – manpower – which helped transform the small pin-pricks of the original clearances into the bases of flourishing monastic economies. For not only did monks and their houses provide the foci for existing rural communities, but they were also often instrumental in founding new ones. In the tenth century, as we shall see, this process was generally limited to bringing unused land into cultivation; in the eleventh, monastic resources provided the means for the extension and improvement of estates on a scale which few but the richest laymen could emulate.[73]

Monasteries, then, had their part to play in the demographic history of the tenth and eleventh centuries and it is interesting to conjecture how many originally secluded houses may have flourished because they were situated within reach of areas where it is very likely that the population was already rising, such as the coastlands of Asia Minor, the hinterland of Thessalonike and some areas of southern Italy. Though the relationship between population levels and the number of monastic vocations is difficult to quantify, few agrarian communities could have supported the growth in monasticism evident in the tenth century unless their own demographic resources had been increasing. But this increase

[72] *Kellerana*, introduction, pp. 11–12. For other references to monastic clearances in southern Italy, see Guillou, 'Italie byzantine', pp. 26ff.
[73] See von Falkenhausen, *Dominazione bizantina*, pp. 187, no. 26; 197, no. 45, for the privileges to the Monastery of the Theotokos of Refuge. The ability of the monastic houses to acquire manpower is discussed in chapter 7.

in the monastic population must also be seen in another light. For just as the rulers of the Byzantine state called upon existing monastic communities for their spiritual aid to extend the frontiers of orthodox rule, so, too, could they be used to strengthen the spiritual ties which bound the empire together.

The new growth of Greek monasticism in south Italy in the tenth century was part and parcel of the reconquest of the area from the Arabs and the reassertion of Byzantine power in the face of the challenge from the Latins. Greek monks were deliberately 'implanted' into areas of mixed populations, as in Bari, where in 1032 the Latin archbishop Byzantius of Bari and Canosa was ordered by the katepan Pothos Argyros to consecrate and give lands to a church dedicated to SS Maria, John the Evangelist and John the Baptist, which was then to be populated by orthodox monks brought into the city from a community at Turi, some 4 km away. The increase in monastic foundations in Macedonia and Bulgaria in the eleventh century was an integral part of the consolidation of Byzantine rule in those areas after the defeat of the Bulgarian tsars at the beginning of the century. The process of 'Byzantinisation' begun by the 'high profile' missionary activity of Constantine and Methodios, or the conversion efforts of St Nikon Metanoeite and St Peter of Argos, was inexorably, if less dramatically, carried forward by the monastic houses.[74]

It was the capacity of monks to play such a diverse variety of rôles within all levels of Byzantine society, and, indeed, to reach both its higher and lower echelons when the secular church often could not, that made them such a potent force. But the fortunes of individual monastic houses – as distinct from the institution itself – varied greatly during the tenth and eleventh centuries. There are a number of explanations for these variations; monasteries were, for instance, just as vulnerable to freaks of climate or enemy attack as were lay communities. But the most important factor contributing to the steady growth in the personnel and territorial resources of any house, especially after the death of a charismatic founder had lessened the first wave of enthusiasm centred on him, was the establishment and continuation of lay patronage. Without this, however prestigious the original founders of the houses might have been, their houses were destined at best to an ephemeral existence and, at worst, to quick extinction. The services that the monks could perform for lay society had, as their corollary, the support that the laity had to give to monastic institutions in order to ensure their survival and growth.

---

[74] For Greek monks in Bari, see Guillou, 'Italie byzantine', p. 28 and von Falkenhausen, *Dominazione bizantina*, p. 201, no. 52.

CHAPTER FIVE

Piety, patronage
and politics

◆

THE TRADITION OF PATRONAGE and donation in Byzantium was one of the most obvious aspects of its classical heritage. The coming of Christianity to the empire in the fourth century did not bring with it a new ethic of donation, though it emphasised the virtues of charity towards the less fortunate and taught that the offerings of the poor, however small, were just as admirable as those of the rich. But it did, however, change the direction of patronage, and, to a certain extent its milieu. In the ancient world, the activities of patrons – the 'good rich men' identified by Aristotle – were mainly confined to cities and chiefly comprised monumental donation: walls, theatres, temples, baths and what might broadly be summed up by the phrase 'bread and circuses': conspicuous expenditure to demonstrate high rank in society and the possession of wealth. With the coming of Christianity, 'monumental' donation, which had declined in the late antique period, once more became a favoured form of patronage, especially for the imperial power and the senatorial aristocracy; the plethora of churches and other religious and charitable institutions which sprang up throughout the empire is eloquent testimony to this tendency.[1]

Another change in emphasis was in the endowment of monuments

---

[1] See for general discussion, R. Morris, 'The Byzantine aristocracy and the monasteries' in M. Angold (ed.), *The Byzantine Aristocracy* (British Archaeological Reports, International Series, 221, Oxford, 1984), pp. 112–37 and 'Monasteries and their patrons in the tenth and eleventh centuries', in J. F. Haldon and J. Kouloumides (eds.), *Perspectives in Byzantine history and culture*, published as *BF*, 10 (1985), 185–231. The motives for ecclesiastical building and endowment are well discussed (albeit in the Italian context) in B. Ward-Perkins, *From classical antiquity to the middle ages. Urban public building in northern and central Italy, AD 300–850* (Oxford, 1984, reprinted 1987), especially pp. 70–84. On charity, see J. Herrin, 'Ideals of charity, realities of welfare: the philanthropic activity of the Byzantine church', in R. Morris (ed.), *Church and people in Byzantium* (Birmingham, 1990), pp. 151–64.

outside the great urban centres of the empire: shrines, pilgrimage sites and rural monasteries, such as the great Monastery of St Catherine on Mount Sinai, as isolated a spot in terms of human habitation (although not, of course, in terms of spiritual connotations) as one might find in the Byzantine world. By the ninth century, donation and patronage had long come to be exercised in both an urban and a rural setting and this development had been made possible by a gradual change in the rôle played by donation in Byzantine society. Once a particular virtue, almost a duty of the governmental classes of the Graeco-Roman cities, it became one of the mechanisms by which spirituality might be expressed by men and women of vastly differing social classes wherever they lived. For emphasis came to be laid not so much on the value of the gift itself, but on the act of giving.[2]

Patronage (a subject too vast to be discussed here in any detail) was, of course, a two-way relationship which could exist between equals or between those of unequal social status. In the context of the patronage of religious institutions, including monasteries, it is important to bear in mind that the donors of money, lands and privileges were, whatever their status in the secular world, of an inferior status in the spiritual context. The patrons in these relationships were, on the highest level, Christ, the Virgin and the saints to whom the houses were dedicated and, of lower spiritual rank, although more immediate spiritual influence, perhaps, the monastic founders (some, as we have seen, having distinct claims to sanctity) who possessed *parresia* with the Deity. The clients were those who hoped to achieve a number of spiritual benefits by making a donation, however small, to a religious institution. Monastic patronage was, if anything, more praiseworthy than the building and endowment of churches (although this, too, was a pious act which benefited the soul), since it helped to support an institution which was considered the highest form of life in the world. We need, therefore, to examine the ways in which Byzantines felt these spiritual benefits could be acquired and of what they were thought to consist.

The ethic of good works may be defined in two ways. The first is essentially active and externally directed. The actions of an individual, whether virtuous or wicked, may be evaluated and 'credited' or 'debited' to his spiritual account. His ultimate fate is seen to depend on his existing achievements. Alternatively, one can, with Max Weber, interpret individual actions (such as patronage) as 'symptoms and expressions of an

---

[2] For a general survey of the development of Christian architecture, see C. Mango, *Byzantine architecture* (London, 1986), chapters 4 and 5; Patlagean, *Pauvreté*, chapter 5, for early Byzantine patronage. G. H. Forsyth and K. Weitzmann, *The Monastery of St Catherine on Mount Sinai*, I, *The fortress of Justinian* (Ann Arbor, Mich., 1973).

underlying ethical personality'. When the motives which lay behind Byzantine piety in general, and donation to monasteries in particular, are examined, a mixture of these two motives is clearly apparent. On the one hand, the old classical virtue of *philanthropia* was seen as a mark of 'proper' behaviour, especially in rulers; on the other, the performance of good works, however humble, increased an individual's prospects of salvation. And patronage and donation could, of course, take a number of different guises. While the endowment of monasteries and other ecclesiastical institutions with land was undoubtedly the most important in the long term, especially since Byzantine canon law forbade the alienation of land given to the church, and it could thus provide a basis for future growth, pious gifts could take the form of money, the donation of precious vessels and books, and the construction or decoration of monastic houses.[3]

Two important questions arise when the mechanisms of donation are considered: what were the motives for monastic donation in general and what decided the direction in which patronage should be directed? The establishments to which Byzantines gave money and lands were, in fact, fairly strictly defined by a number of criteria apart from that of personal inclination. Fashions in spirituality played their part, as did family and political connections. On the highest level, imperial benefaction was seen as part of the ruler's concern for his people's prosperity and success; the welfare of the monasteries was, in effect, an affair of state. But the whole process of donation and foundation began with questions of individual spirituality and the articulation of religious beliefs in words and actions. We can make some progress in detecting what these were.

Though formal autobiography was rarely written in Byzantium, there are sources which contain elements of this type of writing, in particular, the *prooimia* (rhetorical prefaces) to acts of donation of monastic *typika* (foundation charters), especially those of the great coenobitic houses, which frequently contain details of the lives of their founders and a statement of their motives (or at least their public ones) in setting up these establishments. As with the *topoi* of hagiography, there is no real reason

[3] M. Weber, *Sociology of religion*, translated E. Fischoff (London, 1965), especially p. 154. On *philanthropia*, see two studies by H. Hunger: '*Philanthropia*. Eine griechische Wortprägung auf ihren Weg von Aischylos bis Theodoros Metochites', *Anzeiger der Österreichischen Akademie der Wissenschaften, phil. hist. Klasse* (1963), 1–20 reprinted in *Byzantinistische Grundlagenforschung* (London, 1973), article XIII and *Prooimion: Elemente der byzantinischen Kaiseridee in den Arengen der Urkunden* (Wiener Byzantinistische Studien, I, Vienna, 1964), pp. 143–54. For prohibitions on the alienation of monastic land, canon XXIV of the Council of Chalcedon (451); canon XLIX of the Council *in Trullo* (692); canon XIII of the Seventh Ecumenical Council (787); canon I of the Synod of Constantinople (861), cited by P. de Meester, *De monachico statu iuxta disciplinam byzantinam* (Vatican City, 1942), pp. 151–2, 155–6.

to dismiss the details in them as merely formal rhetorical passages. The writers may have expressed certain views and sentiments in conventional ways; but they did not always express the same sentiments, and they shaped the conventions to suit their particular purposes. While we may suspect that the actual drawing up of the *typikon* was not actually performed by the donor, he (or she) clearly kept a close eye on what was included in a document of such spiritual and legal importance and issued it under his (or her) own name.[4]

We may well ask why it was thought necessary to preface with such autobiographical passages documents whose prime function was to lay down the customs and liturgical practices of the house and to enumerate its lands and other possessions. One answer is that the *typikon* itself was considered part and parcel of the process of gift or foundation; it was a commemoration of the founder in words, just as buildings or other gifts were to be used, among other things, to perpetuate his memory. In this context, the document itself needed to contain enough individual detail to distinguish a particular founder from the general run of pious and generous individuals who might also be associated with the same house at one time or another. In addition, it is probable that although Byzantines do not seem to have considered it proper to write about themselves in the normal course of events, self-justification, or at least explanation, was permissible and, indeed, expected in the spiritual context. The active aspect of the 'good works' ethic in the *typikon*, the act of donation, was prefaced by an *apologia* for the person concerned. It was in order to emphasise the particularity of the circumstances, a prerequisite for a salvation which had no value unless it were personally directed, that the authors of the *typika* described their own earlier lives. While most of the surviving *typika* supply some details about the founders, those of Gregory Pakourianos, Michael Attaliates and Irene Doukaina provide the best examples of personal experiences given in the form of spiritual *apologia*. To them may be added other documents from the eleventh century, the well-known Testament of the Anatolian magnate, Eustathios Boïlas (c. 1059) and those of Symbatios Pakourianos and his wife Kale (1090 and 1098 respectively).[5]

Advancing years was undoubtedly a spur to spiritual patronage, for it is clear from all these examples that the donors were old and, in the nature of things, expected to die in the fairly near future. The intimations of

---

[4] G. Misch, *Geschichte de Autobiographie* (4 vols., Frankfurt, 1949–62), only mentions the autobiographical elements in the *Chronographia* of Michael Psellos and the works of Nikephoros Blemmydes and Gregory of Cyprus, see vol. III, ii, pp. 709–830. For a general survey of monastic *typika*, see Galatariotou, 'Byzantine *ktetorika typika*'.

[5] Testament of Boïlas, p. 265 (Vryonis); p. 21 (Lemerle). The Wills of Symbatios and Kale Pakourianos are *Ivirôn*, II, nos. 44 (1090) and 47 (1098).

mortality in the cases of Attaliates, Pakourianos, Boïlas and Kale Pakouriane (whose husband predeceased her and who had already become the nun, Maria) were heightened by the fact that other members of their families had recently died. Attaliates relates that the beginning of his charitable activity was in response to his wife's dying wish; Boïlas that the deaths of both his wife and one of their sons brought with them a realisation of the indiscriminate nature of death: 'and in the circumstances, the recollection of death continuously spurring me, and having the untimely and unexpected before my eyes, I decided to arrange my affairs'. Kale Pakouriane reported sadly that her marriage to Symbatios Pakourianos had lasted only a short time, for he had died in the prime of life leaving her 'defenceless, inconsolable and alone', since they had no children.[6]

The prospect of approaching death was thus a catalyst of action and Byzantines, like their Western counterparts, felt it to be of paramount importance that they should be spiritually prepared and ready to die. There is clear evidence that they believed that it was possible to predict when this might occur. In a general sense, the Christian should always bear his own mortality in mind and be prepared for death at any moment, for, as the tenth-century Patriarch Nicholas Mystikos pointed out in a letter of sympathy to the *parakoimomenos* (chamberlain) Constantine (whose sister had recently died), death was merely what was proper to human life and was ordained by God to each after his allotted span.[7] Some, like the holy men, were granted the power to predict the day, if not the precise moment, of their own death and that of others, but among the laity expectations were, of necessity, much more imprecise. Old age, illness or the deaths of relatives or friends could all serve as poignant reminders of the instability of life and convince an individual that he (or she) was in the position of a 'moribund' – one who knew, or strongly felt, that he was about to die, but had not yet done so. As Philippe Ariès has cogently put it, 'the moribund alone knows how much time is left to him' and the belief in death casting a long shadow before it was just as widespread in Byzantium as in other parts of medieval Europe.[8]

Boïlas reported that he wished to 'arrange his affairs' and for him, as for the other testators, this took two forms: temporal and spiritual preparation. In secular society, the temporal preparation took the form of the legal disposition of property by testament, or, in the lower echelons,

---

[6] See for general discussion, P. Ariès, *The hour of our death*, translated H. Weaver (London, 1981). *Diataxis* of Attaliates, p. 19; Testament of Boïlas, p. 265 (Vryonis), p. 21 (Lemerle); Pakourianos, chapter 1, pp. 29–33; *Ivirôn*, II, 47 (1098).

[7] Nicholas Mystikos, *Letters*, no. 47 (914–18), pp. 266–75.

[8] Ariès, *Hour of our death*, chapter 1.

by oral disposition before witnesses. The testament, like the *typikon*, was imbued with greater significance than its legal function might suggest.For it was both a 'passport to Paradise' in the sense that it attempted to ensure grace through charitable donation, and a safe conduct on earth, because, by the spiritual dispositions expressed in the document and carried out by the testator's heirs, the enjoyment of the remaining (and otherwise suspect) worldly wealth and property could be legitimised. In the formulation of wills and *typika*, then, the author's preparation for death was of just as much, if not more, significance as the arrangements made for his or her heirs. The opportunity to purge oneself of sin and to reassert one's membership of the Christian community was often a preliminary step towards positive action which might be expected to gain spiritual rewards.[9]

Thus both Attaliates and Boïlas were at pains to stress their orthodox upbringing: 'From childhood, [wrote Attaliates] I was instructed in religion by my faithful parents, who held from *their* ancestors decent and proper attitudes towards God.' Boïlas expressed the same idea: 'I was from the beginning and through my ancestors, of a free estate and sound nature and in all ways Orthodox according to the precept and rule of the seven holy ecumenical councils.' Gregory Pakourianos, a Georgian, used a similar formulation, but with an understandable emphasis on his people's acceptance of Chalcedonian doctrine. Thus donations of land or money to the church later in life were to be seen as actions totally in keeping with their birthright as orthodox believers, the logical culmination of their lives as Christians.[10]

But in all these cases, the donors related an interim stage in their spiritual development, one which had taken up the better part of their lives. They described, in very similar terms, two apparently mutually exclusive factors: their own religious laxity complemented, to their surprise, by distinct signs of supernatural protection and the intervention of God's providence. As Attaliates put it:

> I, throughout my life, have remained scornful of His unutterable patience towards me and His goodness towards me because of my many severe faults . . . For not only did I see His desire and not perform it, and returned the talent given to me without any profit . . . but I was also forgetful of His many gifts and graces and of my happy situation and far from turning aside from evil, I allowed myself to be dominated by bad habits and insensitivity.[11]

---

[9] Byzantine wills are a neglected area of study, but see A. Steinwenter, 'Byzantinische Mönchstestamente', *Aegyptus*, 12 (1932), 55–64.

[10] *Diataxis* of Attaliates, p. 19; Testament of Boïlas, p. 265 (Vryonis); p. 21 (Lemerle); Pakourianos, chapter 1, p. 31.

[11] *Diataxis* of Attaliates, p. 21.

Both Pakourianos and Boïlas echoed this theme of protection, all the more vivid in their cases since they had both, in the course of eventful careers, travelled far from their homelands. For Irene Doukaina, a member of the imperial family, the agent of protection was the Theotokos, the Mother of God herself; the *prooimion* to the *typikon* of her foundation was a panegyric to its dedicatee, both as protectress of Irene and her family and as guardian of the Byzantine people and of the city of Constantinople.[12]

The formalised repentance of such passages was intended to re-establish the credentials of the donors as pious Christians, of crucial importance since their gifts could have no merit unless given in the correct spirit of humility. In recognising and showing gratitude for the divine protection of the past, the intercession of Christ, the Virgin and the saints might perhaps be assured in the future and this explains why the establishments mentioned in the *typika* were often actually granted *to* them just as property might be given or bequeathed to other individuals. Their approval and protection were evoked to protect the foundation from attack, as in the case of the *Diataxis* of Attaliates: 'I sanctify all [my property] to the most great and merciful God and I appoint Him heir [*kleronomos*] and guardian [*pronoetes*] and master of all this donation.' Eustathios Boïlas appointed as administrators of his Testament 'the Lord Pantokrator and Her who bore Him without seed'.[13]

In this context, too, the wording of the penal clauses in these documents is also significant. The 318 Fathers of the Church were invoked as protectors; their anathemata would fall upon anyone who broke the conditions of the gift. Any transgressor would be numbered amongst the Jews and the crucifiers of Christ, thus emphasising that such behaviour would immediately place him outside the community of Christians. The function of these penal clauses was not so much to act as a deterrent to future generations (although their very existence does indicate that contravention or challenge to the terms of *typika* was at least envisaged) as to provide, in the first instance, a further indication of the spiritual worthiness of the donor. The terminology emphasised correct doctrine; opposition would be a dangerous sign of religious non-conformity.[14]

The process of establishing the donor as a worthy candidate for

---

[12] Kécharitôménè, pp. 19–29.

[13] *Diataxis* of Attaliates, p. 25; Testament of Boïlas, pp. 272 (Vryonis), 29 (Lemerle).

[14] For penal clauses, see, for example, *Diataxis* of Attaliates, p. 33. On the 318 Fathers of the Church (those who traditionally attended the First Council of Nicaea), see M. Aubineau, 'Les 318 serviteurs d'Abraham et le nombre des Pères au concile de Nicée (325)', *Revue d'Histoire Ecclésiastique*, 61 (1966), 5–43.

divine favour and his foundation as an establishment deserving of divine protection was often taken further in wills and *typika* by deliberate and formal abandonment of behaviour which was widely practised, but which Byzantines knew in their hearts to be contrary to Christian morality: in particular, the owning of slaves. These were almost always household slaves; mentions of agricultural slaves are extremely rare after the sixth century. In the wills of Kale Pakouriane and Eustathios Boïlas, it is made clear that not only had large numbers of slaves been manumitted and given grants of land on which to establish themselves, but that this had been done some time previously. This was not merely a continuation of the old Roman custom, but a process which was taking place against an background of increasing opposition to the institution of slavery, especially expressed by the church. Landowners such as Boïlas, while unable to rid themselves of the view that slaves were necessary to the running of their households, knew that ecclesiastical disapproval of servitude meant that they should, if possible, cleanse themselves of this moral stain before they died.[15]

Thus the *prooimia* and, indeed, the provisions of wills and *typika*, reflect a determination to make proper preparation for death, a preparation in which donation and endowment had an important part to play. These actions reflected a degree of concern amongst Byzantines about the fate of the soul after death. The Byzantine church maintained that the fellowship and solidarity of Christians was not broken by the death of any of its members. Through the intercession of the living members of the church, the dead might be brought closer to God. But where the Western tradition emphasised, in a rather legalistic manner, the need either to provide 'fruits of repentance' before death or to provide satisfaction in the form of 'purgatory pains' (punishment by fire) afterwards, Byzantine theologians interpreted sin as a moral disease which could be healed by Divine forbearance, rather than a transgression or crime which was to be punished by Divine wrath, and they emphasised that purification after death was to be seen in a more allegorical sense of 'darkness', 'separation' or 'remorse'. They did not allow that any final state of bliss or condemnation could be assigned before the Last Day. But the time between death and the Last Judgement might be rather long and it was what became of the souls of the departed during that time – in the

---

[15] *Ivirôn*, II, nos. 44 (1090) and 47 (1098); Testament of Boïlas, pp. 270–1 (Vryonis), 26 (Lemerle). For an introduction to the institution of slavery in Byzantium, see A. Hadjinicolaou-Marava, *Recherches sur la vie des esclaves dans le monde byzantin* (Collection de l'Institut français d'Athènes, XLV, Athens, 1950) and see Kaplan, *Les hommes et la terre*, pp. 275–7. A Byzantine formula of manumission, which emphasises the master's hope that he will thus obtain divine charity, is published by C. Verlinden, *L'esclavage dans l'Europe médiévale* (2 vols., Ghent, 1977), II, p. 986.

so-called 'middle state' – which exercised the Byzantine imagination and had important practical ramifications.[16]

Although the Byzantine attitude to Purgatory before the debates with the Latins on the subject beginning in the thirteenth century is a neglected area of study, evidence from one of the longer versions of the Life of St Basil the Younger, written in the mid- to late tenth century, suggests that they found an attractive image in the concept of a spiritual journey, taking place, as did earthly journeys, over a period of time and subject, as were they, to bureaucratic controls in the form of toll-gates and taxes. Each of these barriers was thought to be manned by an angelic 'customs officer', and each represented a sin such as falsehood, pride, usury, adultery and fornication; at the latter gate, it was said, the largest number of souls was refused further passage. A worthy soul would pass through each of the gates, especially if his guardian angel were there to argue his case (much like a Byzantine lawyer defending a client), to provide 'payment' in the form of prayers and good deeds of particularly worthy individuals (in this particular case Basil the Younger gives a bag of symbolic *nomismata* to the guardian angels of the worthy lady Theodora 'for I by the grace of Christ am rich and have enough and to spare for my soul'), and to bring forward examples of true repentance and charitable action, such as those detailed in *typika*.[17]

Monastic endowment and donation, then, was a major part of a process of ensuring the maximum amount of intercession for the soul after death. Just as in life Byzantines knew only too well the value of powerful patrons and protectors, so, in death, they hoped that heavenly beings – saints, the Virgin and even Christ Himself – would appear before God on their behalf. Such hopes are clearly expressed in the donor inscriptions to be found in churches and monasteries and, indeed, in the fact that patrons and donors often had themselves portrayed in the presence of their heavenly protectors in the decorative schemes. A number of examples can be advanced from the Cappadocian cave monasteries. In Karanlık Kilise, for instance, the Deesis scene in the main apse shows two figures

[16] See, generally, J. Le Goff, *The birth of Purgatory*, translated A. Goldhammer (London, 1984), but see the doubts of, for example, G. R. Edwards, 'Purgatory: "Birth" or evolution', *Journal of Ecclesiastical History*, 36 (1985), 634–46. Discussion on the Greek teaching on the 'middle state' usually concentrates on the period from the twelfth century onwards; see, for example, C. N. Tsirpanlis, *Introduction to eastern patristic thought and orthodox theology* (Collegeville, Minn., 1991), pp. 68–72, 205–11. The effect of Latin teaching on Purgatory on the later Byzantine church is discussed by J. Meyendorff, *Byzantine theology* (London/Oxford, 1978), pp. 96, 111, 220–2.
[17] For earlier Byzantine views on death and the afterlife, see C. Mango, *Byzantium: the empire of New Rome* (London, 1980), pp. 164–5 and, particularly, G. Every, 'Toll-gates on the air way', *Eastern Churches Review*, 8 (1976), 139–51, especially pp. 142–8.

kneeling at the feet of Christ, both with a similar inscription which on the left reads 'Entreaty of the servant of God, Nikephoros, priest' and on the right refers to a layman, Bassianos. In Direkli Kilise, decorated between 976 and 1025, a donor inscription reads '(For the forgiveness) of the sins of your servant [name lost]'. In Yusuf Koç Kilisesi (dating from the early to mid-eleventh century), three donors are portrayed in attitudes of submission and request: a panel depicting the Annunciation on the north wall of the church includes a small figure kneeling at the Virgin's feet, with the beginning of an inscription 'Entreaty of the servant . . .'. A small, possibly female figure kneels to the left of St Prokopios on the east wall and grips the saint's foot in supplication; a similar figure next to St Demetrios on the south wall stands next to the saint and makes a gesture of request with both hands towards him.[18]

The attitudes in which the donors or patrons were portrayed (kneeling, holding the foot of the saint or extending their arms in prayer towards him) are precisely those used in the secular world to indicate humility and submission. The words of the inscriptions might vary and, indeed, often provide useful indications of the motives behind the donation, but they all had the same aim in view: the wish that the offering of the foundation, the building or its decoration should find favour in Heaven and that spiritual protection, if not reward, might then be forthcoming. This body of aspirations is well summed up in an inscription in the Hermitage of Niketas the Stylite (possibly late tenth century) in a portrayal of John the Baptist, which identifies the donor, the direction of the patronage and its purpose: 'For the glory of the Holy Hierarchy, Eustratios, the famous *kleisourarch* of Zeugos and Klados, divinely inspired, offered this service. Protect him. Amen.' A parallel from another medium can be drawn by reference to an illumination from the tenth-century *Bible of Leo* (Vat. reg. gr. 1), in which Makarios, the *hegoumenos* of an unknown monastery dedicated to St Nicholas, and its founder the *protospatharios* Constantine (Leo's deceased brother) are pictured at the feet of Nicholas himself. The scene is framed by an epigram which requests that the founder may find a speedy path to Paradise and the *hegoumenos* may also be given grace. Thus the purpose of such depictions was not only commemorative, but also supplicatory, and served to remind the onlookers that there was no real barrier between the living and the dead. For although the donors were portrayed in the presence of the saints, who could be thought of as

---

[18] See Rodley, *Cave monasteries*, pp. 53–6 (Karanlık Kilise); A. P. Kazhdan and A. W. Epstein, *Change in Byzantine culture in the eleventh and twelfth centuries* (The transformation of the classical heritage, VIII, Berkeley/Los Angeles/London, 1985), p. 221 (read 'Basil' rather than 'Bassianos'), 95 (Direkli Kilise), 156–7 (Yusuf Koç Kilisesi).

living 'beyond' the earth, the prayers of those left behind to read the dedicatory inscriptions were also solicited.[19]

In many cases, however, assurance was made doubly sure by donors and patrons such as Attaliates or Irene Doukaina embracing the monastic life as they grew older and felt the shadow of death coming closer. But it was a step which could be taken by all ranks in Byzantine society, assuming that they could gain access to a monastic house. The landowner Genesios, who made a will in southern Italy in 1086, may not have been an aristocrat, but the sentiments he expressed tally with those found in the documents drawn up by more august individuals. The reason for drawing up the testament was the familiar one of sickness and 'seeing, as in a mirror, the certainty of my end'. To prepare for this eventuality, Genesios had already entered a monastery and decided 'to separate myself from the confusion of this troublesome world'. This course seems, in fact, to have been particularly popular among aristocratic women, who feared the isolation and loss of influence that would naturally follow upon widowhood, or who wished to make provision for unmarried or widowed female relatives. Irene Doukaina's foundation of the Theotokos Kecharitomene is a prime example of a house where the *typikon* clearly stated that any of the empress's female descendants who wished to enter the monastic house should be allowed to do so. Questions of suitability or novitiate simply did not arise. But it was not only imperial ladies who could take this course. By the time she drew up her own will in 1098, Kale Pakouriane had, as we have seen, already been the nun, Maria for five years, following the death of her husband Symbatios, though it would appear that she followed a monastic life in her own home rather than in a nunnery.[20]

Although the foundation or patronage of monastic houses was often linked to concern for the post mortem fortunes of the founder or his or

[19] The best-known Byzantine attitude of submission is, of course, the *proskynesis*, seen being performed by (probably) the Emperor Leo VI to Christ in the mosaic above the Imperial Door from the inner narthex to the nave of Hagia Sophia in Istanbul; see H. Kähler with C. Mango, *Hagia Sophia*, translated E. Childs (London, 1967), plate 90. For the *kleisourarch* Eustratios, see Rodley, *Cave monasteries*, pp. 187–8. Since the duty of this officer was to command detachments guarding passes, Rodley suggests that 'Zeugos' should perhaps be read as 'Zygos', a pass in the Anti-Taurus range; the whereabouts of Klados is unknown. See F. Hild and H. Hellenkamper, *Kilikien und Isaurien (TIB, v,* 2 vols., Vienna, 1990), i, p. 465. For the *Bible of Leo*, see Cormack, *Writing in gold*, pp. 165–6 and plates 59–60.
[20] *Diatyposis* of the Monk Genesios; Carbone, no. 12 (1086); Kécharitôménè, chapter 4, pp. 37–9. *Ivirôn*, ii, no. 46 (1093). Kale/Maria Pakouriane accepts the position of executrix of her husband's will and indicates that she had already become a nun and surrounded herself with a 'religious entourage', though she still lived in considerable style in Constantinople; see *Ivirôn*, ii, p. 174.

her family and was, perhaps, the single strongest motive for foundation, there were other events which could be thought worthy of similar acts of commemoration. Gratitude for a successful period in office, or, in the case of soldiers, a successful campaign might act as motivating factors. In contrast, improper behaviour could be expiated by donation. In both cases, the donors were eager to place themselves in a proper relationship with God; in the first case that of thanksgiving, in the second, that of repentance. Two well-known monuments admirably illustrate this point. The left apse of the so-called 'Dove-Cote' church at Çavuşin in Cappadocia is decorated with a group of five figures in imperial robes, one of whom stands before a throne. An inscription identifies him as the Emperor Nikephoros Phokas and three of the other figures have been identified as those of the Empress Theophano, Nikephoros' brother the *kouropalates* Leo Phokas, and their father Bardas Phokas. The portrayal of the Phokas family forms part of a triumph scene which is completed by a nearby representation of two mounted figures in procession, who have now been identified as the general (and later emperor) John Tzimiskes and the Armenian commander, Melias. The decoration of the church was commissioned, it is thought, by donors who were probably provincial landowners of relatively humble rank and it commemorated Nikephoros' triumphs – either his access to the throne in 963 or, perhaps more plausibly, the campaigns of 964–5 which culminated not only in the capture of the important Arab-held city of Tarsos, but of important relics of the Cross which had been kept there.[21]

In contrast, early twelfth-century inscriptions in the Church of the Holy Trinity attached to the main church of the Monastery of St Chrysostomos at Koutsovendis in Cyprus (founded c. 1090), clearly indicate that the motives of the donor were those of remorse. One which has survived almost intact declares that the *doux* (military commander) of Cyprus, Eumathios Philokales (already met with as one of the circle around St Cyril Phileotes), 'built unto Thee this church from the very foundations to expiate the wicked actions which he has erred in committing'. The circumstances which led to this act of contrition are obscure, but the post he held on the island would have given ample opportunity for both political and financial peccadilloes. Philokales was *doux* of Cyprus from c. 1092–1102 and from 1110 to before 1118 and although described in glowing terms by Anna Komnene in the *Alexiad*, was characterised in the Life of St Cyril Phileotes as a cruel and

---

[21] See Morris, 'Two faces', pp. 107–8. L. Rodley, 'The Pigeon-house church, Çavuşin', *JÖB*, 33 (1983), 201–39 gives a full description of the monument and N. Thierry, 'Un portrait de Jean Tzimiskès en Cappadoce', *TM*, 9 (1985), 477–84 identifies the mounted figures.

unpitying governor and a 'wolf'. He was also attacked for his rapacity by Nicholas Mouzalon, Archbishop of Cyprus until his resignation in 1110–11, and it has been suggested that Philokales' monastic patronage was a public sign of contrition for his part in this affair. This inscription, then, represents something rather different from formalised repentance at the end of the donor's life.[22]

The occasions for donation might, therefore, vary, but they were usually associated with a moment at which a Byzantine felt that some transfer of his or her worldly goods to a spiritual milieu was advisable. This was a motive which could reach right down to the humblest levels of society, for, as the well-known novel of Basil II (996) put it, even small landowners might decide to devote their property and themselves to the religious life:

> For they say that it happens in many of the villages that the peasant builds a church on his land and with the permission of his fellow villagers, grants it all his property, then becomes a monk and spends the rest of his life there.[23]

Indeed, many of the hermitages and monasteries of Cappadocia were probably not founded by rich and powerful aristocrats, but by the local landowners of the region, who wished to associate themselves with sites (especially those of hermitages) which had already gained some kind of spiritual aura. A detailed study of donor and patron inscriptions from other parts of the empire might well confirm this view, although it would be beset by the perpetual problem of accurately identifying both the names and status of the individuals concerned.[24]

While a personal concern to try to ensure the salvation of his soul was undoubtedly the most pressing motive behind monastic patronage, the Byzantine donor well knew that this was a task which did not end with his own death. His family was responsible for the performance of the instructions contained in his will or *typikon* and these documents themselves very often also reveal a concern for the spiritual welfare of the family group as well as for the individual who had initiated the donation. In this respect, as in others, Byzantines did not care to act alone; they involved the present and future members of their immediate families and expected to be so involved in their turn. In many cases, members of the donor's family retained a very close control over the affairs of monastic

<hr/>

[22] Stylianou and Stylianou, *Painted churches of Cyprus*, pp. 456–63. For Eumathios Philokales, see chapter 4, p. 105 and for his allegedly venal activity in Cyprus, Galatariotou, *Making of a saint*, pp. 192–3, 456–63.
[23] Zepos, I, coll. iii, document XIX, see p. 263.
[24] See Rodley, *Cave monasteries*, chapter 6, pp. 223–53.

houses and were jointly responsible for the maintenance of memorial ceremonies and of prayers for the dead – a vital part of the spiritual services that monasteries performed for their founders.[25]

Family solidarity is, in fact, one of the clearest impressions to emerge from a reading of the eleventh-century *typika* for the new coenobitic foundations. But it was limited in scope; Byzantine donors did not involve distant relatives either in the running of their houses, or in a share of the spiritual benefits bestowed by the prayers of the monks. The *Diataxis* of Michael Attaliates clearly indicated how far its liturgical provisions should extend. Attaliates' first concern was for the upkeep of his own tomb; eight *nomismata* per year were granted to the Church of St George Kyparissiotes in Constantinople for this purpose. Ten *nomismata* were to be paid to the same church to ensure the performance of the correct memorial prayers for himself, his two dead wives Sophia and Irene and his children, Irenikos and Kale, who had also predeceased him. Other donations were to be made to the Monasteries of St Nicholas *tou Phalkonos* (three *nomismata*) and St George and to the Nunnery of St Prokopios (two *nomismata*) – all at Rhaidestos – and the Church of the Theotokos *tes Daphnes* at Constantinople (two *nomismata*). His name was to be entered upon the diptychs (memorial lists) in these houses and *trisagia* (special prayers) were to be said for the emperors in his memory. He also made careful provision that if the monies for these memorials were not paid by his heirs after the second or third request of the *hegoumenoi* concerned, they could be directly deducted from the revenues of his property. But the initial responsibility for these observances was firmly placed on Attaliates' heir (his son, Theodore) and his male descendants.[26]

The same concern for the immediate family can be seen in other similar documents. Eustathios Boïlas stipulated that his parents and children should be remembered and Gregory Pakourianos, although he had no children himself, was still concerned to commemorate the memory of his near relatives: his father, the *archon ton archonton* Pakourianos, who was to be remembered on the Thursday of Easter Week, and his brother Aspasios, who was to be commemorated on the day he had died, the Feast of St Eustathios (20 September). The monks of his house

---

[25] See chapter 6 for family control over monastic organisation. For the extent of family commemorations, see Morris, 'Byzantine aristocracy', pp. 119–23.

[26] *Diataxis* of Attaliates, pp. 35, 45, 47, 49, 55. For the Church of St George *Kyparissiotes*, see Janin, *Eglises et monastères*, p. 70. It was situated in the district of Psamathia. The Church of the Theotokos *tes Daphnes* (Janin, p. 173) was inside the Palace of Daphne, the oldest part of the imperial Great Palace. For the *trisagion* see N. K. Moran, *The ordinary chants of the Byzantine mass* (2 vols., Hamburg, 1975), I, pp. 57–83. See Galatariotou, 'Byzantine *ktetorika typika*', p. 93, note 30 for commemorations in other *typika*.

were abjured not to let his own name be forgotten and to ensure, most importantly of all, that the rites were correctly observed. Pakourianos quoted the New Testament text 'Each shall receive his own reward according to his own labour', and it is clear that the labour consisted not only in the very act of establishing a religious house and in charitable donations associated with it, but in making provision for an annual commemoration of these actions through the memorial liturgies. In all these cases, the familial responsibility was clearly expressed, but only the immediate family was involved. Parents (though sometimes only of the founder), spouses, brothers, sisters and children were commemorated; more distant relatives were only incidentally involved if the founder's direct line ran out. The family concerned here was essentially vertical; it moved up and down the line from generation to generation and there was obvious concern that the power of monastic prayer should be concentrated within fairly narrow parameters – a factor which undoubtedly played an important part in the consolidation of family cohesion and loyalty.[27]

In visual terms, this loyalty was focused on the family tombs which came increasingly to be concentrated in the houses founded or patronised by family members. There is no doubt that, like their Western counterparts, members of the Byzantine aristocracy made great efforts to ensure their own burials not merely within monastic precincts, but actually inside monastic churches. Canon and civil law might dictate otherwise, but spiritual instinct dictated that those who could manage to make such arrangements were eager to be buried in the most sacred area of the most highly regarded spiritual institution, and this meant inside a monastic church. From the mid-tenth century, in fact, even members of the imperial families, who, it might have been expected, would have wished to emphasise their legitimacy by continuing to be buried in the two great imperial mausolea at the Church of the Holy Apostles, began to move towards the creation of private dynastic chapels in their own foundations in Constantinople and after 1028, their tombs were no longer to be found in the Holy Apostles. The development can be seen to have begun with such foundations as the Convent of the Myrelaion (Bodrum Camii) built by the Emperor Romanos I Lekapenos c. 920–2 and the burial place of his wife Theodora (922); his sons Christopher (931) and Constantine (946, whose body was placed in the same tomb as his wife, Helena, who had died at some time after 940) and, ultimately, of Romanos himself, whose

[27] Testament of Boïlas, p. 270 (Vryonis), p. 26 (Lemerle); Pakourianos, chapters 20–1, pp. 95–103, cf. 1 Cor. 3: 8. See the pertinent remark (in the context of fifteenth-century England) in J. T. Rosenthal, *The purchase of paradise* (London, 1972), p. 17: 'Spiritually, if not politically, the family was a nucleated one.'

body was brought in 948 from the island of Prote in the Sea of Marmara where he had died in exile. This tendency became stronger in the eleventh century – Constantine Monomachos, for example, was buried in the monastic complex of St George of the Mangana, which he had founded – and culminated at the beginning of the twelfth century with the foundation of the Monastery of the Pantokrator, a grand series of buildings including a hospital, which had at its centre a chapel containing the tombs of the Komnenoi.[28]

The move by the imperial family groups towards these more private expressions of piety was not only an indication of a change in the way in which they viewed the nature of the imperial system (and the so-called 'family' government of the Komnenoi was the culmination of this process of change), but also echoed what had been noticeable in somewhat less august circles for some time. Many of the cave monasteries of Cappadocia, which were mostly constructed or decorated at the end of the tenth century and the first half of the eleventh, contained burial chambers which were far too small to contain all the members of the community of monks and may well, therefore, have been intended for the families of the monastic founders or benefactors. The founders of the *koinobia* of the eleventh century certainly expected that they would be buried within their houses and those who made particularly generous contributions of money or land expected that they would thus earn burial within the monastic precincts.[29]

The example of Symbatios Pakourianos is a case in point. From his will and that of his wife Kale/Maria, it is clear that specific and detailed arrangements were made whereby he would be buried within the Iviron Monastery on Mount Athos. His own testament declared that his corpse should be transported to the house and buried there, the expenses being undertaken by his widow. She would also provide for the cost of the subsequent commemorations and for the charitable donations which it

[28] For the burials of Byzantine emperors until the eleventh century, see P. Grierson, 'The tombs and obits of the Byzantine emperors (337–1042)', *DOP*, 16 (1962), 3–60 and for those in the Myrelaion, Striker, *Myrelaion*, pp. 6–9. See also Janin, *Eglises et monastères*, pp. 70–6 (St George of the Mangana) and for the Pantokrator complex, P. Gautier, 'Le typikon du Christ Sauveur Pantocrator', *REB*, 32 (1974), 1–145 (or separately printed, Paris, 1974). P. Magdalino, 'Observations on the *Nea Ekklesia* of Basil I', *JÖB*, 37 (1987), 51–66, especially p. 62, demonstrates how this church can be seen as a precursor of the family monastic foundations of the tenth and eleventh centuries.
[29] For monastic burials in general, see Galatariotou, 'Byzantine *ktetorika typika*', p. 96. In Cappadocia burial chambers have been identified at Hallaç (eleventh century) which has three graves and space for two more: Şahinefendi (eleventh century) and Karanlık Kilise (mid-eleventh century) each with two graves; Selime Kalesi (late tenth–early eleventh century): a chamber with one grave in it; Eski Gümüş (tomb chamber c. 1050–1075): two graves in one chamber, see Rodley, *Cave monasteries*, p. 248.

was customary to make on the occasion of a rich man's death. In her testament, Kale/Maria reported that she had indeed arranged for Symbatios' burial at Iviron and that she had paid the monks 7 lb of *chichata* (*nomismata* of some kind, the precise meaning is unknown) for this privilege. At the same time, for the salvation of her own soul as well as his (since she would have been aware that she herself could not be buried on Athos), she granted Iviron an estate at Radolibos (modern Rodolibos) in eastern Macedonia and requested the monks in return to perform commemorative liturgies for her as well. In addition, she made the monastery a gift of two icons to be placed on Symbatios' tomb, a silver cross and two candlesticks.[30]

The siting of a burial within a monastic foundation was thus the culmination of the process of identification of an individual or his or her family with the establishment concerned. It often helped to emphasise existing feelings of local identity. Michael Attaliates' foundations in Constantinople and Rhaidestos, for instance, were built on land which he had purchased from relatives. The Monastery of Christ *tou Panoiktirmonos* (the 'All-merciful') stood on property originally belonging to his sister-in-law, the *protospatharissa* Anastaso; the *ptochotropheion* (poor-house) at Rhaidestos on land originally acquired by his aunt by marriage, the nun Euphrosyne. Similar family or professional associations dictated the choice of churches or monasteries to receive donations or to be entrusted with commemorations. The Church of St George Kyparissiotes was almost certainly a foundation patronised by the Attaliates family; the Nunnery of St Prokopios and the two other monasteries in Rhaidestos were in a town where Attaliates had family and possibly business connections. His devotion to the Church of the Theotokos *tes Daphnes* in Constantinople might have been associated with his senatorial rank, since it was in this church that the emperor, on the 1 January each year, gave laurel wreaths to members of the senate.[31]

---

[30] *Ivirôn*, II, nos. 44; 46; 47 (1090; 1093; 1098) for the Pakourianos gifts to Iviron and the arrangements for Symbatios' burial. The sum given by Kale/Maria for the burial was 7 lb of *chichata*; see *Ivirôn*, II, p. 153, not 7,000 lb, as wrongly printed in the Iverites edition of the Pakourianos wills, which transliterates *chiliadas* (thousands) instead of *chichatas* (see *Ivirôn*, II, no. 47, l. 13), causing an over-calculation of Kale's fortune in coin in M. F. Hendy, *Studies in the Byzantine monetary economy c. 300–1450* (Cambridge, 1985), p. 210.

[31] Monastery of Christ Panoiktirmonos: Janin, *Eglises et monastères*, pp. 512–13; *Diataxis* of Attaliates, p. 25 (land of Euphrosyne), p. 27 (land of Anastaso). For Attaliates' senatorial rank, see *Diataxis*, p. 19, Chrysobull of Michael Doukas (1074) (Dölger, *Regesten*, no. 1005), *Diataxis*, pp. 101–9, p. 103 and R. Guilland, *Recherches sur les institutions byzantines* (2 vols., Berliner Byzantinische Arbeiten, XXXV, Berlin/Amsterdam, 1967), II, p. 74. The growing importance of Rhaidestos and its trade with the Adriatic was discussed by G. I. Bratianu, 'Une expérience d'économie dirigée: le monopole du blé à Byzance au XIe siècle', *B*, 9 (1934), 643–62, especially p. 655, see now A. Harvey, *Economic expansion*

The family's place of origin, though not necessarily of domicile, was another aspect of localism emphasised by the direction of donation. Eustathios Boïlas finally settled in lands on the eastern frontier of the empire, but in his will he made provisions for donations to a church in his birth-place of Cappadocia. Gregory Pakourianos' *Typikon* is perhaps the best illustration of this process of territorial association, for he was establishing roots in a territory far from his homeland in Georgia and initiating local links elsewhere. The establishment of the Monastery at Bačkovo was the culmination of a long process of land acquisition in Thrace and Macedonia, to which the long list of confirmatory chrysobulls which he consigned to the Monastery of Bačkovo and to the Great Church of Hagia Sophia in Constantinople for safe-keeping bears eloquent witness. The property of the brothers Pakourianos (Aspasios and Gregory) was centred on three closely defined geographical regions: that around Stenimachos (in the Rhodope Mountains) including Bačkovo and the lands granted to the monastery; in the Stephaniana region to the south of Serres (modern Serrai) and around Mosynopolis (6 km west of present day Kumutzena on the Thracian coast) in the theme of Boleron, east of Thessalonike. So Gregory's action in donating lands to a monastic house in one of these regions was a sure sign of his own full identification with it. Though he had no children and was not perpetuating family ties in that sense, his prohibition on Greeks entering his foundation was a similarly exclusive action. In his case, fellow countrymen, his Georgian 'kin', were charged with the perpetuation of the memory of the donor, but the process was essentially the same. It reflected the same concern as that shown by Symbatios Pakourianos' wish to be buried in the Georgian Monastery of Iviron. In both cases, the Georgians still achieved burial among their own, but in a newly established 'native land', a replacement for their lost territories in the east.[32]

in the Byzantine empire (Cambridge, 1989), pp. 236–8. Attaliates himself provides the only mention of the attempted establishment of an imperial monopoly of corn sales in Rhaidestos; his might have been amongst the business interests threatened. See Attaliates, pp. 202–4 and H. Antoniadis-Bibicou, *Recherches sur les douanes à Byzance; l'octava, le 'kommerkion' et les commerciaires* (Cahiers des Annales, xx, Paris, 1963), pp. 144, 186, 187. For the location of Attaliates properties, see *Diataxis*, pp. 25–31, Lemerle, *Cinq études*, pp. 101–2 and Kaplan, *Les hommes et la terre*, pp. 336–7.
[32] Testament of Boïlas, p. 271 (Vryonis), p. 27 (Lemerle), for the Church of the Hierarch Modestos (not 'Three Hierarchs', *pace* Vryonis) built by his mother in Cappadocia. Pakourianos, pp. 35–45; 125–31 for the Pakourianos properties and their chrysobulls. For their location, see C. Asdracha, *La région des Rhodopes aux XIIIe et XIVe siècles. Etude de géographie historique* (Athens, 1976) and her gazetteer in Lemerle, *Cinq études*, pp. 176–9. These holdings, and further lands owned by the Georgian monks of Iviron in Thrace and Macedonia (including the donation of Kale/Maria Pakouriane) are further discussed in chapter 8.

Where aristocratic and wealthy patrons were concerned, then, the option of founding and endowing monastic houses was always present. This was particularly true in the eleventh century, when new foundations rather than restoration of existing houses were undertaken both by imperial and aristocratic founders – a matter of some importance given the supposed financial plight of the empire at this time. Conspicuous expenditure, such as the fortune spent by Constantine IX Monomachos on the monastic complex of St George of the Mangana, was emulated by lesser members of the imperial families and by such aristocrats or successful state servants as Attaliates, Gregory Pakourianos or the mysterious monk Timothy who, although officially the second *ktetor* (founder) of the Monastery of the Theotokos Evergetis in Constantinople, was responsible for the construction of 'magnificent' buildings and a church and the endowment of the establishment with books, icons and holy vessels, after the death of the first founder, Paul. While such men might make donations to already existing monastic houses, it was both praiseworthy and, more importantly, within their financial means, to found and endow houses themselves.[33]

But the construction and endowment of great coenobitic houses was certainly not within the economic grasp of the majority of the population. Clearly, less wealthy patrons had either to content themselves with small establishments (such as those described in the novel of Basil II) or to channel their gifts into already existing houses. Again, the factors which determined the direction that this level of patronage took might well be territorial and often reflect the efforts of individuals to strengthen their local ties by making donations to the familiar houses of the area. The hagiographic accounts of the foundations of western Asia Minor provide examples of this tendency, as does the history of the monasteries on Athos. St Paul of Latros' foundation of the Stylos received gifts from a certain Michael, an official in charge of the *basilika ktemata* (imperial lands) round Ephesos. St Lazaros' first foundation on Mount Galesion, the Lavra of St Marina, received gifts from a rich woman from Calabria, Judith, who had recently settled in the area, and from the metropolitan of Ephesos himself. On Kos, the local inhabitants assisted Christodoulos with the construction of his monastery at Pile and much of the landed wealth of the Athonite houses came from the accumulation of the gifts of lesser landowners. In Cappadocia, too, where the few identifiable figures

[33] See C. Mango, 'Les monuments de l'architecture du XIᵉ siècle et leur signification historique et sociale', *TM*, 6 (1976), 351–64, especially pp. 353–5; Evergétis, chapters 2–3, pp. 15–19. See chapters 9 and 10 for the financial position of the empire in the eleventh century.

of donors appear to be people with local connections, the same tendency is apparent.[34]

In the case of both local donors and those who came from further afield, patronage of a particular house often followed naturally upon the creation of a relationship between the *hegoumenos* of the monastery and the individual concerned. It is here that an obvious connection between the activities of the charismatic holy men and the subsequent fortunes of the houses they founded can be drawn. St Lazaros' cure of Eustathios Mitas (uncle of John, the *dioiketes* of Ephesos) was followed by a 'gift' to the saint's monastery; a certain Nikephoros, son of Euthymios, assured by Lazaros of his reinstatement in imperial service after involvement in the revolt of Constantine Barys in the mid-eleventh century, donated 286 *nomismata* in gratitude and Maria Skleraina, the mistress of Constantine Monomachos, donated the considerable sum of 700 *nomismata*, perhaps in appreciation of Lazaros' apparent acceptance of her own irregular moral position. Many examples of lesser amounts could be cited from saints' lives and they serve to emphasise the point that, for the vast majority of Byzantines, gifts to monasteries consisted of relatively small donations, often as a sign of appreciation and recognition of spiritual 'services rendered'. But not all gifts were accepted; those from unworthy sources, such as the gold-embroidered robes offered by Constantine Barys himself to St Lazaros, or the land presented by the courtier Constantine Choirosphaktes to St Cyril Phileotes, do not seem to have found favour with the holy men concerned. The acceptance of a donation of money or other gift thus served as important a purpose as its offering, for it contributed to the process of the recognition of the donor as a worthy Christian.[35]

The acceptance of the spiritual 'suitability' of donors by those who were recognised as following the highest form of the spiritual life was of particular significance at the imperial level. Imperial foundation and donation to monastic houses was expected by holders of the office, but the direction this took was often indicative of a deliberate attempt to ensure a form of spiritual continuity similar to that political stability implied by the nature of the imperial office. Imperial patronage was just as much subject to the spiritual inclinations of the ruler (whether male or female) or his own local loyalties as was that of other donors, but there could be another,

---

[34] Life of St Paul the Younger, chapter 30, p. 140; Life of St Lazaros, chapter 33, p. 519; chapter 34, p. 520; *Hypotyposis* of Christodoulos, p. 63 and Vranoussi, *Hagiologika keimena*, pp. 100–7. The accumulation of Athonite land-holdings is discussed in chapters 8 and 9.

[35] Life of St Lazaros, chapter 103, p. 540; chapter 106, p. 541; chapter 245, p. 584 for donations accepted; chapter 105, p. 540 for the refusal of the gift of Constantine Barys and Life of St Cyril Phileotes, chapter 34, pp. 143–6 (370–2) for that of Constantine Choirosphaktes.

political dimension to his generosity. The general monastic duty to pray for the fortunes of the emperor and his subjects (regardless of the individual merits of the holders of power) was often reciprocated by the continuation of patronage begun by political opponents by those who later ousted them from power. Imperial patronage of particularly powerful houses (such as the Lavra on Mount Athos) was thus usually continued by each holder of the imperial power simply as a function of his office.

In the appendix the donations and privileges to major monastic centres granted by individual rulers of the period have been tabulated, although the information cannot be considered complete. It does, however, indicate a remarkable continuity in state patronage of the most important monasteries. But, in addition, more precise information on individual imperial monastic preferences does exist. It is well known, for example, that the Emperor Nikephoros Phokas' novel of 964, while castigating the great coenobitic houses for their excesses of wealth and land, clearly expressed his admiration for the inhabitants of 'the so-called *lavrai*', a monastic system familiar to him from visits to Michael Maleïnos on Mount Kyminas and his own interest in the affairs of St Athanasios' foundation on Athos. His lavish patronage of the Lavra there was a direct consequence of this approval. Similarly, Constantine Monomachos' grants to the Nea Mone on Chios and Nikephoros Botaniates' patronage of Christodoulos' monasteries on Kos and Patmos indicate support for the monastic ideals of their founders. Alexios Komnenos, though described by Nicholas Kataskepenos as a generous patron of all monastic houses – something of an exaggeration – was said to have particularly admired 'those on the mountains' and took a personal interest in their welfare. Apart from his mediation in disputes concerning Athos, he concerned himself with the affairs of the little-known 'Mountain of the *Kellia*' (Mount Pelion in Thessaly) and at one time asked St Christodoulos to become its spiritual director. On the other hand, Romanos Lekapenos, Constantine Monomachos and others clearly combined admiration for the asceticism of the holy mountains with an acceptance of the virtues of the great coenobitic houses.[36]

But although each emperor had his own favoured style of monasticism and patronised houses according to his own inclinations, each clearly considered it part of his imperial duty to continue donations made by previous rulers. This was, as we have seen, particularly noticeable in the

---

[36] See chapter 4, p. 108 for prayers for the emperor and the welfare of the state. For Nikephoros Phokas' monastic inclinations and the Novel of 964, see chapter 7. Life of St Cyril Phileotes, chapter 47, p. 232 (457–8) (Nicholas Kataskepenos' comments on Alexios Komnenos); the 'Monastery of the *Kellia*' is discussed in chapter 2, p. 50.

case of emperors who came to power by usurpation or *coup d'état*. John Tzimiskes, who was present at the murder – if he did not actually commit it himself – of his predecessor, Nikephoros Phokas in 969, was at pains to continue sending privileges and donations to the Lavra on Athos, a house intimately linked with Nikephoros, and was responsible for a chrysobull (the *Tragos*) which both regulated monastic life on the mountain and confirmed the pre-eminent position of that monastery in the Athonite hierarchy. In the eleventh century, Michael VII Doukas confirmed the chrysobulls issued for the Nea Mone on Chios by the man he had over-thrown (Romanos IV Diogenes) and Attaliates' foundations at Rhaidestos and Constantinople were granted chrysobulls by both Michael VII and the man who usurped *his* throne, Nikephoros III Botaniates. Alexios Komnenos continued Botaniates' patronage of St Christodoulos' estab-lishment on Kos.[37]

The continuation of imperial patronage of many of these houses seems surprising at first sight, since the monks within them and their network of lay connections were (as in the Lavra) potentially influential opponents of the enemies of their original patrons. But this in itself was a strong pragmatic reason for not antagonising them and underlying such questions of practical politics lay, in addition, an important question of imperial theory. The uninterrupted continuity of imperial patronage and the diplomatic procedure of confirming the chrysobulls of privilege was just as important a process for the grantors as for the holders of such documents. For it not only gave continued legal protection to the monas-teries concerned and their possessions, but it also conferred legitimacy upon the emperors themselves. Continuing protection of monastic foundations was a reflection of the permanency of the imperial office and, by extension, of the worthiness of the holder.

Imperial patronage was thus, of necessity, more heterogeneous than that offered by lower ranks amongst the laity; but even among the latter it is not possible to discern particularly popular forms of monasticism with

---

[37] For Tzimiskes' involvement in the murder of Nikephoros Phokas, see R. Morris, 'Succession and usurpation: politics and rhetoric in the late tenth century', in P. Magdalino (ed.), *New Constantines: the rhythm of imperial renewal in Byzantine history* (Aldershot, 1994), 199–214. *Lavra*, I, no. 7 (978), although issued by Basil II, recalls the generosity of Tzimiskes, as does *Ivirôn*, I, no. 7 (984), which relates that Tzimiskes granted a *solemnion* of 244 *nomismata* to the Lavra drawn from the fiscal revenues of Lemnos. For the *Tragos*, see chapter 2, p. 45. Eleventh-century confirmatory chrysobulls: Zepos, I, Appendix, document xx (1072), p. 642 (Dölger, *Regesten*, no. 987; Michael VII Doukas for Nea Mone); Gautier, 'Diataxis', pp. 101–9; 109–23 (Dölger, *Regesten*, nos. 1005; 1042; chrysobulls for Attaliates' foundations in 1074 and 1079 from Michael VII Doukas and Nikephoros III Botaniates). Nikephoros Botaniates' chrysobull for Christodoulos' house on Kos is lost, but is mentioned in that of Alexios Komnenos (Dölger, *Regesten*, nos. 1049; 1123): *BEMP*, I, no. 4 (1085), p. 33, l. 11.

any degree of precision. The number of monks entering the Lavra on Mount Athos (estimated at 120 in 973 and 700 by 1045) and already to be found in Lazaros' three foundations on Mount Galesion by the mid-eleventh century (1064) might seem to suggest an upsurge in lavriote-influenced monasticism at this period. But the conclusion would be based on false premises. Though some statistics for the number of places provided for by the founders of the new coenobitic houses do exist (Pakourianos, for example, limited his monks to fifty and Attaliates to seven), any attempt to quantify and characterise the monastic population of the empire in the tenth and eleventh centuries is doomed to failure for reasons of incomplete information. However, the building and endowment of new coenobitic houses in the northern territories of the empire bears witness not only to the improved safety of these areas after the defeats of the Bulgars in the early eleventh century, but also to the migration of easterners who could not now follow traditional patterns of donation at home because of the ever increasing threat posed by the Turks.[38]

One of the most important developments, however, and one which was dependent on the continuing patronage and support of the laity, was the transformation of houses which had begun as spiritual refuges in areas where the eremitic life could be followed (the Athonite houses provide the most obvious example, but the same was true of the houses on Mount Galesion or Patmos) into centres where the rising populations precluded the practice of the more secluded forms of the monastic life. With the increased popularity of hybrid monasticism came the need to extend monastic buildings and to acquire enough land to support the community. The money and manpower resources to aid this process often came from the laity but when they entered monastic hands, they often became, because of their pious purpose, much freer from the restraints which the imperial government attempted to impose upon lay society. As we have seen, political as well as social needs were catered for by the monks and their status as intercessors, men who stood between lay society and the divine, made it difficult to view their wealth or their land-owning in the same way as that of the secular world. The change in the nature of the lavriote-influenced monasticism of the tenth century was a direct consequence of its popularity and its prosperity a testimony to the principle that success breeds success. This was most obvious in the context of the great expansion of land-holdings of these houses and the new ways in which the monastic ordinance to 'be *in* the world but not *of* it' was interpreted.

---

[38] *Lavra*, I, pp. 17; 51; Life of St Lazaros, chapter 246, p. 585.

PART TWO
Protection and survival

CHAPTER SIX
Monasteries and the law

◆

WHILE DONATION AND endowment played a crucial rôle in the establishment of monastic houses, their survival for more than a few years was governed by other factors than the devotion of their founders and the enthusiasm of their immediate patrons. The most important of these was the legal status enjoyed by monastic lands which was the basis of all future prosperity. Without proper legal title to their lands, houses could be deprived of the most useful of their assets – property. Without estates, monasteries could not hope to survive, for both food supply and revenue depended not merely on possession of land, but on a territory adequate to the needs of each house. The safeguarding of their landed endowments and subsequent acquisitions was thus a matter of supreme concern to monastic landowners and the strongest weapon at their disposal was that of the law. Legal precedents were cited to protect and confirm existing territorial conditions, charters were scrupulously reconfirmed at every change of imperial régime, and court cases over disputed lands and rights were a commonplace of monastic life in the larger houses.

In the course of the tenth and eleventh centuries, the conditions under which monastic lands might be held became increasingly complex. This complexity was matched by the evolution of a vast array of terminology which expressed every possible nuance of the legal rights of possession, donation and management. It has often proved difficult to establish precisely what was implied by each of these terms, although it would be mistaken to imply that they could be used interchangeably. In general, they reflected a concern to describe as accurately as possible the precise legal status of each monastery, its lands and its administrators and patrons. As we shall see, a close study of the terms used in specific monastic documents can go a long way towards establishing the legal basis on which each house was run and the particular concerns and demands of its founder – yet more examples of the idiosyncrasy that characterised Byzantine monasticism at this period.[1]

In general terms, however, two aspects of the law are of particular importance to any study of monastic land tenure: the juridical framework within which such land was established and protected, and the legal mechanisms governing its management. But there are certain pitfalls; for while the law which, in theory, applied to monastic land-holdings is relatively easy to establish, the question of whether it was actually put into practice is not. One thing, at least, *is* clear: secular and ecclesiastical law were firmly related. The great legal compilations of Justinian had established that the welfare of ecclesiastical institutions was an imperial concern and subsequent secular legislators always cited the property holdings of the church (including monastic lands) among the subjects within their competence. In the tenth and eleventh centuries, the relationship of secular and ecclesiastical law remained the same: the imperial laws stood powerless if confounded or contradicted by the dogma of the faith, but, conversely, the purely disciplinary canons of the church could be modified both by the promulgation of imperial law and by the granting of imperial exemptions and privileges.[2]

The first concern of both the secular and the canonical legislation of the period was the establishment of the legal liabilities of those who founded monasteries. The so-called *Syntagma canonum*, the most commonly used handbook of conciliar canons which had been updated in 882, quoted a number of canons which placed the responsibility for fulfilling vows to build monasteries squarely on the shoulders of the donors and their families. Building work should be completed within three years in the case of churches, a limit which may also have applied to monasteries too, since the celebration of the liturgy would have been difficult without the existence of a church. If the donor should die, his heirs must see to the completion of the work and their property might be rented or sold so that

---

[1] See, in general, I. M. Konidares, *To dikaion tes monasteriakes periousias apo tou 9ou mechri kai tou 12ou aionos* (Athens, 1979); R. Morris, 'Legal terminology in monastic documents of the tenth and eleventh centuries', *XVI. Internat. Byzantinistenkongress, Akten*, II/2 (published in *JÖB*, 32/3), pp. 281–90 is a short introduction to the problems of terminology, also dealt with by J. P. Thomas, *Private religious foundations in the Byzantine empire* (Dumbarton Oaks Studies, XXIV, Washington, DC, 1987), especially pp. 218–21. Thomas suggests that 'terminological confusion . . . indicates the uneasy transition from old forms of organisation to the new' (pp. 218–19), but it is extremely unwise to assume that highly trained Byzantine legal draftsmen were unaware of the nuances of each of the terms that they used.

[2] R. Macrides, '*Nomos* and *kanon* on paper and in court', in Morris (ed.), *Church and people in Byzantium*, pp. 61–85 for the interaction of secular and canon law in Byzantium. See also N. van der Wal and J. H. A. Lokin, *Historiae iuris graeco-romani delineatio. Les sources du droit byzantin de 300 à 1453*, translated H. Boon (Groningen, 1985).

it could be finished. If they refused to carry out their responsibilities, the *archontes* (leading men) of the neighbourhood should compel them to do so. This joint responsibility (a spiritual version of that in existence for the payment of village tax burdens familiar in the Byzantine countryside by the end of the tenth century) was also emphasised in a Novel of Leo VI (886–912). It supported the canonical ruling that the dependants of a donor stood liable for any monies needed to complete a house, whether or not a will had been left.[3]

Such regulations were derived from the canons of the fourth- and fifth-century councils when there was still a possibility that the heirs of donors might not themselves be Christian and not, therefore, feel morally bound to carry out their relations' intentions. By the tenth and eleventh centuries, however, they can be seen more as citations of the legal basis for long-established social practice. But we cannot always be sure that donors' wishes were always carried out, because the wills and *typika* in which they were expressed were naturally written at the end of the donor's life. Only references to the existence of the houses *after* the donor's or patron's death can indicate beyond all doubt that his wishes had been observed. But the fact that there was no provision in surviving foundation documents and wills for a situation in which the house had *not* even been set up indicates that the donors of the period did not feel it necessary to plan for such a contingency. However, the preservation of such legislation in the canonical collections, while it may simply have been due to the Byzantine habit of preserving long-past legislation almost as an act of faith regardless of contemporary relevance, may also have been for other than purely antiquarian reasons. While the surviving donation documents and *typika* which we possess concern houses founded by those of some social standing, whose heirs were conscious of their social reputation and the need to conform to certain standards of behaviour, many humbler donors and founders may well have had heirs whose conception of what was 'proper' was somewhat looser. The duty of the *archontes* to make sure that vows were carried out probably originally referred to the need for influential landowners to strengthen the resolve of poorer heirs and persuade them to direct money of which they might themselves have made use, into the purposes for which it had been originally intended.[4]

[3] *Syntagma canonum, PG*, 104, cols. 441–976, II.1, col. 564 C-D. P. Noailles and A. Dain, *Les novelles de Léon VI le Sage. Texte et traduction* (Paris, 1944), Novel XIV, p. 55. For the canon law of the late ninth century, see Van der Wal and Lokin, *Historiae iuris . . . delineatio*, pp. 87–9.
[4] Among the houses discussed in chapters 4 and 5, the Monastery at Bačkovo founded by Gregory Pakourianos has survived to the present day; the Monastery of Attaliates (or at least its house in Constantinople) is mentioned in 1094, some seventeen years after

Once a donation had been made, or an establishment set up, a proper distinction had to be drawn between it and the surrounding secular property. The canons decreed that a building once consecrated should remain so even if it were in ruins, but what constituted 'correct' consecration? The *Syntagma Canonum* reflected one of the problems that there had been in the past:

> Certain people give the name of monastery to their own establishments and possessions and announce that they have been dedicated to God and inscribe themselves as masters of the things which have been 'consecrated' and attempt to contrive the creation of the holy merely by the naming of it as such.[5]

The evolution of the so-called 'private religious foundations' in Byzantium, that is those which were set up and administered by private individuals, has been the subject of a major study, but there are particular aspects of the position of privately founded monasteries which do need further emphasis.[6] Although a great deal of legislation declared that all monasteries should be built with the consent of the bishop of the diocese and publicly consecrated by him, it is quite clear that by the end of the ninth century it was possible even for humble individuals to declare their foundations or houses to be monasteries without reference to episcopal authority. Such houses were private property, as opposed to monasteries under the aegis of public institutions, such as the imperial power or the episcopate. Two legal texts from the reigns of Leo VI and Basil II support this view and they may be corroborated by other fragments of evidence. An act from the Lavra archives dating from 1012 states quite baldly that a certain *kouboukleisios* John declared in his will that his ancestral home on the island of Skyros should become a monastery with a church dedicated to Christ the Saviour. A later document from 1016 relates the subsequent unsuccessful attempts of the bishop of Skyros to gain control of the house.[7] Another example can be

the *Diataxis* was drawn up; see P. Gautier, 'Le synode des Blachernes (fin 1094). Etude prosopographique', *REB*, 29 (1971), 213–84, especially pp. 220 and 280. For the signature of an anonymous monk of 'the Monastery of Attaliates' who could have been Michael, first *oikoumenos*, then *hegoumenos* pre-1085, see *Diataxis* of Attaliates, pp. 13–14. The Monastery of the Theotokos Evergetis and the Nunnery of the Theotokos Kecharitomene are both mentioned in documents of the twelfth and thirteenth centuries; see Janin, *Eglises et monastères*, pp. 180–2, 190. But for a salutary example of part of a great twelfth-century monastic complex which started grandly and soon faded out, see E. Kislinger, 'Der Pantokrator-Xenon, ein trügerisches Ideal?', *JÖB*, 37 (1987), 173–9.

[5] *Syntagma canonum*, II.2, col. 577 A–C.

[6] Thomas, *Private religious foundations* (see note 1).

[7] See Kaplan, *Les hommes et la terre*, pp. 295–7. Noailles and Dain, *Léon VI*, Novel XIV, p. 55; Basil II's Novel of 996; Zepos, I, col. iii, document XXIX, 262–72, translated

found in the legal compilation of the *Peira*. The Monastery of Piperatos
(whereabouts unknown) had been founded by an anonymous monk in a
house given to him by a layman. The monastery then passed through the
hands of the future Emperor Romanos Lekapenos and then, somewhat
later, came under the control of a certain *protospatharios* Marianos, a high
court official. At this point, the Patriarch Nicholas (probably Nicholas
Chrysoberges, 979–91) claimed that the monastery should be placed
under patriarchal jurisdiction. His view was dismissed both by the
Emperor Basil II and legal opinion, since, it was maintained, at no time
had the house been 'placed under the authority of the Church'.[8] It was
thus to remain independent and self-governing (*autodespoton*). In the case
of small houses at least, it therefore seems that no episcopal involvement
in their foundation was necessary. And if there was an episcopal ceremony
associated with their consecration, we have no record of it.

The problem is even more complicated in the case of the new houses
founded by the monastic saints. For hagiographers were notoriously
reluctant to mention even the existence of local bishops, let alone to imply
that they had any jurisdiction over the houses their heroes had founded.
Indeed, they often wished to portray these founders as of far more
influence in local society than the bishops and as viewing the values of the
secular church with some contempt. But the hostility sometimes evident
in the sources between monastic and episcopal figures may well have had
another cause – the fact that newly established monastic communities,
especially in remote areas, were not founded with episcopal sanction and
did not subsequently place themselves under the local church hierarchy.
On the contrary, they jealously guarded their independent status. So we
have very little knowledge of the procedure by which the buildings of
these new houses were established as monasteries and, more importantly,
how their churches were consecrated. In the Life of St Michael Maleïnos,
there is a hint that some kind of ceremony took place after the completion
of the Church of the Theotokos built to serve the monks of Mount
Kyminas: a *synodos* (gathering) was held, but it does not seem to have been
the public consecration demanded by the canons. Rather, it was an

P. Charanis, 'The monastic properties and the state in the Byzantine empire', *DOP*, 4
(1948), 53–118, reprinted in his *Social, economic and political life in the Byzantine empire*
(London, 1973), article I, p. 63; *Lavra*, I, nos. 16 (1012) and 20 (1016). See also Malamut,
Les îles, II, pp. 476–7, who interestingly suggests that the quarrel with the bishop was a
consequence of the creation of a monastery from a private house and its subsequent
placing under the care of the Lavra on Mount Athos, thus resulting in the disruption of the
integrity of local village lands.
[8] *Peira*, XV. 4, p. 49 and Kaplan, *Les hommes et la terre*, p. 297. Thomas, *Private religious
foundations*, pp. 154–5, suggests that the house might once have been given a patriarchal
foundation charter. There is no evidence for this.

opportunity for the saint to establish customs (*typoi*) for his house.[9] In the Life of St Lazaros we hear of the saint being sent the gift of a chasuble by the bishop of Phaselis (in Lycia) after he had converted a group of heretics and set up a small community of monks to continue preaching. The bishop was thus not opposed to the setting up of the community, but he does not seem to have been involved in its consecration.[10] Cyril Phileotes, at the end of the eleventh century, was reported to have declared that one reason for the dismissal of a *hegoumenos* could be the lack of a *sphragis* (literally 'seal', but more likely 'seal of approval') from the local bishop. But this probably referred to episcopal approval of the individual concerned; it cannot be taken to imply consecration of the monastery or its church.[11]

The involvement of the local bishop in the consecration of a new monastery was also the public demonstration of his rights and jurisdictions over it. The fact that sources of the tenth and eleventh centuries contain so little evidence for episcopal consecration is an indication that these other rights were no longer so clearly accepted as they might have been in the past. The view put forward by the *Syntagma canonum*, that all sacred establishments should be regulated by the bishops of the district, was the most extreme statement of the secular church's claims. Others saw the question in somewhat less clear cut terms. For some, the important criterion was the size of the establishment, but even here there was a variety of opinion. Leo VI's novel XIV, issued at the end of the ninth century, declared that any establishment containing three or more persons should be considered a monastery and therefore be placed under episcopal jurisdiction. A century later, however, Basil II declared that only houses which contained eight to ten monks should be considered as monasteries proper; smaller ones were simply *eukteria* (oratories) or *euages oikoi* (charitable institutions).[12] The problem was once again the difference between theory and practice. In the twelfth century the theory was still being clearly enunciated by the great canonist, Theodore Balsamon:

> If the founder of a monastery or a church declares in his *typikon* or his *diataxis* that monks and clerics of these houses are not subject to the bishop of the region, let him not be given a hearing, since the divine and holy canons state the opposite.[13]

---

[9] Life of St Michael Maleïnos, chapter 15, p. 560.
[10] Life of St Lazaros, chapter 11, p. 511.
[11] Life of St Cyril Phileotes, chapter 39, p. 173 (399).
[12] *Syntagma canonum* III.4, col. 608 D; x.1, col. 817 and see note 7 above.
[13] Theodore Balsamon, *Comment. in can. viii Conc. Chalc.*, PG, 137, col. 413.

In general, we lack precise information about the jurisdiction of bishops over particular houses in their dioceses, though the Piperatos case would indicate that they were ever watchful to assert their rights. Evidence from the correspondence of the late eleventh-century Archbishop Theophylact of Ohrid also demonstrates that he, at least, did intervene in the affairs of the monastic houses of his archdiocese. He ordered the bishop of Triaditsa to restore an old Bulgar monk to the monastery from which he seems to have been expelled after a dispute and, interestingly, commented that he had only interfered with the bishop's disciplinary rights in the house because he wanted to protect the monks. In another case, Theophylact acted to organise the election of a new *hegoumenos* at a monastery in Serres (rather than simply confirming the choice) as trouble had arisen in the house over the matter. In general, however, it is clear that many houses in the tenth and eleventh centuries were either subject to ecclesiastical figures other than the local bishop (to the patriarch for instance) or did not seem to be subject in any real sense to any secular churchman at all.[14]

Although it has long been recognised that the concern of many monastic founders was to emphasise their ultimate freedom from local ecclesiastical (and, of course, lay) authority, it has often been assumed that their houses were initially subject to some degree of episcopal jurisdiction. As the work of John Thomas has shown, this was certainly not the case. The monastic founders became themselves the true legislators for their houses and established the status of *autodespoton* (independent) for them from the first.[15] Of course, traditional forms of control also survived, though to what extent is unclear. For a fiscal document, dating to the reign of Romanos Lekapenos (920–44) and dealing with the requisitioning of horses from monasteries in the Peloponnese, mentions six different types of monasteries: imperial, patriarchal, archiepiscopal, metropolitan and episcopal as well as *autodespoton*. These terms referred to the type of jurisdiction and authority to which each house was subjected and clearly indicated that in many cases it was not that of the local bishop.[16]

It is extremely difficult to identify the moment at which control over many monastic houses irrevocably slipped away from the hands of the bishops. But it had certainly happened by the end of the ninth

---

[14] See M. Mullett, *Theophylact through his letters: the two worlds of an exile bishop* (doctoral thesis, 2 vols., University of Birmingham, 1981), I, 505–9.

[15] A. Guillou, *La civilisation byzantine* (Paris, 1974), p. 189. See Thomas, *Private religious foundations*, especially chapter 4.

[16] *DAI*, chapter 52, p. 257 and *Commentary*, p. 204. Jenkins dates the document to 921, see 'The date of the Slav revolt'.

century, when the assembled clergy at the Council of Constantinople in 861 discussed a number of important aspects of this development. They added their condemnation of the foundation of monasteries in private houses to that of earlier councils; they criticised what seemed to be a growing practice for landowners to give the name of monastery to any part of their property and then treat it like the rest of their estates, even naming themselves as *hegoumenoi*. They tried to reinstate episcopal rights by requiring an inventory (*brebion*) of the properties granted to newly established houses to be drawn up and left with the local bishops. They encouraged bishops to undertake the repair of dilapidated houses.[17] These moves do not seem to have had any noticeable effect.

Although it is more than likely that there had always been a tension between the understandable wish of lay founders and patrons to keep some influence over 'their' monasteries and the firm dictates of the canons on the subject of monastic consecration, the balance seems to have tipped towards the power of the laity during the period of iconoclasm when monks often fled into the houses of friendly laymen and when iconodule rulers showed their partiality towards monks by taking monasteries under their direct protection. It was also the period when the power of the episcopacy was gravely weakened by divisions over doctrine within its own ranks which seriously affected its ability to assert jurisdictional rights.[18] We know, for instance, that so-called 'imperial' monasteries (*basilika monasteria*) were in existence by the time of the Emperor Nikephoros I (802–11) since he demanded the payment of the *kapnikon* (hearth tax) from them.[19]

To the fiscal document from the Peloponnese may be added increasing evidence of imperial monasteries from the eleventh century. The monk Nikodemos, who built both a bridge and a church in the city of Lakedaimon (Sparta), requested that his church should be managed and protected by imperial officials and that the bishop of the city and his clergy should have no rights in it. The Patriarch Alexios Stoudites complained of the habit of the monks 'of the imperial monasteries' of taking their law cases to secular courts and an act from the Lavra on Athos dated to 1060 indicates that the imperial monasteries were noted in the *brebia* of the imperial office of the *sakellion* in Constantinople in just the same way that the Council of Constantinople had declared they should be preserved in episcopal archives. Thus imperial monasteries

[17] Thomas, *Private religious foundations*, pp. 133–6.
[18] *Ibid.*, pp. 118–25.
[19] Theophanes, pp. 486–7. See Kaplan, *Les hommes et la terre*, p. 295.

were not merely patronised by the emperor, they were, in a very real sense, under his control and formed part of his landed concerns.[20]

It is very likely that the so-called 'patriarchal', 'metropolitan' and 'archiepiscopal' monasteries evolved in much the same way at a time when episcopal power was weak or when a higher power, such as the emperor, could be called upon to intervene. An early example can be found in the Life of St Theodore of Sykeon, where it is reported that the Emperor Maurice (582–602) removed the *hegoumenoi* of the houses Theodore had founded and placed them under the auspices of the Great Church (Hagia Sophia in Constantinople) and thus the patriarch.[21] By the time that the legal compilation until recently known as the *Epanagoge* (*recte Eisagoge*) was composed (?884–6), the right of the patriarch at Constantinople to establish his own *stauropegion* (the act of laying a cross on the site of the monastery and processing round its boundaries, thus affirming dependence) in any province was clearly stated:

> The care and provision of all *metropoleis* and bishoprics, monasteries and churches, and the right of judgement and absolution is the responsibility of each patriarch. But the head [*proedros*] of the Church of Constantinople has the right to grant *stauropegia* in other provinces in which he is not head of the church.[22]

The right of patriarchal *stauropegion* was later upheld by the ubiquitous Theodore Balsamon against the quite understandable objections of bishops and metropolitans and it can certainly be seen in force in the tenth and eleventh centuries. In a *sigillion* for the Monastery of the Theotokos at Demetsana in the Peloponnese (964 or 966), the Patriarch Polyeuktos forbade both bishops and metropolitans to enter it and emphasised its status as a patriarchal house.[23] The Patriarch Nicholas II Chrysoberges granted the Monastery of the Theotokos at Gomatou to the care of the Lavra on Mount Athos in 989 with the proviso that it should return 'to

---

[20] See Feissel and Philippidis-Braat, 'Inscriptions du Péloponnèse', pp. 301–3. *Hypomnema*, no. 2 of Alexios Stoudites (January 1028) in RP, v, 25–32 (Grumel, *Régestes*, no. 834), see p. 29. *Lavra*, I, no. 33 (1060) also denies the right of the metropolitan of Thessalonike to oversee the affairs of the Monastery of St Andrew of Peristerai. For the imperial *sakellion*, see Kaplan, *Les hommes et la terre*, pp. 310–12.

[21] *La vie de Théodore de Sykéon*, ed. and translated A.-J. Festugière (2 vols., Subsidia Hagiographica, XLVIII, Brussels, 1970), I, chapter 82, p. 70; II, p. 225.

[22] *Epanagoge* (*Eisagoge*), II, 10, Zepos, II, 243. For the compilation, see Van der Wal and Lokin, *Historiae iuris . . . delineatio*, pp. 79–82 and Macrides, '*Nomos* and *Kanon*', p. 62.

[23] Theodore Balsamon, *In can. xxxi. Conc. SS. Apost.*, RP, II, 40–2. For Polyeuktos' *sigillion* (Grumel, *Régestes*, no. 791), see MM, v, pp. 250–2, p. 251 and Thomas, *Private religious foundations*, pp. 215–16.

the patriarchal control' if subsequent *hegoumenoi* tried to evict the monks or confiscate the property.[24]

It is quite clear, then, that there was a considerable divergence between the dictates of the long-established canon law on the rights of bishops over the monasteries in their dioceses and the state of affairs actually in existence in the tenth and eleventh centuries. It was possible both to establish a house without episcopal consecration and to maintain it outside the reach of episcopal jurisdiction. Nor was this all. The very existence of the system of 'imperial' monasteries provided an attractive model for both ecclesiastical and lay founders. Without actually going so far as to place their houses directly under the *administration* of imperial officials, they often attempted to gain imperial interest and protection, a situation which often had important practical consequences.[25] But the situation varied from place to place; a particularly strong-minded archbishop, like Theophylact of Ohrid, could always make some practical use of the body of canonical rulings which supported his theoretical rights over the monasteries in his province.

Although the basic legal distinction between lay and ecclesiastical property was maintained in the tenth and eleventh centuries, the precise standing of each monastic house, like the precise type of monasticism practised in it, was often established by the founder. The bewildering array of terminology used to describe the position of each monastery was deployed with two main aims in view: to establish the identity of the possessor (or possessors) of the house and to indicate which other figures might be involved in the administration or management of both the monastery's spiritual life and its landed possessions. A simple, but profoundly important concept lay behind these distinctions, and that was the acceptance that religious houses could constitute private property in the same way as the lay *oikos*. Thus lay founders could have the same freedom to dispose of their ecclesiastical property (so long as it was not secularised) as they claimed over their other possessions. Three aspects of this proprietorship were of particular importance: the right of disposal (by testament, gift or sale); the granting of partial rights in the house and its property and the appointment of others to manage it while the proprietorial rights remained intact. The detailed *typika* of the eleventh century not only provide evidence for the motives and spiritual inclinations of patrons, they are also an invaluable source for the legal mechanisms they employed to protect their foundations.[26]

In terms of disposition, the most important aspect of a *typikon* of foundation was the establishment of the succession to the hegoumenate.

---

[24] *Lavra*, I, no. 8 (989) (Grumel, *Régestes*, no. 802).
[25] See p. 159, below.   [26] See note 1 above.

In many of the large foundations of the eleventh century, the charge of finding a successor to the original holder of the post (usually appointed by the founder) was left to the then *hegoumenos*, sometimes with the assistance of the 'wiser part' of the brethren, the holders of the monastic offices (*diakoniai*). But in some cases the donor himself designated the future *hegoumenoi*. Michael Attaliates expected the post to be handed down amongst his closest male relatives and if this line ran out, to pass to collaterals and, as we have seen, the hegoumenate of Iviron stayed in the hands of one family for about fifty years.[27] The language used was often that employed to designate heirs in the secular world: an act from the Lavra dated to 897 described Euthymios, the *hegoumenos* of St Andrew of Peristerai as 'heir' (the terms *kleronomos* and *diadochos* are both used) of the monastery; another of 993 transferred the island of Gymnopelagision to 'Athanasios of the Lavra, his heirs (*diadochoi*) and all who came after'.[28] On Athos, at least, it became accepted that houses could only pass to the spiritual heirs of those who had founded them, or to whom they had been given. Thus an Act of Xeropotamou (1010), when designating a Lavriote monk Athanasios (not the saint) as *hegoumenos* of the monastery of Bouleuteria, stated that he could only pass it on to his own disciples and heirs, not the spiritual son of the previous *hegoumenos*, the monk Poimen. The rôles of disciple (*mathetes*) and heir were often, in fact, equated. In 1024 the monk Tornik Katakalon was given the right to pass on the Monastery of Pithara on Athos to 'his disciples and heirs wearing the monastic *schema*'. St Paul of Latros confided the care of the Monastery of the Stylos to the monk Thomas; a successor of St Lazaros on Mt Galesion was his spiritual son, Hilarion.[29] The mechanisms of 'spiritual inheritance' thus paralleled those of the secular world and were of great importance in preserving the lasting legal identity of the house. But other aspects of the rights of founders illustrate even more strongly the position of monasteries as legally disposable assets.

They could, for instance, be given away or sold so long as the land remained in clerical hands. The term *dorea* (gift) was usually applied to the land which was donated by the laity to monastic institutions and implied that the donors abdicated their rights in the holding and transferred them to the new owners. The monks of the Monastery of Stylos on Latros, for example, maintained that they had received their property at Messingouma from the Emperor Leo VI *dia doreas* (by gift); vineyards were granted to the Lavra on Athos in 1014 by Constantine Lagoudes and

---

[27] *Diataxis* of Attaliates, p. 39. See chapter 3, p. 81.
[28] *Lavra*, I, nos. 1 (897) and 10 (993).
[29] *Xéropotamou*, no. 2 (1010); *Lavra*, I, no. 25 (1054); Life of St Paul the Younger, chapter 49, p. 178; Life of St Lazaros, chapter 33, p. 519.

his wife 'in absolute gift' (*haple dorea*). But a gift could also transfer one house and its property into the hands of another. In 1030, two monks, Gabriel and Ignatios, made a gift of land previously belonging to houses founded by a certain Nicholas the Hesychast, to the Monastery of the Theotokos at Strobilaia near Karyes on Athos, again in 'absolute grant'. Sometimes, though, what was clearly an act of donation was disguised under a different name: Athanasios of Bouleuteria 'consecrated' (*aphieromene*) his house to the Lavra in 1030 and the Priest John and his son Argentos together with Niketas and Basil, sons of a local *komes*, used the same word to describe their grant of lands at Marathosa near Kyr Zosimo in Calabria to the Monastery of St Maria of Zosimo in 1058 and the same legal action was intended. It did not need to be permanent; in 1085 the Lavra was granted lands known as 'the cells' (*kellia*) in a temporary donation by the Protos of Athos while a dispute about their ownership was settled with the Monastery of Iviron. In a more dubious type of arrangement, the transference of land was sometimes accompanied by the donation by the recipients of a *psychikon* ('spiritual payment' akin to a charitable donation), a mechanism clearly devised to disguise the financial nature of the intermonastic transaction.[30]

The legal freedom to sell or exchange monastic lands so long as they were not deconsecrated also appears in the sources. It applied not only to lands which might have been the personal property of monks before they took on the monastic habit, but also to lands held by monasteries as institutions. The *Tragos* of John Tzimiskes, for instance, allowed each *hegoumenos* on Athos the right to sell or grant his *idios agros* (own field) to whomsoever he chose. This probably referred to the small patch of land cleared and cultivated by the early hesychasts which remained their own property even after the larger houses on Athos had grown up all around them, but there is evidence that entire establishments could be granted in the same way. In 1034, the Monastery of Katadaimon sold its lands on Athos to the *hegoumenos* Theoktistos of Esphigmenou and a document of 1081 from the archives of the Lavra confirms the sale of a property near Prinarion (east of the River Strymon), previously belonging to the Monastery of Kosmidion, to the Latin monks of the Amalfitan monastery. Land could, in fact, pass backwards and forwards a number of times, as witnessed by the fortunes of parcels of land in the region of Magoula on Mount Athos. At the end of the tenth century, the monk Paul Magoulas possessed an *agros* (field) to the south of the Monastery of Iviron, part of which he left to that house. It was then sold by the

---

[30] MM, IV, pp. 324ff.; *Lavra*, I, no. 18 (1014); *Lavra*, I, no. 28 (1030); *Lavra*, I, no. 29 (1030); Trinchera, no. 43 (1058); *Lavra*, I, no. 47 (1085).

hegoumenos Euthymios to the monk Andrew, but it was returned by him to Iviron in 1007 as he felt he was becoming too old to work it.[31]

Closely allied to the procedure of sale of lands was that of exchange (*antallage*). In 1016 or 1017, with the approval of the Athonite authorities, Euthymios of Iviron exchanged lands within the boundaries of the Monastery of Karaba (subject to Iviron) for a field at Galeagra held by one Peter Spanoleontos, *hegoumenos* of the Monastery of St John the Theologian, his cousin, the monk Menas and their uncle, the monk Niketas. But occasionally anything less clear cut than a sale could produce problems later. In the case of the exchange effected between the Monasteries of Stylos and Lamponion on Mount Latros in 987, objections were later raised by the monks of the Monastery of Karyes; questions were asked about the validity of the act and the lack of precise documentation, undoubtedly a consequence of the somewhat vague (and possibly oral) nature of the original transaction.[32]

Of far more consequence in the tenth and eleventh centuries and of growing concern to the secular church authorities, was the ability of monastic proprietors or founders to place their houses under the management of others. These were often laymen and the process thus brought into play important questions of social influence, local power and even imperial preference. In legal terms, when houses passed under the control, but not the ownership, of third parties, a separation occurred in the judicial attributes of ownership. The condition of 'full ownership' (*despotikon dikaion*) brought with it the rights of disposal, gift, sale and bequest that have already been described. It was usually also associated with the qualities of *kyrioteta* and *exousia*, best translated, perhaps, as 'possession' and 'authority'. But when the *management* and not the ownership of property was transferred, clearly some, but not all, of these legal attributes passed out of the hands of the owner. An example from the Acts of the Lavra can make this point more clearly. In 1014, as has been noted, Constantine and Maria Lagoudes made a gift of their lands to the Lavra. But they stipulated that, as long as they lived, they should themselves retain the *exousia* and *despoteia*. In other words, until they died, only the *kyrioteta*, the 'possession', was enjoyed by the ultimate owners. *Exousia* was an active facility: it implied the right to appoint successors to the hegoumenate and the right to build on the property. It could also provide justification for improvements to land (*kalliergemata*). Interestingly, it would appear that it could also be partially held. A Lavriote act of 1024 confirmed that John the Iberian had given up his share of the

---

[31] *Prôtaton*, no. 7 (972); *Esphigménou*, no. 1 (1034); *Lavra*, I, no. 42 (1081); *Ivirôn*, I, no. 14 (1007).
[32] *Ivirôn*, I, no. 22 (1016 or 1017); MM, IV, 308–13; 315–17.

exousia of the Monastery of Pithara (near Karyes) to the monk Cyril, who now enjoyed complete *exousia*.[33]

Was there, though, any real difference in the powers of action possessed by a *despotes* or *despozon* and those enjoyed by a *kyrios* (possessor)? Contemporary Byzantine legal opinion clearly held that there was. But as with episcopal power, there was sometimes a deal of difference between theory and practice and in this case it centred on circumstances in which, technically speaking, the legal rights of the founder or proprietor of a monastic house had been divided, but where, in reality, this division had resulted in a transference of *authority* to the recipient. The terms used to describe such a person – *ephoros*, *epitropos*, *antilambanomenos*, *pronoetes* and the much debated *charistikarios* – all expressed in their various ways aspects of authority, but they all had one thing in common. For they all, in the strict legal sense, 'diluted' the complete powers of the owner and implied the transference of the *exousia* – the power of action and jurisdiction – to the person concerned. There were, however, differences in legal emphasis between these terms and each of them implied a different kind of legal control. In some types of transfer, *exousia* was granted to act in some situations but not in others, and this is where the difference between the various terms employed may be determined. By examining the rôle such figures were expected to play in monastic government, their legal standing becomes much clearer.[34]

One clear group is that of individuals who were entrusted with authority limited either in its scope or its time scale. The *antilambanomenos*, *epitropos* and *ephoros* fall into this category. Their task seems to have been mainly disciplinary: the enforcement of peace between the monks and their *hegoumenoi* and the supervision of the election of a new *hegoumenos* on the death of the previous incumbent, particularly if the latter had not had time to make his wishes known. But in one interesting case on Athos, two such officials were appointed. St Athanasios of the Lavra chose his friend John the Iberian as the 'traditional' *epitropos*; his job was to visit the

---

[33] *Lavra*, I, no. 18 (1014). For the *exousia* to appoint a successor, see the case of Nicholas, *hegoumenos* of the Monastery of St Elias on Athos, who was appointed *hegoumenos* of the Monastery of the Prodromos at Atziioannou and in consequence received this right: *Lavra*, I, no. 19 (1016). Building rights are mentioned in, for example, *Lavra*, I, no. 54 (1101–2) and improvements in *Lavra*, I, no. 9 (981); *Lavra*, I, no. 25 (1024).

[34] See Morris, 'Legal terminology' and for further detailed discussion, H. Ahrweiler, 'La concession des droits incorporels. Donations conditionelles', *Actes du XIIe Congrès International d'Etudes Byzantines* (3 vols., Belgrade, 1964), II, 103–14, reprinted in *Etudes sur les structures administratives et sociales de Byzance* (London, 1971), article I; 'Le charisticariat et autres formes d'attribution de fondations pieuses aux Xe–XIe siècles', *ZRVI*, 10 (1967), 1–2, reprinted in *Etudes sur les structures administratives*, VII; E. Herman, 'Ricerche sulle istituzioni monastiche bizantine: typika ktetorika, caristicari e monasteri "liberi"', *OCP*, 6 (1940), 293–375.

house often and meet the monks (presumably to discuss any grievances) and to oversee, when the time came, the appointment of Athanasios' designated successor – John's own son, Euthymios.[35] But the second *epitropos* was an altogether different figure – the *epi tou kanikleiou* Nikephoros Ouranos, a high court official who was in charge of the authentification of all imperial acts and therefore certainly worked closely with the emperor. Athanasios revealed that he had, in fact, wanted the Emperor Nikephoros Phokas himself to fulfil this rôle, but had not dared to ask him 'because it seemed audacious' and because the emperor was already deemed to be the *epitropos* of all Christians (this did not, however, stop John the Iberian stating that he had asked the emperor to act as *epitropos* for Iviron). This gives us an indication of a further implication of the position of *epitropos* – that of acting as the secular protector of the interests of the monastery in the outside world. Athanasios selected the figure of the *epi tou kanikleiou* for this post because he was in a position to intervene with the imperial administrative bureaux.[36]

The office of the *ephoros*, though similar to that of the *epitropos*, had as its prime concern surveillance over the administration of the landed assets of the monastery and does not seem to have possessed the spiritual authority enjoyed by the *epitropos*. This distinction clearly emerges in the *Diataxis* of Attaliates, where the founder stipulated that, if his direct descendants (designated as *hegoumenoi*) should die out, the post of *hegoumenos* should pass to the then *oikonomos* of the monastery, while that of *ephoros* should remain in the hands of his own collateral descendants. He was thus making a clear distinction between spiritual and temporal administration. It is possible, in fact, that the office of *ephoros* was originally that of the overseer of the monastic lands and their produce. This would perhaps explain why, in what may be an early reference to *ephoroi* (if the supposedly tenth-century Testament of St Nikon Metanoeite is genuine), they are mentioned as receiving payment in kind.[37]

By the mid-eleventh century, there is evidence that the two rôles of *ephoros* and *epitropos* were sometimes being amalgamated. The Emperor Constantine Monomachos' chrysobull to the Lavra of 1052 appointed John the *epi tou kanikleiou* as *ephoros* (not *epitropos*) of the house. This was

---

[35] Activities of *antilambanomene* (literally 'patron'): Kécharitôménè, p. 33 (enforcement of peace between nuns); p. 47 (choice of new *hegoumene*); appointment of *epitropos*: *Diatyposis* of Athanasios, pp. 124–9, especially pp. 124–5.

[36] *Diatyposis* of Athanasios, p. 125. For the *epi tou kanikleiou*, see Oikonomidès, *Listes de préséance*, p. 311.

[37] *Diataxis* of Attaliates, p. 39; Lemerle, *Cinq études*, p. 104; 'Diatheke Nikonos', ed. S. Lambros, *NE*, 3 (1906), 223–8 is printed from an eighteenth-century Venetian source and needs further investigation.

done, as the document states, because of the similarity of his rank to that of Nikephoros Ouranos and he was clearly expected to fill the same rôle. It is not difficult to see why this was done. The estates of the Lavra were by now so extensive that a very real part of the lay protector's rôle would have been to oversee the monastery's landed interests. So the job had also to be entrusted to a figure who held as much authority as possible.[38] References to the *antileptor*, *protastes* and *pronoetes* indicate that they were also protective figures: the *pronoetes* Basil was in charge of the Monastery of Karyes on Mount Latros in 1049, and although we cannot be sure that he was not also the *hegoumenos* (although he should by rights have been designated as such if he had been), his involvement in a quarrel with the neighbouring Monastery of Stylos over disputed land, would suggest that he was certainly the guardian of the monastery's landed estates.[39]

The second group, one which has received much more attention from historians, is that of figures who were granted the total *exousia* and *kyrioteta* of the property concerned (though not, of course, full owner-ship), with no limit being placed on their authority. This category included grants made in *epidosis* (a mechanism for granting one monastery into the hands of another) and the *charistike* by which monastic houses were placed in the hands of a layman.[40] The legal formula by which the *charistike* was granted is quoted (or more likely paraphrased) in the polemic of the eleventh-century cleric John, patriarch of Antioch, against the institution:

> Our majesty, Our Humble Self [referring to the Patriarch] grants to so-and-so the monastery of such-and-such, for example that of Our Lord, God and Saviour Jesus Christ, or of Our Most Blessed Lady, the Theotokos, or of some saint, with all its rights and privileges [*diakaia* and *pronomia*] and all its revenues for the duration of your life, or else for that of two people.[41]

The grant of *charistike*, then, was not intended to be legally equivalent to a gift, and was subject to conditions, particularly those of time. In a probable early example from southern Italy, the *spatharokandidatos* Christopher Bochomakes was granted the control of the imperial monastery of St Peter in Taranto for the duration of his life and that of his son Theophilos. The characteristics of the arrangement are also clearly

---

[38] *Lavra*, I, no. 31 (1052). See also Pakourianos, pp. 59; 85–7 (a passage probably borrowed from the regulations of the Monastery of the Panagiou in Constantinople), for two *epitropoi* who seem to have been in charge both of disciplining the monks and running the estates.
[39] MM, IV, p. 315.
[40] Ahrweiler, 'Droits incorporels', p. 107; 'Charisticariat', p. 11, note 63; Herman, 'Ricerche', p. 329.
[41] John of Antioch, Against the *charistike*, 109–11.

evident in documents of the eleventh century. Michael Attaliates was himself the *charistikarios* of the Monastery of St George at Rhaidestos; his son, Theodore, was to be the second *prosopon* (representative) to whom he had the right to pass on the position. The Theodore Attaliates was also the second *charistikarios* of the Nunnery of St Prokopios (also in Rhaidestos) which he was to receive from the first, Basil Xerades.[42]

In the two testamentary documents left by St Christodoulos of Patmos, the *charistike* is clearly seen as a protective office on a par with the *epitropia* and the *ephoreia*. Christodoulos designated two *charistikarioi*: Arsenios Skenoures, who had given him shelter at Strobilos and subsequently donated lands on Kos, and his own spiritual son, Theodore Kastrisios, an official in Constantinople. On Christodoulos' death, Skenoures was to become *hegoumenos* of the Monastery of St John on Patmos and Theodore Kastrisios was to join him in governing the monastery. The saint's nearest relatives, his nephews, were ordered not to object to these arrangements. It is quite clear that Theodore Kastrisios was intended to hold some kind of disciplinary facility, as those monks who had broken away from the monastery and had left Patmos were abjured, if they returned, to make their repentance to him. As things turned out, Arsenios Skenoures did not come to Patmos and Theodore Kastrisios declined to accept the office of *charistikarios*. He abdicated his right to become *hegoumenos* and the associated powers of a *kyrios* and *exousiastes* to another party, but did not specify to whom.[43]

The patron or owner of a monastic house thus possessed the power to separate the legal aspects of his holding and retain or donate them as he saw fit. The consequences of this freedom of action were extremely important. First, it enabled the best possible separation of the powers of *kyrioteta* and *despoteia* to be made to ensure the survival of the house. It is for this reason that foundation charters in the tenth and eleventh centuries so often insisted that the monastery in question remain *autodespoton* or *eleutherion*, so that the maximum freedom of legal action could be maintained. It also enabled their *hegoumenoi* and their lay advisers and protectors to buy, sell, receive gifts and exchange property to maximum advantage, while still retaining for their houses the

---

[42] Trinchera, no. 9 (999), see von Falkenhausen, *Dominazione bizantina*, p. 188, no. 28; *Diataxis* of Attaliates, p. 47; Lemerle, *Cinq études*, p. 82.

[43] *Diatheke* of Christodoulos, pp. 81–5 (will); pp. 85–90 (codicil), especially pp. 82, 84. *Apotaxis* of Theodore Kastrisios (1094), MM, VI, pp. 90–4. See M. G. Nystazopoulou, 'Ho epi tou kanikleiou kai he ephoreia tes en Patmo mones', *Symmeikta*, 1 (1966), 76–94 and R. Morris, 'Divine diplomacy in the late eleventh century', *BMGS*, 16 (1992), 147–56, especially p. 152 and n. 12 (for discussion of whether we should read Theodore Kastrisios, a surname, or Theodore *kastresios*, the officer in charge of provisioning the imperial table), p. 153.

all-important position of institutions consecrated to God whose property could not be alienated by or to laymen, yet whose welfare was still their concern. Monasteries thus enjoyed the same freedom of action as lay landowners, as well as the added security brought by their sacred status. This was not, of course, a view likely to find favour with bishops and in John of Antioch's polemic Against the *charistike*, there can be found a clear expression of a hostile point of view which had an important influence on patriarchal and imperial thinking at the end of the eleventh century.

> Whoever gives, gives what he possesses and not what he does not own. If you declare that you are granting what you possess, and if you think that God's property belongs to you, then you are putting yourself on a par with God and, as if you were God, you are granting your own possessions in what way you please, and to whom you please. But if you give away what you do not own, what then are you doing?[44]

To grant or give monastic property to a third party was, to him, worse than sacrilege, cupidity or idolatry. As the implications of this attack on accepted Byzantine monastic practice will be discussed at length in chapter 10, suffice it to say at this juncture that John of Antioch's views do not seem to have been widely shared in the tenth and eleventh centuries by those at the 'sharp end' of monastic land accumulation and management.

The monastic houses that have so far been discussed all enjoyed a high degree of legal independence and flexibility. But they were all ultimately subject to the imperial law and it was this law which they used to assert their independence. There were, however, some examples of monastic confederations which evolved their own internal systems of government, which almost set them outside the existing legal structures of the church or the state and created virtually self-governing regions. The holy mountains provide the best example of this last tendency, where the evolution of a central governing body of monks, headed by an elected leader, the Protos, created a specifically monastic form of government for the area concerned. This arrangement was not confined to Athos (an example which still survives) for Christodoulos was appointed to the *prostasia* of Latros and was later offered that of the communities on Mount Kellion by Alexios Komnenos. In addition, the office of Protos of Mount Ganos is known from its seal. But it is from Athos that we possess the clearest information on the workings of the Protos and his officials.[45]

The office of Protos emerged on the mountain at an early period. A *sigillion* of Basil I of 883 mentioned an assembly of monks and, in 908, the

[44] John of Antioch, Against the *charistike*, p. 110.
[45] See chapter 2, p. 50, note 50 for the seal of the Protos of Mount Ganos.

protos hesychastes, Andrew, went to Constantinople to complain about the behaviour of the monks of the Monastery of Kolobos. When Nikephoros Phokas wished to seek out his spiritual father, Athanasios, the *krites* (judge) of Thessalonike charged to find him consulted the Protos of Athos. The council of monks was similarly an early institution; the regulation of the twice yearly meetings (*synaxeis*) being one of the concerns of the *Tragos* of John Tzimiskes. The *Typikon* of Constantine Monomachos of 1045 clearly established that the duty of the Protos and the assembly was to regulate the affairs of the mountain as a whole: to arbitrate in disputes, to distribute imperial *roga* and to allot lands to the various houses. The Protos came to be recognised as the representative of Athos to the civil and ecclesiastical officials of the surrounding region. He confirmed the election of the *hegoumenoi* of the mountain, and, with the aid of elected officials, the *oikonomos*, the *epiteretes*, the *ekklesiarches* and the *dikaios*, regulated the behaviour of the monks at the *synaxeis* and dealt with breaches of monastic discipline.[46] The Protos and his council were also frequently called in to solve disputes concerning boundaries. A common method used in re-establishing disputed boundaries was with the aid of oral testimony and by consulting chrysobulls, in exactly the same way that the secular *krites* and his officials acted. On occasion, the Protos used his discretion to dispose of disputed land as in a case in 1080, when the Protos Paul confiscated the produce of a vineyard claimed by both Iviron and the monastery of Sarabare and arranged for it to be shared when the quarrel had been settled.[47]

It is not clear whether the same conciliar arrangements existed on the other holy mountains, though the emergence of the position of Protos on some of them would suggest that they did. So it can be suggested that the most prestigious monastic regions of the empire (and here one would dearly love to know about the organisation of the populous monastic communities of Cappadocia) ran their own internal affairs and presented a united front to the outside world. In this sense, they were removed from the legal structures of the empire, although in their approach to administration and dispute-solving the monks often imitated the practices of the

[46] *Prôtaton*, introduction, pp. 114–24 and nos. 1 (883) and 2 (908) for early evidence of the Protos. *Life of Athanasios* (A), chapter 46, p. 24; (B), chapter 17, p. 143. *Tragos, Prôtaton*, no. 7 (972); *Typikon* of Monomachos, *Prôtaton*, no. 8 (1045). See *Prôtaton*, introduction, pp. 151–61 for the officers.
[47] Numerous examples survive. See, for instance, *Lavra*, I, no. 17 (1012); Kaspakos v. Atzioannou; *Lavra*, I, no. 21 (1017); Lavra and Philotheou v. monk Eustathios of Magoula; *Lavra*, I, no. 23 (1018–19); Lavra and Karakallou v. Amalfitans; *Ivirôn*, II, no. 42 (1080), for the dispute between Iviron and the Monastery of Sarabare, settled during the Synaxeis of the Assumption (15 August) and St Demetrios (26 October). The procedures for boundary settlements are discussed in Morris, 'Dispute settlement', pp. 134–5, 146.

lay world, even to the extent on Athos of creating a central bureau – the Protaton – to administer matters of concern to the Athonites as a whole. But the self-governing monastic communities also provided a form of communal and elective administration not found in the secular world. It was government which replicated the traditions of monastic houses, with their emphasis on equality and the emergence of leaders whose claims were supposedly based not on the secular criteria of birth, wealth or power, but on the recognition of spiritual strength and natural authority. It also, in the case of Athos, at least, meant that the smaller houses had at least some chance of having their voices heard even though it was often difficult to circumvent the ambitions of the more prestigious houses, such as the Lavra, or Iviron. In fact, the order in which the *hegoumenoi* signed documents issued by the Protaton indicates that there was a hierarchy within the hegoumenate which allowed the larger monasteries with imperial connections a more honourable position than the smaller ones.[48]

The internal government of Athos was an arrangement which was arrived at by removing the monastic community by legal means from some of the normal administrative structures of the empire. It was a recognition, on a large scale, of that freedom that always allowed to monasteries to organise their own internal government. But it did not, of course, apply to the administration of lands held outside the monastic enclaves, in this case beyond the boundary of Athos. Here the imperial writ certainly did run unless a deliberate choice had been made to exempt monastic property from it. The acquisition of 'self-governing' status by the Holy Mountain was achieved by the accumulation of the kind of legal acts which applied to other monasteries but which were not, in their case, intertwined to such significant effect.[49]

For it was legal mechanisms, above all, that by their variety and sophistication allowed the deployment of monastic resources and the involvement of patrons and friendly laymen to best advantage. The fact that monastic property was subject to mechanisms of inheritance, sale and donation remarkably similar to those in the lay world meant that its sacred standing was in no sense a disability. In many ways its consecration provided considerable advantages in that it prevented monastic land-holdings falling completely prey to the vagaries of the secular land market and provided an invaluable check on the activities of both clerical and secular landowners. In the case of the communities of the holy mountains,

[48] See *Ivirôn*, II, introduction, p. 38, where the editors comment on the continuing high status on Athos of Iviron, whose *hegoumenos* usually signed documents under that of the Lavra and before or immediately after that of Vatopedi.
[49] Judicial exemptions are discussed in chapter 9.

their additional spiritual importance enabled them, with the support of the imperial authorities, to remove themselves to a large extent from the legal systems of the secular world. But these were extreme cases. In general, however, whatever difficulties a house might be in, and whatever its precise legal status, the fact of its dedication to God always provided a great deal of freedom of action. The secular authorities did not meddle with monasteries without first taking considerable thought, and in this sense monastic interests always had a psychological advantage when it came to making use of the law.

CHAPTER SEVEN
Fortune and misfortune

———◆———

ALTHOUGH CORRECT LEGAL title was necessary for the foundation of monastic houses and their subsequent endowment with lands and mobilisation of lay supporters, it could not, by itself guarantee them either prosperity or political independence. It is in these two respects that the greatest and most interesting variations may be seen in the landed power of the monasteries at this period. The evidence for the true state of houses and their land-holdings is patchy and varied, but a useful starting point for a retrospective survey of monastic affairs in the tenth century is a consideration of the imperial novels issued wholly or partly on the subject from the mid-century onwards: those of Nikephoros Phokas (964) and Basil II (996). It is now clear that a third, in the past attributed to John Tzimiskes or Basil II, was, in fact, an eleventh-century fabrication.[1] Nikephoros' novel has the distinction of being the only imperial document of the period which deals exclusively with monastic affairs in general and with land-holding in particular. It marks a watershed between the often critical attitude of the emperors of the tenth century towards

---

[1] Novel of Nikephoros Phokas; Zepos, I, Coll. iii, document XIX, pp. 239–52, English translation in Charanis, 'Monastic properties', pp. 56–8. For the now discredited 'novel of Basil II', see Zepos, I, Coll. iii, document XXVI, p. 259; J. P. Thomas, 'A disputed novel of Basil II', *GRBS*, 24 (1983), 273–83 and N. G. Svoronos, *La synopsis major des Basiliques et ses appendices* (Bibliothèque byzantine, Paris, 1964), p. 55, for a discussion of the textual problems and his earlier argument in favour of John Tzimiskes. See now Kaplan, *Les hommes et la terre*, p. 440 and note 327, where, following Svoronos' later research, it is identified as a forgery dating to the reign of Isaac Komnenos (1057–9). For Basil II's novel of 996, see Zepos, I, Coll. iii, document XXIX, 262–72, partial English translation in Charanis, 'Monastic properties', pp. 63–4. The place of these documents in the legal tradition of the tenth century is further discussed in chapter 9, but detailed comment must await the publication of the new editions being prepared by Svoronos at the time of his death.

the growth of monastic estates and the lavish patronage of them by the emperors of the eleventh.[2]

The theme of Nikephoros' novel is that of the incompatibility of wealth and the monastic life. Throughout the document, a clear distinction is made between the justifiable concern of monastic founders and *hegoumenoi* to ensure the survival of their houses and the avarice which had led some to the excessive accumulation of property. The novel purports to be describing the contemporary situation and, 'observing what is happening in the monasteries and the other holy houses', paints a picture of widespread greed reaching almost epidemic proportions:

> They [the monastic authorities] have turned all the attention of their souls to the care of acquiring each day thousands of measures of land, superb buildings, innumerable horses, oxen, camels and other cattle, making the life of the monk no different from that of the layman with all its vain preoccupations.[3]

The first assertion was, then, that there had been widespread accumulation by monasteries of both property and livestock during the period leading up to the promulgation of the novel. The similarity of outlook with the laity, which is amply demonstrated by the legal mechanisms discussed earlier, was commented upon in no uncertain terms. Only a strict adherence to the simplicity of the early fathers of Egypt and Palestine could lead to the true expression of the monastic vocation and the true monastic ideal was that represented by the *lavrai*, for which Nikephoros himself had a deep admiration. No justification of the acquisition by monastic houses of large amounts of property was to be found either in apostolic writing or in those of the Fathers of the Church.[4] The document then castigated the attitude of donors:

> What, then, is the matter with people who, moved by the wish to do something to please the Lord and to have their sins pardoned, neglect thus the easy commandment of Christ, which enjoins them to be free of cares and, selling their property, to distribute the proceeds amongst the poor? But instead of following this commandment, they make it intentionally more difficult and troublesome and subject themselves to more worries by seeking to establish monasteries, hostels and houses for the old.[5]

According to the novel, there had been a noticeable increase in monastic foundations in the years before 964, to such an extent that it was really not

---

[2] See chapter 8 for further discussion.
[3] Zepos, I, Coll. iii, document XIX, p. 249, ll. 19–23, translated Charanis, p. 56.
[4] *Ibid.*, p. 250, ll. 6–10; 18–21, translated Charanis, p. 56.
[5] *Ibid.*, ll. 30–6, translated Charanis, p. 56.

necessary to found any more. The reason for this increase was not at all praiseworthy:

> And moreover, who will not say that piety has become a screen for vanity when those who do good, do so in order that they may be seen by all the others? They are not satisfied that their virtuous deeds be witnessed by their contemporaries alone, but ask that future generations be not ignorant of them.[6]

It is then declared that potential donors should devote their efforts to 'good deeds' and to the monasteries which were already in existence. This was especially necessary at a time when 'there are thousands of other monasteries which have suffered by the passing of time and need much help'. A clear distinction was being made between those monasteries which were prospering (and the implication was that they were few) and the large numbers which had fallen on evil days and were 'in decay, with hardly any part of them left standing'.[7]

Nikephoros went on to declare that it would be far better to donate money to those houses in difficulties, since they could not raise money themselves by selling their lands to the laity. This money could then be used to pay for labour, draught animals and other stock and thus improve the efficiency of the running of the existing property. He forbade the granting of land in any form to monasteries unless the houses concerned could be shown to have lost all their lands. In such cases, enough to provide them with subsistence might be given, but only with imperial sanction. This passage clearly and unequivocally struck at the heart of Byzantine traditions of donation by attempting to curb the right of individuals to choose the direction of their patronage. In addition, he tried to channel donations to particular houses: 'The foundation of cells and so-called *lavrai* we do not forbid. Indeed, we find it praiseworthy, providing that these cells and *lavrai* do not strive to obtain fields and estates beyond their enclosures.'[8]

Apart from his partisan support for lavriote-influenced monasticism, two other important points were emphasised by Nikephoros: first, that the fortunes of monastic houses varied dramatically in the tenth century and secondly, that there was a considerable need for more efficient management of such monastic lands as there were.[9] How true was this

---

[6] *Ibid.*, p. 251, ll. 4–8, translated Charanis, p. 57.

[7] *Ibid.*, ll. 11–13; 35, translated Charanis, p. 57.

[8] *Ibid.*, ll. 19–23, translated Charanis, p. 57.

[9] It is more than likely that Athanasios of the Lavra was in Constantinople shortly before the promulgation of the novel. In any case, Nikephoros' admiration for this style of monasticism is well documented: see chapter 5 and Morris, 'Two faces of Nikephoros Phokas', especially pp. 101–6.

picture? Certainly other imperial documents from earlier in the century had criticised the acquisition of land by 'powerful elements' among which monastic houses and their *hegoumenoi* had been numbered, so accusations of land accumulation were not new nor, significantly, was the imperial government's practice of considering monastic landowners alongside their lay counterparts rather than as a group apart, a commendably realistic attitude.[10] But when considering Nikephoros' accusation of massive land accumulations by monasteries, we immediately come up against an almost intractable problem of evidence. For none of the archives of the great coenobitic houses which Nikephoros doubtless had in mind has survived. We are forced to rely on fleeting references in other kinds of sources and case studies from the eleventh century, which illustrate the potential scope of tenth-century coenobitic land-owning.

The accumulation of monastic estates was clearly well under way long before the tenth century, as the canonical rulings on the subject amply demonstrate. In 802, the Emperor Nikephoros I, in the fifth of his so-called 'vexations', had levied a hearth tax (*kapnikon*) on the *paroikoi* (peasants) on monastic lands and increased their taxes generally. It was clearly worth his while to do so. Monastic houses, especially in the fertile areas around the capital and in Thrace, seemed to be flourishing at the turn of the ninth century, if the report of a Muslim prisoner Harun Ibn-Yahya is anything to go by, although his account of a monastery in Thessalonike dedicated to 'Marqush' (?St Mark) containing 12,000 monks must be viewed as something of an exaggeration.[11] But it is precisely from the region through which Harun travelled that more detailed evidence can be cited for the process of land accumulation in the first half of the tenth century.

Until they were absorbed by Athonite houses, the two monasteries of St Andrew of Peristerai, near Thessalonike and John Kolobos near

---

[10] See chapter 9.
[11] For the activity of Nikephoros I, Theophanes (ed. de Boor), I, pp. 486–7; Thomas, *Private religious foundations*, pp. 128–9, sees this as the reaction of an 'anti-monastic' emperor to the benefactions of his predecessor, Irene; but see Kaplan, *Les hommes et la terre*, p. 299, where it is argued that the exactions only affected imperial monasteries. Thomas points out that Nikephoros I was an ex-logothete *ton genikon* (head of the imperial finances). He was thus well aware of the location of wealth. For Ibn-Yahya's description, see A. Vasiliev, 'Harun ibn-Yahya and his description of Constantinople', *Seminarium Kondakovianum*, 5 (1932), 149–63 and for the Monastery of *Marqush*, p. 162. The date of the journey is disputed but may have been c. 880–90 or in the early years of the tenth century. The identification of the houses mentioned is unclear, though some may have been near the Hebdomon in Constantinople: see A. A. Vasiliev and M. Canard, *Byzance et les arabes* (2 vols, Corpus Bruxellense Historiae Byzantinae, 1–2/2, Brussels, 1935, 1968, 1950), II/2; *La dynastie Macédonienne (867–959). Extraits des sources arabes*, pp. 381–2. A general impression of monastic prosperity is conveyed none the less.

Hierissos, just north of the Athonite peninsula, were both flourishing and independent institutions, well illustrating the tendencies described in the novel of Nikephoros Phokas.[12] The Monastery of Peristerai was founded on the ruins of an earlier church by St Euthymios the Younger in about 870–1. It was a *koinobion* dedicated to St Andrew and by 897 was actively building up its landed estates. The earliest surviving act of the Lavra (March 897) records the sale of land to the monastery by Georgia, widow of Demetrios Tzagastes and her children. In 941, the monastery bought 1,800 *modioi* (c. 180 hectares) of *klasma* (tax relieved) land on the peninsula of Kassandra. In 952, the sale and donation of land and a brickworks near Hierissos to it was confirmed by the *krites* Samonas of Thessalonike. By this time, the house was probably an imperial monastery. Although the fortunes of St Andrew of Peristerai have been overshadowed by those of the Lavra of Athanasios to which it was granted by (interestingly enough) Nikephoros Phokas, it was clearly a rich and powerful house long before the monasteries on Athos began to expand.[13]

Similarly, the Monastery of the Prodromos founded by John Kolobos between 866 and 868 in the *kastron* (fortified town) of Hierissos already possessed lands nearby and at Kamena and Siderokausia by the reign of Basil I. In 886 its possessions were confirmed by Leo VI. It is clear that they were considerable and included small monasteries and large amounts of property on Athos itself. In 927 the monks of Kolobos could be found in dispute with the inhabitants of the *kastron* over lands at Gradiska near the town gates and were already interested in gaining more lands in the direction of the peninsula of Athos.[14] In the normal course of events, as

---

[12] For St Andrew of Peristerai, see *Prôtaton*, pp. 35–6 and for a short description of the monastic church, see Wharton, *Art of empire*, pp. 101–2, 103, figure 4.7, and Mango, *Byzantine architecture*, p. 114, figure 167 (plan), p. 116. For the Monastery of John Kolobos, see *Prôtaton*, introduction, pp. 38–40.

[13] See Petit, 'Vie et office de St Euthyme le Jeune', pp. 192–4. Land accumulation: *Lavra*, I, no. 1 (897); *Lavra*, I, no. 2 (941); *Lavra*, I, no. 4 (952). The location of the lands on Kassandra is discussed by J. Koder, 'Die Metochia der Athos-Klöster auf Sithonia und Kassandreia', *JÖBG*, 16 (1967), 211–24, especially p. 219 and see discussion in Kaplan, *Les hommes et la terre*, pp. 77–8. The importance of *klasma* land is discussed in chapter 8. The 952 sale is analysed by G. Ostrogorsky. 'The peasant's pre-emption right; an abortive reform of the Macedonian emperors', *JRS*, 37 (1947), 117–26 and P. Lemerle, *The agrarian history of Byzantium*, revised English edn., translated G. MacNiocaill (Galway, 1979), pp. 157–60. Evidence for the status of St Andrew of Peristerai as an imperial monastery in *Lavra*, I, no. 33 (1060).

[14] *Prôtaton*, no. 1 (883). Confirmation of Leo VI (now lost) referred to in *Prôtaton*, no. 2 (?908). The land had, in fact, been obtained by false pretences and *Prôtaton*, no. 2 is an imperial act stripping the monastery of most of its newly acquired properties. See Kaplan, *Les hommes et la terre*, pp. 302–23 on the encroachments of Kolobos; further discussion in chapter 9.

has been aptly pointed out by Denise Papachryssanthou, one might have expected that the peninsula of Athos would eventually have come under the control of one of these great houses of the Chalkidike. In fact, the reverse occurred, mainly as a consequence of the paramount place enjoyed by Athonite houses in the hearts of powerful Byzantine patrons of the late tenth and eleventh centuries.[15]

Though evidence from other parts of the empire is scarce, the coastlands of Asia Minor provide another example of a region of monastic land expansion in the early tenth century. During the early years of his monastic profession, Michael Maleïnos passed some time in a monastery on Mount Kyminas. On the death of his father Eudokimos Maleïnos in about 912, he sold his share of the paternal inheritance to his brother Constantine, and gave the proceeds to the house 'to extend that worthy and holy monastery' – precisely the sort of action later to be advocated by his spiritual son, Nikephoros Phokas. But he also later founded a *xenodocheion* (traveller's hostel) on the same mountain, which would not, presumably, have been viewed with the same imperial approval.[16] It was not only the houses of the region that were expanding their holdings. The great monasteries of Constantinople probably controlled many estates in the area. The Monastery of the Myrelaion, for instance, founded in the capital by the Emperor Romanos Lekapenos, owned estates near Miletos possibly given to it soon after 920 when Romanos came to power. By 963, its representatives had come into conflict with Bishop Nikephoros of Miletos, who complained to the emperor that they had appropriated revenues and lands rightfully belonging to the bishopric. Certain *oikoi* (holdings or farms) were later returned. This territorial expansion, or perhaps illegal encroachment, clearly took place in the period that Nikephoros Phokas had under review.[17]

Nikephoros' novel also criticised the insistence of donors on founding new houses and the furthering of proprietorial ambitions not only because this contravened what he maintained was the original simplicity of the monastic life, but also because such actions deprived monasteries in distress of potential assistance. Any accurate assessment of how many there were in the empire is, of course, quite impossible. There are only

---

[15] See *Prôtaton*, pp. 39–40.

[16] Life of St Michael Maleïnos, chapter 11, pp. 557–8; chapter 15, p. 561.

[17] Life of St Nikephoros, chapter 12, pp. 143–4. Striker, *Myrelaion*, pp. 6–10 for a short history of the house. See also Janin, *Eglises et monastères*, p. 352. The *episkepsis* (estate complex) of the Myrelaion in the Thrakesion theme and its controller, John Mitas, are mentioned in the mid-eleventh century: see Life of St Lazaros, chapter 103, p. 540. It included lands in the Maeander Valley, see *BEMP*, II, no. 50. The Myrelaion also controlled the island of Leros until it was granted to St Christodoulos of Patmos, see *BEMP*, I, no. 5, pp. 44–7, especially p. 45. For *episkepseis*, see Kaplan, *Les hommes et la terre*, pp. 319–20.

scattered references in the sources to monasteries in difficulties, partly because the existence of archives and hagiographies are, in themselves, signs of some degree of survival. But a matter upon which hagiographers did comment with approval was the contribution by the saints about whom they wrote to the restoration of old houses which had fallen on bad times – a traditionally worthy act – and although such information could be seen as one of the most characteristic of monastic *topoi*, the specific nature of some of this evidence provides grounds for its reliability.

Even in Constantinopie, the prosperity of houses could not be assured. St Luke the Stylite donated all his wealth to the ailing Monastery of St Bassanios before retiring to his *stylos* at Chalcedon in 935. His help, apparently, came only just in time:

> For this holy monastery, which had been neglected *for a very long time* had almost got to the stage of not calling itself a monastery and was running the risk of becoming a secular residence, when our holy father took charge of it . . . Far from abandoning the buildings of the Holy Bassanios to complete ruin and eternal oblivion, Luke joined this good action to the shining crowd of his other merits.[18]

A similar fate had overcome the once flourishing Monastery of St Mamas when Symeon the New Theologian became its *hegoumenos* in 980:

> The monastery was completely decayed and was no longer a refuge or a shelter for monks but a rendezvous for the worldly . . . Few inhabitants remained, and, as they were lacking in learning, were starved of the Word of God in this desert . . . The monastery was in great need of repair and all the parts which had been destroyed or had fallen down, Symeon had removed, since they were useless, and he reconstructed the monastery.[19]

The symptoms of decline are clear in these two accounts, formulaic though they are: falling revenues so that the fabric could not be maintained – indicative, perhaps, of badly managed estates – decline in monastic numbers and a low intellectual level amongst those remaining; the ruins becoming a rendezvous for immoral behaviour or perhaps squatters, for in reality it was only prosperous and flourishing consecrated buildings that survived as such. The dictates of canon law stood no chance

---

[18] *Life of St Luke the Stylite*, chapter 39, p. 233. For the Monastery of St Bassanios, see Janin, *Eglises et monastères*, pp. 60–1. According to Janin, the monastery was still in existence in the twelfth century and in the thirteenth had a *metochion* in the Genoese quarter of Galata.

[19] Life of St Symeon the New Theologian, chapter 34, p. 46. For the monastery of St Mamas, see Janin, *Eglises et monastères*, pp. 314–19.

against the ravages of time and economic misfortune. If these accounts are to be believed and if houses could decline even in the heart of the capital, how much more serious might the situation have been amongst the small and unassuming houses of the provinces?

Two areas provide examples for examination and a contrasting picture of monastic fortunes emerges from them. In southern Italy, fragmentary evidence from hagiographies and the few remaining archives indicates that many of the houses founded before the more peaceful conditions of the late tenth century often enjoyed only an ephemeral existence. They were clearly small local houses, without much land and in difficult terrain. In the last years of the ninth century, St Leo–Luke of Corleone (d. 910) left the Monastery of Mulae (Mount Mula) near Cassano together with its *hegoumenos* Christopher. They made their way to the region of Merkourion where they built a monastery. After seven years they left again (and what became of the house is not clear) and moved on to Vena (modern Avena) where they built another, which, by the time of Christopher's death, had more than one hundred monks in it. Leo–Luke himself lived the solitary life nearby at Mormanno.[20] About eighty years later, St Luke of Demena is reported to have restored at least three small houses. In about 966, leaving the town of Noe (Noepoli) in Calabria he came to the ruined Monastery of St Julian near the River Agrumento (River Agri) and restored it. But he soon had to abandon his efforts; 'wild tribes from across the Alps' (probably a reference to the Emperor Otto I's invasion in 969) forced them to flee to Armentum (Armento, just north of the valley of the River Agri), but on the way they began the restoration of the hermitage and church of the Theotokos which was later to grow into the Monastery of SS Anastasios and Elias at Carbone. St Luke is also reported as having restored a church dedicated to St Laverinos at Armento.[21] In both these cases, the reasons for the original abandonment of the house are not clearly stated in the texts, but it seems extremely likely that it was associated with the Arab raiding and German and Lombard attacks of the tenth century.

In southern Italy, apart from a brief respite at the end of the tenth century and during the first two decades of the eleventh, the problem of foreign attack was to recur with depressing regularity as a cause for the abandonment of monastic houses. In 1053, Luke 'Tromarchos' (surely the *tourmarches* or military commander) and his brothers Pankratios and Nicholas granted their family foundation of St Andrew in Calabria to the

---

[20] Life of St Leo–Luke of Corleone, II, chapters 7–9, pp. 99–110; III, chapter 16, p. 100.
[21] Life of St Luke of Demena, I, chapter 7, p. 338; II, chapter 9, p. 340; chapter 14, p. 341, see Carbone (History), pp. 281–3.

Monastery of the Holy Trinity at Cava, in the hope that this more powerful house would be able to restore a monastery 'destroyed and burnt in the time of the Franks' – a reference to Norman attacks.[22] Similarly, a document of 1061 from the Carbone archive relates how the monk Hilarion, having been granted a church and monastery within the *kastron* of Trypa (probably Pertosa, near Cerchiara in Calabria) by its patrons, the *spatharokandidatos* John and his brother Nicholas (on condition that he make a somewhat better job of maintaining it than its previous *hegoumenos* Gerasimos), abandoned the attempt when 'our whole country was seized and occupied by heathen hordes and everything came to complete ruin . . . they made a complete end of the army of the Emperor and the whole was chaos'.[23] Monastic fortunes in these regions could thus change in a very short time. In his testament of 1059, the *hegoumenos* Luke of Carbone described not only how he had rebuilt the Church of the Theotokos Cassanites 'which I restored from its ruins' and had built other churches and cells for his monks but also how, 'in the time of the common pest' (the Normans again) he had gained the approval of the leading men of the *kastra* of Rocca Nuova and Battifarano for the building of small houses there in which the brethren could take refuge in times of danger.[24] Clearly, monasteries could be abandoned, rebuilt and abandoned again all within a relatively short space of time and all because of the ever present military threat.

But houses could, of course, be abandoned for other reasons. The early monks of the Monastery of St Nikodemos of Kellerana near Mammola in Calabria were so appalled by the terrain their founder had chosen that they begged to be allowed to move to the Monastery of the Theotokos at Buchita (Prachi) nearby. The saint scotched this feeble plan by taking his brethren to Buchita on the Feast of the Assumption (15 August), whence, appalled by the crowds, they soon returned to the true path of virtuous seclusion. An extreme case, perhaps, but certainly one which indicates a common problem of monastic foundation: that the search for *eremia* might go too far and the physical surroundings of a foundation might simply be too bleak to provide any sustenance in the long term.[25]

---

[22] Trinchera, no. 40 (1053).
[23] Carbone, no. 8 (1061). The document may be referring to the attacks of the Norman Drogo de Hauteville between 1043–53.
[24] Carbone, no. 7 (1059). See von Falkenhausen, *Dominazione bizantina*, 154, note 91 and A. Guillou, 'Des collectivités rurales à la collectivité urbaine en Italie méridionale byzantine (VIe–XIe s.)', *BCH*, 100 (1976), 315–25, reprinted in *Culture et société*, article XIV, see p. 321 for the locations of these towns.
[25] *Kellerana*, introduction, p. 12.

The Italian evidence indicates that the fortunes of monasteries could depend on a number of factors: the political security of a region (or lack of it); the involvement of a village community; the respect in which a founder was held; the pattern of donation (the *hegoumenos* Luke of Carbone gained enough revenue from local gifts to enable him to renovate and re-establish a series of monasteries) and, a phenomenon found elsewhere in the empire, the process by which larger and more successful monasteries were able, by means of the legal mechanisms already discussed, to take over and absorb the less flourishing monasteries and their lands. These ways and means are eloquently demonstrated in a number of examples from the Athonite archives.

Although the existence of the humble houses of Athos is often only revealed at the moment of their annexation by their more powerful neighbours and their fortunes are overshadowed by the prosperity of such great houses as the Lavra and Iviron, they may well (as the few Italian examples would suggest) have been far more typical of the monastic life of the empire as a whole. The Monastery of Monoxylitou provides an example of a house 'deserted and poor', which ultimately came under the control of a more prosperous institution, in this case the Lavra.[26] The fortunes of the Monastery of Pithara near Karyes may stand as a further example. It was founded some time before 976 and was a small, simple establishment qualified by the description of *agridion* (separate farmstead) meaning that it stood apart from the main settlement. It was bought, at some time before 1002, by John the Iberian and one Demetrios Lamares, who then extended it. It came into the hands of the monk Cyril, Demetrios' spiritual son, who in turn passed it on to his disciple, George Charzana, in return for 210 *nomismata*. The case of Pithara thus provides an instance of a humble house being transformed into something rather more valuable, as the purchase price indicates.[27]

A final case, that of the monastic groups of Chaldou in the south of the Athonite peninsula, presents an instance of the way in which eremitic groups could find themselves in difficulties as a consequence of the differing spiritual attitudes of their neighbours. The hesychasts flourished in the mid-tenth century, relying on the aid of other monasteries. But as the great houses began to establish themselves as quasi-*koinobia*, they ran into trouble. Their neighbours refused to give them any more food and,

[26] *Lavra*, I, no. 25 (1024).
[27] *Lavra*, I, no. 12 (996). It is not clear now long the house had been deserted, though since the grant was made by the Protos and the official council of the mountain, perhaps the thirty-year rule for the redistribution of secular *klasma* was being applied by the Athonite authorities. If so, the house had been deserted since c. 960. For the term *agridion*, see Kaplan, *Les hommes et la terre*, pp. 112–15.

rather than disperse, they formed themselves into a *koinobion*, later known – something of a contradiction in terms – as the Monastery of the Hesychasts.[28] This group had earlier clearly enjoyed some kind of centralised organisation, if only for the distribution of food, but it was destroyed not by lack of resources, but by the changing monastic fashions of the area in which the hermits lived. The case may well have had parallels in other parts of the empire where hesychastic groups were being replaced by lavriote influenced *koinobia*; western Asia Minor and southern Italy spring immediately to mind.

As in Italy, political conditions in the northern Balkans cannot have helped monasteries struggling for survival. A major cause of these difficulties, in Thrace in particular, was the depredations of the Bulgarian wars at the beginning of the tenth century. The Patriarch Nicholas Mystikos, in a series of rather stereotyped letters, bewailed the destruction of monasteries and the dispersal of monks which had occurred after the outbreak of hostilities in 912, and although his accounts have more than a hint of the 'atrocity story' about them, there seems little doubt that the lands between Bulgaria and the Aegean, monastic estates among them, suffered considerably from the continual campaigning between 894 and 927.[29] Slav and Magyar raiding parties also penetrated far into the Balkans in the first half of the tenth century.[30] Similarly, Muslim attacks on the coast took their toll of monasteries; the parlous state of a small house on the Island of Gymnopelagision (Pelagonisi in the North Sporades) at the end of the tenth century was due both to continued Muslim raiding and the depredations of the imperial sailors stationed there ostensibly to protect the islanders.[31] The economic repercussions of these invasions were long felt. Much of the land immediately to the north of Athos was deserted by its population in the early tenth century, as its resale as *klasma* in 941 indicates. Those monasteries that survived suffered losses of crops, animals and manpower impossible to recoup without the help of donations of lay patrons. The Monastery of Kolobos, for instance, was assigned forty peasants (*paroikoi*)

---

[28] *Philotheou*, no. 1 (1087), seems to refer to this transformation; we await a modern commentary. It occurred before 991, as *Lavra*, I, no. 17, dating from that year, deals with a question of boundaries involving the Monastery of the Hesychasts, cf. *Prôtaton*, p. 102, note 70. For the later history of the house, see notes to *Lavra*, I, no. 28 (1030).

[29] Nicholas Mystikos, *Letters*, nos. 11 (Winter, 918–19); 14 (July/August 920); 23 (922); 24 (922–June 923); 26 (922–June 923); 29 (923–4).

[30] See chapter 1, pp. 26–8.

[31] *Lavra*, I, no. 10 (993), relates the history of the island in the tenth century. It was bought by the monk Sergios as *klasma* in 973, so its decline must have begun some thirty years earlier, c. 943. See, however, Malamut, *Les îles*, I, pp. 114; 143; II, pp. 397; 462–3, who dates the Muslim attacks to 988–9.

by imperial decree in 959–60 after a Bulgarian attack on Hierissos had dispersed the population.[32]

However, war, though serious, was certainly not the only cause of monastic decline. If Basil II's novel of 996 is anything to go by, then it must be assumed that many monasteries (perhaps even the majority) were very small establishments, often with fewer than ten members. If no more could be found to continue the contemplative life or if, for some reason, the monks ceased to be able to support themselves, then such houses, as Nikephoros Phokas pointed out, could not survive without outside help. While we know nothing precise of the effects of the harsh winters and famines of the early tenth century on the monasteries (save that those in Constantinople at least fulfilled their traditional role as dispensers of imperial charity to the poor) they, too, suffered from the crop failures and harsh weather just as much as the laity.[33]

But varied fortunes in monastic houses were not solely confined to the tenth century. In the eleventh century, while more northerly houses such as those at Bačkovo, Rhaidestos and Stroumitza seem to have been flourishing, others enjoyed only precarious prosperity. On Athos, the process of the absorption of failing houses by more successful ones and the restoration of ruined monasteries by new patrons continued. The Monastery of the old monk Laurentios Paximada at Meleon, having been left 'leaderless and deserted', was granted by the Protos in 1076 to Neophytos, the *hegoumenos* of the Monastery of St Constantine *tou Zebetou* (later Chilandar).[34] The Monastery of Xenophon, founded in the last years of the tenth century and later one of the more prosperous houses on Athos, declined in the course of the eleventh century. Its buildings were restored, decorated and extended only as a consequence of the intervention of the monk Symeon the Sanctified.[35]

Examples may also be cited from outside Athos. Michael Attaliates' small yearly subsidy to the Nunnery of St Prokopios at Rhaidestos was to help a house which had been 'ruined by apostates' – probably a reference to destruction during political violence in the mid–eleventh

---

[32] Much destruction followed the Arab attack on Thessalonike in 904. For the Bulgar attack and the subsequent replacement of *paroikoi*, see *Ivirôn*, II, no. 32 (probably 1059), which lists the lost document by which this was done: *Ivirôn*, I, introduction, pp. 12, 30; and F. Dölger, 'Ein Fall slavischer Einsiedlung im Hinterland von Thessalonike im 10. Jahrhundert', *Sitzungsberichte der bayerischen Akademie der Wissenschaften, phil.-hist. Klasse* (1952), I, 3–28 especially p. 7. The attack probably took place between 943 and 959–60, cf. *Prôtaton*, p. 39.

[33] See *Chronicle of the Logothete*, pp. 908–9 for imperial food doles in the monasteries and Morris, 'Poor and powerful' for the famine and its effects.

[34] Chilandar (*Supplementa*), no. 1 (1076).

[35] *Xénophon*, no. 1 (1083) and see chapter 3, p. 86.

century.[36] Military campaigns were just as much a threat to monastic survival in the eleventh century as they had been in the tenth, for this was, after all, the period at which the monastic structure of Anatolia was irrevocably destroyed. In the northern provinces, the incursions of Petchenegs and Normans took their toll. The Church of the Saviour near Derkos in Thrace, restored by Cyril Phileotes and his brother, the monk Matthew, at the end of the eleventh century 'from non-existence into existence and a good existence at that', may have owed its original decline to its position in the path of Petcheneg attacks.[37]

In fact, monastic prosperity was probably more a localised exception than the rule in the tenth and eleventh centuries. Nikephoros Phokas could point to the contrast between the flourishing houses of his own day and the many that were clinging to survival; so, too, could commentators at the end of the following century. Nicholas Kataskepenos, the author of the Life of St Cyril Phileotes, described, in rather over-flattering terms, Alexios Komnenos' generosity towards monasteries:

> The Emperor ordered through chrysobulls that the corn and oil they needed, together with the cost of transport, should be given to all monasteries, not only to those that were within the capital, but also to those in the vicinity, to the west, to the east, and on the mountains, with the exception of *a few of them that were flourishing*.[38]

Thus a picture emerges of greatly differing fortunes amongst the monastic houses of the tenth and eleventh centuries. Many houses were so small that they could expect only an ephemeral existence; others suffered from the effects of warfare and climatic disaster. So the criteria for the survival and prosperity of a few, often extremely powerful houses, need to be established and analysed. In all cases, the 'reputation' of the house and the ability to attract and retain powerful lay patrons had an important part to play.

Nikephoros Phokas wished money rather than land to be channelled into existing houses, so that those in difficulties would have the wherewithal to provide themselves with workers and animals. He pointed out the folly of acquiring large estates without enough people to work them.

---

[36] *Diataxis* of Attaliates, p. 47. Lemerle, *Cinq études*, 82, note 26 suggests that the destruction occurred during the revolt of Nikephoros Bryennios against Michael Doukas in 1077–8, when Rhaidestos took Bryennios' side; but Gautier has shown (*Diataxis* of Attaliates, p. 46, note 30) that as this revolt began in the autumn of 1077 and the *Diataxis* was drawn up in March of that year, this cannot be the case. He suggests that the damage was caused during the siege of the town in 1047 by Theodore Strabomytes and Marianos Branas; see also Cheynet, *Pouvoir et contestations*, no. 65, pp. 59–60.

[37] Life of St Cyril Phileotes, chapter 21, p. 104 (329).

[38] *Ibid.*, chapter 47, p. 234 (460–1) (added emphasis).

As in all pre-industrial societies, in Byzantium the relationship of labourers to land was crucial. However fertile the land, its maximum productivity could not be attained, still less maintained, without a sufficient supply of workers. Some types of agrarian production, such as vineyards or animal husbandry, employed little manpower; arable farming was far more labour intensive. The clearance of land and the construction of monastic buildings and improvements such as mills and drainage systems also required a substantial pool of labour. Nikephoros' comments give rise to two important questions. First, was there a labour shortage on monastic estates in the years before 964? And secondly, were monastic houses in a better position to gain manpower than the laity?

Alan Harvey's recent work on the Byzantine economy from 900–1200 has presented a strong case for seeing the period as one of overall demographic expansion, although it has to be said that much of his evidence comes from the very monasteries under discussion! So we are still left with the problem that the successful houses from which most of the documentation comes were by definition more able than others to gain or retain labour and thus may present a false picture of a general increase in manpower. In any case, more localised and short-lived demographic changes, such as the barbarian raids of the tenth century or the famines and adverse weather conditions, would have had a far more serious effect on monasteries already leading a very precarious existence, and these have not yet been fully studied.[39]

The description of St Luke the Younger leading his flock in southern Greece away from the Bulgar attack of 918 may stand as an example of this sort of local demographic movement, and similar scenes were doubtless enacted on many other parts of the Aegean coastline, especially in the rich arable area around Thessalonike. Indeed, the *Marcian Treatise*, a tenth-century handbook for tax officials, cited barbarian raiding as the main cause of the flight of small land-holders from their lands. But were such migrations long term and did they leave the areas concerned completely deserted? It is difficult to accept that this was the case. Villages on the frontiers or on the main routes used by raiding parties whether in the Balkans or Anatolia clearly suffered most, but in other places temporary flight would occur as news of a raiding party spread and the population would return as soon as the danger was past. In the areas most attractive and accessible to raiders, such as the Thracian plain and the livestock-rearing regions of the Anatolian plateau, monasteries, constituting easily recognised centres of movable wealth, were probably particularly hard hit in the short term, but, especially in the Balkans, population (and

---

[39] See Harvey, *Economic expansion*, especially chapter 2.

therefore potential labour supplies) was often increased by an influx of Slav and Bulgar settlers.[40]

The sources provide much more assistance in assessing the short- and long-term effects of the climatic disasters of the early tenth century and their aftermath. Although the imperial legislation concerning it is highly rhetorical, the 'great famine' of 928 was clearly a disaster of the first magnitude. It had repercussions on both the local and the state level. Many free peasants were forced to sell their lands to the *dynatoi* (the powerful landed interests among which the monasteries were numbered) in return for food or the means to buy it at inflated prices. What then became of them? Did they migrate away from their home villages? In the areas near Constantinople this was certainly the case, as there was a considerable influx of indigents into the city. In other areas, the crisis of the famine precipitated a social as well as a demographic change. Added to the mortality attendant on the famine came a change in the distribution of labour, an increase in dependent tenures and thus a change both in the geographic concentration of manpower and also in the nature of its control. Availability of manpower was an important underlying factor in the expansion of the successful monastic houses of the late tenth century and it may well be, although we have no evidence of particular cases, that it was in the aftermath of the famine that many monasteries acquired both estates and the manpower to work them. In addition, as traditional centres of charity, they attracted the indigent and perhaps retained some of them as monks or estate workers.[41]

The statement in Nikephoros Phokas' novel that there were 'thousands' of monasteries suffering from a shortage of labour seems, on the face of it, to be in direct contradiction to the accusations of earlier tenth-century emperors that monasteries should be considered as 'powerful' – implying at least a degree of economic prosperity. But the two analyses are not necessarily mutually exclusive; peasants in difficulties would naturally have fled to establishments, such as the villa of the parents of St Luke the Stylite, where they knew (or hoped) they could get help or shelter.[42] The smaller monastic establishments, the already failing houses such as those highlighted by Nikephoros and the peasant foundations of the type later described in the novel of Basil II, shared the fate of the surrounding small landowners. If these humble establishments

---

[40] *Life of St Luke the Younger*, col. 449 (*PG*) and letters of Nicholas Mystikos cited in note 29, above. The *Marcian Treatise* is discussed in chapter 9.
[41] For the legislation following the famine, see Zepos, I, Coll. iii, document VI, p. 215 and reference to it in the eleventh century in *Peira*, IX.1, p. 38. For the selling of the lands to the *dynatoi*, Zepos, I, Coll. iii, document V, p. 210. The tenurial consequences of the famine are further examined in chapter 8. For the poor in Constantinople, see note 33 above.
[42] Life of St Luke the Stylite, chapter 17, p. 201. They lived in the Anatolikon theme.

did constitute the majority of the monasteries of the empire, then Nikephoros' assessment of 'thousands' in difficulty may not be such an exaggeration. And the ability to obtain or attract labour was one of the main criteria of the reputation and efficiency of a house, if not its very survival.

The most available source of labour was the monks themselves. The importance of contemplation was always acknowledged, but a significant feature of the *koinobia* (especially those influenced by Stoudite customs) and the lavriote-influenced houses as well, was the emphasis on physical work. Even *hegoumenoi* could be found working alongside their monks; Athanasios of the Lavra met his death in a fall from a building he was helping to construct.[43] With some subtraction for the old, the sick and those involved in administration, the full monastic complement was available to work for the house. It is therefore of some importance to establish monastic numbers wherever this is possible. In some cases, the number of monks was limited by the founder. Manuel of Stroumitza stipulated that the number of monks in his house should not exceed ten, even if the monastery became more prosperous.[44] Many houses may have been deliberately kept below this number as any excess, according to Basil II's novel of 996, might bring them under episcopal control. The Monastery of Bačkovo was limited to fifty monks (plus the *hegoumenos*) and Attaliates' house dedicated to Christ the Most Merciful in Constantinople, to seven. But in other cases there is evidence of these numbers being greatly exceeded. Athanasios originally stipulated that his *lavra* should contain eighty monks in *kellia*, but later allowed forty more. By 1030, however, the Lavra contained 700 monks and an act of 1102 speaks of 'a great increase in monks', though it does not specify how many. There may indeed have been a thousand monks in the house by the end of the eleventh century, some of whom would have been deputed to man the *metochia* (dependent houses) beyond the mountain.[45]

While this may stand out as the most populous monastery of the period, there were others with more than healthy complements. Iviron increased its numbers similarly dramatically: by the time of John the Iberian's death in c. 1008, the monastery sheltered three hundred monks. Xerochoraphion contained eighty monks at the end of the tenth century, but by the mid-eleventh, the total had risen to three hundred. On a somewhat lower level, the Monastery of Xenophon on Athos contained fifty-five monks in 1083 and, as we have seen, on Mount Galesion, at the death of St Lazaros in 1054, his foundation of the Anastasis contained

43 Life of St Athanasios (A), chapter 234, pp. 112–13; (B), chapters 65–6, pp. 200–1.
44 Stroumitza, p. 72, ll. 28–30.
45 Pakourianos, p. 57; *Diataxis* of Attaliates, p. 59; *Lavra*, I, no. 27 (1030); no. 55 (1102).

forty monks and those of the Soter and the Theotokos twelve each. The evidence from southern Italy is scarcer, but St Leo-Luke's foundation at Vena is reported to have had a population of 100 monks.[46] It is not possible to make any meaningful estimate of the total monastic population of the empire in the tenth and eleventh centuries, still less even to guess what proportion of the total population of the empire it comprised. But from the sparse evidence available, it can be seen that some houses were capable of almost unlimited expansion in numbers as they owned extensive estates while others, like those on Galesion, still maintained a healthy complement of monks, even though they were situated in harsh and uninviting areas.

The rôle of charismatic monastic founders in attracting the early monks to these houses was crucial. Athanasios of Athos must stand as a prime example, although one could also add the names of John the Iberian, Paul of Latros and Lazaros of Mount Galesion to this select list. Their personalities and the type of monasticism they professed were their chief assets in attracting recruits. The hagiographers of the period emphasised as one of the signs of sanctity the ability of holy men to gather others about them and there was thus a direct connection between the spiritual and the economic strength of successful monastic foundations. But although the monks themselves could provide a substantial body of manpower, this might take some years to build up and there might well, initially, have been an unfavourable balance between the amount of land their houses possessed (and its intractability) and the manpower available to work it. It is here that the availability of workers from other sources became an important factor in the development and prosperity of monastic lands.

The main source of labour from outside the monastic ranks came from the dependent peasantry of their estates. They are usually referred to as *paroikoi*, although other terms are also used. In a *praktikon* (fiscal document listing peasant obligations) describing the property granted in 1073 by the Emperor Michael VII Doukas to his brother Andronikos near the Maeander Valley in western Asia Minor, the *paroikoi* were described as *zeugaratoi*, *boidatoi* and *aktemones*. These terms were official classifications on the basis of the number of oxen a peasant owned: the *aktemon* was a peasant without oxen, a *boidatos* possessed one animal and a *zeugaratos* a pair. But Svoronos long ago suggested that the terms also indicated the amount of land they cultivated. Thus, he maintained, the *zeugaratos* had 150 *modioi* (c. 15 hectares), the *boidatos* 100 *modioi*

---

[46] Life of SS John and Euthymios, chapter 26, p. 108; Life of St Nikephoros, chapter 20, p. 150; Hiéra-Xérochoraphion, 7; *Xénophon*, no. 1 (1083); Life of St Lazaros, chapter 246, p. 585; Life of St Leo-Luke of Corleone, III, chapter 14, p. 100.

(c. 10 hectares) and the *aktemon* 75 *modioi* (c. 7.5 hectares). Recently, Michel Kaplan has suggested figures of 75–100 *modioi*; c. 60 *modioi* and c. 12 *modioi*, respectively. These figures should, however, be used only as a rough guide as there were considerable variations throughout the empire, depending on the type of land being allotted.[47]

If a *paroikos* had been settled on his plot for at least thirty years, he could not be expelled by the landowner, but nor (in the tenth century at least) could he alienate it himself. Although the evidence cited is often from a later period, it is generally thought that *paroikoi* could hold land from more than one landowner. They paid rent to their landlord (or landlords) and, increasingly by the eleventh century, paid directly to him state taxes from which the landowner (individual or monastic house) had been exempted by imperial privileges.[48] Sometimes *paroikoi* had to perform labour services for their landlords, but this was not an automatic consequence of paying dues to him. A chrysobull of the Emperor Alexios Komnenos for the Lavra dated to 1081 relates how the monks feared that after the emperor's brother, Adrian, had been granted the state taxes of the peninsula of Kassandra, 'they would be considered as *paroikoi* of the man to whom the state taxes were paid, as though they were not owners of the land for which they paid taxes elsewhere'. The emperor reassured them that, although they no longer paid taxes for this land directly to the state (*demosion*), their tenurial position remained unaltered. The monks were clearly alarmed that they would fall victim to the assumption that with the grant of taxes from an estate came a grant of the services of the peasantry.[49]

The number of *paroikoi* on a given estate, whether monastic or lay, was, in theory, controlled by the state. Only peasants with no land of their own and therefore no fiscal obligations to the state (*ateleis paroikoi*) could be freely settled by landowners looking for more labour. There is evidence that checks were made by imperial officials to identify those landowners who had more *paroikoi* than those to which they were entitled or had gained control of *prosodiarioi demosiarioi* or *demosiarioi paroikoi* (peasants who owed returns to the fisc because they were themselves land-holders or who were dependent peasants on state – usually *klasma* – lands), so there was certainly nothing even resembling a free labour market. Thus it was of great importance to monastic houses to acquire *paroikoi*,

---

[47] *Praktikon* of Michael VII Doukas: *BEMP*, II, no. 50. See N. G. Svoronos, 'Remarques sur les structures économiques de l'empire byzantin au XIe siècle', *TM*, 6 (1976), 49–67, especially p. 5, note 24, Kaplan, *Les hommes et la terre*, pp. 491–2, Harvey, *Economic expansion*, pp. 49–55.
[48] For security of tenure, see Harvey, *Economic expansion*, pp. 45–6 and Kaplan, *Les hommes et la terre*, pp. 268–9.
[49] *Lavra*, I, no. 46 (1084).

particularly *ateleis paroikoi*. They provided not only a source of labour, but of manpower already based on the land in question and familiar with its agricultural problems. If the *paroikos'* payment of state taxes and dues was also assigned to the monasteries, then their treasuries also benefited.[50]

But where did the *paroikoi* of the monastic estates of this period actually come from? Some were clearly already settled on estates acquired by or donated to monasteries, but Ostrogorsky suggested that the *demosiarioi paroikoi* could have been synonymous with the 'poor' (*penetes*) whose difficulties in the tenth century were chronicled by the imperial legislation. He cited two documents to prove the point: one a *sigillion* of the *protospatharios* Symeon, *ekprosopon* of Thessalonike and Strymon to Athanasios of the Lavra (974) and the second, a *sigillion* of the *protospatharios* and *ekprosopon* Theodore Kladon to the Monasteries of Kolobos and Polygyros at Hierissos (975).[51] Both of these officials were taking part in an enquiry to discover how many holders of military estates (*stratiotai*) and *demosiarioi paroikoi* had fled to great estates, especially those of the church. If these *demosiarioi paroikoi* were indeed the long-suffering *penetes*, whose movements on to the lands of their protectors (including monasteries) have already been mentioned, then it could be that the imperial officials were attempting to remedy the consequences of a large-scale migration of their own peasants, forced to abandon their lands by their inability to meet the tax burden that went with them or, in the case of the *stratiotai* to undertake the military service associated with their properties. But there are problems with this interpretation. The two documents are both from the same region of northern Greece and although they both derive from an imperial prototype, there is, unfortunately, no further evidence to suggest that such an enquiry was being carried out in other parts of the empire.

Furthermore, it is simply not the case that the *penetes* referred to in the imperial legislation comprised *only* the *demosiarioi paroikoi*. For the term *penetes* was used in a very general sense by the legislators to indicate all those who were not *dynatoi* and covered a very large variety of social groups. It clearly embraced the *demosiarioi paroikoi*, but was not exclusively composed of them. Many of the *penetes* were peasants who, while paying taxes to the state, and performing general labour services when demanded of them (such as in preparation for a campaign), were not bound to it by any other form of dependency. But among the *demosiarioi*

---

[50] For the status of the various *paroikoi*, see Kaplan, *Les hommes et la terre*, pp. 264–5. Exemptions from taxation are further discussed in chapter 9.

[51] G. Ostrogorsky, *Quelques problèmes d'histoire de la paysannerie byzantine* (Corpus Bruxellense Historiae Byzantinae, Subsidia II, Brussels, 1956), chapter 1. *Sigillion* of Symeon: *Lavra*, I, no. 6 (?974). *Sigillion* of Theodore Kladon: *Ivirôn*, I, no. 2 (September 975).

paroikoi, on the other hand, were *paroikoi* actually living on state lands. So land-holders with only a *fiscal* responsibility towards the *demosion* were thus putting themselves under the protection of the great estates and thereby reducing their social status and becoming liable to labour services and, in addition, in the case of the *demosiarioi paroikoi*, the *demosion* was also in danger of losing both its fiscal dues *and* its resources of manpower.[52]

But although many *paroikoi* may have found their way on to the lands of monastic houses during the crises of the tenth century, the most common source of *paroikoi* for monasteries was probably their donation. When documents speak of the 'gift' of *paroikoi* to a monastic house they do not mean the literal transference of persons on a par with the deportations and resettlements frequently practised in this period.[53] They mean either the allocation of *paroikoi* to the recipient with the gift of an estate, or the increase in the number of the *paroikoi* of a certain estate whose fiscal dues and in some cases labour services would now be transferred from the state to the house in question. In the latter case, a useful measurement of imperial approval is supplied, since only the central government could approve such reallocations of revenue and services. Although publication of new archival material will mean that new data will have to be added, an attempt has been made in Table 1 to present the known gifts and acquisitions of *paroikoi* in this period. The survey has been extended to the end of the eleventh century as a means of placing the tenth in perspective.[54]

Although Nikephoros Phokas may have been right to maintain that some monasteries were suffering from a lack of manpower, this was certainly not the case in certain houses with which he was familiar. The conclusions that can be drawn from Table 1 can only be impressionistic and the preponderance of examples from Athonite monasteries is a consequence of the survival of their archives, but if the other examples from outside the Holy Mountain are considered, and if it is assumed that many other houses of which nothing is known may have enjoyed similar donations and exemptions, imperial munificence of this kind clearly played an important part in ensuring the supply of manpower to monasteries. Again, the link between house and patron, especially if that patron held imperial rank, had definite and beneficial economic consequences.

[52] See Morris, 'Poor and powerful', pp. 17–22.
[53] For deportations and resettlements, see P. Charanis, 'The transfer of population as a policy in the Byzantine empire', *Comparative Studies in Society and History*, 3 (1961), 140–56, reprinted in *Studies in the demography of the Byzantine empire* (London, 1972), article III and Kaplan, *Les hommes et la terre*, p. 451.
[54] See Table 1, pp. 186–8.

Table 1. *Imperial donations of paroikoi to monasteries c. 950–1118*[a]

Athonite houses (or houses which came under Athonite control)

Date	House	Donor	No.	Type	Estate/remarks	Source
945–6 [975, 995, 1059]	Leontia (to Iviron 979–80)	Const. Porph.	36	Oikoi exkoussatoi or ateleis paroikoi	Not known if households or individuals meant	*Iviron,* I, nos. 2, 8; II, 32
945–59 [?1028–34, 1060, 1079]	St Andrew of Peristerai (to Lavra 964)	Const. Porph.	100	Ateleis paroikoi Douloparoikoi	Tzechlianes (nr. Peristerai)	*Lavra,* I, no. 33
945–59 [975]	Polygyros (to Iviron 979–80)	Const. Porph.	20			*Ivirôn,* I, no. 2
957–8 [1059]	Monastery tou Atho	Const. Porph.	70	Ateleis paroikoi	Halikai; Galeai; Dobritza; Dobrodolon (all Kassandra); Psalis	*Ivirôn* II, no. 32
959–60 [995, 1059]	Kolobos (to Iviron 979–80)	Romanos II	40	Ateleis paroikoi	Town and region of Hierissos	*Ivirôn* I, nos. 3, 8; II, 32
959–63 [?964, 974]	St Andrew of Peristerai	Romanos II	22 10	'Not demosiarioi'	Hierissos Nomeristai and other *proasteia*	*Lavra* I, no. 6

Date	Monastery	Emperor	Number	Oikoi exkoussatoi or demosiarioi / Ateleis paroikoi		Reference
Pre-979–80 [1059, 1061]	Iviron	Basil II	60	Oikoi exkoussatoi or demosiarioi		*Ivirôn* II, nos. 32, 33
979–80 [1059, 1061]	Iviron	Basil II	40	Ateleis paroikoi		*Ivirôn* II, nos. 32, 33
Pre-c. 1018	Xenophon	Basil II	12		Monastery ton Hieromnemon	*Xénophon*, no. 1
1057–9 [1078–81, 1081]	Amalfitan (to Lavra 1287)	Isaac I Komnenos		Ateleis paroikoi	Koutariane (nr. Prinarion) ?Bolobisda ?Ramnon	*Lavra* I, no. 43
1079	Lavra	Nikephoros III Botaniates	100	Ateleis paroikoi		*Lavra* I, no. 38
1080	Vatopedi	Nikephoros III Botaniates	50	Ateleis paroikoi	Salama (nr. Peritheorion) Abarnikea (nr. Chrysoupolis) St Paul (Kassandra) Krimota Kyrtos tou Hysmercs (Trantaphyllos)	Vatopedi, no. 2
1101	Iviron	Alexios I Komnenos	100	Ateleis paroikoi	All lands	*Ivirôn* II, no. 52
1104	Lavra	Alexios I Komnenos	80 / 10		Lorotomou Asmalou	*Lavra* I, no. 56

Table 1 (cont.)

Date	House	Donor	No.	Type	Estate/remarks	Source
Houses outside Athos						
1044 [1050, 1060, 1072]	Nea Mone	Constantine IX Monomachos	24	*Ateleis paroikoi*	Kalothekia	Zepos I, Appendix, IV, XII
Pre-1089	Patmos	Alexios I Komnenos	12	Families	Freed specifically from *strateia* Status not clear	*BEMP*, II, no. 54
1099	Patmos	Alexios I Komnenos	12	*Ateleis paroikoi*	Leros	*BEMP*, I, no. 18
1106	Stroumitza	Alexios I Komnenos	12	*Ateleis paroikoi*	Stroumitza	Stroumitza, no. 2
1100–c. 1110	Theotokos Evergetis Cp.	?Alexios I Komnenos (Text names 'Kyr Anthony' = ?*megadoux* John Doukas)	12 16	*Zeugaratoi* *Zeugaratoi*	tou Theophanou (Boleron theme) tou Epiphaniou, nr. Chortokopion (Thrace)	Evergétis, p. 93

Note: *ª*Dates in brackets indicate confirmation of donations.
Among the many chrysobulls granted to Gregory Pakourianos and listed in his *typikon*, there may well have been those assigning *paroikoi*, but their texts have not survived. See Pakourianos, pp. 125–31.

Long before Nikephoros came to power, then, the problems of monastic manpower had already begun to be solved by the donation of labour as well as estates. But another form of assistance was also making the gulf between favoured and popular houses and their less fortunate counterparts more profound. In order to obtain stock, to improve properties and to supplement the manpower available with hired labour, monasteries as much as individual landowners required a steady influx of cash. Selling produce was one obvious source, but for the lay landlord, money might also come from the proceeds of an imperial post or from a share of booty taken in war. But these further options were not usually open to monastic landlords, although those founding monasteries after successful lay careers (like John the Iberian, Gregory Pakourianos or Symeon the Sanctified) could bring considerable fortunes with them. Again, patrons were indispensable. While the details of donations from the laity are sparse in the surviving documents, the case of Iviron demonstrates how a continuing stream of gold could quickly make the fortune of a single monastic house. From the time of its foundation at the end of the tenth century, Iviron was the recipient of large monetary gifts because of its connection with a closely knit ethnic group – the Georgians – whose important rôle in the government and defence of the empire was reflected by the fortunes they made and the generosity of their gifts. As we have seen, John Tornik, returning from his successful campaign against Bardas Skleros, made an enormous donation of 12 *kentenaria* of gold (equivalent to 86,400 *nomismata*) to Iviron. A series of donations noted in the *Synodikon* (commemoration list) of Iviron for the eleventh century, indicate frequent offerings of 200 *nomismata* or more and the Will of Kale Pakouriane also reveals a high level of monetary donation to the house. She gave 7 *litrai* (Byzantine pounds) of *nomismata chichata* (504 *nomismata*) to the house, in return for the burial of her husband, Symbatios, there.[55]

By the end of the tenth century, Iviron itself was spreading largesse throughout Athos. In 979 14 *litrai* of gold (1,008 *nomismata*) were granted to the Protaton for general distribution; in 982–3, another 14 *litrai* (1,008 *nomismata*) followed by a further 28 *litrai* (2,016 *nomismata*) in 984–5. Individual monasteries also benefited: the Lavra of Athanasios received an annual sum of 244 *nomismata*, obtained for them from the Emperor John Tzimiskes by John the Iberian and 600 *nomismata* more for the construction of *kellia* at the Lavra. The Amalfitan monks were assisted

[55] For John Tornik's donation see Life of SS John and Euthymios, chapter 14, p. 93. It was probably in bullion as well as cash. See *Ivirôn*, II, pp. 3–11 for details of monetary gifts recorded in the *Synodikon*. The Will of Kale/Maria Pakouriane is *Ivirôn*, II, no. 47 (1098).

with money to help them build a house.[56] It is impossible to tell how many other houses enjoyed monetary donations on this sort of level. But a useful comparison can be made with the cash made available annually by Michael Attaliates and Gregory Pakourianos to the foundations they had established (Tables 2 and 3).[57]

Attaliates' expenditure was approximately 150 *nomismata* per annum and the breakdown of the list shows that while none of the money was spent in large sums, the small donations for specified purposes could soon build up. Pakourianos' donations, on the other hand, reveal a total of about 2,057 *nomismata* per annum (including the money always to be kept in reserve in the monastery's coffers), to be spent on his foundation at Bačkovo. The amounts noted in the Georgian *Synodikon* of Iviron reveal that benefactions of c. 150–200 *nomismata* were by no means unusual, though very large donations were somewhat out of the ordinary. Attaliates' donations comprised only a fraction of his total revenues (which Lemerle has estimated at 150 *litrai* (10,800 *nomismata*) per annum), so it is possible to suggest that these sorts of donations came to Iviron from men and women of the Attaliates type: rich aristocrats parting with only a fraction of their wealth. Pakourianos, on the other hand, is known to have made over all his estates to his monastery and had no children to claim an inheritance. Thus the Iviron donations of, say, 800 *nomismata* or more could reflect actions on a par with the annual expenditure envisaged by Pakourianos involving the donation of a man's entire wealth in land, bullion and precious objects and the enjoyment of the revenue from it.[58]

Another source of monetary donations, which may be profitably compared with these indications of private charity, was the emperor. Those monastic houses of the empire which enjoyed particular imperial favour were granted *rogai* (annual subsidies) in exactly the same way as annual salaries were paid to administrative officials.[59] This was not only a

[56] For donations from Iviron to other Athonite houses and the Mese (the Athonite central administration), see Life of SS John and Euthymios, chapters 16–17, pp. 94–6 and *Ivirôn*, I, introduction, pp. 35–6.

[57] Tables 2 and 3, pp. 191 and 193.

[58] For Attaliates' wealth, see Lemerle, *Cinq études*, pp. 110–11. Hendy has shown that the Gornoslav hoard of 786 *nomismata* was probably money set aside in 1189 by the Monastery of Bačkovo in accordance with Pakourianos' instructions for payments in 1190, but was lost during the passage of the Third Crusade, see M. F. Hendy, 'The Gornoslav Hoard, the Emperor Frederick I and the Monastery of Bachkovo', in C. N. L. Brooke, B. H. I. H. Stewart, J. G. Pollard and T. R. Volk (eds.), *Studies in numismatic method presented to Philip Grierson* (Cambridge, 1983), pp. 179–91, reprinted in *The economy, fiscal administration and coinage of Byzantium* (London, 1989), article XI.

[59] For *rogai* see Hendy, *Monetary economy*, pp. 190–2, who translates the famous description of the tenth-century western bishop, Liutprand of Cremona, of the distribution of *rogai* to imperial officials in the two weeks before Easter. Harvey, *Economic expansion*, pp. 82–3, characterises all these payments as *solemnia* (diverted fiscal revenues,

Table 2. *Annual monetary grants of Michael Attaliates from revenues of his* Ptochotropheion

Amount (*nomismata*)	Destination	Remarks
House at Rhaidestos and associated houses:		
3	Monastery of St Nicholas	
3	Monastery of St George	Michael Attaliates is *charistikarios*
2	Nunnery of St Prokopios	Theodore Attaliates is second *charistikarios*
2	Monastery of Theotokos of Daphne	
1	Church of Prodromos	
1	Church of Virgin Eleousa	
1	Church of St Michael	
12	To 12 poor on anniversary of his death (1 *nomisma* each)	
6	To chanters on anniversary of his death	
Monastery of Christ Panoiktirmonos at Constantinople		
c. 30	Six poor fed each day at refectory each get 4 *folleis*	
c. 44	Annual *rogai* for seven monks including *hegoumenos*	Theoretical figure. In Attaliates' day only five monks and no *hegoumenos*
15	For *prosphagion* (food to be eaten with bread) for poor	
8	Oil	
24	Expenses on great feast days	
15	Candles, incense, communion wine, bread	
Particular expenses (not necessarily each year)		
3	Eparch of Constantinople	For judicial assistance
3	*hegoumenos* of Stoudios	If he needs to consecrate *hegoumenos*
10	*oikonomos* Michael	
Church of St George Kyparissiotes at Constantinople		
18	Clergy for services at family tombs	

Total: c. 128 *nomismata* each year (of which 39 *nomismata trachea*; 39 *tetartera*)

way for the emperor to strengthen the bonds between the state and its spiritual protectors, but also a means by which he could be seen to be fulfilling his personal duties as a charitable citizen. Table 4 presents data on the payment of imperial *rogai*; the continuation of the payments instituted by his predecessors was a useful method open to an emperor to establish his own legitimacy. Since *rogai* were paid annually and cuts in the payments were almost unknown, they clearly played a major rôle in strengthening the finances of houses fortunate enough to receive them. To them were often added *solemnia* (diverted fiscal revenues), also included in Table 4. It is salutary to note that, by 1057, the Lavra on Athos was receiving from imperial sources *alone* more than the entire monetary revenue that the Pakourianos donations brought to Bačkovo.[60]

Added to these gifts of money came valuable offerings of a more permanent sort: rich silks, books, holy vessels and church ornaments made of precious metals and relics. These were not, perhaps, of such obvious economic significance as the gifts of money, since they could not be openly traded or used as ready cash, but they added inestimably to the reputation of the houses lucky enough to receive them, no mean advantage in a society where power was usually ostentatiously displayed. The wealth might be dedicated to God, but the visual impact of it on monks and laity alike could not but have raised expectations about the spiritual force present within the house.[61]

While the large-scale monetary donations to houses were often remarkable, many houses also enjoyed a steady trickle of income from those entering the monastery. The *apotage*, a donation in cash or kind to be provided by the novice upon entering the monastic life, had been the subject of some criticism as early as the Second Council of Nicaea (787). Later commentators maintained that it had been expressly forbidden by this gathering, but the existence of an entry in the index to a novel of Romanos Lekapenos of 934 forbidding the transfer of lands as *apotage*, but allowing the payment of their selling price indicates that the practice was still current in the tenth century.[62] The payment of *apotage* probably declined during the course of the tenth and eleventh centuries, though

for which see chapter 9), but they are often clearly described as *rogai* which would mean that they were paid out from the private fortune of the emperor, see Hendy, *Monetary economy*, p. 192, note 188 and Kaplan, *Les hommes et la terre*, p. 312.

[60] See Table 4, pp. 194–6. For an example of *roga* being reduced, see Vatopedi, no. 3 (1082) and Harvey, *Economic expansion*, pp. 82–3.

[61] Non-monetary wealth discussed by Hendy, *Monetary economy*, pp. 201–20.

[62] E. Herman, 'Die Regelung der Armut in den byzantinischen Klöstern', *OCP*, 7 (1941), 406–60, remains the most detailed study of the relationship of monastic wealth and the principle of monastic poverty. Index to Romanos' novel of 934: Zepos, I, Col. iii, document v, p. 207. There is no corresponding passage in the text of the novel as published by Zepos.

Table 3. *Annual monetary grants of Gregory Pakourianos for his monastery at Bačkovo and associated hostels*

Amount (*nomismata*)	Destination	Remarks
Rogai (for purchase of habits, etc. paid Easter Day)		
36	*hegoumenos*	
300	Celebrant priests	20 *nomismata* each
	2 *epitropoi; skeuophylax; ekklesiarches* 'most notable brethren'	20 *nomismata* each
225	15 monks 'of second class'	15 *nomismata* each
200	20 monks 'of third class'	10 *nomismata* each
?30	*paroikoi* who act as servants at *xenodocheia*	Rate of 'third class monk' mentioned for Stenimachos. Also paid at St Nicholas and Marmarion?
20	Schoolmaster-priest at Monastery of St Nicholas (nr. Petritzos?)	
Memorials (payments for commemorations, anniversary feasts etc.)		
72	Monks	Anniversary of death of brother Aspasios
24	Monks, strangers poor	Anniversary of death of brother Aspasios
72	Monks	Anniversary of death of Gregory Pakourianos himself
24	Monks, strangers, poor	Anniversary of death of Gregory Pakourianos himself
24	Poor	Anniversary of death of Pakourianos' father
6	Monks	Anniversary of death of first *hegoumenos* Ceremony to be held on Feast of Gregory the Theologian
Other		
180	Monks, priests, poor	Twelve Great Feasts; Dormition of the Virgin; Feasts of St John the Baptist and St George
Total: 1,213 *nomismata* per annum[a]		

Note: [a]Twelve *nomismata* each were also paid to the monks and priests on the day of the election of a new *hegoumenos*.

Table 4. *Donations of rogai and solemnia to monastic houses*[a]

Date	Donor	Beneficiary	Amount	Source
920–44	Romanos I Lekapenos	Olympos Kyminas Athos Barachios/Mykale Latros Chryse Petra	1 per monk	Theoph. cont., VI, chapter 27, pp. 218–19; chapter 44, p. 430; Chronicle of the Logothete, p. 320; Chronicle of George the Monk, p. 910; Chronicle of Pseudo-Symeon, p. 744
?920–44	Romanos I Lekapenos	Athos	216	Life of Athanasios (B), chapter 34, p. 166
?944		Mon. of Panteleimon (Constantinople)	?	Theoph. cont. VI, chapter 50, p. 433
c. 961	Romanos II	Lavra	432	*Typikon* of Athanasios, p. 104
c. 961	Romanos II	Lavra	100	*Lavra*, I, Appendix II
963–9	Nikephoros II Phokas	Kyminas	?	*Typikon* of Athanasios, p. 102
963–9	Nikephoros II Phokas	Olympos	?	*Typikon* of Athanasios, p. 102
964	Nikephoros II Phokas	Athos	288 (total now 504)	Life of Athanasios (A), chapter 104, p. 50; (B), chapter 34, p. 166
964	Nikephoros II Phokas	Lavra	244	*Typikon* of Athanasios, pp. 114–15; Life of Athanasios (A), chapter 50 (no amount); (B) chapter 34, p. 166

Date	Emperor/Founder	Recipient	Number	Source
Pre-972	John Tzimiskes	Lavra	244	Typikon of Athanasios, pp. 114–15; Life of Athanasios (A), chapter 116, p. 56; (B) chapter 36, p. 169. Ivirôn, I, no. 6 (984) Life of John and Euthymios, chapter 16, p. 94
1042–55	Constantine IX Monomachos	Vatopedi	80	Vatopedi, no. 3 (1082)
[1056–7]	Michael VI]			
[1057–9]	Isaac I Komnenos halved the sum]			
1045	Constantine IX Monomachos	Nea Mone, Chios	72	Zepos, I, Appendix, VII
[1078]	Michael VII Doukas]			
[1080]	Nikephoros III Botaniates]			
1042–55	Constantine IX Monomachos	Iviron	72	Ivirôn, I, p. 7
1042–55	Constantine IX Monomachos	Iviron	72	Ivirôn, I, p. 57
1046	Constantine IX Monomachos	Olympos monks in Constantinople	30 mil.	Zepos, I, Appendix, VIII
1046	Constantine IX Monomachos	Nea Mone monks in Constantinople	30 mil.	Zepos, I, Appendix, VIII
?c. 1054–5	Constantine IX Monomachos	Iviron	60 [72]	Ivirôn, II, no. 38 (1065); Vita S. Georgii Hagioritas, chapter 31; Ivirôn, I, p. 7
[1065]	Constantine X Doukas]			
1057	Michael VI	Athos	720	Lavra, I, no. 32 (1059)
1057	Michael VI	Lavra^b	216	Lavra, I, no. 32 (1059)
1058	Isaac Komnenos	Nea Mone	24	Zepos, I, Appendix, XV
[1078]	Michael VII Doukas]^c			

Table 4. (*cont.*)

Date	Donor	Beneficiary	Amount	Source
[1080]	Nikephoros III Botaniates]			
pre-1079	?Michael VII Doukas	Iviron	592 (total)	*Ivirôn*, II, no. 41 (1079)
[288 *nomismata* had been suppressed pre-1079]				
1079	Nikephoros III Botaniates	Iviron	304 (total)	*Ivirôn*, II, no. 41 (1079)
1079	Nikephoros III Botaniates	Attaliates' houses	12	*Diataxis* of Attaliates, p. 121
1084	Alexios I Komnenos	Monastery of Myoupolis	422	Armstrong, *Life of St Meletios*, chapter 49
?1093	Alexios I Komnenos	Patmos	24	*BEMP*, I, no. 8, p. 82

Notes:

a Dates in brackets indicate confirmation of donations. All amounts in *nomismata* unless otherwise indicated.

b *Lavra*, I, no. 32, reveals that by 1057 the Lavra received 2,232 *nomismata* per annum from imperial donations alone.

c In 1078 the amount confirmed for the Nea Mone was 2 lb of gold (144 *nomismata*), whereas only 96 *nomismata* are directly referred to in the surviving chrysobulls. A copy of the heading to the confirmatory chrysobull of 1080 mentions a *solemnion* of 100 *nomismata*.

Likely and imprecisely documented donations of *solemnia* or *rogai*: Constantine IX Monomachos to Galesion, probably in missing section of Life of St Lazaros; Alexios Komnenos to the *Orphanotropheion* in Constantinople, *Alexiad*, XV, 7, vii, Vol. III, p. 217.

there clearly were houses where its payment was customary. Athanasios of the Lavra defined it as a rent and declared that it should not be payable to the monastery but donated to the poor. Michael Attaliates stipulated that donations should be voluntary but should be used for building, restoration and the purchase of lands. St Lazaros of Mount Galesion, however, in the mid-eleventh century, twice paid an *apotage* of 12 *nomismata* for entry into the Monastery of St Sabas in Palestine and a case in the *Peira*, an eleventh-century legal compilation, indicates that payments were still being made elsewhere. As a result of selling some houses to an Eleousa monastery (possibly in Constantinople), a man had gathered enough money together to pay the *apotage* of a female relative to the Nunnery *tes Choras*. But following a lawsuit, he had to return the price of the houses and since he had no money to do so, the judge declared that the woman's *apotage* had to be returned.[63] From this example, it may be suggested that the *apotage* was not an infallible source of revenue for monastic houses. By the end of the eleventh century, opinion had turned against it to such a degree that it probably provided only a small proportion of monastic income. The *typika* of both the Theotokos Kecharitomene and Theotokos Evergetis houses in Constantinople forbade the exaction of the *apotage*, though that of the Evergetis allowed 'freely given' donations. The final blow was struck by Alexios Komnenos, who declared in a novel probably datable to 1096, that the *apotage* were given and received contrary to the law and must cease. Truly voluntary offerings (*prosenexeis*) could still be given, but must be noted in the *brebia* (inventories) of monastic houses. While entrance payments were doubtless still exacted under this guise, they probably declined in houses which did not wish to risk losing their imperial patrons.[64]

By the time Nikephoros' novel was issued, then, the monasteries of Asia Minor and Athos, at least, had clearly received large amounts of money from both aristocratic and humble sources, which allowed them, as we shall see, both to buy land and to improve it. This did not contradict the emperor's statement that only the *lavrai* should be exempt from the ban on further donations of land, since only cash was involved here, but it does serve to remind us that donation of land was not the only means available to monasteries of acquiring it. But Nikephoros, it will

[63] *Typikon* of Athanasios, p. 119; *Diataxis* of Attaliates, pp. 53, 63; Life of St Lazaros, chapter 16, p. 514; *Peira*, XV. 15, p. 54.
[64] Kécharitôménè, p. 43 and note 39; Evergétis, pp. 79–81. Summary of Alexios Komnenos' novel of 'December of the 5th indiction' (probably December 1096): Zepos, I, Col. iv, document XXXVII, pp. 346–8, but see J. Darrouzès, 'Dossier sur le charisticariat', in *Polychronion. Festschrift für Franz Dölger zum 75. Geburtstag* (Heidelberg, 1966), pp. 150–65, especially pp. 160–1, which publishes a longer version of the document in which the novel is mentioned. It is discussed further in chapter 10.

be remembered, had also declared that the foundation of *lavrai* was praiseworthy, 'so long as these cells and *lavrai* do not strive to obtain fields and estates beyond their enclosures'. However, there is incontrovertible evidence from the period even *before* 964 to indicate that lavriote houses were already beginning to amass property. On Latros, before 955, the Stylos Monastery had exchanged property with the Monastery of Lamponion and probably already possessed a *proasteion* (estate) near Larymon.[65] The most startling instance by far of this tendency is the activity of the monks of the Lavra of Nikephoros' own spiritual father, Athanasios. For by the time the novel was issued, Nikephoros had already confirmed the possession by the Lavra of properties at Melana and Prophourni on the peninsula of Athos and the massive addition to its lands in the Chalkidike brought about by the grant of the Monastery of St Andrew of Peristerai and its lands.

Nikephoros, then, was well aware that the *lavrai* which he characterised as continuing the eremitic traditions of simplicity and poverty were doing no such thing. Why did he choose to turn an official blind eye to these developments? The reason must surely lie in the fact that had he condemned gifts of lands to *all* monastic houses he would have been criticising his own past actions. By keeping up an official pretence that the *lavrai* maintained a different economic outlook from the *koinobia*, he could continue his benefactions and perhaps hope that the type of monasticism he favoured would also benefit from donations diverted from elsewhere. If Nikephoros' legislation is seen more as promoting the fortunes of the *lavrai* than harming those of the *koinobia*, then his actions do not, in fact, provide such a stark contrast with the attitudes of his predecessors and the legislation of his successors.

Until recently, it was thought that the novel of 964 was abrogated after Nikephoros' death by either John Tzimiskes or Basil II. But this was not the case and Nikephoros' legislation remained in force throughout the period. But the very fact that a novel abrogating it was falsified in the mid-eleventh century is an indication of the concern of powerful interests to restore the legality of free gifts of lands to monastic houses. As the 'novel of Basil II' (the forgery) put it:

The law of Nikephoros concerning the churches of God and the pious institutions . . . has been the cause and source of the present evils and of the general upheaval and disturbance. Since its enactment to the present day, no good whatsoever has happened amongst us, but, to the contrary there has been no lack of every kind of misfortune.[66]

[65] MM, IV, pp. 308, 324–5.
[66] Zepos, I, Coll. iii, document XXVI, p. 259 and see the important comments of Kaplan, *Les hommes et la terre*, pp. 440–3.

Again, the close relationship between the welfare of the empire and the fortunes of its spiritual protectors was emphasised.

Even without this evidence, it is clear that Nikephoros' novel seems to have been honoured more in the breach than in the observance, but this, of course, does not detract from its considerable importance as an indication of general trends in monastic land donation in the tenth century. If the emperor was concerned to ensure the survival of vulnerable houses and to curb land donation to *koinobia*, legislation was clearly not the way to do it. Indeed, it is doubtful whether any action on the part of the central government could have put a stop to what was part and parcel of accepted piety. The process of land accumulation which he described continued without any perceptible hindrance and there is no evidence of anyone being taken to court for donating land to the 'wrong' kind of monastery. With the steady influx of both cash and manpower and with considerable legal flexibility at their disposal, the more successful monasteries of the tenth and eleventh centuries were, without doubt, among the most expansionist of the landowners of the time.

CHAPTER EIGHT

Territorial expansion and spiritual compromise

◆

THE PROCESS OF MONASTIC land accumulation was not seriously hindered by Nikephoros Phokas' novel of 964, and this had profound consequences for the spiritual orientation of the monks in the more successful houses emerging during the late tenth and eleventh centuries. For with ever-increasing numbers came problems of management, efficiency and self-sufficiency. In solving these, the principle of *eremia*, although theoretically still of paramount importance, had, in practice, to be modified. The eleventh century saw the culmination of tendencies criticised in the tenth; many monasteries evolved into powerful economic units and their holders became increasingly influential figures. As a consequence, numbers increased and with this expansion came the need for greater supplies of foodstuffs. In addition, the evolution of many monastic houses from small locally based foundations to large property owning units means that the social relationships between such houses and their lay neighbours changed, very often for the worse. Donations from patrons allowed monastic interests a purchasing power and a pool of manpower unavailable to all but the richest lay landowners.

The eleventh century, in particular, reveals a series of paradoxes: the tension between the spiritual tenets of monasticism and the practical realities of survival; the theoretical honour in which monks were held by the laity contrasted with the extended and sometimes vituperative conflicts in which they often engaged with their secular neighbours and the lengths to which the heads of many houses were prepared to go to preserve their privileged economic and legal position – even to the extent of engaging in combat with imperial officials and making use of every advantage which their patronage networks afforded them – in clear opposition to the humility and obedience preached by their calling. Each monastic house confronted these challenges in its own way, although responses to such matters as increases in numbers and the need to acquire new land were often tempered by the dictates of the foundation *typika*. But there are certain areas of activity, certain ways and means of coping with problems which can be generally observed. In particular, the spiritual relationships cemented between monks and laity now often took on a highly practical dimension. For added to the traditional donations of money or land came, in many cases, an active participation by the laity in the protection of the economic assets of the houses with which they were associated. Much of the spiritual compromise arose from the expansion in monastic property holding which took place in this period; a phenomenon which, to a greater or lesser extent, seems to have been visible in many parts of the empire.

Though the extent of the lands of the great rural monastic houses in the eleventh century is striking, and the documents associated with them provide the greatest quantity of evidence, the significant rôle played in both the tenth and eleventh centuries by solitary hermits and holy men with small groups of disciples in putting land under cultivation should not be overlooked.[1] The hagiographies of such saints all include passages describing their struggle against the harsh environment in which they had chosen to settle in their search for *eremia* and the laborious clearance of small plots either by themselves or with the aid of one or two of their first disciples. They are a good example of hagiographical *topoi* being created from recognisable experience. The Life of St Luke the Younger, for example, provides details of the clearances made by the saint in the Peloponnese in the tenth century. He created a small garden in which he grew fruit which was then given to his neighbours. The theft of his hand-mill by a group of sailors indicates that he also grew some grain.[2] A similar example of this type of small-scale cultivation comes from the account of the early years of St Lazaros on Mount Galesion. As we have seen, soon after arriving on the mountain, the metropolitan of Ephesos gave him a small plot of land, upon which Lazaros planted one measure of beans. St Cyril Phileotes, active at the end of the eleventh century, is

[1] Harvey, *Economic expansion*, especially chapters 2 and 4, deals with monastic land-holding in the wider context of the Byzantine economy.
[2] Life of St Luke the Younger, pp. 91; 103 (Martini). For other references to hand-mills, see Harvey, *Economic expansion*, p. 132, and A. A. M. Bryer, 'The estates of the empire of Trebizond: evidence for their resources, products, agriculture, ownership and location', *Papers given at the Twelfth Spring Symposium of Byzantine Studies, Birmingham, 1978*, published in *Archeion Pontou*, 35 (1979), 370–477, reprinted in *The empire of Trebizond and the Pontos* (London, 1980), article VII, see especially plate 26. The importance of kitchen gardens in supplying nutritional variety in the Byzantine diet is emphasised by M. Kaplan, 'L'économie paysanne dans l'empire byzantine du Ve au XIe siècle', *Klio*, 68 (1986), 198–232, 207, and *Les hommes et la terre*, pp. 63–4.

also reported to have cleared a small plot in a pine forest near Derkos in Thrace and to have grown vegetables on it.

Further examples can be provided from Italy. Around the year 983, the monk Jonas cleared land around the town of Tricarico in Lucania and then installed freemen (*eleutherioi*) on it to cultivate it. By 998, the settlement was referred to as a *chorion* and was still in existence in 1023. The Life of St Luke of Demena tells how the saint was first a hermit in the lavra of St Elias Spelaiotes near Reggio but how, many years later at the age of about 55, in the mid-tenth century he restored the Church of St Peter at Noe (Noepoli), cleared, planted and tilled the previously abandoned fields until 'after seven years the desert was no more a desert'. The early monks of Kellerana in Calabria, alarmed as they were by the harshness of their surroundings, did eventually succeed in eking out a living there. Indeed, Guillou has pointed out that many southern Italian place names indicate monastic origins: Cersosimo (the Byzantine Kyr Zosimos) and Colobraro-Cironouphrio (Kyr Onouphrios) being but two examples.[3]

Not only did the holy men act as oases of spirituality, but their clearances, initially on a small scale, probably added up to a considerable contribution to the increase of lands under cultivation in the more intractable parts of the empire. With the growth of their houses came the expansion of their properties from these humble beginnings and the part played by Byzantine monks in bringing uncultivated or deserted lands into use in the tenth and eleventh centuries can certainly be compared with the better known efforts of their Western counterparts at the same time.[4] Such small-scale efforts continued throughout the period, often alongside the much more extensive and better organised expansion of the larger houses. The Athonite archives, while they provide a wealth of evidence for the inexorable rise of a few great houses in the eleventh century, also provide numerous examples of such individual endeavour, sometimes with surprising consequences. The monk George Chelandris had brought an abandoned plot under cultivation 'through his own labour', but decided to seek another one nearer the sea to 'assure his own tranquillity'. He found purchasers in 982 for his old property, none other

---

[3] Life of St Lazaros, chapter 34, p. 520; Life of St Cyril Phileotes, chapter 23, pp. 109–10 (334). For Italy, see Guillou, 'Notes sur la société dans le katépanat d'Italie au XIe siècle', *Mélanges d'Archéologie et d'Histoire*, 78 (1966), 439–65, reprinted in *Studies in Byzantine Italy* (London, 1970), article XIII, see p. 453; and Guillou, 'La Lucanie byzantine. Etude de géographie historique', *B*, 35 (1965), 119–49, reprinted in *Studies in Byzantine Italy*, article X, see p. 139. Life of St Luke of Demena, p. 338; Carbone (History), p. 281; *Kellerana*, introduction, p. 12.
[4] See, for example, G. Duby, *Rural economy and country life in the medieval West* (London, 1968), and Kaplan, *Les hommes et la terre*, pp. 531–40.

than John the Iberian and John 'the *synkellos*' (John Tornik), the founders of the Georgian monastery, who were engaged in bringing the Monastery *tou Klementos* back to life. The precise size of George's plot is not known, but it is described in the document as 'small'. It commanded the astounding sum of 100 *nomismata* and the reason for this is not far to seek. The property was 'near the lavra of the Iberians' and the Georgian monks did not wish a 'stranger' to hold it. They were clearly in the process of consolidating their land-holdings around their new centre of activity.[5] So it is often in the context of their acquisition by greater houses that we hear of the existence of these small plots, often ceded by their owners in order to ensure support from a larger house in their old age or bought by more powerful monastic elements in order to consolidate their property. The importance of the supplies of ready cash at the disposal of the latter is clearly evident.

The increase in the landed power of larger houses had already begun in the tenth century and was to gather pace in the eleventh. A flow of ready money from lay donations and imperial *rogai* ensured that monasteries with a growing reputation and the lay patronage that went with it were able to take advantage of times when land prices were particularly low. This was the case in the mid-tenth century when large areas of *klasma* land came under monastic control. This land, abandoned by its owners, then subject to a lightening of tax (*sympatheia*), and finally, after thirty years, reverting to the state (*demosion*) to be resold, was an investment with singular advantages. On the one hand it was cheap: the price, according to a tenth- or eleventh-century treatise, was to be not more than twenty-four times the tax payable on the land before it was abandoned. On the other, with a sufficient supply of labour, the land could soon be brought back into a state of profitable cultivation, since the future land tax payable to the state (*libellikon demosion*) was (initially) to be only one-twelfth of the original tax.[6]

Sales of *klasma* land in Macedonia in the early tenth century provided the basis of the territorial fortunes of a number of monasteries in the region as well as the occasion of conflicts with neighbouring lay communities who were not unnaturally also interested in the opportunity to acquire land cheaply. An early act from the archives of the Protaton (908)

---

[5] *Ivirôn*, I, no. 3 (982). For George Chelandris, clearly a man of some social consequence since he was a bearer of a message from the Athonites to the Emperor Basil II (between 976 and 979–80), Commentary, p. 115. He was still alive in 985.
[6] The mechanism of the *klasma* is discussed by Harvey, *Economic expansion*, pp. 67–9 and in N. Oikonomidès, 'Das Verfalland im 10.–11. Jahrhundert. Verkauf und Besteuerung', *Fontes Minores*, VII (Forschungen zur Byzantinischen Rechtsgeschichte, XIV, Frankfurt, 1986), 116–18, reprinted in *Byzantium from the ninth century*, article V, and see the important discussion of Kaplan, *Les hommes et la terre*, pp. 399–408.

guaranteed free access to the *klasma* lands in the region of Hierissos to all the 'neighbours' – in this case the monks of the Monastery of Kolobos as well as the inhabitants of the town of Hierissos. It is very likely that the monks had tried to claim these lands as their own property and impose an 'access tax' on them. Given the fact that *klasma* lands could not be resold for thirty years, they must have been abandoned in about 870.[7]

The circumstances which had led to these disturbances in tenure, notably Arab and Bulgar raiding, were still serious about the year 910, since further large-scale sales of *klasma* in the region were made some thirty years later in 941–2. The *demosion*, in the person of the tax assessor (*epoptes*) of the theme of Thessalonike, Thomas Moirokouboulos, sold *klasma* on the peninsula of Kassandra to the Monastery of St Andrew of Peristerai near Thessalonike. It was made up of a series of properties amounting to an area of 1,800 *modioi*. Of this, 1,200 *modioi* were already again under cultivation (thus being of particular value) leaving only 600 *modioi* that had to be brought back into use. The price was only 36 *nomismata*: 50 *modioi* per *nomisma*. In contrast to the large purchase the monastery was able to make, a much smaller parcel in the same area was sold to a private individual, Nicholas 'son of Agathon'. He was able to afford only 100 *modioi*; the superior monetary and manpower resources of the monastery were clearly evident.[8] *Klasma* lands around Hierissos were also being bought up in these years. Evidence from the archives of the Monastery of Xeropotamou indicates that the self-same Thomas Moirokouboulos sold 950 *modioi* of *klasma* in this area to thirteen peasants. The price was again 1 *nomisma* per 50 *modioi*. But they were not to hold it for long. In 956, the land was re-assessed, the price was doubled and at this point Xeropotamou gained control of it. The monastery was able to find the extra 19 *nomismata* demanded by the state, whereas the association of peasants clearly could not manage this extra sum.[9]

The relative ease with which some monasteries found the resources to buy up *klasma* lands was one of the causes of the increasing tension between them and their neighbours. An act of the Protaton, also dated to 942, set about establishing a boundary between the Athonites and the local laymen. The need to take action was pressing, since the monks claimed that the territory of Hierissos only comprised the settlement itself and not any lands nearby, thus increasing the amount of *klasma* land to which the monks could lay claim. The Hierissiotes, however, claimed that their *enoria* (district) stretched as far as the Zygos Ridge on the peninsula

---

[7] *Prôtaton*, no. 2 (908).
[8] *Lavra*, I, nos. 2 (941); 3 (941), *Prôtaton*, no. 4 (942). The purchase of Nicholas, son of Agathon is mentioned in *Lavra*, I, no. 3 (941).
[9] *Xéropotamou*, no. 1 (956); see Harvey, *Economic expansion*, p. 61.

of Athos. In the event, a compromise was reached, but it is clear that the possession of *klasma* lands (or at least the right to buy them) was a matter of great interest to both parties.[10]

There does not seem to have been another dispersal of *klasma* lands in Macedonia comparable with that of 941–2 until the end of the eleventh century, a circumstance which would indicate the prevalence of peaceful conditions in the region until mid-century.[11] Parcels of *klasma* land were disposed of from time to time; the Monastery of Iviron bought some in the region of Dobrobikea at some time before 1029 (when it was confiscated). It does not seem to have been a particularly successful purchase (or perhaps its systematic exploitation had been interrupted by the confiscation) as it was granted a *sympatheia* in the second half of the eleventh century.[12] But by then a more serious problem of abandoned lands was clearly emerging. Again, monastic interests profited from the situation. The Amalfitan monastery, the community of Benedictine monks on Mount Athos, experienced problems with its tenants at Koutariane in the Strymon theme:

> Because of continued vexations [probably exactions in kind of food and animals by the imperial armies moving westwards to fight the Normans] the inhabitants of this *chorion* have almost vanished or moved away and the Amalfitani are having difficulty in claiming their fiscal charges.[13]

The monastery was already in possession of many of their abandoned holdings. Clearly the situation was such that only large and prosperous houses could profit from the further availability of *klasma* lands. For the smaller, without the resources to work it, its possession could prove a burden.

Thus when another larger-scale distribution of *klasma* took place at the end of the eleventh century, the Athonite evidence, at least, does not indicate any great enthusiasm on the part of the monasteries to purchase any. In fact, an act of 1082 concerning *klasma* concerns not its purchase but the *gift* by the Emperor Alexios Komnenos of 334 *modioi* of *klasma* to a certain Leo Kephalas. The land later came into the possession of the Lavra, but it was not initially bought by the house. Leo Kephalas was being rewarded for his military services to the state. So too was the Georgian general Gregory Pakourianos whose impressive list of docu-

---

[10] The dispute is discussed in detail in Morris, 'Dispute settlement', pp. 131–5.

[11] Evidence from central Greece indicates that *klasma* lands were being sold in the mid-eleventh century at higher prices, indicating some competition for it in a more peaceful period, see Harvey, *Economic expansion*, p. 59.

[12] *Ivirôn*, I, no. 30 (second half of eleventh century). Harvey, *Economic expansion*, p. 61.

[13] *Lavra*, I, no. 43 (1081).

ments recording his landed assets, included two *libelloi* for ex-*klasma* lands in the *choria* of Eudokimou and Kotresi respectively (whereabouts unknown, but probably in south Bulgaria or Thrace), a *praktikon* describing his lands in the region of Mosynopolis (modern Messoune) and the receipt of the *oikonomos* concerned for the payment of the *libellikon demosion* there. It is likely, therefore, that as Oikonomides has suggested, *klasma* land was somewhat more expensive at the end of the century and that, rather than being bought up by local farming interests, it was given as a valuable reward to servants of the state. It was perhaps now too expensive an investment for monasteries which were, in any case, already well endowed. But the evidence is scarce.[14]

If the purchase of *klasma* land was one aspect of Athonite expansion in the tenth century, another more striking development was the extensive land clearances undertaken towards the end of the century. St Athanasios was granted two barren areas on Athos in quick succession by the Protos. The first, the promontory of Platys, was described in 991 as 'of no use to the community, useless and unprofitable', but by 996 a *metochion* of the Lavra with its own *kellia* had been established there. So successful was this scheme that Athanasios was then given a ruined monastery, Monoxylitou, specifically because of the expertise he and his monks had shown in cultivating Platys. This may also be one of the reasons why the aged monks Kosmas and Luke chose to consign the Island of Gymnopelagision to his care.[15]

The type of activity undertaken by the lavriotes is vividly portrayed by Athanasios himself in his *Typikon*. He describes the physical labour of land clearance, the digging, tree felling and grubbing out of bushes and scrub. Then followed the quarrying of stone for churches and monastic buildings and finally the planting of crops and vines. On the face of it, this kind of activity seemed to fly in the face of Nikephoros Phokas' strictures against monastic expansion, and there are indications in this text that Athanasios was aware of the possibility of criticism. He stated that it was not his intention to buy up land and improve it, as the laity did. He emphasised the concept of self-sufficiency so clearly evident in the novel of 964. He ordered his monks not to establish *proasteia* beyond the *metochion* of Mylopotamos (their first clearance some 15 km from the Lavra), where *kellia* and a church dedicated to St Eustathios had been built. No more *kellia* were to be built or land cultivated south of the

---

[14] *Lavra*, I, no. 44 (1082). For Leo Kephalas, see G. Rouillard, 'Un grand bénéficiaire sous Alexis Comnène: Léon Képhalas', *BZ*, 30 (1930), 44–50. The Kephalas 'dossier' is reconstituted in the Commentary to *Lavra*, I, no. 65. Pakourianos, pp. 127, 129. The *libellos* was a document confirming the sale of *klasma* land by the state to a private individual.

[15] *Lavra*, I, nos. 9 (991), 12 (996), 10 (993).

Lavra, so that the seclusion of the hesychasts could be preserved. It was not, Athanasios maintained, the place of monks 'to concern themselves with goats and sheep'.[16] This statement is puzzling, given that Athanasios had already accepted the estates of St Andrew of Peristerai, authorised large-scale clearances on the mountain and promoted the expansion of the Georgian house. It may be that in his *Typikon* he was referring only to the mountain of Athos and was making efforts to preserve a more simple way of life there, or that he was deliberately paying lip-service to Nikephoros' novel in order to deflect criticism. But whatever his expressed wishes, Athanasios' own actions clearly belied this statement of monastic principle.

From the earliest moment of foundation, then, it proved impossible to reconcile the economic demands of a flourishing foundation with the oft-repeated spiritual goals of solitude, poverty and simplicity. It is a paradox particularly evident in the eleventh century, when the search for *eremia* (they maintained) led Arsenios Skenoures to Kos, Christodoulos to Patmos and Bishop Manuel to Stroumitza. But in all these cases, their activities resulted in the *increased* population and prosperity of the regions concerned and, in many cases, the concept of *eremia* became an active rather than a passive one. It was used not merely to assert the monastic need for seclusion but to impose this condition to the detriment of the rights of neighbouring communities. The fortunes of the Monastery of St John on Patmos and the lands associated with it may stand as an example.

It is not absolutely clear whether the island of Patmos was completely 'inaccessible, deserted and lacking in water' (as Christodoulos himself declared) when the saint arrived there in 1088. He had good reasons for maintaining that the island would be a good place for the exercise of the eremitic life, but it is unlikely that even he would have wished to settle in a place where the harsh environment would have doomed his enterprise to failure from the first. But there is no doubt that the population of the island did not begin to rise significantly until Christodoulos began to import labour. By 1090–2, twelve families of *paroikoi* were present, comprising forty-one adults and young people, to whom should probably be added an unknown number of younger children. This was the beginning of a sustained population growth, which, by 1270, had reached some 400 (on Patmos and its neighbouring island Kalymnos). The arrival of the early lay settlers may be directly attributed to the economic needs of the Monastery of St John, since these *paroikoi* were required to work for the monastery on five days of the week; but continued migration was also a consequence of the almost uninterrupted presence of the monks.

[16] *Typikon* of Athanasios, pp. 105–14, 118, 121.

The main danger came from pirates, but the physical defences of the monastery and the spiritual protection of the monks served to strengthen the morale of the population. The settlers remained on the island and were later joined by those fleeing from Turkish attacks.[17] A similar type of repopulation may have been taking place at roughly the same time at the Monastery of the Theotokos Eleousa at Stroumitza where its founder (or refounder) Bishop Manuel declared that the house was only repopulated after his efforts.[18]

The recultivation of the *klasma* lands and the opening up of deserted lands and uncultivated areas had very similar results in economic terms. In fact, Alexios Komnenos' grant of the whole Island of Patmos to Christodoulos, free from taxes rather than with reduced payments, has much in common with imperial gifts of *klasma* in the late eleventh century.[19] So the initial colonisation of deserted or abandoned lands was itself a mark of monastic success to which resources of money and man-power had already made their contribution. It was a process necessary to their survival. But for successful houses where the numbers of monks rose rapidly, the territorial expansion which then became necessary soon brought with it a change in monastic priorities and outlook.

A principal concern was the feeding of the monastic population. Their diet was simple and subject to traditional monastic prohibitions. We can begin to reconstruct it from the mentions of food allowances contained in *typika* and other monastic documents, although it has to be borne in mind that the purpose of these allowances was spiritual as well as dietary. They indicated what was suitable for the particular type of monastic life being led as well as what should be provided from existing monastic resources. But the absence from many of the documented allowances of basic foods such as beans, suggests that they may simply have been notices of minimum requirements or reminders of grants to be made in specific cases. So it is not surprising that the quantities allotted to the monks vary considerably from document to document. As can be seen from Table 5, allowances might vary from a hermit's diet consisting entirely of beans, to the more generous quantities of food provided for in the *Typikon* of Bačkovo. Items commonly mentioned were clearly bread, supplemented by vegetables, especially beans, oil and wine. Cheese was also sometimes mentioned, although meat and fish rarely and usually only in the charitable hostels associated with monastic houses. But we know from

---

[17] *Hypotyposis* of Christodoulos, p. 64. For the debate over the condition of Patmos at the end of the eleventh century, see P. Karlin-Hayter, 'Notes sur les archives de Patmos comme source pour la démographie et l'économie de l'île', *BF*, 5 (1977), 189–215 and Malamut, *Les îles*, I, p. 152; II, pp. 398, 481 and see pp. 217–220, below.

[18] Stroumitza, p. 71, ll. 28–71.

[19] *BEMP*, I, no. 49 (1088).

other sources that monasteries did possess animals and can suggest that dairy products (if not meat) formed an important part of the monastic diet.[20]

One of the criteria for measuring the degree of success enjoyed by a house was, therefore, its ability to produce or obtain enough of these basic foodstuffs to feed the monks, and if numbers expanded this inevitably meant an expansion in territory. Thus the marked expansion in the land-holdings of the more successful monasteries in the eleventh century and their participation in the land and food markets had as one of its basic causes the simple need to feed more monastic mouths. Even the most strongly held beliefs about the virtues of solitude and lack of contact with the world could not survive the demographic pressure brought about by the spread of the fame of some houses and their founders. The principles of lavriote-influenced monasticism were simply incompatible with the realities of survival.[21]

It is impossible to generalise about the agrarian conditions necessary for the survival of monastic houses, for a variety of growing conditions (even for staples) could be found within the empire. For instance, vineyards at Smyrna (Izmir) were estimated in 1943 to yield four times as much as those in Nikomedia (Izmit). The vineyards of Chios were famous throughout the medieval period; those of the Chalkidike certainly not. Similarly, the olive cannot be grown in Thrace and Macedonia except on the coast and a few inland places, so that the great coenobitic houses of this region, such as Bačkovo, would have had to make sure they possessed land in these regions, or else, in this case, be prepared to buy oil on the open market or make use of the fat from their cattle.[22]

Another important factor was the relationship between the numbers in a monastery, the labour they provided or had at their disposal and their own level of consumption. Higher manpower might mean higher levels

---

[20] See pp. 210–11 (Table 5). There are problems of measurement, however. The varying capacities of the *monasteriakos modios* (monastic *modios*) and monastic food allowances in general are discussed by M. Dembinska, 'Diet: a comparison of food consumption between some eastern and western monasteries in the 4th–12th centuries', *B*, 55 (1985), 431–62, especially Table 1, where she estimates the monastic *modios* at 13.5 litres. The weight in kilograms would vary according to the weight per litre of each commodity, hence, on her estimation, 0.80 kg per *modios* for grain; 1.20 kg for legumes and 0.90 kg for oil. Svoronos, however, estimated the *modios* concerned at 12.8 litres: see N. G. Svoronos, 'Remarques sur les structures économiques', p. 60, note 38. E. Schilbach, *Byzantinische Metrologie* (Handbuch der Altertumswissenschaft, xii/4, Munich, 1970), estimates the *monasteriakos modios* at 13.6 litres.

[21] For monastic numbers, see chapter 7, pp. 181–2.

[22] Naval Intelligence Division, *Handbook for Turkey* (2 vols., London, 1942), ii, pp. 142–3. *Handbook for Greece* (3 vols., London, 1944–5), ii, p. 66; Harvey, *Economic expansion*, pp. 143–7 and Kaplan, *Les hommes et la terre*, pp. 33–5 discuss the production of wine and oil.

Table 5. *Monastic food allowances in the tenth and eleventh centuries*
(amounts per annum unless otherwise stated)

House/area	Date	Recipient	Grain	Bread	Cheese
Myrelaion	After 922	Poor		3,000 loaves	
Athos	c. 972	Hermits	5 *modioi* each		
Athos	1016	Retired hermit, Symeon	30 *modioi*		
Athos	1024	George, *hegoumenos* of Pithara			
Athos	1030	Athanasios of Bouleuteria			8 cheeses
Athos	1030	3 servants	6 *modioi* each		
Galesion	c. 1050	Stylite Kerykos			
Attaliates' foundations	1077	Pilgrims and poor		104 *modioi*ᵃ	
Rhaidestos	1077	12 poor	72 *modioi* (6 each)		
		6 chanters		6 *modioi*	
Constantinople	1077	Poor		52 loaves	
		Indigents	12 *modioi* each		
		Hegoumenos	51 *modioi*		
		Oikonomos	36 *modioi*		
		Monks (5)	150 *modioi* (30 each)		
		Liturgical use	18 *modioi*		
Athos	1083	Esaias *hegoumenos* of Monastery of Prophet Elias			
Bačkovo Hostels at Marmarion and St Nicholas	1083	Poor and travellers	4 *modioi* per day		
Stroumitza	1085–6	Monks			
Lavra	1101–2	Monk, Damian	12 *modioi*		

Vegetables	Oil	Meat	Fish	Other	Wine	Source
						Theoph. cont., VI, 44, p. 430; Kedrenos, p. 319 *Typikon* of Athanasios, p. 115
6 *modioi*					50 *metra*	*Lavra*, I, no. 19
				100 *nomismata* for food		*Lavra*, I, no. 25
8 *modioi* chick peas	2 *bitinas*			12 *modioi* olives; 1 lemon tree	13 *metra*	*Lavra*, I, no. 28
						Lavra, I, no. 28
9 *modioi* beans						Life of St Lazaros, p. 556
					52 *metra*[a]	*Diataxis*, p. 49
						Diataxis, p. 49
						Diataxis, p. 49
						Diataxis, p. 47
						Diataxis, p. 47
3 *metra* (dry)		some	some		36 *metra*	*Diataxis*, p. 69
					30 *metra*	*Diataxis*, p. 69
					120 *metra* (24 each)	*Diataxis*, p. 69
	150 *litrai*				18 *metra*	*Diataxis*, p. 71
					3 *metra*	*Xénophon*, no. 1
					4 *metra* per day	Pakourianos, p. 111
2 *missoi* dry and fresh (3 days a week) 3 *missoi* dry and fresh (4 days)						Stroumitza, p. 86
3 *modioi* (dry)	12 *litrai*			1 *megarikon* honey	40 *metra*	*Lavra*, I, no. 54

[a]General allowances given at all Attaliates' foundations

211

of cultivation and production, but it also meant higher levels and more varied types of consumption. Technical improvements and the use of specialised equipment could, of course, make considerable difference to the productivity of land. The most important of these were irrigation schemes and if this is borne in mind, the number of monastic disputes about the ownership or use of streams is not surprising. Water was perhaps the most important commodity of all. But disciplined clearance, fencing and the construction of mills and presses for wine and oil on the spot (all covered by the general Byzantine term of *kalliergemata*) could reduce the level of losses from animals, theft and transport costs and thus increase production.[23]

A final general consideration to be borne in mind before some specific monasteries are examined is the vexed question of specifically monastic attitudes to land management and investment. As Michel Kaplan has cogently argued, the strictures of Nikephoros Phokas against monastic land acquisition simply for the prestige that this was thought to bring and without due consideration of the problems of exploitation, seem to indicate that many *hegoumenoi* held a rather simplistic view of the consequences of land accumulation. To possess land was one thing; to manage it efficiently or to increase its yields was quite another. The fact that, by the eleventh century, many monasteries had need of lay protectors who, like Michael Psellos, could assist them with cash donations for improvements to their lands and refurbishment of their buildings, does seem to indicate that profitable management of, and investment in lands did not enjoy a high priority in these houses. A marked exception, however (and it may be possible that it was in fact the rule, since our view is gravely compromised by the lack of comparable evidence) was the houses on Athos. Here, large-scale acquisition was combined with shrewd exploitation. The same was true of the houses founded by laymen – particularly those of Attaliates and Pakourianos – where concern to obtain high returns for cash investments and to increase the efficiency of the estates was again manifest. In all these houses, the often rapid growth in numbers demanded a more flexible attitude than

23 Tools and improvements (*kalliergemata*) are discussed by Harvey, *Economic expansion*, p. 159 (irrigation), pp. 122–3 (ploughs), pp. 123–4 (tools), pp. 128–34 (water and donkey mills) and Kaplan, *Les hommes et la terre*, pp. 46–52 (tools, ploughs and mills), pp. 65–9 (*kalliergemata*). The *Life of Athanasios* (A), chapter 81, p. 37 and (B), chapter 25, p. 152, both relate how the saint created an irrigation scheme and directed both the excavation of channels and the construction of two water-wheels. *Lavra*, I, no. 17 (1012), relates a dispute over the use of river water between the two small houses of Kaspakos and Atziioannou. *Lavra*, I, no. 57 (1108?), is an act of the Protos John Tarchaneiotes (or Trachaneiotes) ordering the Lavra and the Monastery of Isidore to share the use of a spring at Karyes, the 'capital' of Athos.

the traditional Byzantine satisfaction with the concept of *autarkeia* or self-sufficiency.[24]

How did all these considerations work out in practice? Only fragmentary evidence, culled mainly from hagiographies and incomplete archives, exists for the holy mountains of western Asia Minor. Of the houses on Latros, only the Stylos Monastery provides any documentary evidence and the monastic archives of the other holy mountains of the region (save Hiera-Xerochoraphion) are lost. The roughness and solitude of Latros and Galesion in particular were what had attracted the holy men to them in the first place. The areas were not completely desolate, however, for there are numerous springs on the lower slopes of Latros and in the ravine where the Stylos Monastery was built. In the nearby river valley, a plain extending for some eight to ten kilometres supported fruit trees, vines and olives. Fish were abundant in the lake.[25] Although the exploitation of these riches was not the initial aim of the founders of the *lavrai*, the fact that they did eventually expand their property into these areas indicates not only a descent from the mountains in a literal sense, but also a descent from principle. A document of April 987, regulating a dispute between the Monasteries of Stylos and the Theotokos of Lamponion, indicates that the process had already begun. For as a condition of the settlement, the Stylos Monastery received 100 *nomismata* which it intended to use for the purchase of thirty-three female water-buffalo, not only an indication that it now possessed lands near the Lake of Herakleia or in the Maeander Valley but also that it had immediate access to dairy products.[26]

The records of this dispute are patchy, but indicate that even some thirty years before its settlement, the Monastery of the Stylos was beginning to consolidate its property into more easily managed parcels. At the heart of the dispute was the question of the exchange of lands between the two houses, possibly agreed verbally by Paul of Latros at some point before 955. There were then complaints that the monks of the Theotokos Monastery had settled *paroikoi* and their wives on lands which now belonged to the other house – a clear attempt to bring the land into cultivation. The matter was apparently settled (after complaints to the local judge, the *krites*) by the adjudication of the Patriarch Nicholas Chrysoberges, but was raised again in 1049, indicating that the Stylos Monastery was determined to keep control of this new property, almost certainly down in the lakeside plain.[27]

There are further clear indications of the territorial expansion of the

[24] Kaplan, *Les hommes et la terre*, pp. 564–7.   [25] Wiegand, *Der Latmos*, pp. 6, 8, 13.
[26] MM, IV, p. 310, ll. 3–14.
[27] The affair was disentangled by Janin, *Grands centres*, pp. 442–5, documents 6–12.

Stylos Monastery in the eleventh century. It possessed an olive grove at Messingouma near Larymon which, by the beginning of the twelfth century, it was maintaining (erroneously) had been given by the Emperor Leo VI, but which may, nevertheless, have figured among the earliest of its possessions.[28] By February 987 it owned lands at Drakontiou and, a hundred years later, *agridia* at Krinos, Borradi and Garsika (location unknown). In the thirteenth century, the monastery possessed lands north-west of Smyrna, at Bare, but it is not clear at what date they were acquired.[29] These land acquisitions may indicate that the Stylos Monastery needed to acquire lands to feed the monastic community at the end of the tenth century, but we have no means of knowing whether the lands in question were bought, or whether they were donated by pious benefactors. Either way, the reputation and influence as well as the size of the house was increasing.

But an indication that the acquisition of more productive land was of great concern to the houses of western Asia Minor is given in many of the hagiographies dealing with the saints of the region, for they contain numerous instances of their heroes' abilities to overcome food shortages. The Life of St Paul the Younger relates an incident on the Sunday after Easter, when the Monastery of the Stylos had used up its stocks of wine, flour, oil and vegetables. The *oikonomos*, in despair, consulted the saint, who told him that there was no cause for alarm. Shortly afterwards, two mules laden with wine, cheese and eggs, sent by the Bishop of Amyzon, arrived at the monastery. There are similar incidents concerning Galesion in the Life of St Lazaros: shortages of bread, wine, cheese and pulses were remedied by miraculous replenishment of the stores or the unexpected arrival of gifts. Evidence from southern Italy, too, indicates that shortages of food were frequent. Two episodes in the Life of St Sabas concern the miraculous filling of oil storage jars when supplies ran out and St Elias Spelaiotes' monks in their cave near Seminare are reported to have suffered from food shortages when more recruits came to join them.[30]

---

[28] MM, IV, 324–5. The reference to the donation of land at Messingouma by Leo VI is in a document probably to be dated to 1127, see Janin, *Grands centres*, 447, no. 21. Since Paul of Latros died on 15 December 955 and his foundation dedicated to the Theotokos was established c. 920–30, Leo VI (d. 912) could not have made donations to it.

[29] For the estate at Bare, see H. Ahrweiler, 'L'histoire et la géographie de Smyrne entre les occupations turques (1081–1317), particulièrement au XIIIe siècle', *TM*, 1 (1965), 1–204, reprinted in *Byzance: les pays et les territoires* (London, 1976), article IV, p. 57 and note 23; p. 99 and note 148.

[30] Life of St Paul the Younger, chapter 29, p. 137. Life of St Lazaros, chapters 209, p. 572; 212–14, pp. 572–3. Life of St Sabas, chapter 38, pp. 163–4; Life of St Elias Spelaiotes, VI, chapters 40–3, pp. 864–5.

In the case of Galesion, two of the main causes of shortages were the large numbers of visitors given hospitality in the *xenodocheion* (monastic hostel) and the day-to-day charity dispensed by Lazaros himself. The *xenodocheios* (hostel keeper), doubtless desperately trying to make ends meet, was reproached by Lazaros for suggesting that visitors should be asked to leave after spending three days in the hostel. The principles of monastic charity prevailed, in this case, over the exigencies of the monastic economy. Charity was not only dispensed in this formal way; the Life contains a curious account of St Lazaros giving a 'chit' to a poor man who had come to him, which the latter was to take to the *kellarites* (store-keeper). It entitled him to a goat, four measures of wine, oil, vegetables, cheese and bread. In both cases, there was an assumption on the part of the laity that the monastery was a place where food could be found and requested, implying a healthy state of surplus, but the reaction of the *xenodocheios* must lead us to question whether this was always so.[31]

The monasteries of Galesion could certainly not, at first, support themselves from the produce of the land around them. Neither grain nor wine, still less the olive, would have flourished on Galesion. In fact, although Lazaros himself made provision for any surplus from the estates (*proasteia*) to be sent to Bessai (which being built on land given by the emperor was thus removed from the authority of the metropolitan of Ephesos), he clearly did not expect there always to be one. The monk Cyril told the author of the Life of St Lazaros of 'shortages and diffi-culties'. The year before Lazaros died (1053), his monasteries were hit by famine. This is not to say that the houses on Galesion possessed no productive land. The Life of St Lazaros relates how monks journeyed to Lydia 'to one of the *proasteia* of the house', to get wine. Vineyards are also mentioned on their estate at Komothona, which was probably near Ephesos. The monastery also owned lands at Barbatziona: *oikos* (farm-stead) Philippikos and Pentakrene and *paroikoi* to work them, but these do not seem to have been large or productive enough to supply all their needs.[32]

The same type of conditions applied on the other holy mountains which shared the same geographical characteristics: Olympos, Kyminas and Mykale. The original mountain environment of the monks could support only a few hermits living a frugal life. But as the houses

[31] Life of St Lazaros, chapter 146, p. 551; chapter 150, p. 552.
[32] Life of St Lazaros, chapters 246–7, pp. 585–6; 210, pp. 572–3. Komothona was near the *chorion ta Boulgarin*, which itself was not far from Ephesos, see Ahrweiler, 'Smyrne', p. 21 and note 96; p. 149. Life of St Lazaros, chapter 243, p. 584 describes two monks super-vising the ploughman. Kaplan, *Les hommes et la terre*, pp. 306–8, for the organisation of the Galesion estates.

expanded, so the need to obtain lands in the valleys increased. In the case of Mount Mykale, for instance, the Monastery of Hiera-Xerochoraphion possessed lands in the region of Sampson (the ancient city of Priene) in the fertile Maeander Valley and was probably able to support its large numbers in the mid-eleventh century.[33] As soon as the fame of the founders of the *lavrai* of Asia Minor began to attract monks and visitors, they were faced with the problems of food supply. The hagiographies depict a hand to mouth existence which, at times, was only rescued from disaster by gifts of food and 'divine intervention', surely a metaphor for the same thing. The houses had to survive on the goodwill of their neighbours and on buying food on the open market. It was only as a consequence of the purchase and gift of land and obtaining the labour to work it that adequate food production could be assured. The ability to do this depended to a large extent on the receipt of *rogai* and other monetary donations and the acquisition of *paroikoi* or hired labour, and it could not be done without compromising the eremitic and ascetic principles of the founders.

The monastic foundations of the Aegean islands were also set up as a consequence of the search for *eremia*, and it is therefore not surprising to find them presenting a similar pattern of development to the houses which had been their inspiration. Two examples of monastic expansion in the Aegean may serve to prove the point. The Nea Mone on Chios was established in the mid-eleventh century on an island which, even today, possesses only a small proportion of cultivated land (some 20 per cent of the total area) on which fruit, olives and mastic trees flourish, but little grain. By 1044, it had obtained estates on the west coast of Asia Minor at Kalothekia (at least 12,000 *modioi*) and Eucheia (c. 20,000 *modioi*) on the peninsula of Erythrai. It also possessed a *metochion* at Perama. But although possession of these lands may have gone some way towards ensuring the grain supply of the monastery, the Nea Mone depended on imperial gifts of wheat for its survival. Constantine Monomachos granted a yearly allowance of 1,000 *modioi* of corn, first taken from the imperial estate of Helos, north of Smyrna and then from that of Bessai, near Ataia in Bithynia. We can, perhaps, assume, that sufficient olives, grapes and fruit grew on the island to support the monastic population.[34]

---

[33] Hiéra-Xérochoraphion, pp. 5–6.
[34] For a short general description of the island, see C. Bouras, *Chios* (Athens, 1974) and for the history of the monastery, *Nea Mone on Chios*. Zepos, I, Appendix, document IV, pp. 615–18 for Erythrai. The possession of Kalothekia was confirmed in 1049 and 1050, see Zepos, I, Appendix, documents XI, pp. 634–5; XII, p. 635. For their probable location, see Ahrweiler, 'Smyrne', pp. 65–8. For Constantine Monomachos' gifts of corn, Zepos, I, Appendix, document XIV, p. 637. Ahrweiler, 'Smyrne', p. 65, locates Helos. For Bessai, see chapter 2, note 28 above.

The second example from the Aegean, that of the fortunes of the Monastery of St John the Theologian on Patmos, provides a rather more precise picture of a monastic economy at work. When the island was granted to Christodoulos in 1088, a *praktikon* (land survey) was made on behalf of Nicholas Tzanzes, the *krites* and *anagrapheus* of the Cyclades, by his delegate, George Granatos. Its details are shown in Table 6.[35] Granatos wrote of 'an impenetrable forest of brushwood and pines, a lack of water and a wasteland'. Only 627 *modioi* were cultivable out of a total of 3,860 *modioi* of taxed land. Only 160 *modioi* could be ploughed; the rest of the land had to be broken up with spades and hoes and it has thus been recently estimated by Elisabeth Malamut that three-quarters of the lands were, in Byzantine terms, of third-class quality. There were only about twenty dry pear trees and no other trees, fruit bearing or otherwise. In his chrysobull of 1088, Alexios Komnenos had himself described Patmos as 'a poor island, but potentially most fertile for the production of *spiritual* fruit' – an indication, surely, that Patmos fulfilled the theoretical requirements of eremitic monasticism. It may be that at the time of year (August) that the *praktikon* was drawn up, Patmos would have been at its most uninviting, with the seasonal springs dried up, but there is little doubt that the landscape was perennially harsh.[36]

The increase in the productivity of Patmos was thus a direct consequence of the efforts of the monks and their *paroikoi*. Olive groves, vines and fig trees were planted by Christodoulos and a successor in the hegoumenate, Sabas, spent 25 *nomismata* on young plants. Animals were pastured too; by the end of the eleventh century sheep and goats' cheeses were being exported from the island. But Patmos was never to become a highly productive island and when Athanasios of Antioch declared in his Life of St Christodoulos, written about 1156, that Patmos now flourished as a direct result of the saint's efforts, he was indulging in something of an exaggeration.[37] There was always a problem of bread supply and Alexios Komnenos ordered that 300 *modioi* of wheat (to which was added a *roga* of 24 *nomismata* per annum) should be supplied each year by the *doux* of Crete. John Komnenos added 100 further *modioi* in 1119. By the end of the twelfth century, if not earlier, the Monastery of St John had acquired lands at Nesi, near Psychro on Crete, which, to a certain extent, replaced these donations and thereby broke the agreement of April 1088, by which it was stated that Christodoulos and his spiritual heirs should not gain

---

[35] See p. 219.
[36] *Praktikon* of George Granatos: *BEMP*, ii, no. 51, pp. 37–40; chrysobull of Alexios Komnenos (1088): *BEMP*, i, no. 6, pp. 59–63. See Malamut, *Les îles*, ii, p. 398.
[37] Vranoussi, *Ta hagiologika keimena*, p. 188.

any other lands in the islands than those granted to them by Alexios Komnenos.[38]

Spiritual compromise, then, became most necessary when matters of survival were at stake. But did Christodoulos know that it would be impossible to achieve self-sufficiency from the Patmos lands alone? Even before the exchange of his previously held properties on the island of Kos for the entire island of Patmos had been effected, Christodoulos had already received lands on the nearby islands of Leipsos and Leros. There is no reason to believe that he intended to establish a monastery on either of them. He may well have been envisaging holding more productive agricultural areas in association with an island, Patmos, which closely conformed to eremitic conventions.[39] For Leros is a much more fertile island than Patmos, possessing a lighter soil and several springs. The lowland areas in the south around Temeneia, where the monks of Patmos possessed estates, are particularly well watered and may have supported cattle. The monastic estate of Parthenion, in the north of the island, was in a region of soft ground and natural springs. It was one of the larger estates of the area; at 6,050 *modioi*, it was more extensive than the territory of two neighbouring villages, Polouphoute (present day Plephoute) at 5,618 *modioi* and Kourounon (1,458 *modioi*). The monastery also possessed an estate at Temeneia. The proportion of taxable land to total area was higher than that on Patmos, indicating a more viable agrarian economy, and the level of pasture land was also higher. The island of Leipsos, though not as productive as Leros, supported cattle in Christodoulos' day. In the *praktikon* describing the monastery's holdings, 400 *modioi* of arable were mentioned, not all of it good quality, but since there were also one or two pairs of oxen, the land could be worked and brought up to a higher level of productivity.[40]

It is difficult to believe that the Monastery of St John would have

---

[38] Chrysobulls of Alexios Komnenos: MM, VI, p. 107 and *BEMP*, I, no. 8 (1119), p. 82, ll. 17–18. Doles of grain discussed by Malamut, *Les îles*, II, pp. 385–6. The grain allowance originally came from the imperial property (*episkepsis*) near Chandax (modern Heraklion). In 1176 Manuel Komnenos replaced the grant (by now of 700 *modioi* of corn from the *episkepsis* in Crete) with one of 2 lb of *nomismata* (144 *nomismata* in coin) per year.

[39] Chrysobull concerning Leipsos and Leros, May 1087 (*BEMP*, I, no. 5); *Pittakion* ordering registration of documents concerned, June 1087 (*BEMP*, I, no. 46); *Pittakion* of Anna Dalassene confirming donation and ordering notification to imperial bureaux concerned, June 1087 (*BEMP*, I, no. 47); *praktika* of Eustathios Charsianites, *strategos* and *pronoetes* of Samos, July 1087 (*BEMP*, II, no. 52) and April 1089 (*BEMP*, II, no. 53). Donation of Patmos, April 1088 (*BEMP*, I, no. 6); *pittakion* ordering registration by interested imperial bureaux, April 1088 (*BEMP*, I, no. 48); *pittakion* of Anna Dalassene, May 1088 (*BEMP*, I, no. 49); *praktikon* established by Nicholas Tzanzes and revised by George Granatos, August 1088 (*BEMP*, II, no. 51).

[40] For Leros, see Malamut, *Les îles*, I, pp. 240, 281; II, pp. 398–9. For Leipsos, *ibid.*, I, pp. 240, 281; II, p. 391.

Table 6. *Properties of Monastery of St John the Theologian, Patmos, c. 1100*[a]

Place	Property	Extent	Nature	Source
Patmos		3,860 *modioi* of which		*BEMP*, I, no. 5
		627 *modioi*	'Cultivable'	
		160 *modioi*	'Ploughable'	
Leipsos		400 *modioi*	Arable	MM, VI, p. 41
			Pasture	
			Mountain	
			Church of St Nicholas	
			Stable for oxen	
Leros	*Proasteion* of Temeneia	259 *modioi*	Arable	*BEMP*, II, no. 52
			Church with dome	
			Tower	
			Eukterion of Theotokos	
			Barn	
			Barn for straw	
			Stable	
			Lodgings for *misthioi*	
			Lodgings for *paroikoi*	
			Olive Press	
			Well	
			Spring	
			4 almond trees	
			10 pomegranate trees	
			11 quince trees	
			4 fig trees	
			12 carob trees	
			156 olive trees	
			326 oak trees	
			3 pear trees	
	Proasteion of Parthenion	6,050 *modioi* of which		
		409 *modioi*	Arable	*BEMP*, II, no. 52
			Church of St George	
			Well	
			Wine press	
			3 climbing vines	
			1 pomegranate tree	
			10 olive trees	
			Wild olive trees	
			5 oak trees	
			1 fig tree	
			24 carob trees	
			3 pear trees	
			Half *kastron* Pantelion (later all)	

Note: [a]Where no precise figures are given these are not known

219

survived more than a short period without its possessions on these islands, and Anna Dalassene's and Alexios Komnenos' action in granting them is an important example of imperial patronage supplying what the chosen monastic environment could not. The process by which Christodoulos requested and obtained specific lands in the Aegean reveals a deliberate strategy in which the spiritual demands of *eremia* could be deployed by the monks when necessary. In a particularly blatant example, existing communal rights to pasture belonging to the villagers of Leros were disrupted when the Patmiote monks were granted grazing lands at Parthenion for their exclusive use on the grounds of the preservation of their solitude; the understandable refusal of the neighbouring lay communities to countenance this overturning of traditional rights by continuing to use the pasture in question for their own flocks led to ultimately successful appeals by the monks to higher lay authority.[41]

The intervention of an influential patron (again the emperor) was also necessary to provide the monastery with its lifeline of survival – the ships which are mentioned as early as 1088. The house required boats to keep in contact with its estates on neighbouring islands, but those mentioned in the documents were clearly more than just a means of communication. In 1088 Christodoulos was granted exemption from taxes and services for a ship of 500 *modioi* capacity, which he had yet to have built. By the time of his death, the monastery possessed four more exempted ships: one *koutroubin*, two *platydia* and one ship of unknown size in which the saint and his followers later fled to Euboea from Turkish attacks. These were allowed to traffic in all parts of the empire without payment of taxes and there were doubtless others which were subject to state dues and taxes. The origin of this uneremitic commerce must be seen in the need to import corn: the ship of 500 *modioi* may well have been used to bring the imperial grain allowance of 300 *modioi* from Crete. But other goods, such as salt, almonds, cheese and dried meat were exported and this commerce does indicate a significant move away from simple survival.[42]

If the early years of Christodoulos' foundation on Patmos provide an example of the way in which a charismatic monastic founder could ensure the survival of his house against the natural odds, the fortunes of the more influential of the Athonite houses also demonstrate the power of certain favoured institutions – a power which could transcend the initial challenges of the terrain by a judicious mixture of spiritual association and political influence – to expand beyond any territorial limits that the

---

[41] See R. Morris, 'Divine diplomacy in the late eleventh century', for imperial patronage. The dispute at Parthenion is further discussed in chapter 9.
[42] Karlin-Hayter, 'Notes sur les archives de Patmos', pp. 310–15 and Malamut, *Les îles*, II, pp. 446–9 discuss the size of the boats.

eremitic tradition might have dictated and to become land-holders of wealth and prestige. The continuing publication of the archives of the Athonite monasteries now makes it possible to trace in some detail the fortunes of the estates of certain houses – particularly the Lavra and Iviron – and to present some revealing case studies concerning the methods by which estates were accumulated as well as the justifications for this process presented by the monks. As far as these great Athonite houses were concerned, the possession of extensive property, although clearly dictated to some extent by monastic need, was something more than that. The possession of large estates added to the prestige of the house and marked the esteem in which its inhabitants were held; by the eleventh century this meant that some houses owned far more land than was necessary for survival.

In many ways, the development of the Athonite monastic estates (map 3) followed a similar pattern to that apparent in western Asia Minor and the Aegean. Although the peninsula of Athos provided the kind of rough terrain and seclusion which first attracted the early hesychasts and then presented a suitable place of refuge to St Athanasios, within easy reach lay the rich agricultural areas of the Chalkidike and southern Macedonia (map 4). The growth in monastic numbers – there may have been over three thousand monks on Athos by the end of the tenth century – was one of the driving forces behind the early expansion of property beyond the Holy Mountain itself. Before the coming of Athanasios, the monastic inhabitants of the mountain seem to have been virtually self-sufficient in food, but a certain measure of clearance had already begun. The writer of the Life of Athanasios (A) gives an erroneous impression of a wild and forbidding area which supported no crops and where the inhabitants led a frugal existence, feeding themselves on fruit and only obtaining corn and millet on those rare occasions when pilgrims came to seek the blessing of the hesychasts and brought small supplies.[43] The work of clearance and cultivation had already begun before Athanasios' arrival. For the saint himself wrote in defence of his own clearances at Mylopotamos that other Athonites before him had cleared fields and planted vineyards. The monk Nicholas, however, the author of the Life of St Peter the Athonite written c. 970–80, commented on the regrettable desire of the Athonites of his own times for possession and expansion.[44]

The importance of ensuring the supply of wine to the Lavra was,

---

[43] Life of Athanasios (A), chapter 38, pp. 18–20, echoed in (B), chapter 13, p. 139. The author of the earlier Life (A) could not have known what conditions were really like at this time, since he was writing about c. 1000–1010. He was describing a 'suitable state' for hesychasm, see *Prôtaton*, pp. 70–1.

[44] *Typikon* of Athanasios, p. 106. *Prôtaton*, pp. 20, 71.

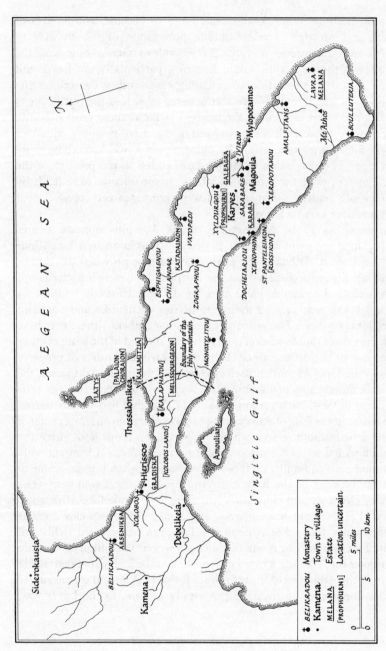

AEGEAN SEA

Siderokausia

BELIKRADOU
ARSENIKEA
KOLOBOS

BELIKRADOU

GRADISKA
Hierissos

Kamena

Debilikeia

PLATYS

[PALAION
CHORAION]

Thessalonikea

[KALAMITZIA]

[KALAPHATOU]

[KOLOBOS LANDS]

MELISSOURGEION

Amouliane

Singitic Gulf

N

ESPHIGMENOU

CHILANDAR

KATADAIMON

ZOGRAPHOU

VATOPEDI

Boundary of the
Holy mountain

MONOXYLITOU

XYLOURGOU
[PROPHOURNI]

Karyes,
SARABARE
KARABA

DOCHEIARIOU

XENOPHON

ST PANTELEIMON
[ROSSIKON]

GALEAGRA
IVIRON

Magoula

XEROPOTAMOU

Mylopotamos

AMALFITANS

Mt Athos

LAVRA
MELANA

BOULEUTERIA

BELIKRADOU   Monastery
Kamena   • Town or village
MELANA   Estate
[PROPHOURNI] Location uncertain

0   5 miles   10 km.
0   5   10 km.

Map 3 Monasteries of Athos

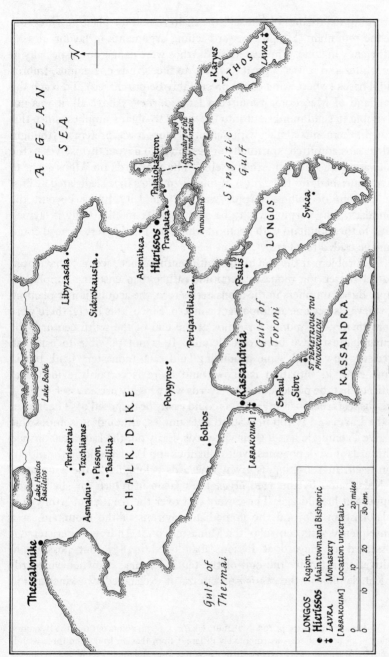

AEGEAN

SEA

ATHOS

*Karyes

LAVRA*

Boundary of the
Holy mountain

Singitic

Gulf

Palaiokastron
Pravlaka*

Hierissos *

*Arsenikea

Amouliane

LONGOS

*Sykea

Libyzasda*

Lake Bolbe

Siderokausia*

Perigardikeia*

Psalis*

Gulf of

Toroni

CHALKIDIKE

*Pobgyros

Kassandreia

ST DEMETRIOS TOU
PHOUSKOULOU *

*Sibre

KASSANDRA

Lake Hosios
Basileios

*Peristerai

Asmalou * * Tzechlianes

*Pisson

*Basilika

*Bolbos

[ABBAKOUM] ?*

*St Paul

Thessalonike *

Gulf of

Thermai

LONGOS Region

Hierissos * Main town and Bishopric

LAVRA + Monastery

[ABBAKOUM] Location uncertain

0   10   20   20 miles

0   10   20   30 km.

Map 4 The hinterland of Athos

according to Athanasios himself, the main reason for planting vineyards on the mountain. He put forward telling arguments in favour of self-sufficiency in wine. The seas around Athos were dangerous, especially in the winter and it was 'a great distance' to the islands of Lemnos, Imbros and Thasos (where wine could presumably be purchased). To reach the mainland of Macedonia required a long journey. Above all, it was not advisable to send monks out into the world to obtain supplies, since this brought them into contact with the laity. Hence it was preferable (though, Athanasios admitted, spiritually undesirable) to devote themselves to the cultivation of vines on Athos itself.[45] The vineyards on Athos seem to have flourished, for the *Tragos* of John Tzimiskes (972) legislated against the custom of selling surplus wine to the laity living beyond the boundary. Any surplus was to be sold to other monks. Only if laymen came to the mountain with goods of which the monks were in need could wine be traded for them.[46]

The problem at the end of the tenth century, then, seems to have been that of preserving monastic rectitude rather than ensuring supplies of wine. But as numbers in the monasteries rose, the acquisition or planting of vineyards became an important concern. Since, as is likely, there were more than 3,000 monks on Athos at the end of the tenth century, the demand must have been considerable. It is not possible to establish precisely how much wine producing land each monastery held, but in some cases its situation is known and there is certainly evidence to indicate that the possession of vineyards was a highly prized asset, mainly, one suspects, because any surplus could easily be disposed of. The houses of the Lavra and Iviron may stand as examples, although it is impossible to give a complete list of their vineyards. Early on, the Lavra established vineyards at Mylopotamos, Metrophanous and Bouleuteria on the mountain itself. In 1065, it was given vineyards belonging to the Monastery of Kalaphatou by the aged *hegoumenos* Jacob in return for shelter and support in his old age. These were just over the frontier of Athos near Palaiokastron. Beyond the immediate environs of the mountain, as a consequence of its control of the Monastery of St Andrew at Peristerai, it possessed a vineyard at Pisson, abandoned in 897, but possibly in cultivation again by the end of the tenth century; it owned vineyards at Katadaimon in the *chorion* of Zitetza; it exchanged two vineyards at

---

[45] *Typikon* of Athanasios, p. 105. Malamut, *Les îles*, I, p. 30, points out that the Byzantine notion of distance at sea was completely different from that on land. The three islands named by Athanasios were *perceived* to be a long way away and indeed could be so if the seas were high or the winds treacherous. As the crow flies, Athos to Thasos is about 60 km; Imbros about 130 km and Lemnos c. 60 km.

[46] *Prôtaton*, no. 7 (972), ll. 95–100.

Sykea for one on Longos and another (location unknown) with a wine-press and lands at Pravlaka for yet more vines.[47]

The Monastery of Iviron, another of the larger houses on the Holy Mountain, was also concerned to expand its ownership of vineyards. In an interesting episode in 1015, it was able to engineer the acquisition of vineyards at Thessalonikea on the peninsula of Platys, by mobilising some of the considerable liquid assets which it then enjoyed. Euthymios, son of John the Iberian, specifically asked for this property, which had previously been administered by the Protaton and which, in the year in question, was estimated to produce revenues of 34 *nomismata* per year. There was probably considerable opposition from the *hegoumenoi* of the other Athonite houses who had gathered at the Easter *synaxis* or assembly, for some nine days elapsed between Euthymios presenting his request and the drawing up of two documents agreeing to it. In both documents, mention was made of the particular service which John the Iberian had contributed to the Holy Mountain: all his life he had shown his love for the Athonite community, never ceasing to spend money on it or give benefits to it, or to individuals. He had made financial donations to assist with the building of the church of the Protaton and had given liturgical objects and vestments. But, as the earlier document reveals, at first only the *hegoumenoi* of the Lavra (whose links with Iviron were still close at this period) and of Xeropotamou were willing to agree with the Protos. Euthymios, who had agreed to compensate the Protaton to the tune of 34 *nomismata*, raised his offer to 100 *nomismata* at which point another forty-one *hegoumenoi* were willing to sign. However, the affair was not yet over. A second document, drawn up very shortly after the first, indicates that Euthymios had to double the sum. It was then agreed that the money should be distributed amongst the Athonite houses according to the proportion of the annual imperial *roga* which each received.[48]

Vineyards, then, were a commodity that large monasteries would go to some considerable lengths to acquire and it was large and influential houses which could find cash at short notice to close such deals. For the Iviron purchase of 1015, the first 100 *nomismata* at issue were described as *holotrachy* (indicating that they were newly minted) and Euthymios seems to have had no difficulty in pledging (on the same day) a further large

---

[47] Vineyards of the Lavra; *Typikon* of Athanasios, p. 105; *Lavra*, I, nos. 26 and 27 (1030); *Xéropotamou*, no. 1 (1010) indicates that the Metrophanous vineyard was later given away. *Lavra*, I, nos. 26 and 27 (1030) for Bouleuteria. Vineyards outside Athos: *Lavra*, I, no. 34 (1065) for Kalaphatou; *Lavra*, I, no. 1 (987): Pisson; *Lavra*, I, no. 18 (1014): Katadaimon and Zitetza; *Lavra*, I, no. 24 (1018), for the vineyards at Longos.

[48] The documents concerned are *Ivirôn*, I, nos. 20 and 21 both drawn up on the same day: 19 April 1015. They indicate that some hard bargaining took place.

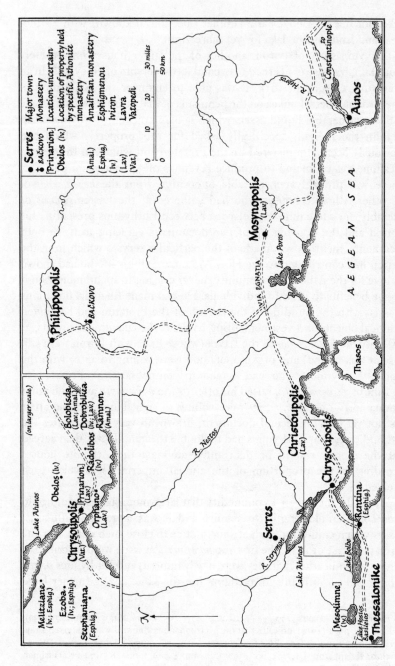

Map 5 Athonite land-holding in Macedonia, tenth to eleventh centuries

sum. Already productive vineyards were naturally valuable, but there are also examples of an even more costly process, the establishment of new ones. Only those houses with large cash surpluses could afford both the expenses of clearance and improvement and the purchase of young plants. The Lavra was one such. At Bouleuteria, 520 *nomismata* was invested in planting vines and in restoring the church, *kellia* and other buildings – a considerable sum. At the Monastery of Xenophon, a 'great vineyard' was planted by the rich restorer of the house, the ex-*megas droungarios* (a high legal official), Stephen, well known in the monastic world as Symeon the Sanctified. So while it is likely that all the Athonite houses possessed small vineyards like that of the humble Monastery of the Prophet Daniel with its six *modioi*, the more powerful houses deliberately set out to acquire or establish more. It is one of the areas in which much of their *roga* and cash donations were spent.[49]

The possession of olive groves was similarly prized. A gift of land supporting 300 olive trees near the Monastery of St Nicholas tou Chrysokamerou was made at the beginning of the eleventh century by the *hegoumenos* to his cousin, Xenophon, the founder of the house that was to bear his name, and, at the end of the century, Symeon the Sanctified was responsible for the establishment of more plantations of olive trees on the property of Xenophon. But a more typical olive grove was probably that of the Monastery of Skamandrenos, which possessed some fifteen trees in 1083. While the establishment of new vineyards on or near Athos was a productive possibility, the same cannot really be said for olives and only those monasteries with land a fair distance outside the mountain would have found it possible to be self-sufficient in oil. The monetary allowances for the monks were intended to buy commodities such as this.[50]

Grain crops were not found on the mountain in large enough quantities for the areas where they grew to become the object of purchase and dispute. The necessity of obtaining the vast quantities needed to feed the inhabitants of the larger monasteries was the main motivation behind the expansion of the richer Athonite houses into the territory around Hierissos, into the Chalkidike and further afield into southern Macedonia. The main areas of Athonite expansion have been plotted on map 5. Initially, powerful houses like the Lavra and Iviron obtained lands on the plains of Basilika south of Thessalonike, where olives, mulberries and vineyards now flourish, as they may also have done in Byzantine

---

[49] *Lavra*, I, nos. 26 and 27 (1030); *Xénophon*, no. 1 (1089). For the Monastery of the Prophet Daniel, *Xénophon*, no. 1 (1089), and introduction, p. 16.
[50] *Xénophon*, introduction, pp. 7, 16; A payment in kind drawn from the olive trees of Skamandrenos was to be fixed at 15 *litrai*, not more than one *litra* per tree.

times, and on the other two peninsulas of the Chalkidike: Kassandra and
Longos. Kassandra was probably the more fertile as it eventually
possessed a larger number of monastic estates and dependent houses
(*metochia*) than Longos. Its economy was mainly pastoral though both
peninsulas still support bee-keeping – perhaps the source of the honey
which makes its appearance in the allowance for the monk Damian in
1101–2.[51]

The expansion of monastic land-holding into the Chalkidike marked
the moment at which the concept of *eremia* was irrevocably compromised
as far as the Athonite monks were concerned. It can be explained by the
need to make use of the varied opportunities this area afforded for
agriculture and animal husbandry. But the acquisition of lands further to
the east, on the coastal plain stretching from Serres to Constantinople,
indicates a far more ambitious aim: to obtain property in one of the most
important agricultural areas of the empire. From map 5, it can be seen
how Athonite property converged on the area between Serres and the sea
and on the coastal plain between the rivers Strymon (Struma) and Hebros
(Maritza). The most striking feature of this process was the speed at
which the Athonite houses gained property far beyond the environs of
the Holy Mountain. By 964, for example, the Lavra possessed lands as
far away as Chrysoupolis. By the end of the eleventh century, the Lavra's
properties in the theme of Boleron-Strymon-Thessalonike amounted to
some 47,052 *modioi* and in 1115 its lands stretched as far afield as the out-
skirts of Thessalonike in one direction and Derkos in Thrace in another.[52]

A similar picture emerges from a study of the expansion of Iviron, even
though the house suffered a difficult period in the mid-eleventh century
when much land was confiscated after the implication of the *hegoumenos*
George I in a plot against the Emperor Romanos III Argyros in 1029.
Until 980, the only possessions held by the Georgian monastery were the
lands on Athos of the old Monastery of Clement on which they built their
house. But an imperial chrysobull of 979–80 granted them important

[51] See map 4, p. 223. The work in progress of Jacques Lefort will eventually provide a full
guide to the historical geography of this region, see the first volume, *Villages de Macédoine*,
I: *La Chalcidique occidentale* (Travaux et Mémoires du Centre de Recherche d'Histoire
et Civilisation de Byzance, Monographies, 1, Paris, 1982). For two old but still useful
geographical surveys, see A. G. Ogilvie, 'A contribution to the geography of Macedonia',
Geographical Journal, 55 (1920), 1–30 and map facing p. 72; *ibid.*, 'Physiography and
settlement in southern Macedonia', *Geographical Review*, 11 (1921), 172–91 and map
facing p. 126. See Koder 'Die Metochia der Athos-Klöster', for a discussion of monastic
holdings in the Chakidike. For Damian's allowance, see Table 5.
[52] Hendy, *Byzantine monetary economy*, p. 25 and map 4; pp. 85–90 and map 19 discuss the
agricultural potential of the coastal plains of Thrace and Macedonia and the interest in
obtaining land there displayed by monasteries and lay magnates in the eleventh century.
For the Lavra's lands in this region, see *Lavra*, I, nos. 50 (1089), and 60 (1115).

groups of lands, which were already in monastic hands and which could well have been considered under Nikephoros Phokas' category of run-down estates needing further investments (something which the Georgians were well able to do, loaded down as they were by the booty brought back by Tornik from his successes in 979). They comprised lands originally held by the Monastery of the Virgin at Abbakoum on Kassandra and in the Chalkidike proper; those of the Monastery of the Prodromos at Leontia near Thessalonike and in the Chalkidike and those of the Monastery of the Virgin of Chabounia (also known after its founder Demetrios Pteleotes as *tou Pteleotou*) near Polygyros also in the Chalkidike. Of considerable interest, however, is the fact that all these houses had, by 979, come under the control of yet another, the Monastery of Kolobos.[53]

It was the acquisition of this monastery and its lands, against considerable opposition from other Athonite interests, which marked the rise of the house of Iviron to prominence on Athos. Its grant by the Emperor Basil II was clearly a mark of imperial favour as a delegation of Athonites (including John the Iberian) had already requested in vain in 972 that the monastery should be handed over to their control. On the accession of Basil II in 976, the request was repeated and again refused; the *hegoumenos* of Kolobos, Stephen, retaliating to these monastic 'take-over bids' by refusing to allow the Athonites their customary hospitality at his monastery when they visited Hierissos. It was only when Tornik himself asked for the house, on his return from Iberia in 979–80, that it was granted and then to him personally rather than to the Athonites as a whole, a matter which caused considerable outrage, one of the early manifestations of the anti-Georgian prejudice which spread through the mountain in the eleventh century and which was only staved off in the tenth by generous monetary donations to the Protaton. With this house came two groups of land: near Hierissos and more importantly in the valley of the River Strymon near Ezoba. By the end of the century they owned at least 80,000 *modioi* of land, far above the subsistence needs of the house. Thus the pattern of expansion set by the Lavra was also followed by Iviron.[54]

The early part of the eleventh century saw a continued expansion in the lands of Iviron, many of them acquired by purchase, though we know that, as in the case of the lands at Thessalonikea, there was often lively opposition from other Athonite monasteries. Iviron obtained further

---

[53] The estates of Iviron are discussed in detail in *Ivirôn*, I, introduction, pp. 25–59, pp. 70–91, especially p. 42 for the 'time of troubles' of the mid-eleventh century, and *Ivirôn*, II, introduction, pp. 21–3, 26–33.

[54] *Ivirôn*, I, introduction, pp. 25–32.

lands beyond the mountain, at Debelikea and Dobrobikea for instance, but this happy process was brought to a sharp halt in 1029 at the beginning of the 'time of troubles', which had as its most serious initial consequence the confiscation by the state of much of the land of Iviron as a punishment for the disloyalty of the *hegoumenos* George I. Rival landowners, such as the bishop of Ezoba, also grasped the opportunity to lay claim to lands previously held by Iviron. In many another house this might have spelled the beginning of the end, but it is a mark of the strength of the patronage network (both Greek and Georgian) which supported the monastery and the access which this gave to the highest authorities of the empire, that repeated lobbying resulted in the restoration of the confiscated lands in 1041 and the recognition in the *Typikon* of Constantine Monomachos that the *hegoumenos* of Iviron should be considered one of the 'chief *hegoumenoi*' whose views should be sought by the Protos. By the end of the century, Iviron had consolidated its estates on Athos; on the peninsula of Platys; near Hierissos; on the isthmus of Athos; to the north and west near Kamena and Arsenikea; in Kassandra and the western Chalkidike; near Ezoba in the lower Strymon valley and on the Aegean coastlands east of the river. By 1100, they had also gained control of the important Radolibos estate as a consequence of the bequests of Symbatios and Kale Pakourianos.[55]

This territorial expansion, paralleled to a lesser extent by other houses on the mountain was in part a consequence of the increase in Athonite numbers and the growing spiritual influence of the monks, but also, too, of the tacit abandonment of their seclusion on the mountain. The claims to *eremia* could none the less still be advanced as a rationale for land acquisition, as in 1013, when the Protos and the assembled *hegoumenoi* granted 'uninhabited and uncultivated land' at Palaion Choraion near Chelanden so that the Georgian monks 'could install themselves there in solitude'. This is an indication, perhaps, that attempts were being made to salvage some of the principles which had led to the establishment of the houses on Athos. If so, it was a losing battle in the long term.[56]

The controversies surrounding the pasturing of livestock on the mountain were another aspect of this continuing debate. Before the arrival of Athanasios, Athos had supplied pasture for the flocks of the inhabitants of Hierissos and a refuge for them in times of attack. By the time of the *Tragos*, two areas of difficulty had emerged. The first was

[55] *Ivirôn*, I, introduction, pp. 45–9, 55, note 57. For the Pakourianos donations at Radolibos, see chapter 5, pp. 135–6. The documents concerned are *Ivirôn*, II, nos. 47 (1098), 48 (soon after December 1098), 51 (1103), and are discussed in detail by J. Lefort, 'Le cadastre de Radolibos (1103), les géomètres et leurs mathématiques', *TM*, 8 (1981), 269–313 and *ibid.*, 'Radolibos: population et paysage', *TM*, 9 (1985), 195–234.
[56] *Ivirôn*, I, no. 18 (1013).

the united opposition of the Athonite monks to the use of Athos as pasture by the neighbouring laity; the second, arguments over the possession of animals by the monasteries themselves. The opposition to lay access, though expressed as a wish to preserve eremitic solitude, was a means of asserting *de facto* monastic control over the peninsula. But the interhouse arguments about the ownership of livestock seem to have had little but jealousy behind them. There is little mention in other tenth-century sources of the ban on female animals contained in the *Typikon* of Athanasios for the Lavra and certainly in evidence by the time of the *Typikon* of Monomachos (though this argument may have been put forward), and hostility to the possession of animals was probably based on the far more basic enmity of the smaller houses towards the expansionism of the larger.[57]

Various attempts to legislate on the question seem only to have exacerbated the situation, since those houses with access to imperial or patriarchal ears were allowed privileges in the holding of livestock not afforded to other houses. In 972 the Lavra was the only house permitted to own a pair of oxen (to be used to propel a machine invented by Athanasios for the kneading of dough), ostensibly because of the number of monks, but in reality as a consequence of the patronage of John Tzimiskes. It was granted three more pairs of oxen in 1045. Vatopedi appears to have been the only other house permitted to possess oxen in this period. The main difficulty, however, was the regulation of the flocks and herds kept on Athos. Although the *Tragos* forbade the entry of flocks on to the mountain, an act of the Lavra of 991 reveals the presence of animals on the heights of the mountain and even individual monks seem to have owned them – the aged Athanasios of Bouleuteria who put himself under the protection of the Lavra in 1030 was allowed to keep his horse. The *Typikon* of Monomachos dealt with the question again in 1045 and declared that goats and sheep were to be expelled from the mountain. The possession of cattle was allowed (but only to the Lavra) so long as the animals were kept twelve miles away from any monastery and their herdsmen were Lavriotes.[58]

These conditions give the first indication of a problem that was to cause considerable discord on Athos at the end of the eleventh century: the increasing presence of nomadic shepherds, mainly Vlachs, in the hinterland of Athos and their steady incursion on to the mountain itself. There were some three hundred families of them on Athos by the end of the century. It is clear that the Athonites considerably benefited from their presence, for not only did they provide large amounts of willing labour,

---

[57] *Typikon* of Athanasios, p. 113; *Lavra*, I, no. 2 (941). See Morris, 'Dispute settlement', for the boundary disputes which were going on at the same time.
[58] *Prôtaton*, nos. 2 (972) and 8 (1045). *Lavra*, I, no. 27 (1030).

but also quantities of cheese, milk and goats' hair cloth. Their continued presence on the mountain, through rising discord, until their expulsion in c. 1105, is an indication of the demand for dairy products from close at hand which could supplement the diet of the large number of monks that there now was. But the livestock holdings of the Monastery of Xenophon, a flourishing house but not one of the largest at the end of the eleventh century, indicate a more than adequate number of animals in some fortunate houses. In 1083 Xenophon possessed at least 14 pairs of oxen, 100 horses and asses, 130 buffalo, 150 cows and 2,000 goats and sheep on its estates beyond the mountain to support fifty-five monks. It was the smaller houses, with little access to land beyond the mountain, which were probably most loath to see the departure of the Vlachs, even though their presence (and especially that of their womenfolk) broke the conditions of the *Typikon* of Monomachos and offended many of the more spiritually minded monks.[59]

The need to ensure adequate food supplies also lay behind the numerous disputes between Athonite houses over the question of fishing rights. Fish was an important supplement to the basic diet and a vital source of protein. In 1010 the Lavra promised not to stop other houses fishing at Bouleuteria and in 1015, Iviron was warned not to try to prevent other Athonite monks from fishing at Kalamitzi. Fishing rights were precious as evidenced by the ferocity of many of the disputes concerning the construction of small landing stages and boat-sheds, since these constituted a claim on the fishing grounds at sea and were often the only legal 'toe-hold' of the inland houses on the coast.[60]

One particularly violent episode on Athos took place in the late 1040s, when the monks of the Monastery of the Holy Apostles of Dometiou tore down a boat-shed erected by the monks of the Monastery of Xylourgos on land which they had previously granted for the purpose in return for a payment of 5 *nomismata*. Serious though this offence doubtless was, it is somewhat surprising to learn that a complaint was immediately made to the Emperor Constantine Monomachos by Joannikios, the *hegoumenos* of the Monastery of Xylourgos. It was, in fact, in response to an imperial *graphe* addressed to the Protos, that the monks of the Holy Apostles were ordered to be fined. Instead, their *hegoumenos* gave a small plot of land for

[59] The Vlach question is dealt with in the *Diegesis merike* a series of documents (in dire need of re-editing) assembled probably before 1109, in Meyer, *Haupturkunden*, pp. 163–84, especially pp. 163–70. See the discussion in M. Gyóni, 'Les vlaques du Mont Athos au début du XIIe siècle', *Etudes Slaves et Roumaines*, I (1948), 30–42. For a general history of the Vlachs (which only briefly deals with this controversy), see T. Winnifrith, *The Vlachs: the history of a Balkan people* (London, 1988). See further discussion in chapter 10. For monastic animals see *Xénophon*, no. 1 (1083); *Xéropotamou*, no. 2 (1010).
[60] *Xéropotamou*, no. 2 (1010); *Iviron*, I, nos. 20 and 21 (1015).

the construction of another boat-house as a *psychikon* (spiritual gift) to Joannikios, in return for 6 *nomismata* on the understanding that his monks could not extend their territory further than the boat-shed. Both sides were probably in the wrong. The monks of the Holy Apostles had indeed pulled down the structure, but possibly because the Xylourgos monks were using it as a pretext to extend their cultivation – a matter which was put a stop to in the final agreement. The *psychikon* was a device to cloak the commercial nature of the transaction in monastic respectability.[61]

The example of Athos illustrates the need for territorial expansion which accompanied a growth in numbers, but an expansion which clearly did keep pace with the demand for staple foodstuffs. The period at which some of the houses began enjoying a surplus (although individual groups, such as the hermits of Chaldou, might still experience difficulties) may be indicated by the first references to trading by the monks. There was, as has been noted, already a surplus of wine by 972 and there was an active trade in this commodity before 1000, for a lost document of Basil II legislated against a commerce in wine which was being carried out with Constantinople 'and other places'. His orders had little effect. The *Typikon* of Monomachos, as with many other issues concerning Athos, proposed a compromise. Ships of up to 300 *modioi* capacity were permitted to sail as far as Thessalonike to the west and Ainos to the east to sell Athonite produce; larger ships were to be broken up. But there were exceptions – boats held by imperial permission – which clearly referred to that owned by the Lavra of 6,000 *modioi* capacity granted to them by Basil II and subsequently given to Iviron. Excepted, too, was the ship owned by Vatopedi with the written permission of the council of *hegoumenoi* and that owned by the Amalfitan monks which enabled them to receive supplies from their compatriots in Constantinople. These restrictions probably had little effect on the profitability of the trade in wine and other goods, since both Thessalonike and Ainos (at the mouth of the River Maritza) were centres of communication with the Slav world.

By the end of the eleventh century, the Lavra possessed seven ships, with a total capacity of 16,000 *modioi*, although by 1102 only two or three of them were left. In that year, Alexios Komnenos allowed them another four of a total capacity of 4,000 *modioi* with the right to replace them when necessary. The value of this imperial privilege lay not so much in the capacity of the ships – for they were all of relatively small draught – but in their exemption (*exkousseia*) from naval duty. This was to hold true even if a time of peril should come to the empire, and ordinances were made to suppress the exemptions of other houses. As in the case of

---

[61] *Pantéléèmôn*, no. 4 (1048), for the boat-shed dispute. The *psychikon* is discussed in chapter 6, p. 156 and note 30.

Patmos, imperial concern and patronage provided the Athonite monasteries with a privileged economic dimension and helped them to expand their interests beyond their own immediate territory.[62]

The Athonite experience, then, was that a few powerful houses, rich in patrons and in cash, were able to surmount the problems forced upon them by rising monastic professions and by the difficulty of extensive cultivation of the mountain itself. They bought, or were given large tracts beyond the mountain and they jockeyed for influence and prestige within the mountain itself. In the process, the Athonites began to break the rules they had made for themselves: they traded (especially in wine); they introduced animals; they requested ships and, at the end of the eleventh century, they became embroiled in the Vlach controversy, the effects of which were to seriously damage their reputation. As with the mountains and islands of the western Aegean, the sites of *eremia* could not remain totally segregated from the world and spiritual compromise was the only effective outcome.

In the lands of Thrace and Macedonia, the great eleventh-century *koinobia* were subject to no such difficulties and compromises. Here the houses that we know about were great family foundations, endowed by members of the imperial family, or by powerful individuals such as Attaliates and Pakourianos. For this reason, the process of accumulating land was much shorter. The houses were endowed from the outset with property, and since their numbers were often specifically linked by their *typika*, it is clear that their founders intended from the first to tailor the size of their houses to existing resources. In addition, such monasteries were not intended to stand as remote and eremitic places; they entered into the mainstream of Byzantine provincial spiritual life and were always much more closely linked to the surrounding lay community. Here it is not so much the question of self-sufficiency that was at issue, as that of the efficiency and potential to produce a surplus of each individual house.

Modern studies of the historical geography of the Rhodope Mountains and the geographical details provided in the *Typikon* of Bačkovo (Pakourianos' foundation) have established the areas of his monastery's main holdings in Bulgaria and Thrace. They fell into three main territorial groups: the first, consisting of lands originally belonging to Gregory Pakourianos' brother, Aspasios, north and west of the River Strymon (Struma); the second, south of Philippopolis (Plovdiv) and the third north

---

[62] *Ivirôn*, I, no. 6 (984). This is a rare example of the partial 'gift' of a chrysobull to a third party. The exemption for the boat was transferred, but not for the 25 *oikoi* also mentioned in the document. See also *Prôtaton*, no. 8 (1045), *Lavra*, I, no. 55 (1102) and, for exemptions, chapter 9.

of Mosynopolis around the monastery itself (see map 6).[63] We do not know what became of Pakourianos' extensive holdings in the eastern provinces of the empire; the monastery may have derived revenues from them. The precise extent of the holdings in Europe is not known, but we do know that on the estate at Petritzos there were some forty-seven *despotika zeugaria*. If, as has been suggested by Catherine Asdracha, this term refers to the land of the monastery as opposed to the private property of their *paroikoi* and if (as she estimates, following Svoronos) one *zeugarion* is estimated at 150 *modioi*, then a territory of some 7,050 *modioi* (c. 705 hectares) was under cultivation here on the monastery's behalf. Asdracha has calculated (though on the basis of a surface *modios* of 1,100 m² rather than 1,000 m²) that, taking into account a yield of 1:3 and biennial or triennial rotation, this land would have produced between 10,575 and 14,100 *modioi* of grain.[64] She assumes that all the land could be put down to grain, but even if we were to halve this amount, the production would still have been in the region of 5,282–7,500 *modioi* per annum. The grain allowance of the monks of Bačkovo is not known, but we know that there were fifty monks in the house. If their allowance was akin to that of the monks of Attaliates' foundation in Constantinople or the Lavra on Mount Athos, say 30 *modioi* each per annum, then their requirements would have been about 1,500 *modioi* per annum, easily obtainable from the land they possessed.

A similar surplus is evident when the charitable foundations attached to Bačkovo are examined. The *xenodocheion* of Stenimachos distributed two *modioi* of corn each day (730 *modioi* per annum), requiring a cultivated surplus of between 365 and 486 *modioi* according to Asdracha's calculations. The other two *xenodocheia* of Marmarion and St Nicholas each gave away one *modios* of grain per day so the total grain dole of the three houses taken together was thus 1,460 *modioi* per annum. This, Asdracha estimates, would have required an area under grain of between 730 and 972 *modioi* depending on the kind of rotation practised. These figures represent only a part of the production of the villages of Stenimachos, Srabikion and Prilongion. But the fact that Pakourianos was able to grant such a generous allowance to the poor each day must be the most telling indication of the prosperity of his lands. Those situated in the coastal areas clearly produced a comfortable surplus of grain.[65]

---

[63] Asdracha, *Région des Rhodopes*, discusses their location. See also Lemerle, *Cinq études*, pp. 115–91 and Kaplan, *Les hommes et la terre*, pp. 337–8.
[64] Lemerle, *Cinq études*, p. 175, note 146 maintains that Pakourianos' eastern holdings were 'worthless' in 1083, but does not provide evidence to prove the point. For extent and yields of European property, see Asdracha, *Région des Rhodopes*, p. 183. For the *zeugaratos*, see chapter 7, p. 182, note 47.
[65] Asdracha, *Région des Rhodopes*, p. 184.

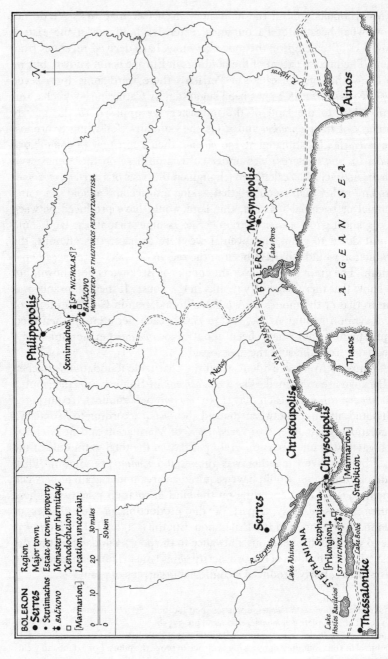

Map 6 Foundations of Gregory Pakourianos

BOLERON   Region
● Serres   Major town
● Stenimachos   Estate or town property
✝ BAČKOVO   Monastery or hermitage
□   Xenodocheion
[Marmarion]   Location uncertain

0   10   20   30 miles
0   50 km

Philippopolis

Stenimachos

[ST NICHOLAS]?
□ BAČKOVO
MONASTERY OF THEOTOKOS PETRITZONITISSA

R. Nestos

R. Hebros

Ainos

Mosynopolis

BOLERON

Lake Poros

VIA EGNATIA

AEGEAN SEA

Thasos

Serres

Christoupolis

Chrysoupolis

[Marmarion]

Srabikion

R. Strymon

STEPHANIANA

Stephaniana

[Prilongion]

[ST NICHOLAS]?□

Lake Achinos

Lake Bolbe

Lake Hosios Basilieios

Thessalonike

It is not so clear that the same was true for wine. The three *xenodocheia* together required 1,460 *metra* of wine each year since we know they were granted four *metra* per day. One might be tempted to assume that this could easily have been provided from their properties, but Stenimachos was too high up to produce wine and it is only the presence of houses associated with Bačkovo on the warmer coastlands that suggests that the foundations were self-sufficient in wine. As on Athos, the monks were able to vary their diet with fish and vegetables. The Lake of Ahinos (since drained) was near the two *xenodocheia* of Marmarion and St Nicholas, and the monks also possessed land around the Lake of Poros.[66] Dairy products as well as draught animals were provided from the considerable livestock possessed by the house. In 1083 these amounted to 110 horses and mares with foals, 75 asses, 4 buffalo, 2 calves (buffalo?), 47 pairs of oxen (working all the lands), 72 cows and bulls, 238 ewes, 94 rams and 52 goats. It would appear that pastoralism played a relatively small rôle in the economy of the Pakourianos lands, but the number of horses and asses mentioned would suggest that these were bred for sale.[67]

There can be no doubt that given their vast and scattered endowments, the monks of Bačkovo and the other Pakourianos foundations had little difficulty in supporting themselves. Again, the development of trade around their houses is indication of their prosperity. Pakourianos declared in his *Typikon* that a fair should take place outside the monastery each Easter Sunday. The monks were to buy their habits and sandals there with the *roga* annually given to them. It is difficult to believe that the monks did not also take advantage of the occasion to trade their surplus foodstuffs and animals. The village of Stenimachos began developing into an important small town on the trade route into Bulgaria at the end of the eleventh century and the monastery had clearly acted as a catalyst in this process.[68]

Pakourianos' monastery was particularly well endowed because the founder and his brother had been rich enough to invest in (or had been fortunate enough to have been given) prime farm land in Thrace. The same is true of Attaliates' houses and the Evergetis Monastery in Constantinople. Again, the level of the charitable donations made must indicate the expectation of a surplus. This is particularly true in the case of Attaliates' foundations, where we have information about the annual charitable food doles as well as the allowances for the monks (see Table 5). The total amounts required by this regimen were c. 650 *modioi* of grain;

---

[66] *Pakourianos*, chapter 2, p. 37; Lemerle, *Cinq études*, p. 153; Asdracha, *Région des Rhodopes*, p. 199.
[67] *Pakourianos*, p. 125.
[68] *Pakourianos*, chapter 9, p. 69; Asdracha, *Région des Rhodopes*, p. 162.

18 *modioi* of bread; 21 *metra* of dry vegetables; 256 *metra* of wine and at least 150 *metra* of oil.[69] The estates which were to provide this were not numerous, since Attaliates did not leave all his lands to his house, though they were all situated in the plain of Thrace. It is precisely because his foundations were not well endowed with lands that Attaliates also assured them a flow of revenue in the form of rents (see Table 2, p. 191). The drain on the resources of Attaliates' houses (as on Galesion) came not so much from the consumption of the monks, who were, after all, limited to seven, but from the demands of travellers and the poor. Any foundation near Constantinople, or on one of the major routes to the city, was bound to suffer more demands than those further afield. The fact that his houses soon fell into obscurity suggests that Attaliates did not make enough provision for the charitable activities of his monks, though he was careful to stipulate that the number of monks and donations could be increased only if resources were extended. Initially, however, the house with its seven monks was probably self-sufficient.[70]

Of the estates of other coenobitic monasteries of the period little is known. The Evergetis Monastery possessed lands in the theme of Boleron at Theophanous (where they had twelve *paroikoi zeugaratoi* suggesting an estate of c. 1,200–1,800 *modioi*) and at Epiphaniou near Chortokopion (sixteen *paroikoi zeugaratoi*, therefore possibly c. 1,600–2,400 *modioi*). The location of these estates is not precisely known, though the theme embraced the territory between the lower reaches of the Rivers Nestos and Hebros. At the end of the eleventh century, the Monastery at Stroumitza held 162 *modioi* around its buildings and another 500 *modioi* at Kristovitza. Since Bishop Manuel, the founder of Stroumitza, declared that the land around the monastery was waste in 1085, it comes as no surprise to read of the establishment of vineyards and of a mill in a document of 1106. The monastery also possessed animals: 150 cows, 40 sheep and 16 oxen. This relatively modest property would have been enough to maintain the ten monks stipulated by the founder.[71]

From this survey of monastic economies two main patterns of development emerge. The first, that of the houses of the holy mountains and those that attempted to continue their traditions, is that of an inevitable process of expansion as a result of the popularity of their founders, an expansion which the pressure of feeding the monks made all the more necessary but which was also a consequence of sustained donation. Since the areas initially chosen for their *eremia* could not support large

---

[69] *Diataxis* of Attaliates, p. 69.
[70] *Ibid.*, p. 59.
[71] Evergétis, p. 93; Stroumitza, introduction, pp. 28, 71; Stroumitza, nos. 1 (1085) and 2 (1106).

communities, their solitude had to be either abandoned or compromised. It thereafter became the privilege of a few monks, rather than the prerogative of the many. In spiritual as well as in economic terms, these developments meant a growing contact with the secular world and an unavoidable participation in its affairs. The second pattern, that epitomised by the great *koinobia*, reflects a spiritual tradition which accepted the place of the monks 'in the world but not of it', and was thus not subject to such a profound compromise of principle. For the *hegoumenoi* of these houses the duty was clear: the fulfilment of the charitable and memorial dispositions of the founders and the maintenance of enough monks to do so from the resources placed at their disposal.

In both groups, however, there were houses which flourished and those which did not. The appearance of *charistikarioi* in some houses was an indication of a degree of economic difficulty. Elsewhere, the hermits of Chaldou on Athos, for example, paid the penalty for their stubborn adherence to unfashionable monastic principles. In some cases, the decline of the houses was out of the control of the monks. The Turkish incursions to the west coast of Asia Minor and the emergence of the Turks as a powerful maritime threat at the end of the eleventh century were factors beyond the foresight of any monastic leader. But in many cases, the nexus of personal links already existing between the patrons and the foundations found its expression in many aspects of economic life. It is clearly evident in the endowment of the Monasteries of Pakourianos and Attaliates by generous patrons. In the case of the lavriote-influenced houses, the process was more subtle. It began with the pious donation of land or *rogai* in admiration of the individual founder. It continued with the grant of *paroikoi*, or permission to own animals and to build ships. With these advantages, houses thus favoured could continue the process of expansion themselves, as the uncertainties of the early years of foundation were removed, and, in the case of imperial patronage, resources were continually at their disposal.

But such favours were not evenly distributed. On Athos, the Lavra accumulated by far the largest body of these signs of imperial approval and thus became the most powerful house on the mountain. It stands as the best example of what could be achieved when the highest possible level of patronage, that of the emperor, was given as a continuous duty by the holder of that position. The houses on Latros, Patmos and Chios were less remarkable examples of the same phenomenon. In contrast, Iviron, though receiving immense cash donations from the Georgian pious, only intermittently enjoyed imperial favour and suffered from the growing rivalry of Georgians and Greeks on Mount Athos. However, the fortunes of many of the lavriote-influenced houses were clearly of prime concern to the emperor and the highest echelons of his administration. But in giving economic and legal expression to their piety, the rulers of Byzantium were, as we shall see, responsible for diluting the resources of their own power and, by these acts of generosity, helped to exacerbate the very problems which brought the empire into crisis and disunity in the eleventh century.

CHAPTER NINE

The challenge to central authority

◆

B Y THE END OF THE ELEVENTH century, the estates of the great monasteries had evolved into powerful economic units. In some areas, the extent of their lands put them on a par with the lay aristocracy, and, unlike them, they enjoyed peculiar advantages. Although they might be subject to the same ravages of climate and the same difficulties of geography, their estates were rarely subject to confiscation for political reasons or subject to the demands of inheritance. Abundant supplies of cash and labour enabled them to expand and to play an important part in the economic life not only of the neighbouring regions, but also further afield. Lay patronage fuelled monastic development and imperial support in particular was a crucial factor in transforming self-sufficient monasteries into highly profitable ones. The motives of piety, patronage and personal friendship which lay behind this generosity have already been discussed. But what were the political and economic consequences of such actions? The question that has to be asked is a simple one, although it has many ramifications: given the difficulties of ensuring the power of the central government over an empire of such extent and ethnic variety, did the existence of stable and economically powerful monastic units within the Byzantine state compound the problems of administration and give a further dimension to the already existing problems of regionalism? And if this was the case, how could the power of the organs of central government, both lay and ecclesiastical, be reasserted over them?

The political stability of the empire depended on the efficient working of two fundamental elements of central government: taxation and justice. They constituted the practical means by which both emperor and patriarch exercised their authority. If these were found wanting, then their power would exist in name only. A third element, that of the armed forces, was linked to both the fiscal and judicial structures. For without revenue, the army could not defend Byzantium, still less extend its frontiers, and without justice, the provinces could easily disintegrate into an anarchy which no army could control. Equally important was the rôle of the fiscal and judicial officials in expressing the authority of the emperor. Tax collectors and judges operated in his name and were perpetual reminders of the sometimes distant, but none the less potent, power of Constantinople.

To a lesser extent, the patriarchal officials performed the same service for the head of the church, for increasingly in the tenth and eleventh centuries, the patriarch's ruling was sought on judicial and administrative questions affecting ecclesiastical institutions. He himself began to emphasise his claims to moral stewardship over the clergy and monks of the entire empire and, as a consequence, over the administration of their foundations. Another authority eager to maintain its influence in the countryside was the episcopate. But this, as we have seen, was steadily being deprived of its force in the monastic sphere by the actions of the charismatic founders and independent minded patrons. It suffered, too, from the increasing claims of the patriarchate. Three powers, then, emperor, patriarch and bishop, each made varying (and sometimes conflicting) financial and jurisdictional claims over the monastic houses. How crucial these claims were to the maintenance of central authority may be appreciated from the study of a period – the tenth century – when there was a series of crises in the relationship between the imperial government and those with influence in the provinces.[1]

The social crisis of the tenth century has frequently been analysed by historians of Byzantium, but few have concentrated on the rôle played by monastic landowners. The imperial legislation of the period clearly included churchmen and monks among those it described as 'the powerful' (*dynatoi*), and against whom the imperial government was apparently pitting all its forces. A novel of the Emperor Constantine Porphyrogennetos, issued in 934, identified the ecclesiastical *dynatoi*: 'the most holy metropolitans, archbishops, bishops, *hegoumenoi*, *archontes* [high-ranking officials] of the Church and those who protect and control the charitable institutions'.[2]

At the root of imperial alarm, as subsequent legislation indicates, was an inability to control the growing disruption of the tenurial and fiscal structure of the empire. The two were closely interlinked. For two contemporary handbooks for fiscal officials, the so-called *Marcian Treatise* and that known as the *Vademecum of a Byzantine Tax Official*, reveal a system which was based on the identification of the village

---

[1] See chapter 5 and pp. 244–6 below.
[2] Morris, 'Poor and powerful' and Kaplan, *Les hommes et la terre*, pp. 359–72, 388–443 discuss the literature and survey the problems.

community (*chorion*) with the basic fiscal unit (*homas*). For tax purposes, a global amount (*rhiza*) was assigned to each village and each land-holder within it (*telestes*) was assigned a share of the total to pay, according to the extent and quality of his land. This, together with any supplementary taxes or exemptions to which he was liable, was noted in his entry (*stichos*) in the local cadaster. As a check, however, the total number of *modioi* in the village was divided by the amount of the *rhiza*, giving a sum of so many *nomismata* per *modios*. This rate, known as the *epibole*, could then be applied to the holdings of each *telestes*. If, when the *epibole* was operated, it was found that a land-holder held fewer *modioi* than his tax payment indicated, then any appeal he might make for a lessening of his burden might be supported. It was, however, rather more likely that extra purchases of land had *not* been declared and, if this were so, the mechanism of the *epibole* would reveal it. All the land in the village was included in the measurement, although some of it might not be subject to the application of the *epibole*. *Idiostata* (lands standing by themselves), for example, were not included in the general cadasters. They might be *klasma* lands, or areas which had not previously been taxed. New areas of settlement beyond the existing boundaries of the community were also classed as *idiostata*. So, too, were lands which were totally exempt from tax. The various types of *idiostata* were noted in separate cadasters (*isokodikes*) and had one important factor in common: although their area was included in the general village measurement, their owners did not share in the joint responsibility of the *telestai* to provide the total tax required by the state (*demosion*). This principle of joint responsibility was the mainstay of the Byzantine tax system. It ensured that if one tax-payer could not pay his due, his fellow *telestai* would, between them, make up the sum. The *demosion* would not be deprived of its revenue for it would be provided by this surcharge – the *allelengyon* – and the fact that idiostatic lands were not subject to the *allelengyon* made their possession attractive.[3]

Although the geographic unity of the village was not always identical

---

[3] For the *Marcian Treatise* and a detailed discussion of the Byzantine tax system, see F. Dölger, *Beiträge zur Geschichte der Byzantinischen Finanzverwaltung besonders des 10. und 11. Jahrhunderts* (Byzantinisches Archiv, IX, Leipzig/Berlin, 1927), pp. 113–23. For the so-called *Vademecum*, J. Karagiannopoulos, 'Fragmente aus dem *Vademecum* eines byzantinischen Finanzbeamten', in *Polychronion. Festschrift Franz Dölger* (Heidelberg, 1966), pp. 318–34. Both these treatises are translated in C. M. Brand, 'Two Byzantine treatises on taxation', *Traditio*, 25 (1967), 35–60, 48–57 (*Marcian Treatise*), 57–60 (*Vademecum*). For a definition of the *chorion*, see Kaplan, *Les hommes et la terre*, pp. 95–105, and for the *homas*, pp. 186–7. On the *epibole*, see N. G. Svoronos, 'L'épibolè à l'époque des Comnènes', *TM*, 3 (1968), 375–95, reprinted in *Etudes sur l'organisation intérieure, la société et l'économie de l'empire byzantin* (London, 1973), article V and Kaplan, *op. cit.*, p. 207. For *idiostaton*, *Marcian Treatise*, p. 116 (Brand, pp. 49–50), *Vademecum*, p. 322 (Brand, pp. 58–9).

with the fiscal *homas*, the two were interrelated enough for the imperial
administration to become alarmed at any wide-scale tenurial upheaval.
The writers of the imperial edicts were at great pains to emphasise that
they were not acting purely to protect the revenues of the *demosion*, but
rather to ensure the equitable treatment of the lesser rural landowners
with their more influential fellows. But in reality, the entire fiscal system
of the provinces was based on the premise that conditions in the countryside would remain constant for long periods. The *epoptai* (tax officials)
often did not visit the villages to check the cadasters and the rate of *epibole*
for spans of thirty years at a time and the process by which *klasma* might
be reassessed for taxation purposes also took a similar period. The administration could not adequately cope with sudden or widespread alterations
in the ownership of land in the countryside, though it was often aware of
them; the effort of rewriting the cadasters would, in itself, have been a
daunting task.[4]

In the first half of the tenth century the imperial government was
seeking to prevent any major changes in the distribution of landed
property, even though circumstances within the empire made this
inevitable. The earliest legislative documents indicate that exchanges
and sales of land were becoming more frequent at this period. In 928,
Romanos Lekapenos forbade the alienation of land, under whatever
pretext, to the *dynatoi*, including those holding high positions in the
administrative hierarchy as well as churchmen and *hegoumenoi*. He
forbade them to 'make new purchases or hirings or exchanges in any
villages or fields (*agroi*) in which they [the *dynatoi*] do not already possess
land'. By 'land' was originally meant the total of village properties subject
to the *epibole* (*hypotage*), but a later interpolation added *idiostata*
(including *klasma*) to the definition. The imperial government enforced
this ruling by ending the practice of free alienation of land established
by the Emperor Leo VI (886–912) and returning to the older system of
preemption right (*protimesis*). This allowed the 'relatives' of the seller of a
parcel of land thirty days in which to bid for the property. By 'relatives'
were meant not only the kin of the seller, but his *syntelestai* ('co-holders')
– those who held land in the same *homas* and contributed tax to it.
Although the *dynatoi* who were *syntelestai* were initially not excluded
from this arrangement, the legislation was later tightened to forbid all
alienation of land to them. If they acquired land from any *penes* (and
since the economic status of the *penes* – literally a 'poor man' was
never precisely defined, this could mean anyone who was not on the
list of *dynatoi*), it had to be returned. Initially, this was to be without

---

[4] Visits of *epoptai*: *Marcian Treatise*, p. 116 (Brand, p. 49). Selling of *klasma*: *Marcian
Treatise*, pp. 118–23 (Brand, pp. 52–7); *Vademecum*, pp. 321–2 (Brand, p. 58).

compensation, but later legislation allowed for the repayment of the purchase price by the *penetes*.[5]

The imperial government was also concerned at the methods being employed by the *dynatoi* to gain control of lands. By 934, accusations of coercion and violence were beginning to appear in the documents: the *penetes* had been subject to 'pressures', the villages were 'rent by strife and by internal arguments about land'. The maintenance of stability (if not the status quo) in the village communities was thus the prime object of the imperial government in the first half of the tenth century. Though often expressed in highly rhetorical terms, its object was clear:

> The settlement of many inhabitants [on the land] is a most useful state of affairs. It assures contributions to the *demosion* and the upkeep of the army. These things will be entirely lacking if the people are abandoned.[6]

Although the early legislation against the *dynatoi* was severe, modifications were soon introduced. One of the most important from the monastic point of view was the *prostaxis* (instruction) of the *patrikios* and *koiaistor* Theophilos, issued in 947. For it tacitly admitted that there were some groups who were far less dangerous than their designation as *dynatoi* might have suggested. It advised a different approach towards ecclesiastical *dynatoi* such as bishops, who were still to return land which they had illegally obtained and the 'poorer monasteries', if the latter could be shown not to have used force in their land transactions. The property was still to be returned to its previous holders, but the erstwhile owners could receive back both the purchase price and any expenditure they might have incurred on *kalliergemata* (improvements). The imperial bureaucrats had recognised the reality of greatly varying monastic fortunes.[7]

Between 947 and Nikephoros Phokas' novel of 964, the concern of the imperial authorities was centred on the problem of the *stratiotika ktemata* (soldiers' estates), the lands granted by the state in return for military service by their holders or members of their families. In a sense, their eagerness to make sure that these estates were not alienated and that the services associated with them were not lost, was merely another aspect of a concern for the preservation of existing rural structures. But a further dimension was added by the fact that many new groups of *stratiotai*

---

[5] Zepos, I, col. iii, document II, pp. 198–204, especially p. 202 for the *protimesis* right. For its dating to April 928, see Kaplan, *Les hommes et la terre*, pp. 415–16. The problem of identifying the *penetes* is discussed in Morris, 'Poor and powerful', pp. 14–20. Arrangements for repayment of purchase price: Zepos, I, coll. iii, documents V, 206–14; VI, 214–17.

[6] Document V, p. 209.

[7] Document VI, 214–17 for *kalliergemata* and see Kaplan, *Les hommes et la terre*, pp. 427–8.

(holders of military estates) were being established as a consequence of the Byzantine military advances of the tenth century, groups who seemed loath to commit themselves to the permanent settlement on designated land which the system implied. A novel of Constantine Porphyrogennetos, datable to the mid-950s forbade the *stratiotai* to sell their estates:

> No one may buy any of these estates, especially not an official, or a metropolitan, or a bishop or a monastery or any other charitable institution, or any other *dynatoi* as far down in rank as a *scholarios*.[8]

It spoke of a 'complete convulsion of society' which had taken place 'only a short time ago' and which had been characterised by the seizure of the *stratiotika ktemata* by *dynatoi* and the treatment of their previous owners like slaves. Further instructions were later issued by Nikephoros Phokas to a specific group of newly established holders of *stratiotika ktemata*, the 'volatile and unreliable Armenians'. They were not to leave their estates before three years had passed and they were not to alienate them to monasteries or other *dynatoi*.[9]

Imperial determination to protect the structure of the village communities was manifested in another direction by Basil II. In his novel of 996, which reimposed all the most stringent prohibitions against alienating lands to the *dynatoi*, the rigid application of the *protimesis* right and the payment of the *allelengyon* by the *dynatoi*, he, also, as we have seen, denied the rights of bishops to claim control over the small village *eukteria* with fewer than eight or ten religious. The villagers' rights over their humble houses were not to be eroded under the pretext of episcopal jurisdiction.[10]

The themes of the imperial legislation of the tenth century were thus the preservation of the fiscal, military and social homogeneity of the provincial *choria*. All the emperors of the tenth century shared these preoccupations and even Nikephoros Phokas had to disguise his patronage of the *lavrai* under the guise of charity to humble institutions

[8] Zepos, col. iii, document VIII, 222–6, especially p. 223, see Kaplan, *Les hommes et la terre*, 429–36.
[9] Document VIII, pp. 225–6. Zepos, col. iii, document XVIII, 247–8 and see Kaplan, *Les hommes et la terre*, p. 249 where, however, he characterises them (I think mistakenly) as soldiers from the Armeniakon theme. The Monastery of Lagape was specifically mentioned in Nikephoros Phokas' document, see H. Grégoire, 'La lieu de naissance de Romain Lécapène et de Digénis Acritas', *B*, 8 (1933), 572–4, reprinted in *Autour de l'épopée byzantine* (London, 1975), article X/2.
[10] See chapter 6, p. 150 and N. G. Svoronos, 'Remarques sur la tradition du texte de la novelle de Basile II concernant les puissants', *ZRVI*, 8 (1964), 427–34, reprinted in *Etudes sur l'organisation intérieure*, article XII.

which could not present any danger. That concern was still being expressed in the eleventh century is illustrated by the existence of a section in the legal compilation known as the *Peira* devoted to cases arising from the application of Basil II's novel of 996. From the forceful language of the imperial laws and edicts, it would appear that there was very real cause for alarm about the activities of the monastic *dynatoi* as well as their lay counterparts. But bearing in mind the highly rhetorical language of the laws and the political motivation that clearly lay behind them, how justified were successive imperial governments in including *hegoumenoi* in the lists of *dynatoi* and seeing them as major challengers to the stability of the rural fiscal communes?[11]

The process of land accumulation by monastic houses was, of course, well under way by the time Constantine Porphyrogennetos' novel was issued in 928. There is no direct evidence to show that property was sold by the *penetes* to the monasteries as a direct consequence of the recent disasters of the 'great famine' of 927–8 and the 'long winter' which may have preceded it, but erosion of the village communities by powerful interests can certainly be cited from this period.[12] A classic case is that of the relationship of the inhabitants of the *kastron* of Hierissos with their monastic neighbours on Mount Athos. By the 940s the competition for *klasma* lands, was, as we have seen, a manifestation of a growing hostility between monks and laity, but the foundations for this particular quarrel had been laid long before as the Hierissiotes and the inhabitants of neighbouring villages found their traditional access to the pasture lands of the mountain increasingly blocked. The way in which the boundary was established between Athos and the secular world vividly illustrated why the legislators wrote of *dynatoi*, for the Athonite monks, originally only one element in the region of Hierissos, soon became the most influential and were certainly not averse to using their power.

By 883, the Emperor Basil I had recognised the corporate existence of the hesychasts on Athos, had freed the monks from the attention of imperial officials and had forbidden private individuals, peasants and shepherds from entering the mountain. In 908, Leo VI forbade the Monastery of Kolobos (an imperial monastery, it should be recalled) from taking tax from those wishing to pasture their animals on the mountain, presumably as a way of denying the house any control over access to the mountain by more recent monastic arrivals. Thus, within twenty years,

---

[11] *Peira*, IX, pp. 38–40.
[12] See chapter 7, p. 177. The two events are usually associated, but there are some grounds for redating the 'long winter' of the chroniclers to 933–4 (unless there was another very cold spell in the early tenth century, which is not out of the question); see Morris, 'Poor and powerful', p. 8, note 28 (a view, I am glad to say, now supported by Kaplan, *Les hommes et la terre*, p. 421, note 234, p. 461 note 104).

the rights of those with traditional interests in the peninsula had been curtailed or removed and the claims of the monastic newcomers maintained. The attempts by the Athonites to establish a permanent frontier, crowned with success in 943, meant that they had usurped not only the usufruct (*chresis*) but also the *despoteia* of the mountain. They had even attempted to have the *enoria* (fiscal district) of Hierissos redefined to their own advantage.[13]

By this process the Athonites radically altered the structure of the *koinosis* (communal holding) of Hierissos and its region by depriving it of one of its most important communal assets – the pasture of Athos – and by acquiring large areas of *klasma*. They had established themselves as major landowners in the region between the Zygos Ridge and Hierissos. The most interesting aspect of the whole affair, however, is the clear imperial responsibility for these developments, all taking place in the period of ostensible anxiety about the activities of the *dynatoi*. Without the chrysobulls establishing the frontier and denying the traditional right of access of the *syntelestai*, the growing influence of the Athonites would have been curbed.

It was not just within the boundaries of Athos that monastic influence reigned supreme. A document from the archives of Iviron dated to 982 relates that in the past the inhabitants of Hierissos had frequently clashed with the monks of the Monastery of Kolobos (which in 979–80, it will be remembered, had been granted to Iviron) and had often had recourse to both local judges, to *strategoi* (provincial governors) and even to judges in Constantinople. Each side had alternately won and lost cases but, the document pursued, they were now on good terms. The agreement that was being made in 982 was, in fact, the settlement of an extremely long-running dispute which had at its origin the refusal of the Hierissiotes to pay land tax for land they rented from the Monastery of Kolobos at Gradiska at the gates of the town. In 927, the monks complained that the laymen had not done so for four years (though they did not explain why) and the matter was settled by the judge of the theme of Thessalonike, Samonas, who fined the townsfolk 40 *nomismata* and gave them two years to pay up or risk eviction. In 942–3 the very same parcel of land was granted to the Hierissiotes as part of the general settlement with the Athonites concerning the frontier. The land was of some 2,000 *modioi* in extent and in exchange for one parcel of 1,000 *modioi* the inhabitants gave a property called St Nicholas and for the other 1,000 *modioi*, 30 *nomismata* in cash. By 982 Iviron (as the successor to Kolobos) had renounced claims to Gradiska, but in the process had discovered the existence of other Kolobos lands at Longos about which there was dispute. The Hierissiotes

---

[13] *Prôtaton*, nos. 1 (883), 2 (908), 5 and 6 (943).

had originally held this land on a twenty-nine-year lease (after paying 100 *nomismata* entry fine) and had then wanted to buy it; this was refused by the then *hegoumenos* of Kolobos and his monks. The Hierissiotes complained, the case went as far as Constantinople and Constantine Porphyrogennetos ordered an imperial official, one Constantine Karamallos, who at the time was in Thessalonike, to go to the region and sort matters out. He confirmed the possession of St Nicholas to the Hierissiotes, but ordered the return of Longos. After continuing strife, the *hegoumenos* Stephen of Kolobos leased the land at Longos for twenty-nine years (this in about 958) but in 982 the Hierissiotes seem to have been asked to give it back with some five years of the lease still left to run. They were offered their 100 *nomismata* back plus a 'sweetener' of 50 *nomismata* – the only problem being that they did not want to return the Longos property at all. They had planted many vines there, they said, so they offered another property in exchange. It is surely no accident that this property was near that of St Nicholas, already obtained by Iviron, and thus helping to consolidate its territories. In addition, the Georgians were to have access to pasture on uncultivated properties at Longos and to hold a specifically named pasture area at Tlaka as well as a brickworks nearby.[14]

While it would be an exaggeration to maintain that the Iviron monks swept all before them in this series of land disputes and settlements, their behaviour certainly does conform with that associated with the *dynatoi*. The kinds of disputes mentioned would not normally have been heard by anyone more grand than the thematic *krites* or his nominated officials; the fact that they went as far as the imperial court was a consequence of the status of the Iberians, not that of the townspeople of Hierissos. By 982, the Georgians were certainly enjoying considerable imperial patronage, so the judicial cards were likely to be stacked in their favour. As for the aim of the exercise, the Kolobos monks were not prepared to allow the non-payment of dues (for whatever reason) even though the settlement by Samonas is remarkably lenient towards the laity, which makes one suspect that their reasons for not paying were tenable ones. The Iberians wanted first to make sure that every property appertaining to the Monastery of Kolobos would safely pass into their hands and, secondly, to consolidate their property at St Nicholas while not giving up all rights to Longos. We are left very much with the feeling that the Hierissiotes made the best of a bad job and were continually struggling to maintain the lay status of the lands they held.

[14] *Ivirôn*, I, no. 1 (927), a document originally from the Monastery of Kolobos, for the dispute at Gradiska and no. 4 (984) for its settlement. More lands there later came under the control of Iviron, see *Ivirôn*, I, no. 12 (1001). *Prôtaton*, no. 5 (942/3) for the frontier of Athos.

Other communities were also struggling to maintain their territorial integrity and their rights. The inhabitants of the village of Siderokausia were holders of various properties at Belikradou and Arsenikea, where the Monastery of Kolobos also had lands. The relationship of the parcels was complex and there had been a delineation of them in the reign of the Emperors Leo VI and Alexander (that is between 886 and 912). By 995, when a document of Nicholas, *krites* of Strymon and Thessalonike, was drawn up, relations between the two parties were extremely bad. The legal officer clearly knew who he thought was ultimately to blame, for in a most interesting preamble, he commented on the activities of the monks. Certainly, he wrote, they had need of material sustenance so that the body could come to the aid of the soul, but, he added 'it sometimes happens that material necessities lead them to do wrong to their neighbours'. The list of complaints was devastating: the men of Siderokausia had come to court 'all shouting at once as rustics do' that the monks had brought in animals which had damaged their lay neighbours' crops. The crops trodden upon did not germinate well and those that did put up shoots were at once trampled. The animals also ate the harvest. More seriously, the monks claimed the whole of the village of Arsenikea and had established their own *paroikoi* to work the land. The laymen countered that the monks indeed owned 'Upper' (*Ano*) Arsenikea but not 'Lower' (*Kato*) Arsenikea where they had wrongly installed water mills. The monks riposted by showing the judgements of previous imperial officials: Constantine Karamallos (again) before 958 and Nikephoros Hexakionites *strategos* of Thessalonike in about 963.

The *krites* Nicholas' firm reaction indicates that he believed that the monks had acted unlawfully. He did not, unfortunately for us, actually cite the legislation against the *dynatoi*, but his judgement was as severe as any suggested by it. The monks were to leave Kato Arsenikea, their *paroikoi* were to be expelled and their huts burnt. They were to take no produce from there and were only to bring their cattle to pasture from 1 July to the end of September (after the harvest and before the new sowing). They could keep the six water mills (certainly *kalliergemata* or 'improvements' in Byzantine terms and for which some compensation could be allowed even to *dynatoi*) and vegetable gardens which they had established, but must create no more. The inhabitants of Siderokausia, however, could have access to the water from the mill-race for periods of twenty-four hours at a time, in order to water their own plots. They would have access to the higher ground controlled by the monks to gather fruit, chestnuts and acorns. The pig was clearly important in the local economy, for as well as the regulation of the gathering of acorns – archetypal pig fodder – the monks were to share in the payment of pig tax (*balanistron*) with the villagers. On the face of it, matters were reasonably amicably sorted out, but in fact the basic problems, those of monastic ambitions to expand holdings, to introduce their own workers and to keep cattle rather than to preserve the traditional methods of cultivation in the area, were not addressed.[15]

In the cases from Athos and its hinterland, the monastic interests concerned well merited the epithet of *dynatoi*. The monks had the money to make the purchases which began the process of breaking up the village communities and changing the nature of their economy; they had the financial resources and the contacts at a thematic and Constantinopolitan level to make sure that no disputed claim would ever go against them until every avenue had been tested. Above all, monasteries were institutions: they would outlive the most dogged individual opponents and could only be matched by determined communal action, such as that presented by the Hierissiotes. By the very nature of their calling, they could claim the support of all 'right-thinking' lay folk.

For the increasing monastic insistence on *eremia* was also an important factor in weakening the established rights of the lay inhabitants of villages. The boundary of Athos was drawn up to ensure the 'seclusion' of the monks and to spare them contacts with worldly elements invading their solitude and when, in 1089, a dispute concerning what had been communal grazing land arose between the monks of the Monastery of St John of Patmos and the inhabitants of two *choria* bordering their property of Parthenion on Leros, the matter was again resolved in the monks' favour by imperial intervention to preserve their *eremia*. They were awarded more property in the region so as to increase their claims on the pasture, rights to which, as we have seen, they then graciously gave up 'of their own free will, so that their own future seclusion could be assured'. In other words, they would undertake not to pasture animals on the land, but had effectively blocked the local villagers from doing so as well. This kind of behaviour was precisely that which the legislation against the *dynatoi* aimed to curb. Yet in all these cases, encroachment on the rights and lands of lay neighbours was supported by state power and often legalised by imperial chrysobulls. They are illustrations of a theme which became increasingly common in the course of the tenth and eleventh century: that of the imperial power itself aiding selected institutions to circumvent the spirit, if not the letter, of the law.[16]

The laws of the tenth century were concerned not only with the fact of

[15] *Ivirôn*, I, no. 9 (995). Kaplan, *Les hommes et la terre*, pp. 193–4, points out the interest of this *collective* action by the villagers of Arsenikea.
[16] See chapter 8, *BEMP*, II, no. 52, 51–60 for the account of the quarrel written by the imperial official Eustathios Charsanites and the action he took to solve it; *BEMP*, II, no. 53, 72–4, especially p. 73 for the 'renunciation' of the pasture land.

disruption in the rural communes, but also with the methods used by the *dynatoi*. The accusations of force might have applied less to ecclesiastics than to the lay powerful, though a metropolitan of Patras in the Peloponnese was accused in the early tenth century of forcibly acquiring the lands of *stratiotai*.[17] Far more common, however, was the use of false claims or trickery either to increase a monastery's share in the holdings of the *koinosis*, or, conversely, to escape from its fiscal responsibilities. A number of cases in the *Peira*, some of which may well date from the tenth century, demonstrate the remarkable ingenuity shown by the monastic *dynatoi* and they also illustrate one of their most telling characteristics: their grasp of the intricacies of Byzantine fiscal practice, the complexities of the cadasters and systems of land measurement and inspection which only a degree of literacy could bring. This is not to imply that the *penetes* were always unlettered peasants ignorant of their rights. But although many small landowners did possess documents which established their position in the community, their perception of their rights was probably based far more on oral tradition, brought into action, for instance, in the establishment of boundaries. Indeed, it is significant that Basil II's novel of 996 contained a clause which forbade the oral testimony produced by *dynatoi* to prevail against that of the *penetes*.[18]

This clause was actually cited in a case involving the inhabitants of the *chorion* of Gordion Kome (ancient Juliopolis/Basileion, modern Nallihan) and the monks of the neighbouring monastery of Neastou Kome. Some 122 years before the case came to court (and therefore at the beginning of the tenth century), the local metropolitan, one Phagitzes, had sold some monastic lands in the *chorion* to the lay inhabitants – a somewhat dubious procedure in itself. The monks still retained lands outside the village in a new settlement (*choraphion*) and some pasture. The case arose because the monks claimed that they still possessed lands within the *chorion*. The judge declared that written evidence showed no sign of them possessing such land and although oral witnesses were produced by the monastery the case was dismissed 'for the novel declares that they, being *dynatoi*, cannot prevail in testimony against the *penetes*'. So there were obviously opportunities for influential or respected members of the community (such as monks) to prevail upon others to make false or mistaken oral testimony. But far more ingenious methods were sometimes used to challenge the cadasters, the final proof of the ownership of land.[19]

[17] Darrouzès, *Epistoliers byzantins*, ii, no. 5, 102.
[18] Zepos, I, col. iii, document XXIX, p. 266.
[19] *Peira*, XXIII. 3, pp. 85–6 and see Kaplan, *Les hommes et la terre*, pp. 75–6, p. 100. For the location of Gordion Kome on the River Sangarios (modern Sakarya under the present-day

For a masterpiece of deception is revealed in another case from the *Peira*, interesting also for the fact that it contains a rare example of an episcopal monastery. The metropolitan of Claudiopolis (modern Bolu) reclaimed a property of the Monastery of Blachnas which had previously been granted (probably for rent) to a certain Eusebios, who had paid neither the rent nor the land tax. It lay within the village of Rhyakia, but it was *idiostaton* and therefore, as the presiding judge was careful to point out, did not belong in the fiscal entity (*homas*) of the village. But a problem had arisen: the boundary markings of the property had been destroyed. The judge ordered that they should be re-established, with the aid of the cadasters and oral witnesses. This was particularly necessary since the *praktikon*, the official description of the property, which the metropolitan had presented, and which he claimed had been drawn up by the notary and *krites* Manuel, had neither the latter's seal nor his signature upon it. Forgery was clearly suspected. The judge's officials examined the *isokodikon* and discovered that the monks' land was indeed *idiostaton* and noted what land tax (*demosios kanon*) they were to pay on it. At this stage the case took a further turn, for the metropolitan's officials now referred to the cadastral entries (*stichoi*) for the entire village against one of which it was noted that the holder was 'Daniel the *hegoumenos*'; clearly a parcel of monastic land. But then they declared (and the *Peira* gives their argument verbatim):

> Look in the *stichos* of the monastery and it is written 'Daniel the *hegoumenos* holds this'. But the second *stichos* also has a holder (*telestes*) Daniel. Why do you not assign this to the monastery as well?[20]

The judge retorted that there were doubtless many 'Daniels' in the *chorion* and that the monastery could not claim all the lands assigned to any 'Daniel'. Besides, the *isokodikon* referring to the land originally under dispute did not mention that the holder of the second parcel had been a *hegoumenos* and since this designation had not been found, this *stichos* must, logically, belong to a layman. The case seemed clear cut, but took a further twist when a second judge discovered a collection of *ekstichia* (individual copies of cadastral entries), in which it appeared that the same *telestes* 'Daniel' *had* indeed been assigned five *stichoi*, before only one of which had the word *hegoumenos* been written. What to do? The first judge broke the impasse. In his view, taxes were paid, as far as *idiostata* were concerned, according to information contained in *isokodikes*. If the monks

---

Sariyar dam), see K. Belke and M. Restle, *Galatien und Lykaonien* (*TIB*, IV, Vienna, 1984), pp. 181–2. The judge concerned was the *droungarios* of the *velon*, for whom see N. Oikonomidès, 'L'évolution de l'organisation administrative', pp. 133–4.

[20] *Peira*, XV.10, 51–2, especially p. 52.

could show, by oral or written witness, that they paid tax for the other 'Daniel' lands, they might have them. This put the monks and their advisers in a highly embarrassing position, since they ran the risk of proving their claims at the expense of acquiring a heavier tax burden. They fell back on the feeble excuse of accusing their opponents of being *dynatoi*, as they might well have been, by definition, themselves. The judge's reply was that everyone should pay the taxes assigned to them in the cadasters and he was clearly not convinced enough about the presence of more *dynatoi* to invoke any legislation against them. He seemed well in control of the situation, interpreting not just the letter, but the spirit of the laws against the powerful, especially where they aimed to ensure the supply of taxation to the state. But state officials clearly had to be on their toes when confronted with able and determined monastic opponents.[21]

The imperial judiciary also intervened to preserve the *protimesis* or preemption right, another vital weapon in the fight to protect the unity of the *choria*. But strict application of the law was not invariable. While one case in the *Peira* shows a judge ordering the return of land given to the church in order to attempt to circumvent the *protimesis* right with the judgement that no property subject to legal dispute could be consecrated, an earlier and well-known example from Athos shows suspiciously indecisive action by the judge concerned and this in 952, when the laws on *protimesis* had only recently been promulgated.[22] In this case, the *krites* of Thessalonike, Samonas (again), gave judgement in a case involving the donation of lands and the sale of a brickworks by the *klerikos* David to Stephen, *hegoumenos* of the Monastery of St Andrew at Peristerai, and thus, by definition, a *dynatos*. The neighbouring landowners, including a retired officer, the *droungarios* John, complained and declared that they wished to 'restore the imperial legality', by which was probably meant the *protimesis* right. It should indeed have applied in this case, but the judge's verdict was somewhat surprising. He declared that the neighbours on three sides of the disputed property were themselves *dynatoi* (the fourth side may have been the sea), so that there were no *penetes* to claim the *protimesis* right. He thus interpreted 'neighbours' in a strictly geographical, rather than a fiscal sense. However, he specified a delay in the sale of four months, which suggests that time was being allowed for other *penetes*

---

[21] For the second judge, *Peira*, xv.10, p. 52. *Ekstichia* are discussed by N. G. Svoronos, 'Recherches sur le cadastre byzantin et la fiscalité aux XIe et XIIe siècles: le cadastre de Thèbes', *BCH*, 83 (1959), 1–166, reprinted in *Etudes sur l'organisation*, article III, see pp. 58, 63, note 1.
[22] *Peira*, v.10, 20–1. For the Athos case, *Lavra*, I, no. 4 (952). It is discussed by Ostrogorsky in 'Peasants' pre-emption right', by Lemerle, *Agrarian history of Byzantium*, pp. 157–60 and Kaplan, *Les hommes et la terre*, p. 431.

to present themselves. But it was little more than a diversionary tactic. The property passed to St Andrew of Peristerai and ultimately to the Lavra. The neigbouring *dynatoi*, understandably outraged by a fellow *dynatos* being so favoured, were powerless to stop the act. At best, this was a case of favouritism between *dynatoi*; at worst, it suggests that the thematic judge was not willing to enforce the law against one of the more powerful monasteries in the region.[23]

Governmental concern to preserve the preemption right continued in the eleventh century and so did attempts to protect the holdings of the *stratiotai*. In a case settled in 1056 concerning the rival claims of the Athonite Monastery of St Panteleimon and a certain Phasoulos to lands on Kassandra which they had both been given in Phasoulos' father's will, the continuation of payment of the *strateia* (the commutation for military service) was a major point of issue. It was settled by a dubious procedure by which Phasoulos 'ceded' (not sold) half of the sixteen *modioi* of land claimed by the monks, but continued to pay the *strateia* for all of it so that the *stratiotikon ktema* had not, technically, been alienated. Phasoulos was paid the immense sum of 10 *nomismata* for the eight *modioi* of arable which he had 'ceded'. While the letter of the law had been complied with, its spirit required that all the property comprised in a soldier's estate should continue to produce revenue to support either a soldier or the payment of *strateia*. There was no guarantee that the single payment Phasoulos received would have been enough to maintain that responsibility in the future. But the fact that both parties baulked at actually alienating the *stratiotikon ktema* must indicate that the laws were still being strongly enough enforced to make men wary of being seen to break them.[24]

Such evidence as we have, then, suggests that the imperial government had good grounds for suspicion of the monastic *dynatoi* in the tenth century, that the measures taken to protect the lay inhabitants of the rural communes were still being applied in the eleventh century and that there were at least some successful prosecutions. In some cases, as the *Peira* evidence reveals, the fiscal and judicial officials operated with a high degree of independence and efficiency, but in others, such as on Athos and Patmos, where imperial interest was high, matters were sometimes rather different. The paradox of the actions of imperial officials being circumvented by imperial interests became increasingly obvious in the

[23] St Andrew of Peristerai could not, as Lemerle maintains, belong to the category of 'poorer monastery' allowed more lenient treatment in 947, see *Agrarian history of Byzantium*, p. 159, note 2, as the land accumulations discussed in chapter 7 demonstrate: see p. 170.
[24] *Dionysiou*, no. 1 (1056).

eleventh century, though this varied from reign to reign. But an important general development was the emergence of areas and properties where such officials were legally prevented from operating, where exemptions from fiscal or judicial control, issued by the imperial power, meant, in practice, the existence of a large degree of autonomy.

By the tenth century, exemption from taxes had long been established as a method of patronising churches and monasteries. The *Marcian Treatise* explained the process of *logisima* by which lands might be completely or partially freed from taxes and all record of them struck out, erased or even literally torn out of the cadasters. They had long been in existence: 'They [the *logisima*] came into existence in former times at the hands of long deceased emperors and up to the reign of Lord Leo "the Wise" as he is called.'[25] Leo VI instituted an inspection of all the *logisima* of the empire and ordered them to be checked and noted in the documents of the government offices concerned. The *logisima* were of two main varieties: the *prokatespasmena logisima* were exemptions from taxes granted to charitable hostels, churches and monasteries; *solemnia logisima* were revenues from lands not owned by the establishment concerned which were diverted to them by the *demosion*. The author of the *Marcian Treatise* indicated that they could replace the direct cash subsidies – the *solemnia*:

> A *solemnion logisimon* is when the emperor, instead of a *solemnion* given to such-and-such a holy establishment, having been invited by the *proestos* [meaning the *hegoumenos*] or the functionaries or the monks in the holy establishment, ascertains the same value of public revenue from village lands *not* owned by the same pious house, so that the exempted money is supplied by the villagers to that holy house.[26]

A third device was that of the *autourgon logisimon* (sometimes shortened to *tourgon logisimon*), by which a monastery, though not formally exempted from taxation, was allowed to keep its own taxes.[27]

The origins of the practice of tax exemptions are obscure, though since the *Marcian Treatise* declared that they were particularly intended to aid ecclesiastical institutions, they may well have originally only applied to them. The earliest surviving examples of monastic exemptions were phrased in general terms. By the mid-tenth century, Athos was already freed from the attentions of the officials of the *demosion*, though the means by which this had been achieved are not at all clear. Exemptions

---

[25] *Marcian Treatise*, pp. 117–18 (Brand, pp. 50–2).
[26] For *solemnia* see chapter 7, pp. 192; 194–5 and *Marcian Treatise*, p. 117 (Brand, p. 51).
[27] *Marcian Treatise*, p. 118 (Brand, p. 52).

for the Athonites were confirmed in the *typika* of John Tzimiskes and Constantine Monomachos, which freed them from all *epereiai* (literally 'burdens'). But it is clear that they only applied to the area within the boundary of the Holy Mountain, while lands held outside Athos were originally subject to taxation and the imposition of dues and services. It is, unfortunately, impossible to establish whether the holy mountains of Asia Minor were also exempted from taxation, since no documents establishing such privileges in this period have survived from their archives.[28]

In economic terms these early exemptions were of no great significance to the fortunes of the *demosion*, for the revenue obtainable from the remote areas first sought out by the tenth-century lavriote founders was negligible. But the practice of tax exemption took on a much more serious aspect when it was applied to large, fertile or economically flourishing areas. It was in the eleventh century that many monastic estates reached a high point of prosperity and it is in this period, too, that the exemptions reached their most widespread and elaborate form. A series of imperial chrysobulls, mostly concerning monastic houses, lists the fiscal (and judicial) exemptions in full.[29] The taxes and dues mentioned in the documents fell into three categories: money payments, labour services and dues payable in kind, such as the provision of food and lodging for imperial officials on the road and *matériel* for the imperial armed forces. A large variety of dues and services are mentioned in these stereotyped lists, but they do not, however, help with the solution of the most important problem, namely whether houses were exempted from the basic land tax, the *demosios kanon*. The crux of the matter is the interpretation of the word *epereia* or 'burden'. For some commentators, such as Ostrogorsky, this meant exemption from all fiscal burdens, including the *demosios kanon*, but for others, including Svoronos and, more recently, Kaplan, it referred to the extra charges and dues levied on land over and above the basic fiscal responsibility and the supplementary taxes (*parakolouthemata*) levied according to the level of the *demosios kanon*: the *dikeraton*, *hexafollon*, *synetheia* and *elatikon*. The problem is of paramount importance, since, if it is assumed that all the houses which enjoyed *exkousseia kathara* (complete exemption) paid no land tax, then the large and flourishing estates which many of them owned by the end of

---

[28] *Prôtaton*, nos. 7 and 8 (972 and 1045).
[29] G. Ostrogorsky, 'Pour l'histoire de l'immunité à Byzance', *B*, 28 (1958), 165–254 and more recently, Harvey, *Economic expansion*, pp. 103–13. There are rare lay examples from this period: Leo Kephalas, a trusted lieutenant of Alexios Komnenos was granted a series of exemptions from taxes and dues in kind, lists of which have survived because his lands passed into the hands of the Lavra, see chapter 8, p. 206, note 14; *Lavra*, I, nos. 44 (1082), 45 (1084), 48 (1086) and 49 (1089).

the eleventh century would have made no contribution whatsoever to the finances of the central government.[30]

There are two cases outside Athos where it seems clear that the monastery concerned was freed from the *demosios kanon*. In 1044, when Constantine Monomachos endowed the Nea Mone with lands in Asia Minor, he declared that the properties concerned were to be considered *idiostaton* and to have their own *isokodikes*. This, in itself, was a privilege, but the emperor went further. The lands were to be granted a *sympatheia* (tax relief) on the *demosion*. It is difficult to see what else he could have meant but the *demosios kanon*, especially since the relatively high figure of 6½ *nomismata* was mentioned as the amount to be exempted. In a confirmatory chrysobull of 1053, the monastery's lands on Chios were freed from the attentions of any *epereiastai* (collectors of dues and services), so that they should remain undisturbed 'to speak with God on behalf of the world'.[31] In the same way, the properties of the Monastery of St John the Theologian on Patmos also seem to have been freed from the *demosios kanon*. The gifts of the lands on Leipsos and Leros were made in 1087 on the understanding that they would not be subject to the *demosion*. They were not to be inscribed in either the *kodikes* (registers) of the *demosion* or those of the Myrelaion, the previous owner of the lands. In 1088, the same kind of complete fiscal immunity was granted to the lands on Patmos itself, for Alexios Komnenos ordered that they should be free from the demands of all imperial bureaux and that all returns should be cut and 'struck out' in red ink in the relevant records – a procedure very similar to that granting *prokatepasmena logisima*. Further proof that exemption from the land tax was at issue here is provided by a document dated to May 1088, in which the emperor, after receiving representations from Christodoulos, reiterated that the monastery was not subject to dues and that 'if any trace [of taxes or dues] remains by accident in the

---

[30] See Kaplan, *Les hommes et la terre*, p. 356, note 513. As Harvey points out (*Economic expansion*, p. 113), the comprehensive lists of exemptions in the eleventh-century chrysobulls may indicate that many of them were now being commuted to money payments and thus had to be individually designated. For the *parakolouthemata*, see Svoronos, 'Cadastre de Thèbes', pp. 81–3. Until the late eleventh century the *dikeraton* was levied at the rate of 2 *keratia* per *nomisma* of *demosios kanon*; the *hexafollon*, levied on all land paying basic land tax of more than ⅔ *nomisma*, at the rate of 6 *folleis* per *nomisma* of *demosios kanon*; the *synetheia* payable at the rate of 1 *miliaresion* per *nomisma* of basic tax of 1–5 *nomismata*, then at the rate of 1 *nomisma* on *demosios kanon* from 6–10 *nomismata* and so upwards. The *elatikon* was levied at 1 *miliaresion* on sums from 1–5 *nomismata*, and at 6 *miliaresia* on sums from 5–10 *nomismata*. The *synetheia* and *elatikon* taken together were not to exceed 10 *nomismata*.

[31] The lands concerned were Kalothekia and Eucheia, see chapter 8, p. 216: Zepos, I, Appendix, document IV, 615–18, especially p. 616. The *protimesis* right was also 'removed' from these lands, document XIII, pp. 636–7.

documents without having been noticed, these dispositions will be considered suppressed and will be crossed out in red ink'.[32]

The occasions upon which we can be confident that *kathara exkousseia* meant precisely that are few, and it is not safe to assume exemption from the basic land tax unless, as in the case of the houses on Athos, Chios and Patmos, it was specifically mentioned. For on many monastic estates which enjoyed a considerable degree of fiscal exemption, the *demosios kanon* was clearly paid. The fear of the Lavriote monks that the handing over of *telos* (tax payment) for their lands on Kassandra to Adrian Komnenos (brother of Alexios) would render them his *paroikoi* in the eyes of the law indicates that the 'complete exemption' they had been awarded for these lands did not include the land tax. Similarly, the monks were assured in 1092 that they had nothing to fear from the officials of another brother, Isaac Komnenos, if they continued to pay the *telos* for their property at St Andrew of Peristerai. The page from the cadaster concerning the taxes paid by the small Monastery of Kalliergou for its *metochion* at Hierissos was actually quoted in a document of 1079 by the *anagrapheus* (tax official) John Kataphloron and indicates that it was paying *demosios kanon* and all the supplementary taxes as prescribed in the *Marcian Treatise*. A similarly precise example also survives for the property of St Demetrios on Kassandra belonging to the Monastery of St Panteleimon.[33]

Even in documents where a comprehensive list of *exkousseia* was given, the *demosios kanon* often remained to be paid. Michael Attaliates complained in 1075 that his estates were being 'pillaged' by officials gathering *epereiai* (in this case certainly taxes in kind), and, as a consequence, was granted a chrysobull freeing him from their attentions by the Emperor Michael VII Doukas. But he was still to give his accustomed rate of *demosia* and other *telesmata*, a clear reference to land taxes and the other taxes calculated on them. Even when some of these lands were granted to his monastic foundations, the arrangements remained the same. Nikephoros Botaniates confirmed the exemptions granted by his predecessor, but reiterated that land taxes must be paid. In the case of the layman Leo Kephalas, too, a grant of exemption from taxes on some *klasma* lands at Derkos, granted by Alexios Komnenos in 1082, did not include the *demosion*, which he was still to pay at the rate of $4\frac{7}{12}$ *nomismata*.[34]

---

[32] *BEMP*, I, nos. 5 (May 1087) and 6 (April 1088). See Ostrogorsky, 'Immunité', p. 188. For the cancelling of dues: *BEMP*, I, no. 49 (May 1088). Ostrogorsky, 'Immunité', p. 189.
[33] *Lavra*, I, nos. 46 (1084) and 51 (1092). Cadastral entry for Kalliergou: *Lavra*, I, no. 39 (1079). *Pantéléèmôn*, no. 3 (?1044).
[34] Chrysobull of Michael Doukas (March 1075); *Diataxis* of Attaliates, pp. 101–9, especially p. 103. Chrysobull of Nikephoros Botaniates (April 1079); *Diataxis* of Attaliates, pp. 109–23. *Lavra*, I, no. 44 (1082).

In both these cases, and in many others, the exemptions simply referred to the dues in cash and kind and the labour services which were levied in addition to the land tax. They were extremely comprehensive and it is possible that monastic landowners and their lay counterparts were more eager to gain freedom from them (or their monetary commutation) than from the *demosios kanon* which, after all, might remain unaltered for thirty years or longer. This is evident in the case of the monks of the Athonite house of Vatopedi. The house had received a *solemnion* of 80 *nomismata* under both Constantine Monomachos and Michael VI, but it had been halved by Isaac Komnenos. It was raised again to 72 *nomismata* by Alexios Komnenos. The monks also owned two properties on Kassandra for which they paid 19 *nomismata* in state taxes. In 1082, the monks requested the emperor to allow them the 19 *nomismata* (the process of *autourgion logisimon*) in place of the *solemnion*. At the same time they begged that he would forbid the local fiscal and judicial officials access to their possessions. For, they maintained, the judges often took 20 *nomismata* or more from them as *chreia* (payments to support travelling officials) and *antikaniskion* (money in lieu of food dues to officials). They clearly felt that the freedom from dues in cash and kind payable to officials would more than compensate for the loss of their *solemnion*.[35]

The aim of monastic houses was to rid themselves of as many of these extra taxes and services as they could and thus entirely devote their resources to increasing the prosperity of their own estates. The effects on the efficient working of the Byzantine administration, both civilian and military, are difficult to calculate. The loss of the land tax in some not very fertile areas (such as Athos or Patmos) was perhaps not a matter of great significance – though it did mark an important departure from principle – but the loss of those dues and services which supported the administration in the provinces and the army in the field was far more serious. What the holders of exemptions did not provide, other land-holders, or the central government, must have. In the late eleventh century, when Byzantium was under constant attack from Turkish forces in the east and from the depredations of nomads and the Normans in the Balkans, and when, as the exemptions themselves indicate, mercenary armies had to be recruited, paid and fed, the burden falling on those who did not enjoy exemptions was severe. Among these must be numbered those unable or temporarily unsuccessful in making use of the ties of patronage to maintain fiscal advantage. If the case of Theophylact, archbishop of Ohrid at the end of the eleventh century, is anything to go by, those who held lands in militarily sensitive areas (as were his in the northern Balkans) could expect a never ending struggle with the agents of the

[35] *Vatopedi*, no. 3 (1082).

demosion and even the ignoring of *exkousseia* granted to houses under their control.[36]

With the augmentation of revenues that the holders of *exkousseia* enjoyed, there often came freedom from the attentions of judicial officials of the empire. The communities of the Holy Mountain enjoyed a distinctive legal status within their boundaries, but they and other famous houses also came to enjoy a certain degree of judicial exemption for their properties elsewhere. The chrysobulls granted to Michael Attaliates stipulated that the imperial judges were not to have access to his monastic lands; Bačkovo and its dependencies were freed from the judicial as well as the financial control of the metropolitan of Philippopolis; the monks of Stroumitza were 'not to be troubled by imperial or clerical judges, either those of the archbishop of Bulgaria or of the bishop of Stroumitza'. But perhaps the most striking example of judicial immunity was that awarded by Constantine Monomachos to the Nea Mone on Chios in 1045. In order to preserve the monks' *eremia* 'so that they may live the angelic life', no thematic judges were to have entry to the island:

> The God-loving monks in the aforesaid monastery shall not be taken to any court for any reason concerning their lands and those on them. For only the imperial court [*bema*] shall issue judgements about such things.[37]

The example of the Nea Mone is of great assistance in revealing the real aim of obtaining judicial exemptions. It certainly meant that, in the local sphere, monastic control over their lands and tenants was complete, but it did not mean that the monks were, or intended to be, beyond the reach or, indeed, the aid of the law. Rather, they sought to have their complaints heard and dealt with at the highest possible level. The monks of Chios were actually given permission to do this by the emperor, but recourse to him, and sometimes the patriarch, was common practice in other monastic establishments. As monastic founders pointed out in their *typika*, it was the duty of the emperor to protect the interests of the monastic houses and as well as exercising this general guardianship, the ties of spiritual kinship or patronage often meant that the emperors involved themselves in conflicts on behalf of favoured houses or groups.

The period immediately preceding the issue of the *Tragos* of John Tzimiskes shows this kind of relationship in action on Athos. The conflict

---

[36] See M. E. Mullett, 'Patronage in action: the problems of an eleventh-century bishop', in Morris (ed.), *Church and people in Byzantium*, pp. 125–47, especially p. 128, note 16, for Theophylact's complaints about the disregarding of an *exkousseia* for the Monastery at Pologos by imperial fiscal agents.

[37] Chrysobull of Michael Doukas, p. 103; chrysobull of Nikephoros Botaniates, p. 111, see note 34, above. Pakourianos, p. 45; Stroumitza, documents 1 (1085) and 2 (1106). For Chios, Zepos, I, Appendix, document VII, 629–31, especially p. 630.

between the Lavriotes and the other Athonites about the conduct of spiritual life on the mountain was of crucial importance, since it marked the final defeat of the hesychasts and allowed the process of building and land acquisition begun by Athanasios to continue. Both parties appealed directly to the emperor and all were agreed that such matters should not become the province of 'worldly courts' (*kosmika kriteria*). John Tzimiskes appointed Euthymios, the *hegoumenos* of Stoudios, to investigate

> so that affairs should not be set in order by the representatives of the *archontes* [local officials] and matters discussed amongst themselves or alleged against them should not become common knowledge. For the *kosmikoi* [men of the world] do not understand spiritual affairs.[38]

The *Typikon* of Monomachos emphasised that the Protos and his council were to make up the body which should deal with conflicts on the mountain and deplored the fact that Athonites had been taking their grievances to lay judges. But it is significant that, when Athos was torn by the Vlach controversy at the end of the eleventh century, the judicial organisation of the Protaton was unable to make peace. The party in favour of the expulsion of the Vlachs, led by John Balmas, the *hegoumenos* of the Lavra, complained directly to the Emperor Alexios Komnenos and the Patriarch Nicholas Grammatikos. A similar example may be cited from Latros, for when Christodoulos, then *hegoumenos* of the Stylos Monastery, came under attack from his own monks and those of other houses, he appealed for help directly to the Patriarchs Kosmas, Eustratios Garidas and Nicholas Grammatikos.[39]

An interesting pattern emerges from these cases. Clearly, the monks of the holy mountains and other houses preferred, if possible, to administer justice for themselves. But if this proved impossible, they did not turn of choice to the secular or ecclesiastical justice of the surrounding areas, although they were sometimes forced into local courts by their neighbours. Instead, they made use of the ties of patronage linking them to the capital to invoke the most influential assistance that they could, that of the emperor or the patriarch. While such action might strengthen the influence of an individual holder of either of these offices, it did nothing to consolidate the power of the institutions concerned. For intervention on this personal basis only served to emphasise the peculiar standing of the monks and houses concerned. Their removal from the administrative structure of the empire and from the control of imperial officials

---

[38] *Prôtaton*, no. 7 (972).
[39] *Prôtaton*, no. 8 (1045); *Diegesis merike*, pp. 163–70; MM, VI, pp. 30–1, see Vranoussi, *Hagiologika keimena*, pp. 90–6.

was, ultimately, extremely damaging to the imperial and patriarchal power.

Imperial fiscal and judicial immunities continued to be awarded to monastic houses throughout the eleventh century, but opposition began to be strongly expressed to the possession of such exemptions by the *charistikarioi*, the lay holders of *exousia* and *kyrioteta* over monastic houses. Although the history of the *charistike* has been shrouded in much rhetoric (both in the Byzantine period and today), it should be borne in mind that it was but one of the many legal methods by which authority and control over monasteries could be delegated. The problem at the end of the eleventh century was twofold: in the first place, there was concern that the *charistikarioi* were abusing their position as protectors of monastic interests and, in the second, both patriarch and emperor began to see the danger of allowing widespread immunities and this concern became focused on the obvious target of the *charistike*. In addition, the difficult military circumstances that the empire found itself in at the end of the eleventh century, and the consequent spiritual self-examination that this brought about, were conducive to the rise of a new kind of morality, one which emphasised the essential difference between churchmen and laity and which recalled the highest authorities of the empire to their duty to preserve untainted the rights and possessions of those who had consecrated their lives to God.[40]

The *charistike*, as we have seen, was originally an institution intended to benefit monastic houses. John of Antioch, in his treatise *Against the Charistike* described the origin of this type of grant:

The emperors and patriarchs transferred monasteries and poor houses which had been destroyed or were falling into ruins into the hands of important men, not in the way of a gift, or a worldly benefit, but in order that they should be restored and made of spiritual use.[41]

He was not clear when the practice had first begun, for although he mentioned the iconoclast emperors, he did not make clear whether he thought they had instituted the *charistike*, or whether it had been introduced as a means of repairing the damage to monasteries which they

[40] For the nature of the grant of *charistike*, see chapter 6, pp. 146 and note 1; 148 and note 34. Thomas, *Private religious foundations*, pp. 157–66; pp. 186–213 discuss the *charistikarioi* in detail but omit consideration of the valuable contributions of M. Kaplan, 'Les monastères et le siècle à Byzance: les investissements des laïques au XIe siècle', *Cahiers de Civilisation Médiévale*, 27/1–2 (1984), 71–83 and S. Varnalidou, *Ho thesmos tes charistikes (doreas) ton monasterion eis tous Byzantinous* (Byzantina Keimena kai Meletai, XXI, Thessalonike, 1985).
[41] John of Antioch, Against the *charistike*, p. 109.

had allegedly caused.[42] In fact, it was probably an institution introduced in the ninth and tenth centuries to help the fortunes of the poorer monasteries. The Patriarch Alexios Stoudites, writing in 1027, indicated that two factors had played their part in its growth: the aspirations of lay landowners to expand their influence and the declining fortunes of some monasteries. Lay elements, jealously eyeing the possessions of the monasteries, gained control of them by promising to take better care of them than had their inmates and grants were made by the patriarch and bishops on this understanding.[43]

Alexios Stoudites clearly indicated that the *charistike* had first been introduced by churchmen as a mechanism to benefit the establishments concerned, and in many monasteries this was indeed the case. One of the most famous of the eleventh-century *charistikarioi*, the historian Michael Psellos, apparently did his best to improve the houses of which he was *charistikarios*. In a letter to the *krites* Zoma of the Opsikion theme, he detailed the improvements which he proposed to make to the Monastery of Medikion in Bithynia: 'I will purchase cattle and acquire flocks, I will plant vineyards, divert rivers and exploit springs . . . and from a hundred measures of wheat, I will double or more than double the yield.'[44] This might all seem rather rhetorical, but there is evidence that he also intervened on behalf of the houses of which he was *charistikarios* with local and fiscal officials, to protect them against excessive charges and to forward their cases in boundary disputes.[45] In fact, *charistikarioi* such as Psellos and Michael Attaliates, acted on behalf of the lesser houses in precisely the same way as the emperor did for the holy mountains and the other establishments he favoured. Their aims were the same: to lessen as far as possible the control of the provincial administration, whether it be ecclesiastical or lay.

For the power of the *charistikarioi* was not disinterested. They always enjoyed some revenues from the monastic lands they controlled once the expenses specified in the founders' *typika* had been disbursed, and in some cases apparently mercilessly exploited them. The *Typikon* of St Mamas (1159) described in vivid terms the damage that the house had

[42] *Ibid.*, pp. 105–7.
[43] Alexios Stoudites, *Hypomnema*, no. 1 (1027), RP, V, 20–4, p. 21.
[44] K. A. Sathas, *Mesaionike Bibliotheke* (7 vols., Athens/Paris, Vienna/Paris, 1872–94), V, no. 29, pp. 263–5.
[45] For example, intervention on behalf of the Monastery of Homonoia in a boundary dispute: *Michaelis Pselli scripta minora*, ed. E. Kurtz and F. Drexl (2 vols., Milan, 1936–41), II, no. 60, 92–3; defence of the Monastery of Megala Kellia (Opsikion theme) against the jurisdiction of the thematic judge, *ibid.*, II, no. 108, 137. G. Weiss, *Oströmische Beamte im Speigel der Schriften des Michael Psellos* (Miscellanea Byzantina Monacensia, XVI, Munich, 1973), pp. 145–53, provides a list and see Kaplan, 'Les monastères et le siècle', pp. 73–4.

suffered 'through the insatiety and shamelessness of the *charistikarioi* who had held it from time to time and who, like wolves grasped ravenously upon it'.[46] It had become not so much a means of providing help for monasteries in decline as of exploiting well-established houses. But the temptation to explain this development as another sign of the activities of the *dynatoi* should be resisted; there is some evidence to suggest that the first initiative to obtain a *charistikarios* may have come from the monasteries themselves. Michael Psellos reported that he had been requested by the monks of Mount Ganos to accept the *prostasia* (the office of Protos) and he referred in a letter to an unidentified *hegoumenos*, to a request from the latters' monks that he should become the *kyrios* of their house.[47]

It was the spectacle of prosperous houses being removed from the fiscal and judicial control of the ecclesiastical administration that brought matters to a head. The main onslaught came at the end of the eleventh century, though John of Antioch reported that Patriarch Sisinnios (996–8) had already attempted to stop grants of *charistike*. His action had been countered by the Patriarch Sergios in 1016, who had maintained that both monasteries and potential benefactors would be unfairly penalised if the *charistike* were to be banned. He declared that it was only uncanonical to grant monasteries to the control of the laity if they were going to be transformed into secular dwellings, an action which can be seen not so much as indicating approval of *charistikarioi*, as a pragmatic admission that neither the patriarch nor the bishops possessed the funds to help all the houses that were in need. But by the end of the eleventh century, financial considerations of another sort were plaguing the church. Under the pressure of invasions in both the eastern and western provinces, the dues payable to provincial bishops were increasingly difficult to extract and the number of areas which could support their bishops was drastically reduced as the contemporary influx of clerics into Constantinople reveals. It was, therefore, imperative for the church authorities in the provinces to gain control of every source of revenue which they considered legitimately theirs.[48]

Hostility to the *charistikarioi* was primarily instigated by high-ranking members of the secular church, such as John of Antioch himself, and, as we shall see, their arguments were based more on high moral considerations than on the practical needs of monasteries. But the attack did form part of a more widespread tendency in the second half of the

[46] S. Eustratiades, 'Typikon tes Mones tou hagiou megalomartyros Mamantos', *Hellenika*, I (1928), 256–311, 257. Quotation, translated Charanis, 'Monastic properties', p. 76.
[47] Sathas, V, no. 150, 398–9; *Scripta Minora*, II, no. 104, 190–1.
[48] For patriarchal legislation concerning the *charistike* in the tenth and early eleventh centuries, see Thomas, *Private religious foundations*, pp. 160–71.

eleventh century: the increased willingness of imperial officials to challenge the fiscal and judicial claims of powerful houses and the renewed attempts by patriarchal and episcopal officials similarly to claim what they perceived to be their rights. The increasing number of serious legal cases which the powerful Athonite monasteries such as the Lavra and Iviron became involved in, and in which they found that automatic assistance from the imperial power was not now to be relied upon, is an indication of this changing climate. This is not to say that the ingrained habits of patronage and special pleading were overthrown in a moment; immunities and privileges were still granted on a wide scale. It simply became unwise to assume that financial and judicial claims would be accepted by the central authorities simply because they came from long-respected houses. In this respect, the late eleventh century presents a considerable contrast with the tenth for now, instead of using the majestic (but often ineffectual) powers of legislation to counter the attempts of monastic interests to withdraw themselves from the structures of the state, the imperial government began more strongly to support the efforts of its long-suffering officials. Rhetoric was buttressed by action and the result was an important period of active imperial and patriarchal intervention in monastic affairs.

CHAPTER TEN

The Komnene reaction

—————◆—————

THE END OF THE ELEVENTH century has aptly been described as a 'turning point' in the history of Byzantium. Under the pressure of the incursions of Normans, Petchenegs and later Crusaders in the European themes and of the Turks on the eastern frontier and in Anatolia, the defences of the empire began to buckle. Debasement and inflation, a constant threat throughout the century and much more serious after 1070, were fuelled by the need to find more cash to pay the ever increasing mercenary forces of the Byzantine army. The great days of victory of the late tenth and early eleventh century were long since past, and commentators of the period sought long and hard for explanations for the failure of Byzantine military forces. The provincial aristocracies, already flexing their muscles in the tenth century, increasingly controlled access to the imperial power, especially after the death of the Empresses Zoe and Theodora, the last representatives of the Macedonian line.

It was yet another scion of a powerful house (or rather group of houses), Alexios Komnenos, who, by managing to obtain the imperial office which he achieved by *coup d'état* in 1081, instituted a more stable period of imperial government which was to last until the end of the twelfth century. The changes which he introduced in the style of government, in the financial and judicial organisation of the empire and in the church have often led to his being characterised as a great reformer. But throughout all these activities, one theme stood out: the need to reassert the legal rights of the emperor, whether it be in the sphere of church or of financial administration and, in this sense, he was something of a conservative. Since a considerable body of material concerning monastic affairs dates from Alexios' reign, it is also a suitable moment to examine the imperial response to the growing legal and economic power of the more successful monasteries. It was a response also associated with an important period of patriarchal activity, for both powers were equally concerned to reassert rights which had been seriously eroded in the turbulent political conditions of the mid-eleventh century by using the weapons enshrined in both secular and canon law to identify and attack abuses.[1]

Alexios' concern to reassert and strengthen his legal rights can certainly be illustrated by his part in the campaign against the *charistikarioi*. A major source for this question is, as we have seen, John of Antioch's treatise *Against the Charistike*, but it is a document which should be treated with some care as it uses the most extreme polemic possible against the institution. It also needs to be taken in the context of other attacks mounted by this particularly choleric churchman against the emperor, the theme of which was that moral turpitude of all sorts lay at the root of the empire's military difficulties. John, of course, used all the rhetorical weapons that he could find, but an analysis of his basic arguments does enable us to get some idea of the kind of criticisms (both moral and practical) which were being levelled at the *charistikarioi*.[2]

Essentially, the appointment of lay administrators inevitably meant the perversion of the monastic life, which, as John eloquently put it was 'a holy society, which, for [Christ's] sake, had renounced the world and the affairs of the world . . . and had joined itself to Christ and clung to Him'.[3] The power of the *charistikarios*, he maintained, undermined the authority of the *hegoumenos*; monastic discipline and the all-important virtue of obedience were lost,[4] and there was even a danger of the *hegoumenos* losing control over the admission of monks into his house. For John maintained that *charistikarioi* often overrode the customary three years of novitiate, by issuing written instructions about admission:

> We have placed such-and-such as a brother in such-and-such a monastery; receive him, *hegoumenos*, tonsure him and give him cells for his stay and his rest. Let him also receive what all the other brothers receive. Make a copy of our present ordinance and give it to him by way of a guarantee.[5]

---

[1] For a succinct survey of Alexios Komnenos' reign, see Angold, *The Byzantine Empire*, pp. 92–149. The collection of studies in M. E. Mullett and D. Smythe (eds.), *Alexios I Komnenos* (Belfast Byzantine Texts and Translations, v, forthcoming) will shed new light on this important reign. For financial matters, see note 46.

[2] See John of Antioch, Against the *charistike*, *passim*, summarised by Thomas, *Private religious foundations*, pp. 186–92 and P. Gautier, 'Diatribes de Jean l'Oxite contre Alexis Ier Comnène', *REB*, 28 (1970), 5–35, dated by Gautier to February/March 1091. The career of the Patriarch John V Oxites is traced in *ibid.*, 'Jean V l'Oxite, patriarche d'Antioche. Notice biographique', *REB*, 22 (1964), 128–57. It is interesting to note that John's elevation to this post probably took place after he had composed these virulent attacks. Gautier suggested that his appointment might have been a move to get John out of the way, but it was, after all, a position of considerable prestige in the church.

[3] Against the *charistike*, chapter 11, p. 111.

[4] *Ibid.*, chapter 14, pp. 119, 121–3.   [5] *Ibid.*, p. 121.

Here John was exposing a practice about which we know very little: the insistence by lay patrons on the admission of certain individuals to the monastic life, which was linked to another about which it would be interesting to know more, that of the acceptance of 'lay brethren' (*esomonitai* or *exomonitai* depending on whether they lived inside or outside the monastery), who seem to have been spiritual pensioners and who received support from the monastery itself but were not subject to the authority of the *hegoumenos*. It is difficult to know who such people were, but they might have been trusty and long-serving lay retainers rewarded by monastic patrons with this assurance of food and shelter in their declining years, or simply those being granted this particular monastic 'perk' among other privileges. In both cases, John complained that the *charistikarioi* and, interestingly, emperors (perhaps a reference to the use of monasteries as detention centres for political prisoners and inconvenient members of the imperial families) were imposing their candidates on monastic houses with catastrophic results:

> And inside the holy monastery, O scandal!, the lay brothers [*kosmikoi adelphoi*] slaughter animals, eat meat, indulge in amateur dramatics and freely practise every kind of profane activity.[6]

The unfortunate monks were forced to submit to these abominations by force of necessity: 'They put themselves servilely at the disposal of the *charistikarios*, their hands are tied (as they say), and they obey his orders and his profane wishes like so many slaves, without even knowing whether they have a Superior of their own.'[7]

If these accusations were true – and it is almost impossible to find specific evidence to back them up – then matters would have given contemporaries grave cause for concern. More convincing are John of Antioch's strictures on the economic management of the *charistikarioi*. He complained that the pious intentions of founders had been violated:

> That the properties consecrated to God by the Christ-loving emperors, by the bishops, by leading men, by monks and by the laity, that is to say monasteries, hospices and hospitals are now being granted by men to men along with the lands that belong to them, in spite of the powerful curses with which their founders, in their testaments, struck down anyone who attempted such a thing.[8]

[6] *Ibid.*, p. 123. The verb used is *tragoidousi*, translated by Gautier as 'font du theâtre', although it might perhaps mean 'indulge in over-emotional behaviour'! See Thomas, *Private religious foundations*, pp. 188–9, for a discussion of *exomonitai* and *esomonitai*.
[7] Against the *charistike*, chapter 14, p. 128.
[8] *Ibid.*, chapter 8, p. 107.

He maintained that the new masters were notoriously mean; the *charistikarios* 'grants to the Holy Church and to the monks the smaller portion of the total [revenue], giving it to them as if it were his personal alms and only after much pleading'.[9]

It is impossible to know how widespread such abuses were, especially since, for rhetorical purposes, John maintained that *all* monasteries were in the hands of *charistikarioi* 'with the exception of a very small number of them and a few more recently founded houses', something which was palpably untrue, as founders such as Attaliates and Pakourianos could have testified.[10] But the very concern of late eleventh-century patrons to create houses that were *autodespoton* and, in Pakourianos' case, the warning against interference by his relatives, strongly suggest that the likelihood of pernicious lay control was anticipated in some quarters. There were certainly general complaints about this from patriarchal officials in the 1080s; specific cases were brought to light by Metropolitan Niketas of Athens in 1089 and Metropolitan Constantine of Kyzikos in 1116 and, as we have seen, enough accusations of 'asset stripping' continued through the twelfth century to give some credence of John of Antioch's remarks. Certainly one of the matters which most concerned the patriarchate and provincial bishops was the loss of revenues to which they were entitled.[11]

However, before considering the patriarchal and imperial response to the specific problem of the *charistikarioi*, it is necessary to pause and examine the validity of the view that this formed part of a more general Byzantine 'reform movement' in which Alexios Komnenos found it politic to play a part after his sacrilegious behaviour in 1081 when, under the pressure of financing an army struggling to contain the Norman menace in the western Balkans, he had authorised the melting down of holy vessels and church decorations made of precious metal and provoked a storm of protest in the church.[12] There certainly was a monastic aspect to the crisis over the holy vessels, for a letter of Leo, metropolitan of Chalcedon and Alexios' fiercest critic on this matter, probably written in the summer of 1082, urged the emperor to:

[9] *Ibid.*, chapter 14, p. 119.
[10] *Ibid.*, chapter 9, p. 109; chapter 11, p. 113. Gautier (p. 108, note 45) quotes Lemerle's view that 'recently founded houses' might refer to the Athonite monasteries, but this would be stretching somewhat the meaning of 'recent'.
[11] Thomas, *Private religious foundations*, pp. 221–4. John of Antioch, Against the *charistike*, p. 118, note 58 and, for specific cases, Thomas, *Private religious foundations*, pp. 201–21. Niketas of Athens, who wanted to overturn grants to laymen made by his senile predecessor Constantine of Kyzikos, concentrates on the damage grants in *charistike* were creating in the finances of his see.
[12] Thomas, *Private religious foundations*, chapters 6 and 7, especially pp. 192–3 and 203–5, where the bibliography on the 'holy vessels affair' is discussed.

Observe the holy monasteries and see how many have been sacked! How many houses of asceticism have lost their ornaments? How many altars have been stripped of their beauty and are like stripped corpses . . . ? If you wish for written witness, seek out the *dikaiomata* [legal documents]; they will speak and will not hide the truth, some declaring that they have been torn to shreds, others that they have been scratched out, yet others that they have been completely altered and transformed. Who could stand against so many witnesses? Who would refuse to hear them? Who would not admit the truth that all proclaim?[13]

Unfortunately, we are in no position to gauge how widespread the stripping of monastic treasures was, since the matter is not mentioned in the surviving archives of Athos (or of any other monastery for that matter) and the only house specifically mentioned as having suffered was the Church of St Mary of the Chalkoprateia in Constantinople. But enough had certainly happened for the emperor to be forced to make amends. He issued a chrysobull in 1082 declaring that such measures would not be repeated and, at a synod in 1084, promised compensation for those monasteries and churches which had suffered loss. However, if, as has been suggested, Alexios planned to make further seizures of church vessels in 1091, then the matter cannot have had such catastrophic results in the 1080s as to preclude this particular financial option ever being considered again.[14]

Alexios Komnenos and Leo of Chalcedon were formally reconciled at the Synod of Blachernai in 1094 and it is this event, according to John Thomas, that 'enabled the emperor to commit himself gracefully to moderate reform . . . allowing concentration on the greatest outstanding problem, the reform of the *charistikarioi*'.[15] In fact, the attention of both Alexios Komnenos and his patriarchs had been turned towards this question from the earliest years of his reign and if, as Gautier suggested, John of Antioch's tirade against the *charistikarioi* was written between 1088 and 1092, it was a response to the moves which had already been made by the highest secular and ecclesiastical authorities of the state, rather than the instigation of them. But in contrast to the violence of

---

[13] V. Grumel, 'Les documents athonites concernant l'affaire de Léon de Chalcédoine', *Miscellanea G. Mercati*, 3 (published as *Studi e Testi*, 128, (1947) 116–35, especially p. 125). The connection between ornaments and vessels and written *dikaiomata* is not immediately obvious. Perhaps Leo was referring in an over-dramatic way to losses of vessels reflected by the necessary strikings out in monastic *brebia* (lists of possessions), which commonly included them.

[14] For St Mary of the Chalkoprateia, see *Alexiad*, v.2, vol. II, pp. 10–13. Alexios Komnenos' chrysobull of 1082; Zepos, I, coll. iv, document XXII. For the suggestion that Alexios was planning another seizure in 1091, see P. Gautier, 'Synod des Blachernes', p. 214.

[15] Thomas, *Private religious foundations*, p. 205.

the language used by John of Antioch, the imperial and patriarchal
documents about the *charistike* (details of which were later gathered
together in one 'dossier' at the beginning of the thirteenth century),
concentrated on practicalities, on attempting to monitor the real situation
and on re-establishing legality.[16]

As early as March 1084, responding to a report from the Patriarch
Eustratios Garidas, Alexios issued an instruction (*lysis*) ordering the
restitution to Hagia Sophia of lands granted in *epidosis* to monasteries
that were not subject to it. In other words, the property of patriarchal
monasteries was not to be granted to those which did not hold this
status.[17] At some point before January 1086 the Patriarch Nicholas
Grammatikos ordered his *chartophylax* (official in charge of documents)
to insert in any grants of donation a nullity clause to be activated in the
case of non-registration of the details of the property (*brebia*) with
the patriarchate within six months. On 28 January 1086, however, the
measure was tightened up: no grants would be registered unless they were
accompanied by an inventory of the property of the monastery
concerned.[18] In May 1087, the patriarch placed the acts made by his
predecessors under the same control, for he decreed that they could not
be registered without a new permission issued by himself.[19] Three years
were to elapse before any further patriarchal legislation on this subject.
What was its direction and effect thus far?

The patriarchal authorities were being mobilised, with imperial
support, to re-establish their control over patriarchal monasteries and to
ensure that, if they were placed under lay administration, the lists of
their property deposited in Constantinople would prevent large-scale
mismanagement and alienation. But grants in *charistike* were *not* ended
and the whole exercise has a legalistic and administrative ring about it. We
are in no position to know whether this flurry of activity was sparked off
by the independent (but contemporary) scandal over the holy vessels,
especially since it was not, after all, *charistikarioi* who were accused of
melting them down, but the emperor himself. There may well have been
a highly charged atmosphere in ecclesiastical circles in the early 1080s in
which the patriarchate became extremely sensitive to any alleged lay

---

[16] See John of Antioch, Against the *charistike*, p. 85 and Thomas, *Private religious foundations*, pp. 186; 203 for discussion of John of Antioch's treatise (Thomas dates it to after 1090). Darrouzès, 'Dossier sur le charisticariat', pp. 151–7 for the establishment of the correct order of the documents and their relationship with imperial and patriarchal legislation.

[17] Darrouzès, 'Dossier', no. 3, p. 159 (163). Page numbers in brackets refer to French translation.

[18] Darrouzès, 'Dossier', no. 2, pp. 158–9 (162–3).

[19] Darrouzès, 'Dossier', no. 5, pp. 159–60 (164).

misdemeanours; but any direct connection between the controversy spearheaded by Leo of Chalcedon and Alexios Komnenos and this essentially bureaucratic activity on the part of the patriarch has yet to be established.[20]

If the items of the 'dossier' are complete (and although the order of the items is chronologically incorrect it does seem to have been compiled by someone with a specific interest in the matter), the next ecclesiastical decree about the *charistikarioi* was issued on 18 January 1090. In it, the *megas sakellarios* and the *chartoularioi* of the Great Church (all high officials of the patriarchate) simply restated the patriarchal *pittakion* of 1086, which would seem to indicate that there had been some difficulty in enforcing it. This is illustrated by a short note in the dossier relating to objections expressed by the beneficiaries of grants of *charistike*. This, in its turn, brought forth an imperial *lysis* annulling any imperial documents which they might make use of to question patriarchal demands.[21] It was closely followed by a patriarchal ruling on 22 May 1094 that only three months was to be allowed for the registration of monastic properties with the patriarchate. Not much was new about this second wave of activity, but then not much seems to have been achieved by the first. But the aim was still clearly to protect the position of the patriarchal monasteries, and the relationship between patriarch and emperor was still that of support by the secular power for measures instigated by the church.[22]

If, as Thomas argues, the Synod of Blachernai, which took place at the end of 1094, initiated a period of imperial concern with the *charistikarioi*, there was little to show for it. For again it was the Patriarch Nicholas Grammatikos who made the next move in a series of actions which demonstrate a new initiative on the part of the central administration of the church. At some time between May 1094 and December 1096, he ordered his officials to make a census of all patriarchal monasteries to discover their real situation.[23] Such was the prevarication and obstruction that they encountered, that the imperial officials composed a formal complaint (doubtless with patriarchal approval) which was submitted to the emperor:

> Having begun [our enquiries] we experienced great difficulties with certain individuals. For some presented documents of immunity which ordered that no *sakellarios* or any ecclesiastical official should be allowed to enter. Others presented acts of donation specifying that until the passing of

[20] *Pace* Thomas, *Private religious foundations*, pp. 192–9.
[21] Darrouzès, 'Dossier', document 2, p. 159, ll. 10–14 (163, ll. 13–16), document 4, p. 159 (163).
[22] Darrouzès, 'Dossier', no. 1, pp. 157–8 (161–2).
[23] Darrouzès, 'Dossier', no. 6, pp. 160–1 (164–5).

273

two lives or of one (which was rarer) absolutely no one could enter [the monasteries] and exercise the least right. As for those who have received the monasteries in *epidosis*, they will in no wise allow mention to be made of the presence in their house of a *sakellarios* or other ecclesiastical functionary.[24]

It is in the imperial response to these complaints and the questions the officials put to him about the conditions under which the patriarch should have access to monasteries, that we can distinguish a sea-change in Alexios Komnenos' attitude. In the novel which he issued in December 1096, he not only emphasised the right of the patriarch to have access to patriarchal houses at all times (with the exception of those granted in *epidosis* to other monasteries) but followed this up with the statement that the patriarch enjoyed rights of *epiteresis* (oversight) and *diorthosis* (correction) over all houses in the patriarchate of Constantinople, regardless of their legal status. He could make a visitation if spiritual faults or immorality were suspected. In the case of monasteries granted in *epidosis*, as *ephoreia* or in *oikonomia*, the patriarch could compel their holders to make restitution for any diminution of property and restore any buildings which had been damaged or destroyed and those that had been irrevocably ruined should be taken back into patriarchal control.[25]

While Alexios was clearly widening the scope of potential patriarchal intervention into the affairs of monastic houses by allowing it on moral grounds, he did not abolish the *charistike*, nor is there any evidence that the Patriarch Nicholas Grammatikos wanted him to. Alexios and the patriarch well knew that the institution was now ingrained in the traditions of lay patronage and, when successful, it could benefit the houses concerned. While admitting that the advantage of this arrangement may have lain with the *charistikarioi* and that while it existed there was always a potential for abuse, it is salutary to recall the comments of twelfth-century churchmen on the matter. Theodore Balsamon, as we have seen, thought the arrangement perfectly legitimate; Eustathios, archbishop of Thessalonike, went further. In the course of a generalised attack on the state of the monasteries of his province in the late twelfth century (absence of learning, ignorance and greed were themes which he returned to time and again), he pointed out that the appointment of lay *archontes* to the management of large monasteries was beneficial, because it meant that 'the ascetics could devote themselves to divine deeds'. In independent houses, he noted, the monks had to perform both ecclesiastical and lay functions and that 'they hold in their hands the

---

[24] Darrouzès, 'Dossier', no. 6, p. 160 (164).
[25] Zepos, I, coll. iv, document XXXVII, 347–8. For the legal terminology, see chapter 6.

scales of injustice and counterfeit coins instead of the Psalter and holy books'.[26]

The contrasting views of John of Antioch and Eustathios of Thessalonike on the question of the *charistikarioi* had, of course, much to do with their attitude towards their various Komnene rulers. John had nothing much good to say about Alexios Komnenos and therefore attacked an institution which Alexios refused to outlaw; Eustathios was, in general, a supporter of Alexios' grandson Manuel, himself a vocal critic of contemporary monastic life. If the distortions caused by this political dimension are taken into account, the matter of the *charistikarioi* can be seen not so much as an argument about high moral and theological principles with which Alexios chose, eventually, to associate himself, but a question of practicalities. Should the ruler support the secular church in its attempts to recover lost assets and reassert the claims of jurisdiction which, as we have seen, were consistently challenged or ignored during the tenth and early eleventh centuries, or should he allow monasteries to go their own way, even if a corruption of the 'life of the angels' would inevitably ensue? In supporting the patriarchal action over the *charistikarioi*, it seems, at first, as if Alexios Komnenos took the former view.[27]

Nothing, however, was that simple. While the emperor gave general support to patriarchal claims for moral oversight over all monasteries, when it came to particular cases where the imperial power had a special interest, then matters could be rather more complicated. The problem of dealing with the dissension and scandals on Mount Athos is a case in point. Unfortunately, the documents concerning Athonite dealings with both patriarch and emperor are gathered together in a muddled hotch-potch of memoranda, the so-called *Diegesis merike*, apparently compiled in Constantinople c. 1180 and dealing with a number of problems which troubled the Holy Mountain at the turn of the eleventh and twelfth centuries.[28]

The first matter was that of the Vlach herdsmen and their families (including female persons and animals, both long prohibited in the monastic enclosures on the Holy Mountain) who had been welcomed by certain monks at the end of the eleventh century. They provided, as we have seen, a supply both of manpower and of dairy produce and

---

[26] *Eustathii Metropolitae Thessalonicensis Opera*, ed. G. L. F. Tafel (Frankfurt, 1832, reprinted Amsterdam, 1964), p. 244, ll. 33–61. His arguments are summarised in Kazhdan and Franklin, 'Eustathius of Thessalonica', especially pp. 150–5.
[27] Kazhdan and Franklin, 'Eustathius of Thessalonica', p. 154.
[28] For the *Diegesis merike*, see chapter 8, p. 232, note 59. It is unfortunate that the archives of the *Prôtaton* (in which we might have expected to find some mention of these troubles) are completely lacking from 1045–1178/9: see *Prôtaton*, p. 266.

wool.[29] An opposing group, led by the *hegoumenos* of the Lavra, John Balmas, unable to force the removal of the Vlachs by the Protaton, complained to the Patriarch Nicholas Grammatikos. He, according to the memorandum drawn up on the subject by the Protos John Trachaneiotes (or Tarchaneiotes) and thus before 1109, then warned the Athonites, as their moral supervisor, to mend their ways, but did not, apparently, order the removal of the Vlachs, but rather advised that no more should come in and that their flocks should be banned from the mountain. It is not clear when this took place; 1101–2 or 1104–5 seem the most likely dates. But it was certainly in accordance with the right of patriarchal moral jurisdiction over all houses accepted by Alexios Komnenos' novel of December 1096, stopping short, it appeared, of directly interfering with the long-accepted (and imperially maintained) right of the Holy Mountain to conduct its own affairs and to settle its own disputes internally. But this was not the end of the matter.[30]

According to a memorandum apparently by John Balmas himself, who was not content with the cautious attitude of the patriarch, he (Balmas) then forged a patriarchal *entole* or 'formal instruction' which ordered the Athonites to banish the Vlachs. Violent protests about this apparent interference in internal affairs were brought to the emperor and he began to investigate. He sent a letter to Nicholas Grammatikos complaining first that his action had led to strife on the mountain and a depopulation of the monastic community and, secondly, but more significantly, that the patriarch had no right to interfere. The patriarch, pursues the memorandum, had replied by detailing the serious moral lapses which were implicit in the Vlach affair (including the horror of Vlach women dressed as men) and which, he claimed, would have given him the right to intervene on moral grounds, but, he added, he had not done so. He had merely issued *parangelias* (instructions) and *epitimeseis* (criticisms) but asked the emperor, in his rôle as protector of the Holy Mountain to add his weight to the campaign to get rid of the Vlachs.[31]

[29] *Diegesis merike*, pp. 163–70. These matters had been clearly dealt with in the *Tragos* of John Tzimiskes and the *Typikon* of Constantine Monomachos. It was not until the reign of Manuel Palaiologos, however, that, in 1406, the emperor forbade the possession of female animals on the mountain as a whole, see *Prôtaton*, introduction, pp. 107–9.

[30] For John Balmas' complaint, *Diegesis merike*, pp. 181–2; for the patriarch's description of his actions, pp. 167–8, see especially p. 168, ll. 10–11. The problem of the dating, which depends on the order of the late eleventh-century Protoi of Mount Athos, is discussed by J. Darrouzès, 'Listes des Prôtes de l'Athos', in *Millénaire du Mont Athos*, I, 407–47, especially pp. 413–14. Skoulatos, *Personnages byzantins*, no. 160, pp. 253–6, comments on the personality of Nicholas Grammatikos and dates these events to c. 1104.

[31] *Diegesis merike*, pp. 181–2 (John Balmas' confession), pp. 165–6 (Athonite protests), pp. 166–7 (Alexios Komnenos' letter to Nicholas Grammatikos ordering withdrawal of the *entole*), p. 168 (Nicholas Grammatikos' moral arguments and denial of the *entole*).

But the affair rumbled on. Further delegations of Athonite monks came to Constantinople attempting to 'find out the truth' about the *entole* until, in 1111, according to another entry in the *Diegesis Merike*, an extraordinary scene took place at the deathbed of the Patriarch Nicholas Grammatikos. The monk John Chortaïtinos (*hegoumenos* of the Monastery of Chortaïtou near Thessalonike) related how, on business concerning his own house in Constantinople, he had been requested by the emperor to go with sundry courtiers to the patriarch and find out once and for all about the much-maligned *entole*. He demurred, saying that he feared the curse of the dying patriarch, at which point Alexios agreed to accompany him. The text here records a scarcely credible dialogue between emperor and patriarch at the end of which the patriarch was able to produce records in his own hand in which the offending *entole* did not appear. Balmas, also hearing of the imminent death of the patriarch, then came to him and confessed the forgery.[32]

There are many problems left to be elucidated about these accounts, not least the fact that the sick-room of the Patriarch Nicholas Grammatikos seems to have been somewhat overcrowded with important figures in the drama, all of whom (if they are to be believed) happened to be in Constantinople at the same significant moment. Of far more importance, however, and central to our understanding of what the Patriarch Nicholas Grammatikos was actually doing, is the fact that, contrary to the denials preserved in the *Diegesis merike*, there is evidence that he did issue an *entole* or formal instruction to the Athonite monks. A document from the Archives of the Protaton dated 1178–9 contains a request from a monk who had left the mountain because he had felt that the patriarchal ban on the innocent (in the Vlach affair) mixing with the guilty had made monastic brotherhood on the mountain impossible, and who now wanted permission to return to pass his last days on Athos. If monks had felt it necessary to distance themselves from erring brethren, then they were clearly acting on something far more serious than patriarchal admonitions and advice.[33]

Given the support of Alexios Komnenos for such patriarchal moral intervention in 1096, it seems entirely logical that Nicholas Grammatikos

---

[32] *Diegesis merike*, pp. 177–80 (John Chortaïtinos' account). Although the possibility that John Tarchaneiotes (Trachaneiotes) and John Chortaïtinos were one and the same was suggested by Gyóni, 'Les vlaques', pp. 35–6, this is not a satisfactory solution. The Monastery of Chortaïtinos was quite near enough to Athos to know of its problems: see Darrouzès, 'Listes de prôtes', p. 413 and Beck, *Kirche und theologische Literatur*, p. 233.

[33] *Prôtaton*, no. 10 (1178–9). Both this document and one of the last notes in the *Diegesis merike*, a patriarchal *lysis* reasserting Athonite independence, are associated with the Patriarch Chariton whose patriarchate lasted only one year from 1178–9. The monk concerned must have been of advanced age.

should have used these powers when the Athonite scandals came to his notice. But why should he have denied doing so? We can only guess that the violent protests of the Athonites about patriarchal interference in their internal affairs, the fact that these protests were brought to the emperor and the subsequent imperial reminders about the special status of the Holy Mountain, led him to find it politic to deny his legal action, while maintaining his moral involvement. In this case, then, any claim of patriarchal oversight over the Holy Mountain was firmly rebuffed, but it is clear that the patriarchal strictures were taken so seriously by many monks as to cause a migration away from the mountain. While Alexios Komnenos certainly intervened to reassert Athonite independence, he does, however, seem to have supported the patriarch in the general tenor of his actions. But long-established imperial ties with Athos made it impossible for him to go the whole hog.

But Alexios' attitude to Athonites does not seem to have been unfailingly sympathetic. In the accounts of another scandal, entangled with that of the Vlachs in the *Diegesis merike*, distinct imperial irritation was clearly evident. In this case, Alexios was responding to the (possibly separate) delegations of monks who had come to Constantinople to complain about the presence on the mountain of children and eunuchs, both expressly forbidden by the *Typikon* of Constantine Monomachos in 1045.[34] After apparently holding a vigorous debate with them (the details of which we cannot verify), Alexios lambasted them as 'false hesychasts' for daring to leave their monasteries without the permission of the Protos, a matter which was against the 'laws of the fathers' and the imperial edicts. The image of a soldier, flogged, tonsured and led before his fellows in wooden fetters because he had dared to go to Constantinople without permission of his superiors, was invoked.[35] He then sent them to the Patriarch Nicholas Grammatikos with a letter warning the patriarch that the monks were annoying him and were bidding fair to suffer an unpleasant punishment for importuning the emperor:

> If you can, help them! Otherwise, I want to slit their nostrils and send them back, so that the rest will learn what the Emperor's command is.[36]

In two further documents associated with the Protos Hilarion, the matter of the children and eunuchs was mentioned again as part and parcel of the continuing strife on Athos caused by the presence of ignorant men and disruptive elements some of whom were learned and 'came from the palace'. The Patriarch Nicholas Grammatikos wrote to

---

[34] See above, note 29, and *Diegesis merike*, pp. 170–3.
[35] *Ibid.*, p. 171, ll. 25–7.   [36] *Ibid.*, p. 172, ll. 20–4.

Alexios Komnenos that the 'hagiorites' (meaning the traditionally minded Athonites) should not have to 'cultivate' *sebastoi* (high-ranking officials) and 'men from the palace' in a desert spot, by which he presumably meant that the virtues of *eremia* and the simple spiritual life were being compromised by the presence of sophisticated and unsubmissive newcomers. This looks like an interesting example of the social friction caused by monastic expansion. But who could he have meant?[37]

It would be a great deal easier to resolve this problem if we were sure about the date at which the complaints were being heard in Constantinople. It used to be thought that the monk Hilarion was Protos of Athos at the beginning of Alexios' reign, before John Balmas who can be dated to 1096. But persuasive arguments have been put forward for dating Hilarion to the years 1109–?16. Since the Patriarch concerned is Nicholas Grammatikos, this would narrow the period down to between 1109 and 1111, when he died.[38] In fact, the complaints probably rumbled on throughout Alexios' reign. But his sensitivity (not to say irritability) on the subject may well have had a rather more personal cause. For, as we shall see, when Alexios' own patronage and friendships were involved, then his general support for the legal organs of the state bureaucracy and the patriarchate tended to become rather lukewarm.

This is particularly evident in the matter of the eunuchs on Mount Athos. For in one particular case, at the beginning of his reign, Alexios clearly and deliberately contravened the prohibition against their presence. For he insisted on the reinstatement of the monk Symeon the Sanctified in his Monastery of Xenophon. Symeon, it will be remembered, had enjoyed a successful legal career in earlier life and had gained the rank of *megas droungarios*. He arrived on Athos with three companions in the summer of 1078 (at the latest), and was allowed to settle in the ruined Monastery of Xenophon. The gift of 25 lb of *nomismata trachea* that he then made for the upkeep of the church of the Protaton was not unusual, except, perhaps, in its generosity. What was unusual, to say the least, was the fact that Symeon and his group were all eunuchs. Their initial acceptance can, surely, only be explained by the size of the 'offering' to the Protaton. At some point before 1081, Symeon and his group were expelled; the 'arrogance' of his young followers expressly mentioned as having caused difficulties at the Athonite *synaxeis*. Their subsequent movements are unclear, though they may have gone to Thessalonike, since Symeon is reported to have founded a monastery for eunuchs there. Did they head back to Constantinople?

---

[37] *Ibid.*, pp. 174–5; especially 175, ll. 32–5.
[38] Grumel, *Régestes*, nos. 958 and 959 dated Hilarion's holding of the post of Protos to the 1090s, but see Darrouzès, 'Listes des prôtes', for strong arguments in favour of 1109–?1116.

Were they among the wandering monks, some of them described as
'rhetors and learned' (certainly a description that would fit a lawyer)
and 'from the palace', who were the objects of criticism in the *Diegesis
merike*?[39] We only know that Symeon was well known to Alexios and had
been employed by him in the summer of 1078, when Alexios was still
megas domestikos (commander-in-chief), and when Symeon was still on
Athos, to try to persuade the rebel Nikephoros Basilakios to surrender
from his refuge in Thessalonike.[40]

On Alexios Komnenos' accession to the imperial throne, Symeon
'hastened to plead his cause before him' and, as a result, was reinstated in
the Monastery of Xenophon in 1089. In addition, an imperial agent,
Theodore Senacherim, was sent to supervise the execution of the
imperial command, which was read out at the Great Synaxis. Symeon was
then formally forbidden to leave Athos without permission of the Protos
and the prohibition against eunuchs, beardless youths and female animals
was again asserted. It was also established that the next *hegoumenos* of
Xenophon should be chosen by the monks of the monastery and installed
by the Protos. Underneath this apparent reassertion of the regulations of
the Holy Mountain, it is clear that the re-establishment of Symeon was a
deeply humiliating defeat for the Protos and the monastic governors of
Athos. Given this wounding experience and convinced in their hearts of
the righteousness of their cause, it is not surprising that elements among
the Athonite monks continued to bombard emperor and patriarch with
complaints about the moral state of Athos. But the emperor, officially
sympathetic to them, might well have found repeated allusions to the
Xenophon affair embarrassing, hence his sharp reaction.[41]

Perhaps because of the straitened financial circumstances in which he
found himself at the beginning of his reign, Alexios showed a distant
benevolence towards the smaller Athonite houses, but did not go out of
his way to patronise them as his predecessors had done. In 1081, the
monks of the Monastery of Xeropotamou renewed their request for
imperial action against Iviron over disputed lands at Sisikion; they had
been in contact with Nikephoros Botaniates about the matter in 1080 and
do not seem to have envisaged any problem in contacting his successor.
As far as they were concerned, it was business as usual. The Monastery of

[39] See chapter 3, p. 86. For the 'learned monks' and 'those from the palace', see *Diegesis merike*, p. 175.
[40] The historians Nikephoros Bryennios and Anna Komnene both describe this diplomatic mission. While Anna calls the monk concerned Joannikios (*Alexiad*, VII.5–VIII.2; IX.3, vol. I, pp. 31–2, 35), Bryennios names him as Symeon, *hegoumenos* of Xenophon. Since Bryennios was intimately concerned with these events, it is probably he who should be believed: see Bryennios, L.iv, 27, p. 155.
[41] *Xénophon*, no. 1 (1089).

Vatopedi, whose previous *solemnion* of 80 *nomismata* had been halved by Isaac Komnenos, had it partially restored by Alexios and were also given a measure of tax relief. The Iviron archives are virtually non-existent at this period, which makes any assessment of their position difficult, especially any attempt to see how far they had recouped their fortunes after the dark days of the mid-eleventh century. It was, of course, during Alexios' reign (in about 1112) that official copies of documents confirming the extensive gifts made by the nun Maria (the widow Kale Pakouriane) of estates at Radolibos, were made in Constantinople, but this was essentially a private affair.[42]

If it is difficult to see Alexios as a great patron of the monastic houses of Athos, with their reputation of holding the spiritual 'high ground' of the empire, then we must logically ask whether Alexios should be seen as much of a monastic patron at all. We know that he had a series of spiritual fathers; that he joined in family visits to St Cyril Phileotes and that he assisted in the foundation of the Monastery of Christ Philanthropos in Constantinople, in which house he was buried. He also patronised the Monastery of St Mokios in Constantinople, possibly providing it with new regulations.[43] But when we examine the early history of Christodoulos' establishments on Patmos and elsewhere, however, it looks very much as though his mother, Anna Dalassene, took the initiative, though her son was clearly impressed enough by Christodoulos to ask him to undertake the task of reforming monastic life on Mount Kellion.[44] In his dealings with the recently established houses of Stroumitza and Bačkovo, Alexios was no more than conventional; he simply confirmed their privileges in the traditional manner.[45]

It is, in fact, much easier to make a case for the keen monastic patronage of other members of the Komnenos family, notably Anna

---

[42] *Xéropotamou*, no. 6 (1081); Vatopedi, no. 3 (1082), pp. 124–8. For the Pakourianos wills and the estate of Radolibos, see chapter 8.

[43] For visits to Cyril Phileotes, see chapter 5. See Janin, *Eglises et monastères*, pp. 354–8 and Mango, *Art of the Byzantine empire*, p. 227, for the Monastery of St Mokios. For the Monastery of Christ Philanthropos, Kécharitôménè, pp. 133, 139 and Janin, *Eglises et monastères*, pp. 525–7. Alexios' involvement in its construction is mentioned in the 'Chronicle of the Sathas Anonymous', in Sathas, *Mesaionike Bibliotheke*, VII, pp. 177–87, probably the work of the late thirteenth-century historian Theodore Skoutariotes. I am very grateful for the generous assistance of Paul Magdalino on this point and for providing unpublished material on the *Orphanotropheion*.

[44] See chapter 8, pp. 217–20 for the grant of the lands associated with Patmos and chapter 2, p. 50 for Mount Kellion.

[45] For confirmatory chrysobulls, see Stroumitza, nos. 1–3. Pakourianos, pp. 124–31 provides a list of imperial chrysobulls preserved in the Monastery of Bačkovo and in Hagia Sophia, all of which were presumably confirmed by Alexios Komnenos, who considered Pakourianos a close friend: see *Alexiad*, XIV.3, vol. II, p. 83 and Skoulatos, *Personnages byzantins*, no. 78, pp. 112–15.

Dalassene, who founded the monastic church of Christ Pantepoptes (Eski Imaret Camii) about the year 1100; Alexios' wife, Irene Doukaina, the founder of the Nunnery of the Theotokos Kecharitomene as well as the prime founder of the Monastery of Christ Philanthropos; his eldest son, John, the founder of the immense monastic hospital and complex of the Pantokrator (Zeyrek Kilise Camii), and his youngest son, Isaac, who rebuilt the church at the Monastery of Chora (Kariye Camii) in about 1120 and founded, towards the end of his life, the Monastery of the Virgin Kosmosotira at Ainos (Pherrai) on the River Hebros (Maritza) in Thrace (its *typikon* dates from 1151). Alexios' mother-in-law, Maria Doukaina, had herself been responsible for an earlier rebuilding of the Chora church, probably in 1077–81.[46]

However, recent work by Paul Magdalino suggests that we should further examine the monastic 'components' of the complex of the *Orphanotropheion* (orphanage) in Constantinople, founded by Alexios Komnenos in the 1090s. Here the extensive buildings devoted to the care of the old, infirm and disabled were associated with possibly as many as four monasteries: three for women (including one for Georgian nuns) and one for men. Anna Komnene, who gave a long description of the complex, also reported that Alexios assigned valuable properties to the house whenever he came across them; among them were two properties once belonging to the Lavra on Mount Athos. The *Orphanotropheion* may, then, have been Alexios' 'personal' house, and if it was, it is quite possible that the expenditure concerned made him unlikely (at a time of financial stringency) to consider another larger-scale foundation. But it was a different kind of house from the primarily monastic establishments favoured by his relatives or by laymen such as Pakourianos or Attaliates, and was more in keeping with the maintenance of the traditions of imperial *philanthropia*. If, as seems likely, the wealth of the *Orphanotropheion* was based to a large extent on revenues hitherto assigned to defunct charitable institutions and from lands which had come into the control of the state, and thus did not constitute a major financial investment on the part of the emperor, it would provide further evidence of a distinct air of financial caution during the first twenty years of Alexios' reign. Of particular importance for any study of monasticism,

---

[46] For Komnene monastic buildings in general, see Mango, *Byzantine architecture*, pp. 130–7; for Christ Pantepoptes, Janin, *Eglises et monastères*, pp. 513–15. Maria Doukaina and Isaac Komnenos' building activities at the Chora monastery are discussed in R. G. Ousterhout, *The architecture of the Kariye Camii in Istanbul* (Dumbarton Oaks Studies, XXV, Washington, DC, 1987), pp. 15–20, 20–32. The *typikon* of the Theotokos Kosmosotira was published by L. Petit, 'Typikon du monastère de la Kosmosotira près d'Aenos (1152)', *IRAIK*, 13 (1908), 17–77.

therefore, is the need to assess what effects Alexios' financial reforms had upon the wealth, land-holding and administration of monastic houses.[47]

There is much debate among historians about the causes and the course of the successive debasements of the Byzantine coinage in the eleventh century and the consequent financial difficulties in which the Byzantine state found itself. What is clear, however, is that by the time Alexios Komnenos gained the throne in 1081, the imperial *demosion* was far from gaining its proper returns, mainly because of the poor quality of much of the coinage in which they were paid, but also because of the inability of the existing systems of assessment and payment of tax to take account of this phenomenon. Nothing much could be done at the beginning of the reign while imperial attention was still focused on dealing with the invasions of the Petcheneg nomads and the Normans, but in the 1090s the immediate danger to the empire was past and it was at this point that we can see the beginning of a serious attempt at financial management and restructuring. Alexios' reforms were twofold. Firstly, the issuing of a new gold *nomisma*, the *hyperperon* of 20½ carats marked at least the intention to return to a full gold standard, though all sorts of debased coins continued to circulate long afterwards. Other reformed currency issues were associated with it and new mints established to get the coins into circulation. Secondly, in 1106–9, the fiscal system was reformed to take account of the variety of coinage in existence; tax officials were given detailed guidance in the *Nea Logarike* (New Computation) about how to collect sums which bore some resemblance to the true level of the established tax burdens.[48]

The reports of the imperial officials which were included in the legislation reveal how these problems were affecting matters in the provinces. For example, the tax collector Nikephoros Artabasdos, entrusted with the tax farm of Thrace and Macedonia, reported that a variety of monetary equivalents were in use and that some land-holders had managed to get away with paying taxes in coins nominally worth 12 *miliaresia*, but in fact worth a lot less. In 1106–7 he was instructed to collect one *palaion trachy nomisma* (a pre-reform low value *nomisma*) for each *miliaresion*; soon afterwards it became clear that one *aspron trachy nomisma* (a post-reform

---

[47] See P. Magdalino, 'Innovations in government', in Mullett and Smythe (eds.), *Alexios I Komnenos*.

[48] Hendy, *Studies in the Byzantine monetary economy*, pp. 434–5; 513–17 and Hendy, *Coinage and money in the Byzantine empire 1081–1261* (Dumbarton Oaks Studies, XII, Washington, DC, 1969) who debates the views of C. Morrisson, 'La dévaluation de la monnaie byzantine au XIe siècle: essai d'interprétation', *TM*, 6 (1976), 3–48 and 'La Logarikè: réforme monétaire et réforme fiscale sous Alexis I Comnène', *TM*, 7 (1979), 419–64. See Harvey, *Economic expansion*, chapter 3, for a cogent exposition of the major problems.

electrum – silver/gold alloy – coin) was to be collected for each existing *miliaresion* of tax. A heavy increase in taxation was thus levied. In addition, Alexios' officials were instructed to make adjustments to the system of collection of supplementary taxes which led to a standardisation of payments which could amount to a rate of about 34 per cent on the basic tax, higher than had been paid previously.[49]

If any further evidence were needed that Alexios' efforts to regain the rightful revenues of the *demosion* (by means of the tax census of 1087–8 and the coinage reforms of 1092) bore swift fruit, it is amply provided by material from the Athonite archives showing the anguished reaction of those monasteries with extensive land-holdings to the efforts of the imperial officials to establish the level of taxation to which they were truly liable and later to adjust their payments to realistic levels by use of the formulae of the *Nea Logarike*. There were a number of issues at stake, all of which had ramifications for monastic economies. As we have seen, the fiscal system had been thrown into disarray by the progressive debasements of the *nomisma*, which meant that tax payments were often being made in coin of a very low real value. There had been previous efforts to remedy this and other financial malpractices (such as the holding of far greater amounts of land than that covered by existing tax payments) before Alexios came to the throne. The somewhat mysterious confiscations of monastic land undertaken by Isaac Komnenos (1057–9), though reported by the historian Michael Attaliates as having the aim of raising money for military campaigns, were also, it was said, intended 'to free the "neighbouring" farmers [a clear reference to *syntelestai*] from the meanness and greed of the monks' and to concentrate monastic minds on spiritual matters. Though we have no precise details as to which monasteries were involved, it does look as though matters affecting the fiscal unit of the rural *choria* may have been used as justification for a measure which, according to Michael Psellos, had received some general support.[50]

There is no doubt, however, that a new air of purpose is evident in Alexios Komnenos' reign but the doggedness of the imperial officials was met by the opposition of equally determined monastic administrators. Rights and exemptions were brandished at every turn and the number and variety of the documents cited in many cases testifies to a highly literate and skilled bureaucracy on both sides. The establishment of the

---

[49] Harvey, *Economic expansion*, pp. 90–1, 97–9.
[50] See Attaliates, pp. 60–2; Michael Psellos, *Chronographia ou histoire d'un siècle de Byzance (976–1077)*, ed. and translated into French by E. Renauld (2 vols., *Collection byzantine*, Paris, 1926–8), VII.60, vol. II, p. 120. For the process of tax assessment, see chapter 9.

fiscal liability of the Lavra is a case in point. Sometime between 1044 and 1050, the Lavra's tax payment had been fixed at 46⅞₄ *nomismata per annum* by the *anagrapheus* Andronikos.[51] In 1079, when the effects of debasement had become only too clear to the imperial authorities, the Lavra's assessment was increased by another *anagrapheus*, John Kataphloron, to 79¾ *nomismata*, the aim of which seems to have been to compensate for the poor coinage in which the payments had hitherto been made. The monks were not prepared to support the increase and thus began a series of arrangements of some complexity between the monks of the Lavra and the officials of the *demosion*. We can, without becoming too enmeshed in the small print of the documents concerned, identify both main areas of conflict and the tactics employed by both sides.[52]

First, it was clearly important to establish how much land the Lavra really held. In 1088–9, the *hegoumenos* had stated that the Lavra held 42,705 *modioi*. This turned out to be far from the case, as we shall see, and it is somewhat surprising that his word was initially taken on the matter. It was surely a reflection of the prestige of the house. This all came out during the process of the establishment of the *epibole* by the *krites* and *anagrapheus* Niketas Xiphilinos, who was instructed by Alexios to apply a rate of 535½ *modoi* per *nomisma* in order to cover the total payment of 79¾ *nomismata* set in 1079. But Xiphilinos now discovered, after measuring them, that the true extent of the Lavra's lands was just over 47,051 *modioi*.[53] In addition, the Lavra had consistently refused to pay the established tax of 79¾ *nomismata*. From 1079–1088/9 the monks had not done so and had been allowed to keep the extra lands which should have provided the increased payment. All this was now supposed to change and the Lavra, if it persisted, was only to keep land approximating to the 46⅞₄ *nomismata* it was prepared to pay. But after Xiphilinos' discovery of the true extent of the land-holdings, he was, of course, forced to change the rate of the *epibole*. This new sum worked out at 590 *modioi* and one *litra* per *nomisma*. Under this calculation, the land covered by the tax Lavra was prepared to pay amounted to 26,671½ *modioi*, some 1,800 *modioi* more than that which they would have held under the previous rate of *epibole*, but still implying a considerable surplus of land which should have passed to the *demosion* since it was not covered by tax. Xiphilinos therefore attributed 20,380½ *modioi* to the *demosion*.[54]

In allowing the Lavra to keep the additional 1,800 *modioi*, it might be

---

[51] *Lavra*, I, no. 50 (1089).
[52] *Lavra*, I, no. 50 (1089). See Harvey, *Economic expansion*, pp. 92–101.
[53] *Lavra*, I, no. 50, ll. 14–22. For Byzantine land measurement methods, see J. Lefort, R. Bondoux, J.-C. Cheynet, J.-P. Grélois, V. Kravari and J.-M. Martin, *Géometries du fisc byzantin* (Réalités byzantines, IV, Paris, 1991).
[54] *Lavra*, I, no. 50; Svornons, 'Epibolè', p. 378.

thought that Alexios was taking a quick way out of a dispute that had dragged on for too long. But when his further actions are examined, it does look as though he was making a special case for the Lavra. In addition to the gift of land, he also agreed that the tax for the estates of the Lavra should remain for ever at the level imposed by Andronikos (46¾₄ *nomismata*). This marked one loss to the *demosion*. There was more: in 1094, after another official, Gregory Xeros had discovered that the Lavra was still holding a surplus of 11,000 *modioi* to its officially established level, the emperor first of all allowed them to keep 8,000 *modioi* of it by making an imperial gift and then, it would appear, did nothing to prevent them keeping it all. In 1109, the last document in the dossier concerning the lands of the Lavra was established after Alexios' reform of the fiscal system in 1106–9 and after examining it, we can begin to draw some conclusions about the fortunes of the Lavra during this long period of imperial enquiry and assessment. In 1107–8, another imperial gift of 16,000 *modioi* had been made from the surplus land which the monastery still held, but it was also at this time that two estates, those of Peristerai and Tzechlianes, were assigned to the *Orphanotropheion*, at first sight a victory for the imperial officials; but the monks successfully petitioned for additional land to be assigned to them to correspond to the tax payments previously made on these two estates.[55]

Thus a series of exemptions, exchanges, donations and tax adjustments, meant that, in 1109, the Lavra enjoyed the legal possession of some 47,052 *modioi* of land (essentially what Xiphilinos had found in 1088–9) and with a tax burden of 32¾₄ *nomismata*, somewhat *less* than that established as long ago as the 1040s. If, as Harvey suggests, the taxes were still being paid in low value, pre-reform *nomismata*, this would have been another advantage for the monks.[56] The end result was certainly in the Lavra's favour, as, indeed, had been some of the methods by which it had been arrived at. Among the unconventional (not to say illegal) procedures which had been allowed in the Lavra case was that by which the tax for the Lavra estates had been fixed as a global sum, regardless of the areas where these lands were situated and the local rates of *epibole* that should have applied in the case of each individual estate. This also meant that the unity of the existing *choria* was being disregarded; in a sense, the Lavra properties were being gathered together to constitute one large, imaginary *chorion*.[57]

Other houses also seem to have been able to exploit their imperial

---

[55] *Lavra*, I, nos. 50, 52 (1094), 54 (1106), 58 (1109). Harvey, *Economic expansion*, pp. 99–100.
[56] Harvey, *Economic expansion*, pp. 100–1.
[57] Svoronos, 'Epibolè', *passim*.

connections. In 1088–9, as part of his full-scale enquiry into Athonite land-holding, the hapless Niketas Xiphilinos confiscated two estates, Perigardikeia and Atoubla belonging to the Monastery of Docheiariou. He was immediately overruled by Anna Dalassene. Alexios, however, initially supported his official and Atoubla was once more made forfeit since no tax at all seemed to be being paid for it. At this point, the monks sent a *deesis* (request) to the emperor, which may have been conveyed in writing as well as orally, although a monastic delegation would have been involved either way. They were successful. The emperor issued a *pittakion* in February 1089, which allowed the monks to keep both estates, plus some 'extra' land which Xiphilinos had already sold to them, and, a most useful additional privilege, permitted them to go on paying 'the tax which they had always paid'. In other words, in an arrangement similar to that which was to be made with the Lavra, no account was to be taken now, or in the future, of any land which might be added to these two estates.[58]

Why was Alexios apparently so willing to allow these monasteries to circumvent the actions of his own officials? An important point to make at the outset is that the very fact of imperial investigation on this scale into monastic land-holding was a new departure and marked a willingness to ignore – in the interests of the *demosion* – any immunities from the attentions of imperial officials which these houses might hitherto have enjoyed. The continuing visitations by imperial officials and some of the initial decisions that Alexios made indicate that he was well aware of what the monks were up to, yet, in the end, he seems to have given in to their demands. Was he simply worn down by monastic importuning? The evidence from the *Diegesis merike* seems to indicate that Alexios was made of sterner stuff and could robustly rebuff monastic delegations when he wished to do so. But Alexios was loath to antagonise his mother, upon whom he greatly relied during the dangerous first decade of his reign, and thus acquiesced in her wishes concerning Patmos and Docheiariou. And family loyalty also played a part in the compromises over Athonite land-holding. For they should be seen in the context of the wider property holding situation in Thrace and Macedonia. It was here, as we know, that Alexios had already made wide-ranging grants to his brothers Adrian and Isaac and to other such loyal supporters as Leo Kephalas, who had had confirmation of a gift of *klasma* land near Derkos (originally given to him by Nikephoros Botaniates) granted by Alexios,

---

[58] *Docheiariou*, no. 2 (1089) is an *isokodikon* (official copy) of two documents: a *pittakion* of Alexios Komnenos of February 1089 and a *prostaxis* of Anna Dalassene of 25 March 1089. The *isokodikon* was given to Niketas Xiphilinos on 29 April 1089 and he then presented it to the monks.

probably in return for services rendered during his *coup d'état* in 1081. In addition, Kephalas was given more lands in recognition of his success in holding the town of Larissa against the onslaughts of the Norman Bohemond in 1082–3. Adrian Komnenos was granted all the *demosion*'s land on Kassandra at some point before 1084 and in 1092, Alexios had reassured the Lavriotes that he would defend the rights of the *metochion* of St Andrew of Peristerai against the 'vexations' of the agents of his brother Isaac, who were clearly active in the region.[59]

It has been suggested that the impetus for the re-examination of the assessment of Xiphilinos (which led to the enquiry of Gregory Xeros) and which was based on suggestions that the *demosion* was not receiving its just returns under Xiphilinos' adjustment of the *epibole*, may have come from the agents of Isaac Komnenos. If this was indeed the case, and imperial relatives and clients were becoming important landowners in precisely those areas in which Athonite landed interest was strongest, the concessions made to powerful monasteries may have been part of a policy of soothing ruffled feathers in an area in which Komnenan family involvement was on the increase.[60] Where family concerns came into conflict with those of long-established and powerful monasteries, Alexios was thus forced to compromise and to allow some major irregularities in land-holding and taxation to continue, albeit disguised under the description of 'imperial donation', so that, as one document put it, 'these monks should not undergo the least hardship' and that they could be allowed extra land 'for the health of the soul of the empire'.[61] But there was a new atmosphere abroad. The emperor, mindful of his rôle as protector of the monastic houses of the empire, needed to be circumspect in his actions; other members of his increasingly powerful family may have seen no reason to mute their criticisms of the over-powerful Athonite land owners. There were also other interests equally set upon re-establishing their rights.

For cases from the second half of the eleventh century concerning the affairs of the Monastery of Iviron illustrate how hostile elements, which in other circumstances might have been held at bay by imperial patronage, could now close in on a monastery which had forfeited (albeit temporarily) its claims to imperial favour. As well as the increasing challenges from local lay landowners, two other potentially hostile groups

---

[59] Grants to Adrian Komnenos were complained of in *Lavra*, I, no. 46 (August 1084). For Alexios' assurances of protection against the 'vexations' of the officials of Isaac Komnenos, see *Lavra*, I, nos. 46 and 51 (1092). They refer to lands near Thessalonike. Isaac was given lands near Kalamaria c. 1089, see *Esphigménou*, no. 5 (1095). For Leo Kephalas, see chapter 8, p. 206.

[60] Harvey, *Economic expansion*, p. 94, note 60.

[61] *Docheiariou*, no. 2 (1089).

can be identified: the officials of the local bishops and those of Hagia Sophia (the Great Church) in Constantinople. In a long-running feud with the bishop of Ezoba (in the Strymon/Struma valley), the monks of Iviron tried to reclaim property which had been lost to them as a consequence of the 'time of troubles' of the mid-eleventh century. But they were up against opponents just as well versed in legal niceties as they were themselves, as an examination of the documents in the case amply demonstrates.

By an act drawn up in August 1062, the *krites* of the theme of Boleron, Strymon and Thessalonike, Nicholas Serblias, restored to the house lands which had been usurped by the bishop of Ezoba, including a *metochion* dedicated to the Virgin at Zitenos in the district of Ezoba. The bishop had obtained a *praktikon* from a previous *krites* Michael Serblias 'as a result of false accusations of the disobedience of the monks' – a reference, perhaps, to the accusations of treason against the *hegoumenos* George I, which the Iviron monks denied. He then received two further documents from thematic officials confirming him in possession. In 1062, the *oikonomos* of Iviron, Michael Mertatos arrived (presumably in Thessalonike) with other monks and a selection of documents to prove their claim, including a *praktikon* of the then thematic official George Hexamilites, 'issued at the request of the *hegoumenos* George' (probably George III the Hagiorite, c. 1044–56), which established that the relevant *stichoi* of the *isokodikon* showed Iviron's possession of the *metochion* and its boundaries. Secondly, they produced a confirmation of the earlier document issued by the *kouropalates* John Komnenos. They also had unspecified confirmatory documents issued by various legal officials in Constantinople, the details of which have not survived. Their strongest card was the possession of an imperial instruction of Constantine X Doukas to his *doux* in Thessalonike, Nikephoros Botaniates, telling him that if the monks did possess a chrysobull or the confirmation of John Komnenos, they should be awarded the property. Nicholas Serblias was now carrying out this instruction and Iviron won the case.[62]

Iviron emerged victorious from this particular skirmish, though the case must have been a costly one to maintain, involving as it did repeated trips to Constantinople and Thessalonike. But their enemy was a foe worthy of their steel. Already in 1062 the bishop had been described as one who had 'annexed the fields and vineyards of this *metochion* . . . appropriating them to himself by incessant watchfulness and thanks to his assiduous attendance at courts'. This particular holder of the office, who is not named, was also a *synkellos* and was thus a patriarchal official with considerable experience in dealing with documents. His successor in the

[62] *Ivirôn*, II, no. 35 (1062).

see, Theodoulos, who was in office in 1085, was also concerned to take on the monks of Iviron. In March 1085, an agreement was signed concerning lands belonging to the Monastery of the Cave and its vineyards and other properties near a stream called Kostanitza immediately north-west of Ezoba. The bishop maintained that the Iviron monks had usurped the property, and after an enquiry organised by the officials of the Caesar Nikephoros Melissenos, the governor of the city of Thessalonike (a powerful individual since he was married to Alexios Komnenos' sister, Eudocia, and had once been a rival for the imperial throne), an agreement was finally made. The monks could keep a mill and vineyard associated with the property, but they lost all right to the Monastery of the Cave.[63]

In a rare case involving officials in charge of the provincial property of the Great Church, the same kind of hard-fought contest is evident. Again it was a question of Iviron land being encroached upon by outside interests. In a case which was settled in August 1071, the monks maintained that two patriarchal officials, the deacon Peter and the *protospatharios* John Iatropoulos, who were both *chartoularioi* of the bureau that looked after the property of Hagia Sophia (the *oikonomeion*) and who had previously been collectors of patriarchal dues in the Strymon region, had, with the encouragement of the local *paroikoi*, encroached upon land at Melitziane (c. 4 km north-east of Ezoba) belonging to Iviron and had assigned to it Eunouchou, a neighbouring village. In this instance, the monks had to take their case to a patriarchal tribunal, which sat in Constantinople in January 1071 and which consisted of some extremely distinguished people: the *megas oikonomos* of the Great Church, Joannikios, the metropolitans Theophilos of Heraklea and John of Sardis and two high-ranking laymen, Christopher *ton dishypaton*, the *primikerios* and *hebdomadarios* and Constantine Sideriotes, *ostiarios* and *krites*. Fortunately for them, the monks of Iviron were able to present the official *periorismos* (boundary description) of their lands at Eunouchou and the tribunal found in their favour. The patriarch then nullified the acts of the deacon Peter and John Iatropoulos. In August of 1071, the *hegoumenos* George of Iviron went to the metropolitan of Serres, Stephen, armed with a letter from the *megas oikonomos* Joannikios, which instructed him to take note of the tribunal's decision, to re-establish the boundary and to send a *praktikon* of the property to the relevant patriarchal bureau to end the conflict. After the usual on the spot inspection, the boundary was duly re-established in Iviron's favour.[64]

Apart from the intrinsic interest of this case, which gives us a rare glimpse of the officials of the Great Church at work in the provinces, there are a number of conclusions which arise from it and from other

---

[63] *Ibid.*, no. 43 (1085).   [64] *Ibid.*, no. 40 (1071).

similar cases involving the Athonite monasteries and their property. The first is that, where patronage at the highest level could not be invoked, then it was of vital importance, in any dispute, to be able to provide detailed and accurate documentary evidence of claim. Chrysobulls, legal findings, *praktika*, *periorismoi*, excerpts from cadasters – all were paraded through the courts. No longer was a word in the imperial ear quite enough. Claims had to be buttressed by documents and documents had to be drawn up according to established patterns and norms. Nowhere can the increasing sophistication of the imperial government and the power of the Byzantine bureaucracy, both ecclesiastical and lay, be better seen than in the piles of paper produced in these interminable late eleventh-century disputes. It is not surprising, therefore, that new founders, such as Pakourianos, as well as the *hegoumenoi* of monasteries such as Iviron, were concerned to have the documents enshrining their rights and exemptions listed and safely stored, for the very survival of their houses could come to depend on them.[65]

Secondly, we have to ask whether, in the new circumstances of increasing imperial vigilance over fiscal and legal rights, the monasteries of the empire suffered any serious set-backs to the process of expansion of their power and influence witnessed during the course of the eleventh century. It is a question difficult to answer, since our evidence comes almost entirely from the Athonite archives and it is thus confined to a relatively small geographical area. There were some losses (such as the confiscations of Lavra land to the *Orphanotropheion*), but the general picture seems to be one of increasing monastic influence in the northern themes of the empire. Donations of land (such as the Radolibos estates to Iviron) continued to be made to the Athonite houses. Monetary donations (such as those from Kale and Symbatios Pakourianos) continued to flood in. Attempts by outside interests to claim property or dues were rigorously, and for the most part successfully, resisted. New houses, such as those founded by Attaliates and Pakourianos and the Monastery of the Evergetis in Constantinople all possessed lands in the region to the north of the city, thus increasing monastic influence in the tenurial structure of the area.[66]

In the eastern provinces and in southern Italy, the situation was somewhat different. We know next to nothing about the fortunes of the monasteries of the eastern frontier or Anatolia, but can surely surmise

---

[65] See *ibid.*, no. 41 (1071), where the importance of chrysobulls and their reconfirmation is succinctly put: 'the safety of all these properties was assured thanks to the chrysobulls delivered by previous emperors . . . but the memory of the chrysobulls had been lost in the same way as great deeds which do not have speeches to praise them fall into oblivion.' For Pakourianos' chrysobulls, see note 45, above.

[66] See chapter 8.

that many of them were destroyed. Certainly, the threat (actual or real) of Turkish attack was enough to drive Christodoulos away from Mount Latros and subsequently from Strobilos and even the island of Patmos itself. The destruction of the archives of many of the houses of Asia Minor was not, after all, carried out in isolation. It implied damage to the monasteries themselves and the dispersal of their monks. Though some of the wall paintings of the rock-cut monasteries of Cappadocia have been dated to the late eleventh century and beyond, it is really only on the western and Pontic coasts of Asia Minor and on some of the islands of the Aegean that we can see monastic life continuing, and even there the threat of attack made existence extremely precarious.[67]

In southern Italy, even though the mid-eleventh century brought danger from the activities of rival military forces, there is considerable evidence of Greek monasticism continuing and even, in some cases, flourishing under Norman rule. Indeed, the vast majority of the surviving documents of the Greek houses date from the mid-eleventh century onwards and increase in number in the twelfth. In the published archives of Carbone, for example, there exist only four documents dating from 1007–1050 and ten from 1050–1100, while the remainder, some fifty-four documents, date from the twelfth century. They indicate a considerable interest in the house from the surrounding Norman settlers, including donations and confirmations by Bohemond, Prince of Taranto, the political *bête noire* of the Byzantine empire in the late eleventh and early twelfth centuries, but clearly keen to play his part in the system of local monastic patronage in southern Italy, regardless of the Greek practices of the monks concerned.[68]

Other examples may be added. For although the Monastery of St Nikodemos at Kellerana was given to the newly founded Latin Abbey of the Holy Trinity at Mileto by the Norman Count Roger of Calabria and Sicily in about 1080, it survived as a Greek house until the eighteenth century. In 1457 an inspection by Athanasios Chalkeopoulos and the *hegoumenos* Makarios was received by the *hegoumenos* Benedict and twelve monks. The fabric of the house was reported to be in a good state as were its revenues, though some of the monks were found to be woefully uneducated.[69] A similar history can be suggested for the Monastery of St John Theristes, founded near Stilo in Calabria in the last years of the eleventh

---

[67] Rodley, *Cave monasteries*, pp. 8, 254; Bryer and Winfield, *Byzantine monuments and topography of the Pontos, passim*; Malamut, *Les îles*, I, pp. 91–104.
[68] Carbone, no. 74 (1125) is a confirmation by Bohemond II of privileges granted by his father 'the great Bohemond'. No. 80 (1132), is a confirmation by Roger, King of Sicily, of grants made to Carbone by Robert Guiscard, Bohemond I, Bohemond II and Richard the Seneschal, some of which must, therefore, have dated to the end of the eleventh century.
[69] *Kellerana*, introduction, pp. 3–6.

century. Here, too, the fortunes of the monastery flourished in the twelfth century under the patronage not only of the local Greek families but also the Norman princes and their wives. But it was an insular survival, for contacts with Constantinople were virtually lost and thus the exchange of monks and learning with the eastern provinces dried up.[70]

A third major conclusion must be that patronage, in all its shapes and forms, transcended all the economic and political difficulties of the eleventh century and continued to flourish in the twelfth century and beyond. For even in the darkest days of the late eleventh century, money was still forthcoming from both imperial and private purses for the endowment and support of monastic houses. True, their inhabitants often had to be given a taste of imperial authority, and there was continuing criticism, particularly by secular churchmen of their perceived 'worldly concerns', property holding and corruption by lay influence. But there was never any question about the value to the state of the life they led. No one was ever tempted to 'economise' by stopping monastic patronage. Indeed, why should they have ever thought of it, since, as we have seen, the monastic life was so intertwined in the concerns and was so firmly at the service of the laity?

It is, however, extremely difficult to make any kind of realistic judgement of the style of monasticism most prominent at the end of the eleventh century, not the least because the history of the small village foundations continues to elude us. Certainly, the surviving evidence, particularly of the *typika* of the great aristocratic foundations, would suggest that the coenobitic way had gained most favour. But there is some evidence that 'hybrid' monasteries and their charismatic founders were still to be found. St Cyril Phileotes, though he came to express suspicion of the life of the wandering monks, yet had himself lived it for a time. St Meletios of Myoupolis (Mount Kithairon, near Athens), whose houses were founded c. 1081, seems to have been seeking the kind of 'holy mountain' familiar to his earlier counterparts on Olympos or Latros and received some monetary support from Alexios Komnenos. And Christodoulos himself created in the Monastery of St John on Patmos a monastery in which provision was still made for some ascetics to live apart.[71] In the twelfth century, however, there was a growing and

---

[70] A. Guillou, *Saint-Jean Thériestès (1054–1264)* (Corpus des actes Grecs d'Italie du sud et de Sicile. Recherches d'histoire et de géographie, v, Vatican City, 1980), pp. 15–25.

[71] For St Cyril Phileotes and St Christodoulos, see chapters 2, 3 and 8. For St Meletios, see P. Armstrong, *The Lives of Meletios of Myoupolis: introduction, translation and commentary* (MA thesis, Queen's University, Belfast, 1988) and *The Lives of Meletios of Myoupolis* (Belfast Byzantine Texts and Translations, III, forthcoming). For the *roga* of 422 nomismata (possibly 432 – 6 lb) from Alexios Komnenos, see Harvey, *Economic expansion*, p. 83.

influential view that the best place for monks was in monasteries and that eccentricity and even individuality in the monastic life was doctrinally suspect.[72]

In many ways the history of the relationship between monks and laymen reflected the fortunes of the Byzantine state itself. In the late ninth century, monks were seen as the standard bearers of orthodoxy and the best living practitioners of that 'correct belief' which had helped to sustain the empire through the dark days of external attack and internal heresy. In the tenth, the new foundations and their leaders provided outlets for the growing admiration and enthusiasm of the laity and a chance for them to aspire to the 'life of the angels' on a variety of terms. Monastic saints could offer a network of protection and authority in the provinces precisely when the forces of the imperial administration were still struggling to reassert themselves there. But it was the very successes of this period which led to the corruption of the ideals of the early monastic founders. More peaceful conditions in the empire and the lessening of the danger from enemy attack were only two of the reasons which led to a rise in monastic vocations. Soon it became no longer possible for increasing monastic numbers to be accommodated in restricted physical and economic surroundings and it was, above all, in the tensions over land-holding that conflicts between the monks and their lay neighbours first began to arise.

It was particularly in protecting their landed fortunes that monks began to emulate the legal devices of the lay world and began to draw upon the spiritual networks centred upon their houses and the lasting prestige of their founders. Protectors were called upon and privileges were exacted in the harsh world of the eleventh century, when the tension between the need for an increase in the real resources of the state and the imperial responsibility for the preservation of monastic life throughout the empire was at its height. In the last analysis, Alexios Komnenos, like many a ruler before him, seems to have felt that the spiritual returns provided by monastic intercessions for the survival and protection of the imperial power outweighed the shortfall in financial returns implicit in the monetary endowments and exemptions in which he acquiesced. But the tide was on the turn. For the twelfth century saw not only the powers of the secular government firmly gathered into the hands of the imperial power, but also the increasing imposition of imperial views on spiritual matters. The practitioners of the monastic life became increasingly subject to criticism and rebuke, their individuality stifled in a new era of repression and conformity. Holy men there were, but their continuing

---

[72] See Magdalino, 'Byzantine holy man in the twelfth century', and, most recently, *ibid.*, *The empire of Manuel I Komnenos* (Cambridge, 1993).

popularity in many quarters was against a barrage of criticism from court-orientated intellectuals and the secular church. Where once miracle working, predictions and cures had been admired, now scepticism and fear of charlatans was evident. The monastic saints were deemed to be figures of the past; the present was a world in which the figure of the monk had, for many, lost much of its spiritual aura.

Imperial privileges to monasteries, c. 900–1118

	Athos	Xeropotamou	Lavra	Iviron	Vatopedi	Docheiariou	Xenophon	Amalfitan
Basil I	*							
Leo VI	*							
Alexander								
Constantine VII (913–20)								
Romanos Lekapenos	*	*						
Constantine VII (945–59)	*							
Romanos II	*							
Nikephoros Phokas	*		*					
John Tzimiskes	*		*					
Basil II			*	*			*	
Constantine VIII								
Romanos III Argyros								
Michael IV Paphlago					*			
Michael V								
Zoe								
Constantine IX Monomachos	*		*	*	*			
Theodora					*			
Michael VI	*		*		*			
Isaac Komnenos					*			*
Constantine X Doukas	*		*	*				
Eudocia								
Romanos IV Diogenes								
Michael VII Doukas	*							
Nikephoros III Botaniates	*		*	*	*		*	
Alexios Komnenos	*		*	*	*	*	*	*

Kolobos	St Andrew	tou Atho	Polygyros	Leontia	Olympos	Latros	Kymnias	Chryse Petra	Mykale	Galesion	Chios	Patmos	Attaliates	Stroumitza	Bačkovo
*					*	*	*	*	*						
*	*	*	*	*											
*	*														
					*		*								
					*						*				
										*	*				
											*				
											*				
											*				
											*				
											*		*		*
											*	*	*		*
												*		*	*

Bibliography

———————————◆———————————

Works given in the abbreviations list are not included.

PRIMARY SOURCES

Ahrweiler, H. 'Un discours inédit de Constantin VII Porphyrogénète', *TM*, 2 (1967), 393–404, reprinted in *Etudes sur les structures administratives*, article XII.

Armstrong, P. *The Lives of Meletios of Myoupolis: introduction, translation and commentary* (Belfast Byzantine Texts and Translations, III, forthcoming).

Athanasius of Alexandria, *Life of St Anthony*, translated R. T. Meyer (Ancient Christian Writers, X, Westminster, Md., 1950).

Balsamon, Theodore *Comment. in can. viii Conc. Chalc. PG*, 137.

Comment. in can. viii Conc. Oec. iv, RP, II, p. 236.

Comment. in can. xxxi Conc. SS. Apost., RP, II, pp. 40–2.

Basil of Caesarea, *Constitutiones monasticae*, *PG*, 31, cols. 1321–1428.

Boïnes, K. *Akolouthia hierea tou hosiou kai theophorou patros hemon Christodoulou* (3rd edn., Athens, 1884).

Brand, C. M. 'Two Byzantine treatises on taxation', *Traditio*, 25 (1967), 35–60, pp. 48–57 (*Marcian Treatise*), pp. 57–60 (*Vademecum*).

The Chronicle of Theophanes: an English translation of anni mundi 6095–6306 (AD 602–813) with introduction and notes, ed. and trans. H. Turtledove (Philadelphia, 1982).

Darrouzès, J. 'Dossier sur le charisticariat', in *Polychronion. Festschrift Franz Dölger zum 75. Geburtstag* (Heidelberg, 1966), pp. 150–65.

Epistoliers byzantins du Xe siècle (Archives de l'Orient Chrétien, VI, Paris, 1966).

Delehaye, H. 'Le testament de Jean l'Etranger', in 'Deux typica byzantins de l'époque des Paléologues', *Mémoires de l'Académie royale de Belgique, Classe des lettres*, 13 (1921), 1–213, appendix, pp. 188–96, reprinted in *Synaxaires byzantins, ménologes, typica* (London, 1977), article VI.

'Les femmes stylites', *AB*, 27 (1908), 391–2.

Synaxarium ecclesiae Constantinopolitanae e Codice Sirmondiano (Brussels, 1902).

Bibliography

Dmitrievskii, A. *Opisanie liturgicheskikh rukopisei kharaniashchikhsia v bibliotekakh pravoslavnago vostoka* (2 vols., Kiev, 1895–1901, reprinted Hildesheim, 1965), I: *Typika.*

Dölger, F. *Aus den Schatzkammern des heiligen Berges* (Munich, 1948).

Epanagoge (Eisagoge), Zepos, II.

Eustathii Metropolitae Thessalonicensis Opuscula, ed. G. L. F. Tafel (Frankfurt-am-Main, 1832, reprinted Amsterdam, 1964).

Eustratiades, S. 'Typikon tes Mones tou hagiou megalomartyros Mamantos', *Hellenika*, 1 (1928), 256–311

Feissel, D. and Philippides-Braat, A. 'Inventaires en vue d'un recueil des inscriptions historiques de Byzance. III: Inscriptions du Péloponnèse (à l'exception de Mistra)', *TM*, 9 (1985), 267–395.

Gautier, P. 'Diatribes de Jean l'Oxite contre Alexis Ier Comnène', *REB*, 28 (1970), 5–35.

'L'édit d'Alexis Ier sur la réforme du clergé', *REB*, 31 (1973), 165–201.

'Eloge funèbre de Nicolas de la Belle Source par Michel Psellos, moine à l'Olympe', *Byzantina*, 6 (1954), 9–69.

'Le typikon du Christ Sauveur Pantokrator', *REB*, 32 (1974), 1–45.

Gouillard, J. '*Le Synodikon de l'Orthodoxie*, édition et commentaire', *TM*, 2 (1967), 1–316.

Grumel, V. 'Les documents athonites concernant l'affaire de Léon de Chalcédoine', *Miscellanea G. Mercati*, 3, published as *Studi e Testi*, 128 (1946), 116–35.

Guillou, A. *Saint-Jean Théristès (1054–1264) (Corpus des actes grecs d'Italie du sud et de Sicile. Recherches d'histoire et de géographie*, v, Vatican City, 1980).

Hypotyposis katastaseos tes lauras tou hosiou Athanasiou, in Meyer, *Haupturkunden*, 130–40.

Justinian, *Novellae*, in *CIC*, III.

Karagiannopoulos, J. 'Fragmente aus dem *Vademecum* eines Byzantinischen Finanzbeamten', in *Polychronion. Festschrift Franz Dölger*, 318–24.

Kurtz, E. 'Das Klerikers Gregorios Bericht über Leben, Wunderthaten und Translation der hl. Theodora von Thessalonich', *Zapiski Imperatorskoi Akademii nauk, ist.-fil. otdelenie*, 8th ser. 6/1 (1902), 1–49 (text, 37–59).

Life of St Athanasia of Aegina, ed. and English summary, L. Carras, in *Maistor: Classical, Byzantine and Renaissance Studies for Robert Browning*, ed. A. Moffat (Byzantina Australiensia, v, Canberra, 1984), pp. 199–224 (text, pp. 212–24).

Life of St Irene of Chrysobalanton, ed. and translated J. O. Rosenqvist (Acta Universitatis Upsaliensis, Studia Byzantina Upsaliensis, 1, Uppsala, 1986).

Life of St Nikon, ed. and translated D. F. Sullivan (Brookline, Mass., 1987).

Marcian Treatise, see Dölger, *Finanzverwaltung*, pp. 113–23 and Brand, 'Two Byzantine treatises', pp. 48–57.

Il Menologio di Basilio II (Cod. Vaticanus greco, 1613), 2 vols. (*Codices e Vaticanis Selecti*, Turin, 1907).

Michaelis Pselli Scripta minora, ed. E. Kurtz and F. Drexl (2 vols., Milan, 1936–41).

Bibliography

Michel Psellos Chronographie ou histoire d'un siècle de Byzance (976–1077), ed. E. Renauld (2 vols., Collection byzantine, Paris, 1926–8).

Nicephori Bryennii Historiarum libri quattuor, ed. and French translation P. Gautier (CFHB, IX, Ser. Bruxellen., Brussels, 1975).

Noailles, P. and Dain, A. *Les novelles de Léon VI le Sage* (Paris, 1944).

The Paterik *of the Kievan Caves Monastery*, translated M. Heppell (Harvard Library of Early Ukrainian Literature, *English translations*, I, Cambridge, Mass., 1989).

Petit, L. 'Typikon du monastère de la Kosmosotira près d'Aenos (1152)', *IRAIK*, 13 (1908), 117–77.

Sathas, K. A. *Mesaionike Bibliotheke* (7 vols., Athens/Paris, Venice/Paris, 1872–94).

Speck, P. *Theodoros Studites. Jamben auf verschiedene Gegenstände* (Supplementa Byzantina, I, Berlin, 1968).

Symeon the New Theologian, *Catechèses*, ed. B. Krivochéine, translated J. Paramelle (3 vols., Sources Chrétiennes, 96, 104, 113, Paris, 1963–5).

Chapitres théologiques, gnostiques et pratiques, ed. and translated J. Darrouzès and J. Neyrand (Sources Chrétiennes, 51, 2nd edn., Paris, 1980).

The Discourses, translation of the *Catechèses* by C. J. deCatanzaro (New York, 1980).

The Practical and Theological Chapters and the Three Theological Discourses, translated P. McGuckin (Cistercian Studies, 41, Kalamazoo, Mich., 1982).

Traités théologiques et éthiques, ed. and translated J. Darrouzès (2 vols., Sources Chrétiennes, 122, 129, Paris, 1966–7).

Syntagma canonum, *PG*, 104, cols. 441–976.

Theodori Studitae opera omnia, *PG*, 99.

Theophylacti Achridensis orationes, tractatus, carmina; epistulae, ed. and French translation P. Gautier (2 vols., CFHB, XVI/1–2, Series Thessalon. Thessalonike, 1980).

Three Byzantine military treatises, ed. and translated G. Dennis (CFHB, XXV, Ser. Washington., Dumbarton Oaks Texts, IX, Washington, DC, 1985).

Vasiliev, A. A. and Canard, M. *Byzance et les arabes* (2 vols. in 3, Corpus Bruxellense Historiae Byzantinae, 1–2/2, Brussels, 1935–68), II/2: *La dynastie Macédonienne (867–959). Extraits des sources arabes.*

Veselovskii, A. N. 'Zhitie sv. Vasiliya Novogo', in *Sbornik Otdeleniya Russkogo Yazyka i Slovesnosti Imp. Akad. Nauk*, 46 (1890); 53 (1892), *Prilozheniya.*

La Vie de Théodore de Sykéon, ed. and translated A.-J. Festugière (2 vols., Subsidia Hagiographica, XLVIII, Brussels, 1970).

Vie et office de Saint Euthyme le Jeune, ed. L. Petit, *ROC*, 8 (1903), 168–205.

Vilinskii, S. G. *Zhitie sv. Vasiliya Novogo v russkoi literature* (2 vols., Odessa, 1911–13).

Vita et conversatio sancti patris nostri et confessoris S. Theodori abbatis monasterii Studii, *PG*, 99, cols. 233–328.

Vita S. Georgii Hagioritas, ed. and translated P. Peeters, in 'Histoires monastiques géorgiennes', *AB*, 36/7 (1917–19), 74–159.

Bibliography

SECONDARY SOURCES

Abrahamse, D. deF. 'Women's monasticism in the middle Byzantine period: problems and prospects', *BF*, 9 (1985), 35–58.

Ahrweiler, H. *Byzance: les pays et les territoires* (London, 1976).

'Le Charisticariat et autres formes d'attribution de fondations pieuses au Xe–XIe siècles', *ZRVI*, 10 (1967), 1–27, reprinted in *Etudes sur les structures administratives*, article VII.

'La concession des droits incorporels. Donations conditionelles', in *Actes du XIIe Congrès International d'Etudes byzantines* (3 vols., Belgrade, 1964), II, pp. 103–14, reprinted in *Etudes sur les structures administratives*, article I.

Etudes sur les structures administratives et sociales de Byzance (London, 1971).

'L'histoire et la géographie de Smyrne entre les occupations turques (1081–1317), particulièrement au XIIIe siècle', *TM*, 1 (1965), 1–204, reprinted in *Byzance: les pays et les territoires*, article IV.

Alexander, P. J., ed Abrahamse, D. deF. *The Byzantine apocalyptic tradition* (Berkeley/Los Angeles/London, 1985).

Amand, L. *L'ascèse monastique de Saint Basile. Essai historique* (Maredsous, 1948).

Angold, M. *The Byzantine empire 1025–1204. A political history* (London, 1984).

Angold, M. (ed.), *The Byzantine aristocracy* (British Archaeological Reports, International Series, 221, Oxford, 1984).

Antoniadis-Bibicou, H. *Recherches sur les douanes à Byzance: l'octava, le 'kommerkion' et les commerciaires* (Cahiers des Annales, XX, Paris, 1963).

Ariès, P. *At the hour of our death*, translated H. Weaver (London, 1981).

Asdracha, C. *La région des Rhodopes aux XIIIe et XIV siècles. Etude de géographie historique* (Texte und Forschungen zur byzantinisch-neugriechischen Philologie, XLIX, Athens, 1976).

Aubineau, M. 'Les 318 serviteurs d'Abraham et le nombre des Pères au concile de Nicée (325)', *Revue d'Histoire Ecclésiastique*, 61 (1966), 5–43.

Beck, H.-G. *Kirche und theologische Literatur im byzantinischen Reich* (Handbuch der Altertumswissenschaft, XII/1.2, Munich, 1959).

Belke, K. and Restle, M. *Galatien und Lykaonien* (*TIB*, 4, Vienna, 1984).

Bertaux, E. *L'art de l'Italie méridionale et la fin de l'empire romain à la conquête de Charles d'Anjou*, I–III (Paris, 1903), reprinted with *Aggiornamento*, ed. A. Prandi, IV–VI (Rome, 1978).

Binon, S. *Les origines légendaires et l'histoire de Xéropotamou et de Saint-Paul* (Louvain, 1942).

Bon, A. *Le Péloponnèse byzantin jusqu'en 1204* (Bibliothèque Byzantine, Etudes, I, Paris, 1951).

Bouras, C. *Chios* (Athens, 1974).

Nea Mone on Chios. History and architecture (Athens, 1982).

Bratianu, G. I. 'Une expérience d'économie dirigée; le monopole du blé à Byzance au XIe siècle', *B*, 9 (1934), 643–62.

Bréhier, L. *Le monde byzantin* (3 vols., Paris, 1949, reprinted 1970).

'L'hagiographie byzantine des VIIIe et IXe siècles', *Journal des Savants*, 14 (1916), 458–67.

Brokaar, W. 'Basil Lekapenus', *Studia Bizantina et Neohellenica Neerlandica*, 3 (1972), 199–234.

Bibliography

Brown, P. R. L. *The cult of the saints* (London, 1981).

'The rise and function of the holy man in late antiquity', *JRS*, 61 (1971), 80–101, reprinted in *Society and the holy in late antiquity* (London, 1982), 103–52.

Bryer, A. A. M. *The empire of Trebizond and the Pontos* (London, 1980).

'The estates of the empire of Trebizond: evidence for their resources, products, agriculture, ownership and location', *Archeion Pontou*, 35 (1979), published as *Maure Thalassa. Papers given at the Twelfth Spring Symposium of Byzantine Studies, Birmingham, 1978*, pp. 370–472, reprinted in *The Empire of Trebizond and the Pontos*, article VII.

Bryer, A. A. M. and Herrin, J. (eds.), *Iconoclasm* (Birmingham, 1977).

Bryer, A. A. M. and Winfield, D. C. *The Byzantine monuments and topography of the Pontos* (2 vols., Dumbarton Oaks Studies, XX, Washington, DC, 1985).

Charanis, P. 'The monastic properties and the state in the Byzantine empire', *DOP*, 4 (1948), 53–118, reprinted in *Social, economic and political life*, article I.

'The monk as an element in Byzantine society', *DOP*, 25 (1971), 68–84, reprinted in *Social, economic and political life*, article II.

Social, economic and political life in the Byzantine empire (London, 1973).

Studies in the demography of the Byzantine empire (London, 1972).

'The transfer of population as a policy in the Byzantine empire', *Comparative Studies in Society and History*, 3/2 (1961), 140–56, reprinted in *Studies in the demography of the Byzantine empire*, article III.

Cheynet, J.-C. *Pouvoir et contestations à Byzance (963–1210)* (Byzantina Sorbonensia, IX, Paris, 1990).

Connor, C. L. *Art and miracles in medieval Byzantium: the crypt at Hosios Loukas and its frescoes* (Princeton, NJ, 1991).

Constantelos, D. *Byzantine philanthropy and social welfare* (New Brunswick, NJ, 1968).

Cormack, R. S. 'Byzantine Cappadocia: the archaic group of wall-paintings', *Journal of the British Archaeological Association*, 3rd ser., 30 (1967), 19–36, reprinted in *The Byzantine eye*, article VI.

The Byzantine eye (London, 1989).

Writing in gold: Byzantine society and its icons (London, 1985).

da Costa-Louillet, G. 'Saints de Constantinople aux VIIIe, IXe et Xe siècles', *B*, 24 (1954), 179–263, 453–511.

'Saints de Grèce aux VIIIe, IX et Xe siècles', *B*, 31 (1961), 309–69.

'Saints de Sicile et d'Italie méridionale aux VIIIe, IXe et Xe siècles'. *B*, 29–30 (1959–60), 89–173.

Dagron, G. *La romanité chrétienne en Orient. Heritages et mutations* (London, 1984).

'Quand la terre tremble', *TM*, 9 (1985), 87–103, reprinted in *La romanité chrétienne en Orient. Heritages et mutations*, article III.

Darrouzès, J. 'Le mouvement des fondations monastiques au XIe siècle', *TM*, 6 (1976), 156–76.

'Listes des Prôtes de l'Athos', in *Le Millénaire du Mont Athos*, I, 407–47.

Davies, W. and Fouracre, P. (eds.), *The settlement of disputes in early medieval Europe* (Cambridge, 1986).

de Jerphanion, G. *Une nouvelle province de l'art byzantin. Les églises rupestres de Cappadoce* (3 vols., Paris, 1925–42).

Delehaye, H. 'Les femmes stylites', *AB*, 27 (1908), 391–2.

Les légendes hagiographiques (Subsidia Hagiographica, XVII, 3rd edn., Brussels, 1927).

Les saints stylites (Subsidia Hagiographica, XIV, Brussels/Paris, 1923).

Dembinska, M. 'Diet: a comparison of food consumption between some eastern and western monasteries in the 4th–12th centuries', *B*, 55 (1985), 431–62.

De Meester, P. *De monachico statu iuxta disciplinam byzantinam* (Vatican City, 1942).

Dölger, F. *Beiträge zur Geschichte der byzantinischen Finanzverwaltung besonders des 10. und 11. Jahrhunderts* (Byzantinisches Archiv, IX, Leipzig/Berlin, 1927).

'Ein Fall slavischer Einsiedlung im Hinterland von Thessalonike im 10. Jahrhundert', *Sitzungsberichte der Bayerischen Akademie der Wissenschaften, phil.-hist. Klasse* (1952), 1, 3–28.

Regesten der Kaiserurkunden des oströmischen Reiches von 563–1453 (3 vols., Munich/Berlin, 1924–32, reprinted 3 vols. in 1, Hildesheim, 1976).

Drew-Bear, T. and Koder, J. 'Ein byzantinischer Kloster am Berg Tmolos', *JÖB*, 38 (1988), 197–215.

Duby, G. *Rural economy and country life in the medieval West*, translated C. Postan (London, 1968).

Ducellier, A. 'Les séismes en Méditerranée orientale du XIe au XIIe siècle. Problèmes de méthode et résultats provisoires', *Actes du XVe Congrès Internationale d'Etudes Byzantines* (4 vols., Athens, 1980), IV: *Communications*, pp. 103–13.

Dvornik, F. *Byzantine missions among the Slavs* (Brunswick, NJ, 1970).

Edwards, G. R. 'Purgatory: "Birth" or evolution?', *Journal of Ecclesiastical History*, 36 (1985), 634–46.

Every, G. 'Toll gates on the air way', *Eastern Churches Review*, 8 (1976), 139–51.

Festugière, A.-J. 'Notes sur la vie de saint Cyrille le Philéote', *REG*, 80 (1967), 430–44; 81 (1969), 88–109.

Forsyth, G. H. and Weitzmann, K. *The Monastery of St Catherine on Mount Sinai.* I: *The fortress of Justinian* (Ann Arbor, Mich., 1973).

Foss, C. 'Strobilos and related sites', *Anatolian Studies*, 38 (1988), 147–74.

Frantz, A. *The Church of the Holy Apostles* (The Athenian Agora, XX, American School at Athens, 1971).

Frazee, C. 'St Theodore of Stoudios and ninth-century monasticism in Constantinople', *Studia Monastica*, 23 (1981), 27–58.

Galatariotou, C. 'Byzantine *ktetorika typika*: a comparative study', *REB*, 45 (1987), 77–138.

'Byzantine women's monastic communities: the evidence of the *typika*', *JÖB*, 38 (1988), 263–90.

The making of a saint: the life, times and sanctification of Neophytos the Recluse (Cambridge, 1991).

Gautier, P. 'Jean V l'Oxite, patriarche d'Antioche. Notice biographique', *REB*, 22 (1964), 128–57.

'Le synode des Blachernes (fin 1094). Etude prosopographique', *REB*, 29 (1971), 213–84.

Gedeon, M. 'Mnemeia latreias christianikes en Ganochorois', *Ekklesiastike Aletheia*, 32 (1912), 304, 311–13, 325–7, 352–5, 389–92.

Gero, S. 'Byzantine iconoclasm and the failure of a medieval reformation', in J. Gutman (ed.), *The image and the word: confrontations in Judaism, Christianity and Islam* (Missoula, Mont., 1977), pp. 49–62.

Grégoire, H. *Autour de l'épopée byzantine* (London, 1975).

'La lieu de naissance de Romain Lécapène et de Digénis Acritas', *B*, 8 (1933), 572–4, reprinted in *Autour de l'épopée byzantine*, article x/2.

Grierson, P. 'The tombs and *obits* of the Byzantine emperors (337–1042)', *DOP*, 16 (1962), 3–60.

Grosdidiers de Matons, J. 'Les thèmes d'édification dans la vie d'André Salos', *TM*, 4 (1970), 277–328.

Grumel, V. *La chronologie* (Bibliothèque byzantine, Traité d'Etudes byzantines, I, Paris, 1958).

Guilland, R. *Recherches sur les institutions byzantines* (2 vols., Berliner Byzantinische Arbeiten, xxxv, Berlin/Amsterdam, 1967).

Guillou, A. *La civilisation byzantine* (Paris, 1974).

Culture et société en Italie byzantine (VIe–XIe siècles) (London, 1978).

'Des collectivités rurales à la collectivité urbaine en Italie méridionale byzantine (VIe–XIe s.)', *BCH*, 100 (1976), 315–25, reprinted in *Culture et société*, article xiv.

'Grecs d'Italie du sud et de Sicile au moyen âge: les moines', *Mélanges d'archéologie et d'histoire de l'Ecole Française de Rome*, 75 (1963), 79–110, reprinted in *Studies in Byzantine Italy*, article xii.

'L'Italie byzantine du IXe au XIe siècles: Etat des questions', in Prandi (ed.), *Aggiornamento*, 3–47.

'Italie méridionale byzantine ou byzantins en Italie méridionale?', *B*, 44 (1974), 152–70, reprinted in *Culture et société*, article xv.

'La Lucanie byzantine. Etude de géographie historique', *B*, 35 (1965), 119–49, reprinted in *Studies in Byzantine Italy*, article x.

'Notes sur la société dans le Katépanat d'Italie au XIe siècle', *Mélanges d'Archéologie et d'Histoire*, 78 (1966), 439–65, reprinted in *Studies in Byzantine Italy*, article xiii.

Studies in Byzantine Italy (London, 1970).

Gyóni, M. 'Les vlaques du Mont Athos au début du XIIe siècle', *Etudes Slaves et Roumaines*, 1 (1948), 30–42.

Hackel, S. (ed.), *The Byzantine saint* (Studies Subordinate to Sobornost, v London, 1981).

Hadjinicolaou-Marava, A. *Recherches sur la vie des esclaves dans le monde byzantin* (Collection de l'Institut Français d'Athènes, lxv, Athens, 1950).

Halkin, F. 'L'hagiographie byzantine au service de l'histoire', *Proceedings of the XIII International Congress of Byzantine Studies, Oxford, 1966, Main Papers* (Oxford, 1968), pp. 345–9.

Bibliography

Harvey, A. *Economic expansion in the Byzantine empire* (Cambridge, 1989).

Hausherr, I. *Spiritual direction in the early Christian east*, translated A. P. Gythiel (Cistercian Studies, 116, Kalamazoo, Mich., 1990).

'Vocation chrétienne et vocation monastique selon les pères', in *Etudes de spiritualité orientale*, OCA, 188, Rome, 1969, pp. 403–85.

Hendy, M. F. *Coinage and money in the Byzantine empire 1081–1261* (Dumbarton Oaks Studies, XII, Washington, DC, 1969).

The economy, fiscal administration and coinage of Byzantium (London, 1989).

'The Gornoslav Hoard, the Emperor Frederick I and the Monastery of Bachkovo', in C. N. L. Brooke, B. H. I. H. Stewart, J. G. Pollard and T. R. Volk (eds.), *Studies in numismatic method: essays presented to Philip Grierson* (Cambridge, 1983), pp. 179–91, reprinted in *The economy, fiscal administration and coinage of Byzantium*, article XI.

Studies in the Byzantine monetary economy c. 300–1450 (Cambridge, 1985).

Herman, E. 'Die Regelung der Armut in den byzantinischen Klöstern', *OCP*, 7 (1941), 406–60.

'Ricerche sulle istituzioni monastiche bizantine. Typika ktetorika, caristicari e monasteri "liberi"', *OCP*, 6 (1940), 293–375.

'La "stabilitas loci" nel monachismo bizantino', *OCP*, 21 (1955), 115–42.

Herrin, J. 'Ideals of charity, realities of welfare: the philanthropic activity of the Byzantine church', in Morris (ed.), *Church and people in Byzantium*, pp. 151–64.

Hild, F. and Hellenkemper, H. *Kilikien und Isaurien* (*TIB*, 5, 2 vols., Vienna, 1990).

Holl, K. *Enthusiasmus und Bussgewalt beim griechischen Monchtum. Eine Studie zu Symeon dem Neuen Theologen* (Leipzig, 1898).

Hunger, H. *Byzantinistische Grundlagenforschung* (London, 1973).

'*Philanthropia*. Eine griechische Wortprägung auf ihrem Wege von Aischylos bis Theodoros Metochites', *Anzeiger der phil.-hist. Klasse Österreichische Akademie der Wissenschaften*, 100, 1963, pp. 1–20, reprinted in *Byzantinistische Grundlagenforschung*, article XIII.

Prooimion. Elemente der byzantinischen Kaiseridee in den Arengen der Urkunden (Wiener Byzantinistische Studien, I, Vienna, 1964).

Hussey, J. M. *The orthodox church in the Byzantine empire* (Oxford, 1986).

Janin, R. *La géographie ecclésiastique de l'empire byzantin*. Section one: *Le siège de Constantinople et le patriarcat oecuménique* (2 vols). II: *Les églises et les monastères des grands centres byzantins* (Paris, 1975); III: *Les églises et les monastères [de Constantinople]* (2nd edn., Paris, 1969).

Jenkins, R. J. H. 'The date of the Slav revolt in the Peloponnese under Romanos I', in *Late Christian and medieval studies in honor of A. M. Friend, Jr* (Princeton, 1955), pp. 204–11, reprinted in *Studies on Byzantine history of the ninth and tenth centuries*, article XX.

Studies on Byzantine history of the ninth and tenth centuries (London, 1970).

Kähler, H. with Mango, C. *Hagia Sophia*, translated E. Childs (London, 1967).

Kallistos, Bishop of Diokleia, 'The spiritual father in Saint John Climacus and St Symeon the New Theologian', *Studia Patristica*, 8/2 (1990), reprinted as foreword to Hausherr, *Spiritual direction*.

Bibliography

Kaplan, K. 'L'économie paysanne dans l'empire byzantin du Ve au XIe siècle', *Klio*, 68/1 (1986), 198–232.

Les hommes et la terre à Byzance du VIe au XIe siècle. Propriété et exploitation du sol (Byzantina Sorbonensia, x, Paris, 1992).

'Les monastères et le siècle à Byzance: les investissements des laïques au XIe siècle', *Cahiers de Civilisation Médiévale*, 27/1–2 (1984), 71–83.

Karagiannopoulos, J. (ed.), *Polychronicon. Festschrift Franz Dölger* (Heidelberg, 1966).

Karlin-Hayter, P. 'L'édition de la vie de S. Cyrille Philéote par E. Sargologos', *B*, 334 (1964), 607–11.

'Notes sur les archives de Patmos comme source pour la démographie et l'économie de l'île', *BF*, 5 (1977), 189–215.

Kazhdan, A. P. *Authors and texts in Byzantium* (Aldershot, 1993).

'The Byzantine family of Dermokaïtes: additions to the article by D. M. Nicol in *BS* (1974), 1–11', *BS*, 36 (1975), 192.

'Hagiographical notes', *B*, 54 (1984), 176–92, reprinted in *Authors and texts in Byzantium*, article IV.

'Hermitic, cenobitic and secular ideals in Byzantine hagiography of the ninth century', *Greek Orthodox Theological Review*, 30/4 (1985), 473–87.

Kazhdan, A. P. and Constable, G. *People and power in Byzantium: an introduction to modern Byzantine studies* (Washington, DC, 1982).

Kazhdan, A. P. and Epstein, A. W. *Change in Byzantine culture in the eleventh and twelfth centuries* (The transformation of the classical heritage, VII, Berkeley/Los Angeles/London, 1985).

Kazhdan, A. P. and Franklin, S. 'Eustathius of Thessalonica: the life and opinions of a twelfth-century Byzantine rhetor', in *Studies in Byzantine literature of the eleventh and twelfth centuries* (Cambridge/Paris, 1984), IV.

Kazhdan, A. P. and Maguire, H. 'Byzantine hagiographical texts as sources on art', *DOP*, 45 (1991), 1–22.

Kislinger, E. 'Der Pantokrator-Xenon, ein trügerisches Ideal?', *JÖB*, 37 (1987), 173–9.

Koder, J. 'Die Metochia der Athos-Klöster auf Sithonia und Kassandreia', *JÖBG*, 16 (1967), 211–24.

Kolias, G. *Léon Choirosphaktes, Magistre, proconsul et patrice. Biographie-Correspondance (Texts et traduction)* (Texte und Forschungen zur byzantinisch-neugriechischen Philologie, XXXI, Athens, 1939).

Konidares, I. M. *To dikaion tes monasteriakes periousias apo tou 9ou mechri kai tou 12ou aionos* (Athens, 1979).

Krivochéine, B. *In the light of Christ. St Symeon the New Theologian 949–1022: life, spirituality, doctrine*, translated A. P. Gythiel (Crestwood, NJ, 1986).

Laiou, A. E. 'Observations on the life and ideology of Byzantine women', *BF*, 9 (1985), 59–102.

Lampe, G. W. H. *A patristic Greek lexicon* (Oxford, 1961).

Leclercq, J. 'Monachisme et pérégrination du XIe au XII siècle', *Studia Monastica*, 3 (1961), 33–52.

Lefort, J. 'Le cadastre de Radolibos (1103), les géomètres et leurs mathématiques', *TM*, 8 (1981), 269–313.

'Radolibos: population et paysage', *TM*, 9 (1985), 195–234.

Bibliography

Villages de Macédoine. i: *La Chalcidique occidentale* (Travaux et Mémoires du Centre de Recherche d'Histoire et Civilisation de Byzance, Monographies, I, Paris, 1982).

Lefort, J. and Papachryssanthou, D. 'Les premiers Géorgiens à l'Athos dans les documents byzantins', *Bedi Kartlisa*, 41 (1983), 27–33.

Lefort, J., Bondoux, R., Cheynet, J.-C., Grélois, J.-P., Kravari, V. and Martin, J.-M., *Géométries du fisc byzantin* (Réalités byzantines, IV, Paris, 1991).

Le Goff, J. *The birth of Purgatory*, translated A. Goldhammer (London, 1984).

Lemerle, P. *The agrarian history of Byzantium*, revised English edn., translated G. MacNiocaill (Galway, 1979).

'Les archives du monastère des Amalfitains au Mont Athos', *EEBS*, 23 (1953), 548–66.

Byzantine humanism; the first phase: notes and remarks on education and culture in Byzantium from its origins to the 10th century, translated H. Lindsay and A. Moffat (Byzantina Australiensia, III, Canberra, 1986).

Cinq études sur le XIe siècle byzantin (Le monde byzantin, Paris, 1977).

Leroy, J. 'La conversion de S. Athanase l'Athonite à l'idéal cénobitique et l'influence studite', in *Le millénaire du Mont Athos*, I, 101–20.

'La reforme studite', in *Il monachesimo orientale* (OCA, 153, 1959), 181–214.

'La vie quotidienne du moine studite', *Irénikon*, 27 (1954), 21–50.

'S. Athanase l'Athonite et la Règle de S. Benoît', *Revue d'Ascétique et de Mystique*, 29 (1953), 108–22.

Macrides, R. 'The Byzantine god-father', *BMGS*, 11 (1987), 139–62.

'*Nomos* and *kanon* on paper and in court', in Morris (ed.), *Church and people in Byzantium*, pp. 61–85.

Macridy, T., Megaw, A. H., Mango, C. and Hawkins, E. J. W. 'The Monastery of Lips (Fenari Isa Camii at Istanbul)', *DOP*, 18 (1954), 249–315.

Magdalino, P. 'The Byzantine holy man in the twelfth century', in Hackel (ed.), *Byzantine saint*, pp. 51–66.

'Observations on the *Nea Ekklesia* of Basil I', *JÖB*, 37 (1987), 51–64.

Magoulias, H. 'The lives of Byzantine saints as sources of data for the history of magic in the 6th and 7th century AD: sorcery, relics and icons', *B*, 38 (1967), 228–67.

Malamut, E. 'A propos de Bessai d'Ephèse', *REB*, 43 (1985), 243–51.

Les îles de l'empire byzantin, VIIIe–XIIe siècles (2 vols., Byzantina Sorbonensia, VIII, Paris, 1988).

Mango, C. *The art of the Byzantine empire 312–1453: sources and documents* (Englewood Cliffs, NJ, 1972, reprinted Toronto, 1986).

Byzantine architecture (London, 1986).

Byzantium and its image: history and culture of the Byzantine empire and its heritage (London, 1984).

Byzantium: the empire of New Rome (London, 1986).

'Diabolus byzantinus', *DOP*, 46 (1992), 215–23.

'Historical introduction', in Bryer and Herrin, *Iconoclasm*, pp. 5–6.

'The legend of Leo the Wise', *ZRVI*, 65 (1960), 59–93, reprinted in *Byzantium and its image*, article XVI.

'The Life of St Andrew the Fool reconsidered', *Rivista di Studi bizantini e Slavi*, 2 (1982), published as *Miscellanea A. Pertusi*, I–II, vol. II, pp. 297–313.

'The liquidation of iconoclasm and the Patriarch Photios', in Bryer and Herrin, *Iconoclasm*, pp. 133–40, reprinted in *Byzantium and its image*, article XIII.

'Les monuments de l'architecture du XIe siècle et leur signification historique et sociale', *TM*, 6 (1976), 351–64.

'St Anthusa of Mantineon and the family of Constantine V', *AB*, 100 (1982), 401–9, reprinted in *Byzantium and its image*, article IX.

Mango, C. and Hawkins, E. J. W. 'Report on field work in Istanbul and Cyprus, 1962–3', *DOP*, 18 (1964), 319–40.

Mango, C., Hawkins, E. J. W. and Boyd, S. 'The Monastery of St Chrysostomos at Koutsovendis (Cyprus). Part I: Description', *DOP*, 44 (1990), 63–94.

Mango, C. and Ševčenko, I. 'Some churches and monasteries on the southern shore of the Sea of Marmara', *DOP*, 27 (1973), 235–77.

Martin-Hisard, B. 'Trébizonde et la culte de Saint Eugène (6e–11e s.)', *Revue des Etudes Arméniennes*, n.s., 14 (1980), 307–43.

Ménager, L.-R. 'La byzantinisation réligieuse de l'Italie méridionale (IX–XIIe siècles) et la politique monastique des Normands d'Italie', *Revue d'Histoire Ecclesiastique*, 53 (1958), 747–74, 54 (1959), 5–40, reprinted in L.-R. Ménager, *Hommes et institutions de l'Italie normande* (London, 1981), I.

Menthon, B. *Une terre de légende. L'Olympe de Bithynie* (Paris, 1935).

Meyendorff, J. *Byzantine theology* (London/Oxford, 1975).

Le millénaire du Mont Athos, 963–1963. Etudes et mélanges (2 vols., Chevetogne, 1963–4).

Millet, G. *Le monastère de Daphni. Histoire, architecture, mosaïques* (Paris, 1899).

Misch, G. *Geschichte der Autobiographie* (4 vols., Frankfurt, 1949–62).

Moran, K. *The ordinary chants of the Byzantine mass* (2 vols., Hamburg, 1975).

Morris, R. 'The Byzantine aristocracy and the monasteries', in Angold, *Byzantine aristocracy*, pp. 112–37.

'Dispute settlement in the Byzantine provinces in the tenth century', in Davies and Fouracre (eds.), *The settlement of disputes in early medieval Europe*, pp. 125–47.

'Divine diplomacy in the late eleventh century', *BMGS*, 16 (1992), 147–56.

'Legal terminology in monastic documents of the tenth and eleventh centuries', *XVI Internationaler Byzantinistenkongress, Wien, 1981, Akten*, II/2, published as *JÖB*, 32/2 (1981), 281–90.

'Monasteries and their patrons in the tenth and eleventh centuries', *BF*, 10 (1985), published as *Perspectives in Byzantine history and culture*, ed. J. F. Haldon and J. Kouloumides, pp. 185–231.

'The political saint in Byzantium in the tenth and eleventh centuries', in *Politik und Heiligenverehrung in Hochmittelalter*, ed. J. Petersohn, published as *Vorträge und Forschungen*, 42 (1993), 385–402.

'The powerful and the poor in tenth-century Byzantium: law and reality', *PP*, 73 (1976), 3–27.

'Spiritual fathers and temporal patrons: logic and contradiction in Byzantine monasticism in the tenth century', *Revue Bénédictine*, 103 (1993), 273–88.

'Succession and usurpation: politics and rhetoric in the late tenth century', in P. Magdalino (ed.), *New Constantines: the rhythm of imperial renewal in Byzantine history* (Aldershot, 1994), pp. 199–214.

'The two faces of Nikephoros Phokas', *BMGS*, 12 (1988), 83–115.

Morris, R. (ed.), *Church and people in Byzantium* (Birmingham, 1991).

Morrisson, C. 'La dévaluation de la monnai byzantine au XIe siècle: essai d'interprétation', *TM*, 6 (1976), 3–48.

'La logarikè: réforme monétaire et réforme fiscale sous Alexis I Comnène', *TM*, 7 (1979), 419–64.

Mouriki, D. 'Stylistic trends in monumental painting of Greece during the eleventh and twelfth centuries', *DOP*, 34–6 (1980–1), 77–124.

Mullett, M. E. 'Byzantium: a friendly society?', *PP*, 118 (1988), 3–24.

'Patronage in action: the problems of an eleventh-century bishop', in Morris (ed.), *Church and people in Byzantium*, pp. 125–47.

Theophylact through his letters: the two worlds of an exile bishop (Doctoral thesis, 2 vols., University of Birmingham, 1981).

'Writing in early medieval Byzantium', in R. McKitterick (ed.), *The uses of literacy in early medieval Europe* (Cambridge, 1990).

Nicol, D. M. 'The Byzantine family of Dermokaïtes, c. 940–1453', *BS*, 35 (1974), 1–11.

Noret, J. 'La vie la plus ancienne d'Athanase l'Athonite confrontée à d'autres vies des saints', *AB*, 103 (1985), 243–51.

Nystazopoulou, M. G. 'Ho epi tou kanikleiou kai he ephoreia tes en Patmo mones', *Symmeikta*, 1 (1966), 76–94.

Obolensky, D. *The Byzantine commonwealth* (London, 1971).

Ogilvie, A. G. 'A contribution to the geography of Macedonia', *Geographical Journal*, 55 (1920), 1–30.

'Physiography and settlement in southern Macedonia', *Geographical Review*, 11 (1921), 172–91.

Oikonomidès, N. *Byzantium from the ninth century to the Fourth Crusade* (Aldershot, 1992).

'Das Verfalland im 10–11. Jahrhundert: Verkauf und Besteuerung', *Fontes Minores*, 7 (*Forschungen zur Byzantinischen Rechtsgeschichte*, 14, Frankfurt, 1986), 161–8, reprinted in *Byzantium from the ninth century*, article v.

Les listes de préséance byzantines des IXe et Xe siècles (Le monde byzantin, Paris, 1972).

'L'évolution de l'organisation administrative de l'empire byzantin au XIe siècle', *TM*, 6 (1976), 125–52, reprinted in *Byzantium from the ninth century*, article x.

'The first century of the monastery of Hosios Loukas', *DOP*, 46 (1992), 245–55.

'St George of the Mangana, Maria Skleraina and the "Malyj Sion" of Novgorod', *DOP*, 34–5 (1980–1), 231–45, reprinted in *Byzantium from the ninth century*, article xvi.

Ostrogorsky, G. 'The peasants' pre-emption right; an abortive reform of the Macedonian emperors', *JRS*, 37 (1947), 117–26.

'Pour l'histoire de l'immunité à Byzance', *B*, 28 (1958), 165–254.

Quelques problèmes d'histoire de la paysannerie byzantine (Corpus Bruxellense Historiae Byzantinae, Subsidia, II, Brussels, 1956).

Ousterhout, R. G. *The architecture of the Kariye Camii in Istanbul* (Dumbarton Oaks Studies, XXV, Washington, DC, 1987).

Pallas, D. I. 'Zur Topographie, und Chronologie von Hosios Lukas: eine kritische Ubersicht', *BZ*, 78 (1985), 94–107.

Papachryssanthou, D. 'La vie ancienne de Saint Pierre l'Athonite. Date, composition et valeur historique', *AB*, 92 (1974), 19–61.

'La vie de saint Euthyme le Jeune et la métropole de Thessalonique', *REB*, 32 (1974), 225–45.

'La vie monastique dans les campagnes byzantines du VIIIe au XIe siècles', *REB*, 43 (1973), 158–82.

'L'office ancien de Saint Pierre l'Athonite', *AB*, 88 (1970), 27–41.

Papoikonomos, S. *Ho poliouchos tou Argous Hagios Petros episkopos Argous ho thaumatourgos* (Athens, 1908).

Pargoire, J. 'Mont Saint-Auxence. Etude historique et topographique', *ROC*, 8 (1903), 15–31, 240–79, 426–58, 550–76.

Patlagean, E. 'Ancienne hagiographie byzantine et histoire sociale', *Annales ESC*, 23/1 (1968), 104–24, reprinted in *Structure sociale*, article V.

'Christianisme et parentés rituelles: le domaine de Byzance', *Annales ESC*, 32 (1978), 625–36, reprinted in *Structure sociale*, article XII.

Pauvreté économique et pauvreté sociale à Byzance, 4e–7e siècles (Paris, 1977).

'Sainteté et pouvoir', in Hackel, *Byzantine saint*, pp. 88–105.

Structure sociale, famille, chrétienté à Byzance (London, 1981).

'Theodora de Thessalonique. Une sainte moniale et un culte citadin (IXe–XXe siècle)', in S. B. Gajano and L. Sebastiani (eds.), *Culto dei santi. Istitutioni e classi sociali in età preindustriale* (Rome, 1984), pp. 37–67.

Pattenden, P. 'The Byzantine early warning system', *B*, 53 (1983), 258–99.

Pertusi, A. 'Nuovi documenti sui Benedettini Amalfitani dell'Athos', *Aevum*, 27 (1953), 1–30.

'Rapporti tra il monachesimo italo-greco ed il monachesimo bizantino nell'alto medio evo', in *La chiesa greca in Italia dall'VIII al XVI secolo (Atti del convegno storico interecclesiale, Bari, 1969)*, published as *Italia Sacra*, 20 (1972–3), 473–520.

Petit, L. 'St Jean Xénos ou l'Ermite d'après son autobiographie', *AB*, 42 (1924), 5–20.

Photeinos, G. *Ta Neamonesia* (Chios, 1865).

Pingree, D. 'Gregory Choniades and Palaeologan astronomy', *DOP*, 18 (1964), 135–60.

'The horoscope of Constantine VII', *DOP*, 27 (1973), 219–31.

Prandi, A. (ed.), *L'art dans l'Italie méridionale: Aggiornamento dell'opera di Emile Bertaux* (6 vols., Rome, 1978).

Rodley, L. *Cave monasteries of Byzantine Cappadocia* (Cambridge, 1985).

'The Pigeon-house church Çavuşin', *JÖB*, 33 (1983), 201–39.

Rosenthal, J. T. *The purchase of paradise* (London, 1972).

Rouan, M.-F. 'Une lecture "iconoclaste" de la vie d'Etienne le Jeune', *TM*, 8 (1981), 415–36.

Bibliography

Rouillard, G. 'Un grand bénéficiaire sous Alexis Comnène: Léon Képhalas', *BZ*, 30 (1930), 44–50.

Runciman, S. *The Emperor Romanus Lecapenus and his reign* (Cambridge, 1929, reprinted 1963).

Rydén, L. 'The date of the *Life of Andreas Salos*', *DOP*, 32 (1978), 127–55.

'The *Life* of St Basil the Younger and the *Life* of St Andreas Salos', in *Okeanos: essays presented to Ihor Ševčenko on his sixtieth birthday by his colleagues and students* (Harvard Ukrainian Studies, VII, Cambridge, Mass., 1983), pp. 568–86.

Saward, D. *Perfect fools: folly for Christ's sake in catholic and orthodox spirituality* (Oxford, 1980).

Schilbach, E. *Byzantinische Metrologie* (Handbuch der Altertumswissenschaft, XII/4, Munich, 1970).

Seiber, J. *The urban saint in early Byzantine social history* (British Archaeological Reports, Supplementary Series, XXXVII, Oxford, 1977).

Seibt, W. *Die Skleroi. Eine prosopographische-sigillographische Studie* (Byzantina Vindobonensia, IX, Vienna, 1976).

Ševčenko, I. 'Constantinople viewed from the eastern provinces in the middle Byzantine period', in *Eucharisterion: essays presented to Omeljan Pritsak* (Harvard Ukrainian Studies, III–IV/2, Cambridge, Mass., 1979–80), pp. 712–47, reprinted in *Ideology, letters and culture*, article VI.

'Hagiography of the iconoclast period', in Bryer and Herrin, *Iconoclasm*, pp. 113–31, reprinted in *Ideology, letters and culture*, article V.

Ideology, letters and culture in the Byzantine world (London, 1982).

'On Pantaleon the Painter', *JÖB*, 21 (1972), 241–9, reprinted in *Ideology, letters and culture*, article XII.

Skawran, K. *The development of middle Byzantine painting in Greece* (Pretoria, 1982).

Skoulatos, B. *Les personnages byzantins de l'Alexiade. Analyse prosopographique et synthèse* (Université de Louvain, Recueil de Travaux d'Histoire et de Philologie, 6th ser., fasc. 20, Louvain, 1980).

Špidlík, T. *The spirituality of the Christian east*, translated A. P. Gythiel (Cistercian Studies, 79, Kalamazoo, Mich., 1986).

Starr, J. *The Jews in the Byzantine empire* (Texte und Forschungen zur byzantinisch-neugriechischen Philologie, XXX, Athens, 1939).

Striker, C. *The Myrelaion (Bodrum Camii) in Istanbul* (Princeton, 1981).

Stylianou, A. and A. J. *The painted churches of Cyprus: treasures of Byzantine art* (London, 1988).

Svoronos, N. G. 'L'épibolè à l'époque des Comnènes', *TM*, 3 (1968), 375–95, reprinted in *Etudes sur l'organisation*, article V.

Etudes sur l'organisation intérieure, la société et l'économie de l'empire byzantin (London, 1973).

'Recherches sur le cadastre byzantin et la fiscalité aux XIe et XIIe siècles: le cadastre de Thèbes', *BCH*, 83 (1959), 1–166, reprinted in *Etudes sur l'organisation*, article III.

'Remarques sur la tradition du texte de la novelle de Basile II concernant les puissants', *ZRVI*, 8 (1964), 427–34, reprinted in *Etudes sur l'organisation*, article XII.

Bibliography

'Remarques sur les structures économiques de l'empire byzantin au XIe siècle', *TM*, 6 (1976), 49–67.

La Synopsis major des Basiliques et ses appendices (Paris, 1964).

Talbot, A.-M. 'A comparison of the monastic experience of Byzantine men and women', *Greek Orthodox Theological Reivew*, 30/1 (1985), 1–20.

'The Byzantine family and the monastery', *DOP*, 44 (1990), 119–29.

Thierry, N. 'L'art monumental byzantin en Asie Mineure du XIe siècle au XIVe', *DOP*, 29 (1975), 75–111, reprinted in *Peintures d'Asie Mineure*, article IX.

'Monuments de Cappadoce de l'antiquité romaine au moyen âge byzantin', in *Le Aree omogenee della civiltà rupestre nell'ambito dell'impero bizantino.: La Cappadocia* (Galatina, 1981), pp. 39–73.

Peintures d'Asie Mineure et de Transcaucasie aux Xe et XIe siècles (London, 1977).

'Un portrait de Jean Tzimiskès en Cappadoce', *TM*, 9 (1985), 477–84.

Thierry, N. and Thierry, M. *Nouvelles églises rupestres de Cappadoce: région de Hasan Dagi* (Paris, 1963).

Thomas, J. P. 'A disputed novel of Basil II', *GRBS*, 24/3 (1983), 273–83.

Private religious foundations in the Byzantine empire (Dumbarton Oaks Studies, XXIV, Washington, DC, 1987).

Tsirpanlis, C. N. *Introduction to eastern patristic thought and orthodox theology* (Collegeville, Minn., 1991).

Turner, H. J. M. *St Symeon the New Theologian and spiritual fatherhood* (Byzantina Neerlandica, XI, Leiden/New York/Copenhagen/Cologne, 1990).

Van der Vorst, C. 'Le translation de S. Théodore Studite et de S. Joseph de Thessalonique', *AB*, 31 (1913), 27–62.

Van der Wal, N. and Lokin, J. H. A. *Historiae iuris graeco-romani delineatio. Les sources du droit byzantin de 300 à 1453*, translated H. Boon (Groningen, 1985).

Vannier, J.-F. *Familles byzantines: les Argyroi (IXe–XIIe siècles)* (Byzantina Sorbonensia, VII, Paris, 1975).

Varnalidou S. *Ho thesmos tes charistikes (doreas) ton monasterion eis tous Byzantinous* (Byzantina Keimena kai Meletai, XXI, Thessalonike, 1985).

Vasiliev, A. 'Harun ibn-Yahya and his description of Constantinople', *Seminarium Kondakovianum*, 5 (1932), 149–63.

'The "Life" of St Peter of Argos and its historical tradition', *Traditio*, 5 (1947), 163–90.

Verlinden, C. *L'esclavage dans l'Europe médiévale* (2 vols., Ghent, 1977).

Vlasto, A. P. *The entry of the Slavs into Christendom* (Cambridge, 1970).

Von Falkenhausen, V. 'I bizantini in Italia', in G. Cavallo, V. von Falkenhausen, R. F. Campanati, M. Gigante, V. Pace and F. D. Rosati, *I bizantini in Italia* (Milan, 1982).

La dominazione bizantina nell'Italia meridionale dal IX all'XI secolo (Bari, 1978).

Voulgarakis, E. 'Nikon Metanoiete und die Rechristianisierung der Kreter vom Islam', *Zeitschrift für Missionswissenschaft und Religionswissenschaft*, 417 (1963), 192–269.

Bibliography

Vranoussi, E. 'Les archives de la Néa Moni de Chios. Essai de reconstitution d'un dossier perdu', *BNJ*, 22 (1977–84), 267–84.

Ta hagiologika keimena tou hosiou Christodoulou hidrytou tes en Patmo mones. Philalogike paradosis kai historikai martyriai (Athens, 1966).

Ward-Perkins, B. *From classical antiquity to the middle ages. Urban public building in northern and central Italy, AD 300–850* (Oxford, 1984, reprinted 1987).

Weber, M. *Sociology of religion*, translated E. Fischoff (London, 1965).

Weiss, G. *Oströmische Beamte im Speigel der Schriften des Michael Psellos* (Miscellanea Byzantina Monacensia, XVI, Munich, 1973).

Wharton, A. *Art of empire: painting and architecture of the Byzantine periphery. A comparative study of four provinces* (University Park, Pa., 1988).

Wiegand, T. *Milet. Ergebnisse der Ausgrabungen und Untersuchungen seit dem Jahre 1899*, III/1: *Der Latmos* (Berlin, 1913).

Wiegand, T. and Schrader, H. *Priene. Ergebnisse der Ausgrabungen und Untersuchungen in den Jahren 1895–98* (Berlin, 1904).

Winnifrith, T. *The Vlachs: the history of a Balkan people* (London, 1988).

Zakynthinos, D. 'Kastron Lakedaimonos', *Hellenika*, 15 (1957), 95–111.

Index

Index

John Tornik, 37, 46–7, 81, 85–6, 88,
    189, 203, 229
John, *docheiarios*, 87
John, *droungarios*, 254
John, *epi tou kanikleiou*, 84, 159
John, *kouboukleisios*, 148
John, from Thrakesion, 109
Joseph, metropolitan of Thessalonike,
    14, 18
judges, 248, 252
Julian, St, monastery of, 173
Justinian, 107
Justinianic legislation, 16, 33, 146

Kalamitzi, 232
Kalaphatou, 224
Kale/Maria Pakouriane, 124, 130,
    135–6, 230, 281, 291
    testament of, 123, 127, 189, 230
kalliergemata, 157, 212, 245, 250
Kalothekia, 216
Kalymnos, 207
Kamena, 170, 230
kandidatos, 115
Kaplan, Michel, 183, 212, 257
kapnikon, 152, 169
Karanlık Kilise, 128
Karyes, 175
Kassandra, 170, 183, 204, 228–30,
    255, 259–60
Kastellion, *see* Kastrianon
Kastrianon, 48
Katadaimon, 224
Kataskepe, monastery of, 28
katepan, 85, 118
Kekaumenos, 62
Kellerana, 202
Kerkyra, bishop of, 26
Klados, 129
klasma, 170, 176, 183, 203–6, 208,
    243, 244, 247, 248, 259, 287
kleisourarch, 129
kleronomos, 126, 155
kodikes, 258
koiaistor, 245
koinobion, 16, 22, 25, 32–3, 35, 38, 42,
    45, 49, 52, 54–6, 63–4, 67,

    133, 175–6, 198–9, 209,
    234, 239, 293
koitonites, 77
Kolobos, monastery of, 86, 163,
    169–70, 176, 204, 229,
    247–50
komes, 75, 156
Komothona, 215
Kos, 47, 48, 138, 140–1, 207, 218
    Nea Mone, 49, 66, 140–1, 216, 258,
    261
Kosmas I, patriarch of
    Constantinople, 262
Kosmas Konidiares, 103
Kosmas, *ekklesiarches*, 89
Kosmidion, 156
Kostanitza, 290
Kotresi, 206
kouboukleisios, 148
kouropalates, 85, 131
Koutariane, 205
Kourounon, 218
Krinites, *strategos* of Hellas, later
    Peloponnese, 104
Krinos, 214
Kristovitza, 238
krites, 104, 163, 170, 213, 217, 264,
    285, 289, 290
ktetor, 138
Kyminas, Mt, 11, 35, 39–40, 42–3, 45,
    46, 47, 71, 76, 79, 80, 102,
    108, 140, 149, 171, 215
    church of Theotokos on, 149
kyrios, 157–8, 160, 161, 263, 265
kyrioteta, *see kyrios*
Kyr Onouphrios, 202
Kyr Zosimo, 156, 202
    Monastery of St Maria at, 156
Kyzikos, metropolitan of, 108, 270

Lakedaimon, *see* Sparta
Laodicea, 61
Larissa, 288
Larymon, 198, 214
Latinianon, 29
    tourma of, 118
Latium, 113

Patmos (*cont.*)
Monastery of St John the
Theologian on, 47, 48, 140,
161, 207, 217–19, 251, 258,
281, 287, 293
Paul, St, the Younger, of Latros, 37,
56, 61, 72, 75, 77, 83, 89,
109, 113, 116, 155, 182
foundations of, 50
Life of, 38, 66, 69, 72, 116, 213,
214
Pachomios, St, 16
Pakourianos, *archon ton archonton*,
133
Palaion Choraion, 230
Palaiokastron, 224
Pantoleon, painter, 89
Papachryssanthou, Denise, 171
parakolouthemata, 257
parakoimomenos, 85, 124
paroikos, 169, 176, 182–8, 207, 213,
215, 216, 217, 219, 235,
239, 250, 259
Parthenion, 218, 220, 251
Parthenion, river, 79
pasture, 230, 249, 251
Patras, 61, 109
metropolitan of, 252
patrikios, 75, 85, 245
Paul of Evergetis, 18, 138
Paul Magoulas, monk, 156
Peira, 105, 149, 197, 247, 252–4
Pelion, Mt (Kos), 48
Pelion, Mt (Thessaly), 50, 140, 162
Peloponnese, 57–8, 61, 82, 88, 103,
114, 117, 151–2, 201
theme of, 104
penes, 184, 244–5, 247, 252
Pentakrene, 215
Perigardikea, 287
Perama, 216
periorismos, 290, 291
Peristerai, 286
Persia, 82
Peter, St, of Argos, 59–60, 76, 79,
103, 110, 114, 117, 119
Life of, 66, 113

Peter, St, the Athonite, 43
canon on, 43
life of, 221
Peter Spanoleontos, 157
Peter, deacon, 290
Petchenegs, 28, 111, 178, 267, 283
Phagitzes, metropolitan, 252
Phaselis, bishop of, 150
Phasoulos, 255
philanthropia, 122, 282
Philaretos, St, Life of, 12
Philea, 75
Philippopolis, 234
metropolitan of, 261
Philostratus, 68
Phokis, 27, 52
Piacenza, 112
Pile, 138
pilgrimage, 51, 57, 82, 117
Piperatos, monastery of, 149, 151
Pisson, 224
Plato, *hegoumenos* of Sakkoudion, 14
Platys, 206, 225, 230
Pliska, 25
Po, river, 112
Poimen, *hegoumenos* of Bouleuteria, 44
Polouphoute, 218
Polyeuktos, patriarch of
Constantinople, 153
Polygyros, 229
Pontos, 79
Poros, lake, 237
Pothos Argyros, 104, 119
praktikon, 182, 206, 217–18, 252, 289,
290, 291
Pravlaka, 225
prayer, 73, 108, 133, 140
preaching, 82
predictions, 58, 102–7, 109, 124
Prespa, lake, 26
priests, 93–4
Prilongion, 235
primikerios, 290
Prinarion, 156
proasteion, 198, 206, 215, 219
Prokopios, St, 129
pronoetes, 126, 160

Index